⊚Harden's

In association with

RÉMY MARTIN
FINE CHAMPAGNE COGNAC

The Heart of Cognac

London
Restaurants
2010

"Gastronomes' bible" Evening Standard

Survey-driven reviews of over 1800 restaurants

Put us in your pocket!

Coming soon to your iPhone or BlackBerry

Be the first to know! register at www.hardens.com/pda/launch

© **Harden's Limited 2009**

ISBN 978-1-873721-85-8

British Library Cataloguing-in-Publication data:
a catalogue record for this book is available from
the British Library.

Printed in Italy by Legoprint

Content manager: Alexandra Woodward
Research assistant: Hannah Hodges

Harden's Limited
14 Buckingham Street
London WC2N 6DF

Would restaurateurs (and PRs) please address
communications to 'Editorial' at the above address,
or ideally by email to: editorial@hardens.com

The contents of this book are believed correct at
the time of printing. Nevertheless, the publisher
can accept no responsibility for errors or changes in
or omissions from the details given. The views expressed in
this guide are exclusively those of Harden's Limited.

CONTENTS

RATINGS & PRICES

Ratings

Our rating system is unlike those found in other guides (most of which tell you nothing more helpful than that expensive restaurants are, as a general rule, better than cheap ones).

What we do is to compare each restaurant's performance – as judged by the average ratings awarded by reporters in the survey – with other restaurants in the same price-bracket.

This approach has the advantage that it helps you find – whatever your budget for any particular meal – where you will get the best 'bang for your buck'.

The following qualities are assessed:

F — Food
S — Service
A — Ambience

The rating indicates that, ***in comparison with other restaurants in the same price-bracket***, performance is...

❶ — Exceptional
❷ — Very good
❸ — Good
④ — Average
⑤ — Poor

Prices

The price shown for each restaurant is the cost for one (1) person of an average three-course dinner with half a bottle of house wine and coffee, any cover charge, service and VAT. Lunch is often cheaper. With BYO restaurants, we have assumed that two people share a £5 bottle of off-license wine.

Telephone number – all numbers should be prefixed with '020' if dialling from outside the London area.

Map reference – shown immediately after the telephone number.

Rated on Editors' visit – indicates ratings have been determined by the Editors personally, based on their visit, rather than derived from the survey.

Website – the first entry in the small print (after any note about Editors' visit)

Last orders time – listed after the website (if applicable); Sunday may be up to 90 minutes earlier.

Opening hours – unless otherwise stated, restaurants are open for lunch and dinner seven days a week.

Credit and debit cards – unless otherwise stated, Mastercard, Visa, Amex and Maestro are accepted.

Dress – where appropriate, the management's preferences concerning patrons' dress are given.

Special menus – if we know of a particularly good value set menu we note this (e.g. "set weekday L"), together with its formula price (FP) calculated exactly as in 'Prices' above. Details change, so always check ahead.

HOW THIS GUIDE IS WRITTEN

Survey
This guide is based on our 19th annual survey of what
'ordinary' diners-out think of London's restaurants. In 1998,
we extended the survey to cover restaurants across the rest
of the UK; it is by far the most detailed annual survey of its
type. Out-of-town results are published in our UK guide.

This year, the total number of reporters in our combined
London/UK survey, conducted mainly online, exceeded 8,000,
and, between them, they contributed some 85,000 individual
reports. This is a vast exercise, and we are grateful to Rémy
Martin Fine Champagne Cognac for continuing to support it.

How we determine the ratings
In the great majority of cases, ratings are arrived at
statistically. This essentially involves 'ranking' the average
survey rating each restaurant achieves in the survey – for
each of food, service and ambience – against the average
ratings of the other establishments which fall in the same
same price-bracket. (This is essentially like football leagues.
So expensive restaurants go in one league and cheaper ones
in another. Where the restaurant is ranked in its league
determines its ratings.)

How we write the reviews
The tenor of each review and the ratings are very largely
determined by the ranking of the establishment concerned,
which we have derived as described above. At the margin, we
may also pay some regard to the proportion of positive
nominations (such as for 'favourite restaurant') compared to
negative nominations (such as for 'most overpriced').

To explain why a restaurant has been rated as it has, we
extract snippets from survey comments ("enclosed in double
quotes"). On larger restaurants, we receive several hundred
reports, and a short summary cannot possibly do individual
justice to all of them.

What we seek to do – *without any regard to our own personal
views* – is to illustrate the key themes which have emerged
in our analysis of the collective view. The only exception to
this is the newest restaurants, where survey views are
either few or non-existent, and where we may be obliged to
rely on our own opinions. Unless the review carries the
small-print note "Rated on Editors' visit", however, the
ratings awarded are still our best analysis of the survey
view, not our own impressions.

Richard Harden   **Peter Harden**

SURVEY FAQs

Q. How do you find your reporters?
A. Anyone can take part. Simply register at
www.hardens.com. Actually, we find that many people
who complete our survey each year have taken part
before. So it's really more a question of a very large and
ever-evolving panel, or jury, than a random 'poll'.

Q. Wouldn't a random sample be better?
A. That's really a theoretical question, as there is no
obvious way, still less a cost-efficient one, by which one
could identify a random sample of the guests at each of,
say, 5000 establishments across the UK and get them to
take part in any sort of survey. And anyway, which is
likely to be more useful: a sample of the views of
everyone who's been to a particular place, or the views
of people who are interested enough in eating-out to
have volunteered their feedback?

Q. What sort of people take part?
A. A roughly 60/40 male/female split, from all adult age-
groups. As you might expect – as eating out is not the
cheapest activity – reporters tend to have white collar
jobs (some at very senior levels). By no means, however,
is that always the case.

Q. Do people ever try to stuff the ballot?
A. Of course they do! A rising number of efforts are
weeded out every year. But stuffing the ballot is not as
trivial a task as some people seem to think: the survey
results throw up clear natural voting patterns against
which 'campaigns' tend to stand out.

Q. Aren't inspections the best way to run a guide?
A. It is often assumed – even by commentators who
ought to know better – that inspections are some sort
of gold standard. There is no doubt that the inspection
model clearly has potential strengths, but one of its
prime weaknesses is that it is incredibly expensive.
Take the most famous practitioner of the 'inspection
model', Michelin. It doesn't claim to visit each and every
entry listed in its guide annually. Even once! And who are
the inspectors? Often they are catering professionals,
whose likes and dislikes may be very different from the
establishment's natural customer base. On any restaurant
of note, however, Harden's typically has somewhere
between dozens and hundreds of reports each and every
year from exactly the type of people the restaurant
relies upon to stay in business. We believe that such
feedback, carefully analysed, is far more revealing and
accurate than an occasional professional inspection.

RÉMY MARTIN®
FINE CHAMPAGNE COGNAC

Few business partnerships last as long as the co-operation between Rémy Martin and Harden's. This is based on many things, but particularly on authenticity, integrity and reliability, which are important to both of us.

Harden's derives its authenticity from its annual nationwide survey of restaurant-goers, leading to the creation of the UK's definitive democratic restaurant guides. For Rémy Martin, it comes from three centuries of tradition, our origins in the heart of Cognac and the unique know-how of our cellar-master.

Since 1724, Rémy Martin – the only large cognac house still in family ownership – has produced cognacs of exceptional quality and taste. Alone, we source 100% of our grapes from the very 'heart of Cognac'. The "heart" has its own official designation: 'Appellation Fine Champagne Contrôllée'. "Fine Champagne" indicates a blend of cognac from the two best areas in the centre of the Cognac region, Grande Champagne (at least half the blend) and Petite Champagne.

Champagne lends its name to these two Cognac areas because, like the famous sparkling wine region, the soil is chalky. Over 80% of all the Fine Champagne cognac produced in this designated area is used in Rémy Martin Fine Champagne cognacs.

The result is three main characteristics which distinguish Rémy Martin; the harmony between the complex aromas and the sweetness of the flavours; the elegant richness of the aromas and palate; and the supreme length of the finish.

This is why we believe that Rémy Martin captures the very heart of Cognac and it is this unswerving dedication to quality over nearly three centuries that has led Rémy Martin to become the worldwide leader in the most premium of cognacs.

The Restaurant Rémys

2010 sees a new structure to the Restaurant Rémys. The Rémy Martin VSOP Award for the Best-Rated Newcomer remains the industry's most coveted recognition of up and coming restaurants and Rémy Martin is once again proud to be associated with the development of such a dynamic category.

New to the line up is the Coeur de Cognac Award for Best Dessert – a much overlooked, yet sublime aspect to a complete dining experience. Also new is the Rémy Martin XO Excellence Award for the Best All-Round Restaurant. This award is the result of painstaking analysis of the survey results to identify the true crème de la crème among London's ever more competitive restaurant world.

SURVEY RESTAURANT REMYS

This year, in conjunction with our sponsors Rémy Martin Fine Champagne Cognac, we have introduced three new awards based on the results of the survey.

Rémy Martin XO Award
Best All-Round Restaurant

Winner
 1   **Marcus Wareing at The Berkeley**
Runners-up
 2   Chez Bruce
 3   Le Gavroche
 4   The Ledbury
 5   La Trompette
 6   The Landau
 7   L'Aventure
 8   Clos Maggiore
 9   J Sheekey
10   Barrafina

Coeur de Cognac Award
Best Dessert

Winner
 1   **Marcus Wareing at the Berkeley**
     (Custard tart)
Runners-up
 2   The Ivy *(Iced berries with hot white chocolate sauce)*
 3   Chez Bruce *(Cheeseboard)*
 4   The Wolseley *(Victoria sandwich)*
 5   L'Atelier de Joel Robuchon *(Le chocolat tendance)*

Rémy Martin VSOP Award
Best-rated Newcomer

Winner
 1   **Murano**
Runners-up
 2   Min Jiang
 3   Soseki
 4   Bull & Last
 5   Trishna

SURVEY MOST MENTIONED

These are the restaurants which were most frequently mentioned by reporters. (Last year's position is given in brackets.) An asterisk* indicates the first appearance in the list of a recently-opened restaurant.

1   J Sheekey (1)
2   Chez Bruce (2)
3   Scott's (7)
4   The Wolseley (3)
5   Marcus Wareing at the Berkeley (8)
6   Hakkasan (4)
7   Bleeding Heart (6)
8   Le Gavroche (9)
9= Gordon Ramsay (5)
9= Galvin Bistrot de Luxe (15)

11 Le Caprice (16)
12= The Ivy (10)
12= La Poule au Pot (11)
14 Andrew Edmunds (17)
15 La Trompette (12)
16 The Cinnamon Club (-)
17 Arbutus (13)
18= Zuma (18)
18= maze (28)
20 Oxo Tower (14)

21 Gordon Ramsay at Claridge's (20)
22 L'Atelier de Joel Robuchon (30)
23 Yauatcha (21)
24 Clos Maggiore (-)
25 The Square (19)
26 Benares (26)
27 The Anchor & Hope (22)
28 St John (38)
29 Wild Honey (23)
30 The River Café (33)

31 The Ledbury (35)
32 Locanda Locatelli (25)
33 Le Café Anglais (29)
34 Amaya (34)
35 Corrigan's Mayfair*
36= The Don (36)
36= Bocca Di Lupo*
38 New Tayyabs (-)
39 Moro (32)
40 Murano*

SURVEY NOMINATIONS

Top gastronomic experience

1   Marcus Wareing at the Berkeley (3)
2   Chez Bruce (2)
3   Le Gavroche (4)
4   Gordon Ramsay (1)
5   La Trompette (5)
6   maze (9)
7   L'Atelier de Joel Robuchon (7)
8   The Ledbury (-)
9   The Square (-)
10 Murano*

Favourite

1   Chez Bruce (1)
2   Le Caprice (2)
3   J Sheekey (3)
4= The Wolseley (5)
4= The Ivy (6)
6   La Trompette (4)
7   Galvin Bistrot de Luxe (9)
8   Scott's (-)
9   Moro (7)
10 St John (-)

Best for business

1   The Wolseley (1)
2   Bleeding Heart (3)
3   The Don (2)
4   Coq d'Argent (6)
5   The Square (4)
6   L'Anima*
7   1 Lombard Street (5)
8   Scott's (-)
9   Galvin Bistrot de Luxe (9)
10 St Alban (-)

Best for romance

1   La Poule au Pot (1)
2   Andrew Edmunds (2)
3   Clos Maggiore (5)
4   Bleeding Heart (3)
5   Chez Bruce (4)
6   Le Caprice (6)
7   J Sheekey (10)
8   Marcus Wareing at the Berkeley (8)
9   Galvin at Windows (-)
10 Le Gavroche (-)

Best breakfast/brunch

1 The Wolseley (1)
2 Smiths (Ground Floor) (2)
3 Roast (3)
4 Cecconi's (5)
5 Simpsons-in-the-Strand (7)
6 Electric Brasserie (4)
7 High Road Brasserie (6)
8 Tom's Kitchen (-)
9 Providores (Tapa Room) (8)
10 Automat (-)

Best bar/pub food

1 The Anchor & Hope (1)
2 Churchill Arms (9)
3 The Gun (2)
4= The Eagle (6)
4= The Thomas Cubitt (7)
6 The Narrow (3)
7 Harwood Arms*
8 The Engineer (5)
9= The Anglesea Arms (4)
9= Bull & Last*

Most disappointing cooking

1 Oxo Tower (1)
2 The Ivy (2)
3 Gordon Ramsay at Claridge's (3)
4 Gordon Ramsay (7)
5 The Wolseley (4)
6 Corrigan's Mayfair*
7 Cipriani (9)
8 Le Café Anglais (5)
9 The Warrington (-)
10 maze (-)

Most overpriced restaurant

1 Gordon Ramsay (3)
2 Oxo Tower (1)
3 Gordon Ramsay at Claridge's (4)
4 Cipriani (2)
5 The River Café (5)
6 L'Atelier de Joel Robuchon (8)
7 Hakkasan (6)
8 The Ivy (7)
9 Sketch (Lecture Rm) (9)
10 maze (-)

SURVEY HIGHEST RATINGS

FOOD

SERVICE

£80+

	FOOD		SERVICE
1	Marcus Wareing	1	Marcus Wareing
2	Le Gavroche	2	Le Gavroche
3	The Capital Restaurant	3	The Capital Restaurant
4	Rasoi	4	The Square
5	Roka	5	The Landau

£60-£79

	FOOD		SERVICE
1	Morgan M	1	The Ledbury
2	One-O-One	2	Roussillon
3	The Ledbury	3	Angelus
4	Zuma	4	The Goring Hotel
5	Roussillon	5	Murano

£45-£59

	FOOD		SERVICE
1	Chez Bruce	1	Oslo Court
2	La Trompette	2	Chez Bruce
3	Hunan	3	La Trompette
4	Assaggi	4	Lamberts
5	Amaya	5	Le Caprice

£35-£44

	FOOD		SERVICE
1	Sushi-Say	1	Caraffini
2	Barrafina	2	Frantoio
3	Jin Kichi	3	Brula
4	Sukho Thai Cuisine	4	Sushi Say
5	Babur Brasserie	5	Barrafina

£34 or less

	FOOD		SERVICE
1	Dinings	1	Uli
2	Franco Manca	2	Adams Café
3	Mangal Ocakbasi	3	Hot Stuff
4	Rasa N16	4	Yming
5	New Tayyabs	5	Vijay

SURVEY HIGHEST RATINGS

AMBIENCE	OVERALL
1 The Ritz Restaurant	1 Marcus Wareing
2 Marcus Wareing	2 Le Gavroche
3 The Landau	3 The Landau
4 Le Gavroche	4 The Greenhouse
5 Blakes	5 The Square
1 Rules	1 The Ledbury
2 Scott's	2 J Sheekey
3 J Sheekey	3 Scott's
4 Zuma	4 Roussillon
5 Goring Hotel	5 Morgan M
1 L'Aventure	1 Chez Bruce
2 La Poule au Pot	2 La Trompette
3 Clos Maggiore	3 L'Aventure
4 Belvedere	4 Clos Maggiore
5 Archipelago	5 J Sheekey Oyster Bar
1 Andrew Edmunds	1 Barrafina
2 $ (Dollar)	2 Brula
3 Brula	3 Sushi Say
4 Oak	4 Babur Brasserie
5 Annies	5 El Faro
1 Gordon's Wine Bar	1 Rasa N16
2 Bar Italia	2 Hot Stuff
3 El Pirata	3 Adams Café
4 Fish in a Tie	4 El Pirata
5 Princi	5 Flat White

SURVEY BEST BY CUISINE

These are the restaurants which received the best average food ratings (excluding establishments with a small or notably local following).

Where the most common types of cuisine are concerned, we present the results in two price-brackets. For less common cuisines, we list the top three, regardless of price.

For further information about restaurants which are particularly notable for their food, see the cuisine lists starting on page 246. These indicate, using an asterisk*, restaurants which offer exceptional or very good food.

British, Modern

£45 and over		Under £45	
1	Chez Bruce	1	Tom Ilic
2	Lamberts	2	Harwood Arms
3	The Glasshouse	3	Market
4	The Landau	4	Palmerston
5	Trinity	5	Anglesea Arms, W6

French

£45 and over		Under £45	
1	Morgan M	1	Upstairs Bar
2	Marcus Wareing	2	Brula
3	The Ledbury	3	Terroirs
4	La Trompette	4	Giaconda Dining Rooms
5	Roussillon	5	Cellar Gascon

Italian/Mediterranean

£45 and over		Under £45	
1	Assaggi	1	Salt Yard
2	Murano	2	Dehesa
3	Latium	3	Ristorante Semplice
4	Tentazioni	4	Bocca Di Lupo
5	Oliveto	5	500

Indian

£45 and over		Under £45	
1	Amaya	1	Rasa N16
2	Rasoi	2	New Tayyabs
3	Zaika	3	Ragam
4	The Painted Heron	4	Lahore Kebab House
5	Cinnamon Kitchen	5	Babur

Chinese

£45 and over

1 Hunan
2 Yauatcha
3 Hakkasan
4 Min Jiang
5 Princess Garden

Under £45

1 Mandarin Kitchen
2 Dragon Castle
3 Haozhan
4 Goldfish
5 Harbour City

Japanese

£45 and over

1 Zuma
2 Roka
3 Umu
4 Nobu
5 Nobu Berkeley

Under £45

1 Sushi-Say
2 Dinings
3 Jin Kichi
4 Café Japan
5 Pham Sushi

British, Traditional

1 Scott's
2 St John Bread & Wine
3 Anchor & Hope

Vegetarian

1 Roussillon
2 Mildreds
3 The Gate

Burgers, etc

1 Lucky Seven
2 Haché
3 Ground

Pizza

1 Franco Manca
2 Oliveto
3 The Oak

Fish & Chips

1 Nautilus
2 Golden Hind
3 Fish Club

Thai

1 Sukho Thai Cuisine
2 Esarn Kheaw
3 Addie's Thai Café

Fusion

1 The Providores
2 Champor-Champor
3 Village East

Fish & Seafood

1 One-O-One
2 Mandarin Kitchen
3 J Sheekey

Greek

1 Vrisaki
2 Daphne
3 Lemonia

Spanish

1 Barrafina
2 Moro
3 El Faro

Turkish

1 Mangal Ocakbasi
2 Cyprus Mangal
3 Kazan

Lebanese

1 Chez Marcelle
2 Fakhreldine
3 Pasha

TOP SPECIAL DEALS

The following menus allow you to eat in the restaurants concerned at a significant discount when compared to their evening à la carte prices.

The prices used are calculated in accordance with our usual formula (i.e. three courses with house wine, coffee and tip).

Special menus are by their nature susceptible to change – please check that they are still available.

Weekday lunch

£65+ Alain Ducasse
Gordon Ramsay

£60+ Rib Room
Marcus Wareing

£55+ The Capital Restaurant
Le Gavroche
Launceston Place
The Ritz Restaurant

£50+ Ambassade de l'Ile
Aubergine
Bellamy's
Foliage
Kai Mayfair
L'Oranger
Pearl
Pied à Terre
Tom Aikens

£45+ L'Atelier de Joel Robuchon
Gordon Ramsay at
   Claridge's
The Goring Hotel
Hélène Darroze
Rasoi Vineet Bhatia

£40+ Benares
Bombay Brasserie
The Cinnamon Club
Galvin at Windows
The Ledbury
One-O-One
Roussillon
Sumosan
Texture
Theo Randall

£35+ Babylon
Cheyne Walk Brasserie
China Tang
5 Cavendish Square
Hibiscus
Homage
Momo
Morgan M
Notting Hill Brasserie
Patterson's
York & Albany
Zafferano

£30+ Awana
Brasserie Roux

Cinnamon Kitchen
Criterion
Le Deuxième
Enoteca Turi
Essenza
L'Etranger
The Forge
Frederick's
L'Incontro
Kenza
Lucio
Mews of Mayfair
Michael Moore
Min Jiang
Mon Plaisir
Odette's
The Palm
Quilon
Le Suquet
Tom's Kitchen
Wild Honey

£25+ Arbutus
Artigiano
Atma
L'Aventure
Bar Trattoria Semplice
Bonds
La Bouchée
Boudin Blanc
Bradley's
Brasserie James
Buchan's
La Buvette
Café des Amis
Cantina del Ponte
Charlotte's Place
Daphne's
Fish Hook
Garbo's
Gastro
Goodman
Greig's
The Haven
Inside
Kew Grill
Kiku
The Light House
Mitsukoshi
Northbank
The Palmerston
Paradise by Way of
   Kensal Green
Phoenix Bar & Grill

		£15+	Balfour
	Ristorante Semplice		The Banana Leaf Canteen
	Sam's Brasserie		Café Laville
	Sardo Canale		Café Rouge
	Sonny's		Fish in a Tie
	Tamarind		Isola del Sole
	Vanilla		Lemonia
	Vanilla Black		Rocca Di Papa
	The Zetter		Le Sacré-Coeur
			Saigon Saigon
£20+	The Albion		Tendido Cuatro
	Arch One		Tentazioni
	The Bull		Thai Café
	Chez Liline		Viet Garden
	Don Pepe		Zero Degrees
	Il Falconiere		
	High Road Brasserie	£10+	Diwana Bhel-Poori House
	Koba		Hammersmith Café
	Loch Fyne		Inshoku
	The Lock Dining Bar		Mandalay
	Madsen		Olympus Fish
	La Mancha		El Pirata
	Menier Chocolate Factory		Ragam
	Origin Asia		Sakonis
	Sarracino		
	Tosa		

Pre/post theatre (and early evening)

£45+	L'Atelier de Joel Robuchon		Bradley's
			Brasserie Roux
£40+	Benares		Café des Amis
	Theo Randall		Café du Jardin
			Fish Shop
£30+	Alastair Little		Joe Allen
	Christopher's		L-Restaurant & Bar
	Le Deuxième		Northbank
	The Forge		
	Frederick's	£20+	Yming
	Indigo		
	Tom's Kitchen	£15+	Mon Plaisir
	Wild Honey		
£25+	Ambassador		
	Arbutus		
	Bianco Nero		

Sunday lunch

£45+	Le Pont de la Tour		The Wharf
£40+	Chez Bruce	£25+	Buchan's
	Corrigan's Mayfair		La Buvette
	Odette's		Garbo's
	York & Albany		Ziani
£30+	Artigiano	£20+	Galicia
	Como Lario		Le Querce
	Racine		Le Sacré-Coeur
	Sam's Brasserie		
	The Swan At The Globe	£15+	Sree Krishna
	Le Vacherin		
	Village East		

THE RESTAURANT SCENE

Economy implodes. Openings rise.

This year we record 121 new openings, and 64 closings (listed on pages 20-21) – bizarrely 'normal' figures for a year that saw both the near-collapse of the world's banks and a major decline in UK national income! Openings were actually *up* on the previous year (111), and closings were *down,* to the *lowest* level since our 2001 guide, to stand at not much more than half the record figure (113, 2004 guide)! This year's widely-expected bloodbath just didn't happen.

French hail magnificent defeat

The big news of the past year is another non-event. Three mega-star French imports – *Hélène Darroze, Alain Ducasse at the Dorchester* and L'Ambassade de l'Ile – have now had a full year to show us what they can do for top-end London dining…. *Rien!* The weakest, L'Ambassade, closed as this guide went to press. The *best, Ducasse,* emerged *24th* (out of 33) for food quality in our top (£80+) price bracket (much in line with the *ennui* which permeated most press reviews).

But that's not how it seemed to Michelin, who rushed to anoint the establishment of Ducasse (the world's second-Michelin-starriest chef) as the *second-best in London!* Just a French guide cheerleading *pour la Patrie?* Or more support for those who say Michelin overhypes new ventures from chefs they've already blessed with stars elsewhere?

Trouble at the top

This doling out of questionable Michelin stars tends to disguise the fact that London's top end remains thin, by international standards, and shows little sign of improvement. If you look at the best top-bracket restaurants (pages 14 and 15) it's striking that – *The Landau* aside – they tend to be have been around for some time. (London's 'new' best restaurant *Marcus Wareing at the Berkeley* is old Pétrus by a new name.)

Adding to this sense of drift, a couple of high-achieving chefs chose this year to 'move on' – Eric Chavot from the *Capital Hotel,* and William Drabble from *Aubergine.* And, emblematic of 'trouble at the top', *Gordon Ramsay* – flagship of the f-word chef's international empire – has recorded an unprecedented slide in reporter approval: what had until recently been, for many years, London's best restaurant has suddenly slumped to being unremarkable.

The success of the Ramsay group's new *Murano* – the best opening of the year – proves it can still 'deliver the goods'. However – looking at the sharp decline of *Gordon Ramsay,* and the excruciatingly poor ongoing performance of the pubs – it is also clear that much remains to be sorted out if the business is to get properly back on track. Is the head man prepared to divert enough of his time from TV and celebrity appearances to do what needs to be done? There's no sign of it so far.

Market trends

The following seem to us the trends of the moment:

● many of the most interesting and successful newcomers operate on some variation of a 'tapas' (or other light-bite) format. Informal restaurants of this type are – at long last – bringing high-quality, stylish, non-ethnic dining, within easy financial reach of ordinary restaurant-goers, *even in the heart of the West End*.

● Steakhouses – though still of low relative importance, compared to New York – are currently going through something of a mini-boom.

● East London continues to emerge as a restaurant destination, with Shoreditch the fashionable restaurant frontier. Canary Wharf is finally showing more hopeful signs of evolving as a restaurant destination in its own right, even though most of its new names – such as the forthcoming *Jamie's Italian*, *Roka* and *Wahaca* – are still spin-offs.

● In the mid-range, there appears to be little change taking place in the West End: a sheer shortage of good sites (not least because of the small number of restaurants closing, as noted opposite) may be among the causes.

● There is no real evidence that the credit crunch has put off the better-capitalised sorts of operators (international or domestic) from taking a positive long-term view of London. High-budget forthcoming openings include: from Hong Kong, the two large-scale *Aqua* restaurants; *Galvin la Chapelle*; *The Luxe*; offshoots of *Green's* and *Roka*; and – further out in 2010 – spin-offs from *Hakkasan* and *St John*.

Every year, we select what seem to us personally to be the ten most significant openings of the preceding 12 months. This year, our selection is as follows:

Cinnamon Kitchen	Min Jiang
Bocca di Lupo	Murano
Bull & Last	St Pancras Grand
Goodman	Terroirs
Lutyens	Trishna

Prices

The average price of dinner for one at establishments listed in the guide is £40.73.

Prices have on average risen by 1.6% in the past 12 months. Restaurateurs, however, currently have the temporary benefit of paying a reduced proportion of total bills by way of VAT, so pre-tax prices have in fact increased by some 3.8% year-on-year. This represents a surprisingly modest decline from the 4.7% increase we recorded last year.

OPENINGS AND CLOSURES

Openings (121)

Albion
Abeno NW3
Aqua Kyoto
Aqua Nueva
Arch One
Atari-Ya NW4
The Avalon
Ba Shan
Bar Trattoria Semplice
Il Baretto
The Bathhouse
Bocca Di Lupo
The Bolingbroke
La Bottega SW7
Brinkley's Kitchen
Brompton Bar & Grill
Brouge TW2, TW9
Bull & Last
Byron W12
The Cadogan Arms
Canteen W1
Caponata
Casa Brindisa
Cha Cha Moon W2
Chakalaka W4
The Chelsea Kitchen
Chilango N1, EC4
The Chippy
Coast
Comptoir Libanais W1, W2, W12
Corrigan's Mayfair
Côte WC2, W8
Daylesford Organics W11
Dean Street Townhouse & Dining Room
Dockmaster's House
Dotori
The Drapers Arms
The East Room
Eastside Inn
Ekachai W1
The Establishment SW11
Fat Boys SW14
The Fellow
Fire & Stone W12
500
Forman's
Gail's Bread NW8
Gallery Mess

Galvin La Chapelle
Garufa
Gilmour's
Goodman
Green's EC3
High Timber
Ibérica
Indali Lounge
Jamie's Italian
Keelung
The Kensington Wine Rooms
Kings Road Steakhouse & Grill
Lena
Lower East
Lutyens
The Luxe
Madsen
Marco Pierre White Steakhouse & Grill
The Meat & Wine Co
More
Mrs Marengos
No.20
Noto Kikuya
1001 Nights
Okawari WC2
Ooze W12
The Orange
Osteria Dell'Angolo
The Palm
The Pembroke
Pétrus
El Pirata de Tapas
Port of Manila
Portobello Ristorante Pizzeria
Princi
Le Provence
The Refinery
Le Relais de Venise L'Entrecôte EC2
The Restaurant at St Paul's
Rocca Di Papa
Roka E14
Rosa's
The Rose & Crown
Rossopomodoro WC2

Openings (cont'd)

Rotunda
The Roundhouse
Royal Wok
St Pancras Grand
Santo
Seasons Dining Room
Sophie's Steakhouse *WC2*
Soseki
Sushinho
The Swan & Edgar
A Taste Of McClements
Terroirs
tibits
Tierra Brindisa
Trishna

Tsunami *W1*
twotwentytwo
Ultimate Burger *W1*
Il Vaporetto
Viajante
Villandry Kitchen
Villiers Terrace
Vineria
Wahaca *W12, E14*
Whitechapel Gallery
    Dining Room
The Wine Theatre
Yalla Yalla
The Yellow House
Zeen

Closures (64)

Aaya
Agni
Amato
L'Ambassade de L'Ile
Aperitivo
Aquasia
Arancia *two SE1 branches*
Bar Bourse
Barnes Grill
Bincho Yakitori *SE1*
Bodeguita del Medio
The Brackenbury
Brasserie St Quentin
Bush Bar & Grill
Caldesi
Drones
Eat & Two Veg *N10*
11 Abingdon Road
Eco *W4*
Franklins *SE11*
Freemasons
Giardinetto
Giusto
Greyhound at Battersea
Grille
Haiku
Iznik Kaftan
Lanes (East India House)
Levantine
Lilly's
Lindsay House
Made in China
Mimmo d'Ischia

Missouri Grill
Mosaico
Nanglo
Nosh
Notting Grill
Noto Kikuya
Osteria Stecca
Pacific Bar and Grill
Papageno
Passione
Philpotts Mezzaluna
Picasso's
Pick More Daisies
(Ciro's) Pizza Pomodoro *EC2*
Pomegranates
Rocket *SW15*
Rose & Crown
Rôtisserie Jules *W11*
Royal China Club *NW8*
San Carlo
Seabass *W2*
Singapura *EC3, EC4*
Snows on the Green
Spiga
Tatsuso
3 Monkeys
Tom's Place
Ubon
Vic Naylors
Vino Rosso
Yakitoria

EATING IN LONDON FAQs

How should I use this guide?

This guide can be used in many ways. You will often wish to use it to answer practical queries. These tend to be geographical – where can we eat near…? To answer such questions, the Maps (from page 300) and Area Overviews (from page 264) are the place to start. The latter tell you all the key facts about the restaurants – perhaps dozens – in a particular area in the space of a couple of pages.

But what if you'd like to be more adventurous and seek out new places purely for interest's sake or for a truly special occasion? That's the main point of this brief section – to give you a handy overview of London's dining scene, and also some thoughts as to how you can use the guide to lead you to eating experiences you might not otherwise have found (or perhaps even contemplated).

What makes London special?

This question would once have been easy to answer: London was the opposite of Paris. There you could eat one cuisine only – albeit in all its various regional glories – supremely well. London, like New York, was a city where nothing was done especially well, but at least the scene was cosmopolitan.

Well, London's cosmopolitanism has not gone away, and standards continue to improve across the board, but there are now at least two specialities of particular note. The first, chronologically speaking, was the cuisine of the Indian subcontinent, which is offered in London in greater variety, within a small geographical area, than anywhere else in the world. And the more recent speciality is…British cuisine! London is now the only city where you can consistently eat well in a varied idiom which is clearly British!

Which is London's best restaurant?

It's getting more and more difficult to say, because the old rules – which boiled down to French is Best – seem ever more inappropriate today. But let's stick with the traditional 'haute cuisine' definition. If you want the whole high-falutin' Gallic dining experience, the top all-rounder – no question – is *Marcus Wareing at the Berkeley*. In a rather more traditional style, London's original post-war grand restaurant, *Le Gavroche*, still has a lot going for it.

In a very superior second tier are a number of restaurants which have maintained very high quality for a good number of years, including *Pied à Terre*, the *Square* and the *Capital Hotel*. (and, heading up the reserves, the *Greenhouse*). A recent opening which is beginning to knock on the door of the front rank – and which offers a bit of grand hotel bling thrown in – is *The Landau*. (With that exception, and *Marcus Wareing*, London's hotels offer little truly top-end dining.)

What about something a little more reasonably priced?

You can still have meals of exceptional quality – often memorable ones – a lot cheaper than at the establishments mentioned above.

For top-flight French culinary experiences just below the top tier, price-wise, *Roussillon* (Pimlico) and *Morgan M* (Islington) are the two places most worth seeking out. If you'd like to check out a member of the group associated with worldwide TV star Gordon Ramsay, by far the best group restaurant of the moment is the excellent new *Murano* (Mayfair).

Notting Hill's *The Ledbury* also rates mention. It's part of a fine group of restaurants that have in common the 'hidden' guiding hand of restaurateur Nigel Platts-Martin – this includes not just 'London's Favourite Restaurant', *Chez Bruce* (Wandsworth), but also *La Trompette* (Chiswick) and the *Glasshouse* (Kew), as well as the aforementioned *Square*.

What about some really good suggestions in the heart of the West End?

It used to be difficult to recommend places to dine well in the West End at reasonable cost, but the position has improved hugely in recent years. Names particularly to consider include *Arbutus*, *Giaconda Dining Room*, *Galvin Bistrot de Luxe* and *Wild Honey*. If you're happy to eat in tapas style, add to this list such recent arrivals as *Barrafina*, *Bocca di Lupo*, *Dehesa*, *Sheekey's Oyster Bar* and *Terroirs*.

If you want a little more comfort and style, as well as pretty good food, you're unlikely to go far wrong at the discreet *Caprice* (just behind the Ritz), or its siblings *J Sheekey* (hidden-away in Theatreland) and *Scott's* (a celebrity magnet on one of the grandest streets in Mayfair). These last are hardly bargain suggestions, but they do offer all-round value. For pure theatre, a visitor looking for that sort of style should probably try to eat at the *Wolseley* – the nation's 'grand café', by the Ritz – at some point.

Covent Garden is a tricky area, rich in tourist traps, but is now the unlikely home of a restaurant that's beginning to approach 'destination' status – *Clos Maggiore*.

And don't forget to lunch!

Particularly if you want to eat in the West End, it is very well worth considering whether you can do so at lunchtime, when there are some unlikely bargains available. Restaurants don't come much grander than *Le Gavroche*, for example, and it famously offers a superb-value all-in lunch (even including some very decent wine) for less than many relatively run-of-the-mill establishments end up charging for a basic dinner. For further top value suggestion, see the list on pages 18 and 19.

And for the best of British?

As we hinted above, British food has only very recently emerged from a sort of tourist ghetto. If it's the grand end of that market you're looking for, seek out the Roast Beef of Olde England at *Simpson's-on-the-Strand*. Less impressive in scale, but much better, is nearby *Rules* – a beautiful old-timer, where game is the culinary speciality.

That, though, is not the sort of cooking – often offal-rich and rediscovering historical dishes – that's making British one of the most fashionable cuisines in town. The pioneer establishment of the new-wave Brits – which for so long seemed to be crying in the wilderness often mixed in with 'gastropub' cooking in many people's minds – has become mainstream. Restaurants proper which may be said to be strongly influenced by the style include *Magdalen, Great Queen Street, Hereford Road* and *St John Bread & Wine*. It will probably also feature at the new Heston Blumenthal restaurant to open at the swanky Mandarin Oriental hotel in 2010. But a lot of this sort of cooking is taking place in gastropubs…

What are gastropubs?

These are essentially bistros in the premises of former pubs. They come in a variety of styles. What many people think of as the original gastropub (*The Eagle*, 1991) still looks very much like a pub with a food counter. At the other end of the scale, however, the 'pub' element is almost redundant, and the business is really just a restaurant housed in premises that happen once to have been a pub.

Few of the best gastropubs are particularly central. The reasonably handy location of the *Anchor & Hope*, on the South Bank, is no doubt part of the reason for its crazy popularity. Hammersmith and its environs, for some reason, have a particular concentration, with the *Anglesea Arms* the stand-out performer there. Two new stars are the *Bull & Last* (Kentish Town) and *Harwood Arms* (Fulham).

Isn't London supposed to be a top place for curry?

London, as noted above, has a reasonable claim to being the world's top Indian restaurant city. Leading lights such as *Rasoi, Amaya, The Painted Heron, Benares* and *Zaika* are pushing back the frontiers, but – perfectly reasonably – charge the same as their European equivalents.

What's more exciting in terms of value are the many Indian restaurants where you can eat much more cheaply than you could eat European. There are too many of them to list here – search out the asterisked restaurants in the Indian and Pakistani lists commencing on pages 259 and 261 respectively. Two top names in the East End are, however, almost legendary 'value' experiences – the *Lahore Kebab House* and *New Tayyabs*.

Any tips to beat the crunch?

● The top tip, already noted, is to lunch not dine. If you're a visitor, you'll find that it's better for your wallet, as well as your digestion, to have your main meal in the middle of the day. In the centre of town, it's one of the best ways you can be sure of eating 'properly' at reasonable cost. See the spread on pages 18 and 19.

● Think ethnic – for a food 'experience' at modest cost, you'll still generally be better off going Indian, Thai, Chinese or Vietnamese (to choose four of the most obvious cuisines) than French, English or Italian. The days when there was any sort of assumption that ethnic restaurants were – in terms of comfort, service and décor – in any way inferior to European ones is long gone.

● Try to avoid the West End. That's not to say that, armed with this book, you shouldn't be able to eat well in the heart of things, but you'll almost certainly do better in value terms outside the Circle line. Many of the best and cheapest restaurants in this guide are easily accessible by tube. Use the maps at the back of this book to identify restaurants near tube stations on a line that's handy for you.

● If you must dine in the West End, try to find either pre-theatre (generally before 7.30 pm) or post-theatre (generally after 10 pm) menus. You will generally save at least the cost of a cinema ticket, compared to dining à la carte. Many of the more upmarket restaurants in Theatreland do such deals. For some of our top suggestions, see page 17.

● Use this book! Don't take pot luck, when you can benefit from the pre-digested views of thousands of other diners-out. Choose a place with a ❶ or ❷ for food, and you're very likely to eat much better than if you walk in somewhere on spec' – this is good advice anywhere, but is most particularly so in the West End. Once you have decided that you want to eat within a particular area, use the Area Overviews (starting on p264) to identify the restaurants that are offering top value.

● Visit our website, www.hardens.com, for the latest reviews, and restaurant news.

DIRECTORY

Comments in "double quotation-marks" were made by reporters.

Establishments which we judge to be particularly notable have their NAME IN CAPITALS.

A Cena TW1 £42 ❷❷❷
418 Richmond Rd   8288 0108   1–4A
On "the wrong side of Richmond Bridge" (in St Margarets), this "intimate" Italian has built an impressive following, thanks to its "consistently good" food, "knowledgeable" staff and "lovely" surroundings. / www.acena.co.uk; 10 pm; closed Mon L & Sun D; booking: max 6, Fri & Sat.

The Abbeville SW4 £33 ④④❷
67-69 Abbeville Rd   8675 2201   10–2D
The "relaxed" style helps make this Clapham hang-out a "favourite haunt" for some locals, even if the food does "fluctuate". / www.renaissancepubs.co.uk; 10.30 pm.

Abeno £34 ❸❷❸
47 Museum St, WC1   7405 3211   2–1C
17-18 Great Newport St, WC2   7379 1160   4–3B
66 Heath St, NW3   8–1A NEW
"For something different and fun", try these Japanese okonomiyaki diners – their "tasty" snack food "sounds weird" ("filled omelettes cooked in front of you on a hot plate") but "works well", thanks not least to the "supremely helpful" staff; a new Hampstead branch is due in September 2009. / www.abeno.co.uk; 10 pm - 11 pm; WC2 no booking.

The Abingdon W8 £46 ❸❷❷
54 Abingdon Rd   7937 3339   5–2A
Hidden-away in the lush back streets of Kensington, this "quintessential local" is often noted for its "buzzing" atmosphere and "consistent" standards; grab one of the "spacious booths" if you can. / www.theabingdonrestaurant.com; 11 pm, Mon 10.30 pm, Sun 10pm.

Abokado WC2 £15 ❷④⑤
160 Drury Ln   7242 5600   4–2D
"A brilliant alternative to the lunchtime sandwich"; this small oriental take-away chain ("like Itsu but much better") is roundly praised for its "fresh, delicious and inexpensive" fare, which includes some "excellent sushi and wraps". / www.abokado.com; 7.30 pm; closed Sat & Sun.

About Thyme SW1 £40 ❷❷❸
82 Wilton Rd   7821 7504   2–4B
Much improved in recent times, this "welcoming" Pimlico spot is emerging as something of an unexpected "gem"; the Spanish/French menu includes some "quite unusual" dishes, and the results are usually "very good"; a tapas menu is a recent innovation. / www.aboutthyme.co.uk; 11 pm.

L'Absinthe NW1 £36 ❸❷❷
40 Chalcot Rd   7483 4848   8–3B
"Proper retro-Gallic bistro cuisine" has made a big hit of this "crowded" and "very convivial" Primrose Hill corner spot, where the (French) patron brings a surreal level of authenticity to "the performance of being a French waiter". / 10.30 pm, Sun 9.30 pm; closed Mon.

Abu Zaad W12 £20 ❷❷❸
29 Uxbridge Rd   8749 5107   7–1C
"A small trip to Syria" is on offer to those who visit this "stalwart" café, near Shepherd's Bush market... and at an "unbelievably cheap" price too; "fab juices" and "first-class" mezze and kebabs. / www.abuzaad.co.uk; 11 pm.

The Academy W11   £37   ❷❷❷
57 Princedale Rd   7221 0248   6–2A
"A great neighbourhood stand-by" in a "quiet backwater" of Holland Park – this "traditional pub", with "separate conservatory dining area", serves some "good-value" fare. / www.academybar.com; 11 pm, Sun 10.30 pm; no Amex.

L'Accento Italiano W2   £41   ❸④④
16 Garway Rd   7243 2201   6–1B
"You wouldn't cross town for it", but this "honest" Bayswater Italian has long been a "good neighbourhood place", liked for its "careful" cooking and "decent value". / www.laccentorestaurant.co.uk; 11 pm; closed Sun.

Acorn House WC1   £41   ❸❸⑤
69 Swinton St   7812 1842   8–3D
It has "laudable aims about seasonality and sourcing", but this "overcrowded", eco-friendly training-restaurant, in Bloomsbury, inspires wildly divergent reports – fans talk of "accurate" handling of "fantastic" ingredients, whereas critics say its dishes are way "overpriced", given that they're so "basic". / www.acornhouserestaurant.com; 10 pm; closed Sat L & Sun.

Adam Street WC2   £56   ❸❷❷
9 Adam St   7379 8000   4–4D
"For a quiet business meal", this "relaxing" club dining room – in attractive cellars just off the Strand – makes a "great venue" (open to non-members at lunch, £10 cover charge); the wine selection has some "reasonably-priced gems", arguably outshining the steady British cooking. / www.adamstreet.co.uk; L only (open for D to members only), closed Sat & Sun; set dinner £32 (FP).

Adams Café W12   £26   ❸❶❸
77 Askew Rd   8743 0572   7–1B
By day it's a regular greasy spoon, but at night this "fantastic", family-run Shepherd's Bush "favourite" serves "delicious tajines and couscous" and other "authentic" Tunisian dishes, with great "charm"; for modest corkage, you can BYO. / 11 pm; closed Sun.

Addie's Thai Café SW5   £26   ❷❷❸
121 Earl's Court Rd   7259 2620   5–2A
"Chock-full of oriental customers", this "cramped and uncomfortable" – but "very friendly" – café, by Earl's Court tube, serves "brilliant" food in "true Bangkok style". / www.addiesthai.co.uk; 11 pm; closed Sat L & Sun L; no Amex.

Admiral Codrington SW3   £43   ❸❷❷
17 Mossop St   7581 0005   5–2C
"The menu may not change much, but the food is good" at this "upmarket" Chelsea boozer – a "fun" and "vibrant" location, offering "reliable" cooking. / www.theadmiralcodrington.co.uk; 11 pm.

The Admiralty
Somerset House WC2   £50   ④④④
Strand   7845 4646   2–2D
This is potentially a "lovely" and "calm" dining room, in the historic heart of Somerset House, and it offers a menu "of modest innovation"; it's long been hampered by "stiff" service and a "stifling" atmosphere though, and only attracts a trickle of feedback nowadays. / www.theadmiraltyrestaurant.com; 10.30 pm; closed Sun.

Afghan Kitchen N1 £19 ❸④④
35 Islington Grn 7359 8019 8–3D
For a "cheep 'n' cheerful" snack, the simple curries at this tiny Islington Green café fit the bill nicely; service can be "erratic", though, and dishes can seem "samey". / 11 pm; closed Mon & Sun; no credit cards.

Aglio e Olio SW10 £34 ❷❸❷
194 Fulham Rd 7351 0070 5–3B
A "great Chelsea local" that's "packed to the rafters" (and "unbearably noisy") – the food "doesn't suffer from the popularity", though, and you get "perfect pasta" in "generous portions", and at "excellent prices" too. / 11.30 pm.

Al Duca SW1 £42 ④④④
4-5 Duke of York St 7839 3090 3–3D
This low-key modern Italian has in recent years been a St James's "staple", thanks to its "fair pricing" and its "consistent performance in all dimensions"; too often, however, the verdict is that it's "nothing special" nowadays. / www.alduca-restaurant.co.uk; 11 pm; closed Sun.

Al Forno £30 ④❷❷
349 Upper Richmond Rd, SW15 8878 7522 10–2A
2a King's Rd, SW19 8540 5710 10–2B
You get "pizza with a pulse!", at these "hectic" Italians in Wimbledon Town and Putney, where the staff are "friendly but not OTT"; "perfect for big groups". / SW15 11 pm; SW19 11.30 pm, Sun & Mon 10.30 pm.

Al Hamra W1 £46 ④⑤⑤
31-33 Shepherd Mkt 7493 1954 3–4B
"Dependable Lebanese food" comes "at Mayfair prices" – and with sometimes "uninterested" service too – at this long-established Shepherd Market spot; pleasant al fresco tables. / www.alhamrarestaurant.co.uk; 11.30 pm.

Al Sultan W1 £42 ❸❸⑤
51-52 Hertford St 7408 1155 3–4B
It may look a little "jaded", but this Shepherd Market Lebanese is a "welcoming" sort of place, where the food is sometimes "very good". / www.alsultan.co.uk; midnight.

Al-Waha W2 £33 ❷❶❸
75 Westbourne Grove 7229 0806 6–1B
"Year after year", this "quiet" and unremarkable-looking Bayswater Lebanese has proved itself "unbelievably consistent", thanks to its "extremely friendly" staff and its "delightful" food – "rather like you find in many other Middle Eastern restaurants, just better!" / www.alwaharestaurant.com; 11.30 pm; no Amex.

Alain Ducasse
Dorchester W1 £99 ④❸④
53 Park Ln 7629 8866 3–3A
"What is Michelin thinking, giving it two stars?" – "massive hype meets modest execution", at this "disgracefully overpriced" Mayfair outpost of the mega-starry Parisian über-chef: the set lunch, though, is undoubtedly a "steal". / www.alainducasse-dorchester.com; 10 pm; closed Mon, Sat L & Sun; jacket; set weekday L £65 (FP).

Alastair Little W1 £50
49 Frith St   7734 5183   4–2A
This "café-like" Soho site which was once at the forefront of the 'Modern British' culinary revolution (as it was then called) was closed as this guide went to press; we're told that a relaunch is planned. / 11.30 pm; closed Sun; set weekday L £30 (FP), set pre-theatre £31 (FP).

Alba EC1 £47 ❸②④
107 Whitecross St   7588 1798   12–2A
"An unusual haven, near Barbican" – this "professional" Italian (30 this year) offers a "consistent", if "pricey", formula, which includes "quality" Piedmontese food and an "outstanding" wine list; the interior is "sparse", though, and critics find the whole performance rather "dull". / www.albarestaurant.com; 11 pm; closed Sat & Sun.

Albannach WC2 £52 ⑤⑤⑤
66 Trafalgar Sq   7930 0066   2–3C
"Dressing staff in kilts doesn't make them Scottish", and this large central venue's Caledonian theming convinces few reporters; worse, the "overpriced" mezzanine restaurant "seems like an afterthought" to the "booming" bar below. / www.albannach.co.uk; 10.15 pm; closed Sun.

The Albemarle
Brown's Hotel W1 £72 ❸②❷
Albemarle St   7493 6020   3–3C
More "classic" in style than most hotel dining rooms nowadays, this "cosseting" Mayfair chamber is a "discreet setting for power lunches", or "comfortable" fine dining; it inspires limited feedback, however, suggesting its aim to become a sort of Savoy Grill II isn't quite achieved yet… / www.roccofortecollection.com; 10.30 pm.

The Albion N1 £38 ④❸❷
10 Thornhill Rd   7607 7450   8–3D
A "superb garden" adds to the appeal of this "above-average" gastropub, in a leafy corner of Islington; in particular, the Sunday roasts – which you carve yourself – are "incredible". / www.the-albion.co.uk; 10 pm; set weekday L £24 (FP).

Albion E2 NEW £32 ④❸❷
2-4 Boundary St   7729 1051   12–1B
Sir Terence Conran's very English new café, in Shoreditch, is designed with a "cool urban austerity"; that's not the only thing which makes it "typical Sir Tel" either – "the vibe is good, but the food is hit-and-miss". / www.albioncaff.co.uk; midnight.

Ali Baba NW1 £18 ❸④④
32 Ivor Pl   7723 5805   2–1A
"An Egyptian café transported to the fringe of Regent's Park, complete with Arabic TV programmes, reliable food and family members doing the serving" – that's the deal at this "fairly eccentric" living room-style venture, behind a Marylebone take-away; BYO. / midnight; no credit cards.

Alisan HA9 £31 ❷②④
The Junction, Engineers Way, Wembley   8903 3888   1–1A
"Pretty amazing" dim sum justifies the trek to this "oddly-located" but "friendly" restaurant, by Wembley Stadium; the "lifeless" setting, though, has all the ambience of a "school hall". / www.alisan.co.uk; Mon-Thu 11 pm, Fri & Sat 11.30 pm, Sun 10.30 pm.

All Star Lanes £36 ④⑤❸
Victoria Hs, Bloomsbury Pl, WC1   7025 2676   2–1D
Whiteley's, 6 Porchester Gdns, W2   7313 8363   6–1C
Old Truman Brewery, 95 Brick Ln, E1   7426 9200   12–2C
"Considering they're really bowling alleys", the "good diner fare" and
"excellent booze" on offer at these fun sporting ventures impresses
some reporters; even fans can find them "overpriced", though,
and service can be "poor". / www.allstarlanes.co.uk; WC1 10.30 pm, Fri &
Sat midnight, Sun 9 pm; E1 10 pm; W2 10.30 pm, Fri-Sun 11 pm;
WC1 & W2 closed L Mon-Thu.

Alloro W1 £53   ❸❸④
19-20 Dover St   7495 4768   3–3C
For a "high-quality" Mayfair meal – especially on business –
this "professional" Italian is worth bearing in mind; nowadays, though,
it can seem "extremely expensive", and some reporters find it "over-
rated". / www.alloro-restaurant.co.uk; 10.30 pm; closed Sat L & Sun.

Alma SW18 £37   ④④❸
499 Old York Rd   8870 2537   10–2B
A "lovely" Wandsworth hostelry, tipped for its "great Sunday lunches"
and "exceptional burgers"; avoid during rugby matches.
/ www.thealma.co.uk; 10.30 pm, Sun 9 pm.

The Almeida N1 £46   ④④④
30 Almeida St   7354 4777   8–2D
This large and "anonymous" venture, near Islington's theatre of the
same name, is the D&D group's most obviously Gallic member;
it continues to inspire mixed feedback – the middle view is that it's
"reliable", if somewhat "lazy" and "unimaginative".
/ www.almeida-restaurant.co.uk; 10.30pm, Sun 9pm; closed Mon L & Sun D.

Alounak £24   ❸④④
10 Russell Gdns, W14   7603 1130   7–1D
44 Westbourne Grove, W2   7229 0416   6–1B
"You know what you're going to get", at these "value-for-money" BYO
bolt-holes, in Olympia and Bayswater – "fresh" kebabs, "delicious"
dips and "mouthwatering" bread. / 11.30 pm; no Amex.

Amano £25   ❸⑤❸
More London Pl, (off Weavers Lane), SE1   7407 9751   9–4D
Victor Wharf, Clink St, SE1   7234 0000   9–3C
Sadly it's shrunk in recent times, but this small South Bank chain
offers some handy places for a snack – sandwiches and brunches are
highlights – albeit with somewhat "ropey" service.
/ www.amanocafe.com; Victor Wharf 10.30 pm; More London Pl 7.30 pm;
no Amex; no booking at D.

Amaranth SW18 £26   ❸❸❸
346 Garratt Ln   8874 9036   10–2B
You "must book" for this "no-frills" BYO Earlsfield spot, which
is world-famous locally for its "great-value" Thai fare; the occasional
reporter, however, fears "standards are slipping" (but a revamp
is promised soon). / 11.30 pm; D only, closed Sun.

Amaya SW1 £57   ❶❷❷
Halkin Arc, 19 Motcomb St   7823 1166   5–1D
With its "eye-opening" cuisine (served "tapas"-style) and "striking"
setting, this "brilliant" modern Indian, in Belgravia, is hard to beat;
the staff can occasionally seem "aloof", but they're
"very knowledgeable" too. / www.realindianfood.com; 11.30 pm,
Sun 10.30 pm.

Ambassade de l'Ile SW7
117/119 Old Brompton Rd   7373 7774   5–2B
This bizarre but ambitious Gallic restaurant, in South Kensington, closed just as this guide was going to press.

Ambassador EC1   £37   ❸❷❸
55 Exmouth Mkt   7837 0009   9–1A
"High-quality" cooking and "eclectic" wines have won quite a reputation for this "sincere" (if rather "bare" and "noisy") Clerkenwell three-year-old; standards, however, have been "a bit inconsistent" of late. / www.theambassadorcafe.co.uk; 10.30 pm; set pre theatre £25 (FP).

Amerigo Vespucci E14   £43   ④④④
25 Cabot Sq   7513 0288   11–1C
"One of the better Canary Wharf places" – this old-fashioned Italian is "a good independent spot amongst all the chain operators", and offers a "reasonably-priced" menu. / www.amerigovespucci.co.uk; 11.30 pm; closed Sat L & Sun.

Anarkali W6   £28   ❷❷④
303-305 King St   8748 1760   7–2B
"I went here when I was a boy – now I take my own kids"; this Hammersmith stalwart has long been a local favourite for those in search of "British-traditional" Indian fare, despite dated-going-on-"dreary" décor; it's closed as we go to press, apparently for a refurb, but re-opening is promised soon. / www.anarkalirestaurant.co.uk; midnight, Sun 11.30 pm.

The Anchor & Hope SE1   £35   ❶❸❸
36 The Cut   7928 9898   9–4A
"Crazy-busy", this Waterloo legend is still the survey's No. 1 gastropub, thanks to its "exciting" and "hearty" cooking, from an "offal-centric" menu (with "shades of St John"); "it practically takes bare-knuckle fighting to get a table". / 10.30 pm; closed Mon L & Sun D; no Amex; no booking.

ANDREW EDMUNDS W1   £36   ❸❷❶
46 Lexington St   7437 5708   3–2D
"It's cramped and uncomfortable – I can't wait to go back!"; this "delightfully quirky" Soho townhouse is again voted "the most romantic spot in central London", thanks to its "gorgeous", candlelit, "Boho" ambience and its "cracking, fairly-priced wine list"; the food is "a decent support act". / 10.30 pm; no Amex; booking: max 6.

Angelus W2   £61   ❷❷❸
4 Bathurst St   7402 0083   6–2D
A "magnificent wine list", "enthusiastic" service and "superb" cooking are finally beginning to win real acclaim for ex-Gavroche sommelier Thierry Tomasin's ambitious yearling – a "smart" Gallic pub-conversion, "tucked-away in a little cul-de-sac near Lancaster Gate". / www.angelusrestaurant.co.uk; 11.30 pm.

The Anglesea Arms SW7   £31   ④❸❷
15 Sellwood Ter   7373 7960   5–2B
For a "fine traditional pub", it's hard to better this South Kensington landmark; it serves "good-value" pub grub, but it's the "lovely" ambience and charming terrace that people really go for. / www.angleseaarms.com; 10 pm.

The Anglesea Arms W6 £40 ❷❸❷
35 Wingate Rd 8749 1291 7–1B
This "lovely" (if "cramped") gastropub "classic", near Ravenscourt Park, "continues to delight" with its "inventive seasonal menu" ("amazing for such a tiny kitchen"); it's "better now you can book", and the "engaging" service is much-"improved" on a few years ago too. / Tue-Sat 10.30 pm, Sun & Mon 10 pm; no Amex; no booking.

Anglo Asian Tandoori N16 £24 ❸❶❷
60-62 Stoke Newington Church St 7254 3633 1–1C
A Stoke Newington veteran that's "still the best for a cheap 'n' cheerful curry", thanks not least to the "impeccable" service. / www.angloasian.co.uk; 11.45 pm.

L'Anima EC2 £57 ❷❷❷
1 Snowden St 7422 7000 12–2B
Francesco Mazzei's "exceptional" cooking has helped make this Italian yearling "a breath of fresh air in the City"; with its "sophisticated" and "airy" décor, and its "exemplary" service, it continues to prove itself as "one of the best new openings of the last few years". / www.lanima.co.uk; 11 pm; closed Sat L & Sun.

Annie's £42 ❹❸❶
162 Thames Rd, W4 8994 9080 1–3A
36-38 White Hart Ln, SW13 8878 2020 10–1A
"The lush and boudoir-ish décor is more important than the food", at these "wonderfully atmospheric" and "intimate" west London hang-outs; burgers and brunches are recommended – otherwise the grub's "ordinary". / www.anniesrestaurant.co.uk; 10 pm, Sat 10.30 pm.

Antipasto & Pasta SW11 £33 ❸❷❸
511 Battersea Park Rd 7223 9765 10–1C
"Brilliant half-price nights" – early in the week, when the place is "always packed" – are the time to visit this long-established Battersea Italian. / 11.30 pm, Sun 11 pm; need 4+ to book.

Apostrophe £14 ❸❸❸
Branches throughout London
"Re-inventing fast food with quality!"; converts to this "clean-cut" Gallic chain love its "superb" sarnies, "yummy pastries" and "coffee that rocks"; even fans concede "it's dearer than its rivals", though, and – while still pretty solid – the enthusiasm of survey feedback slipped a bit this year. / www.apostropheuk.com; most branches 6 pm, Sat 5.30 pm; no booking.

Applebee's £38 ❷❸❹
4 Stoney St, SE1 7407 5777 9–4C
17 Cambridge Pk, E11 8989 1977 1–1D
"The highest-quality fish" and "fresh, simple seafood", served in "canteen-like settings" – the formula that's won wide-ranging acclaim for these "buzzy" operations in Borough Market and Wanstead; they're "perfect for lunch". / www.applebeesfish.com; SE1 10.15 pm, Sun 5 pm; E11 11 pm; E11 closed Mon-Tue.

Apsleys
Lanesborough Hotel SW1 £85 ❹❸❸
1 Lanesborough Pl 7333 7254 5–1D
This "ostentatious" conservatory dining room, by Hyde Park Corner, has failed to make any waves in its first year of operation; even some fans concede its oddly "rustic" Italian food "isn't a wow", and critics just decry it as "fake", and "very poor value" too. / www.apsleys.co.uk; 11 pm; booking: max 12.

Aqua Kyoto W1 NEW
240 Regent St   3–2C
An impressively large project on the top floor of the former Dickins & Jones store near Oxford Circus – this Hong Kong-backed late-2009 newcomer will include a sushi bar and a 'sumibiyaki 'charcoal grill'; there will also be a bar, 'Aqua Spirit', and three outdoor terraces.

Aqua Nueva W1 NEW
240 Regent St   3–2C
A late-2009 newcomer – sibling to Aqua Koto (see also) – specialising in 'contemporary northern Spanish cuisine'.

ARBUTUS W1   £48   ❷❷❸
63-64 Frith St   7734 4545   4–2A
"If there were a category 'Best-Value Gourmet Food'", this "sophisticated" (if "bland" and "cramped") Soho bistro might well win it with its "creative" yet "ungimmicky" cuisine (and its "brilliant wines by the 250ml carafe"); the set lunch, in particular, is "a staggeringly good deal". / www.arbutusrestaurant.co.uk; 10.45pm, Sun 9.30 pm; set always available & weekday L £26 (FP).

Arch One SE1 NEW   £36
1 Mepham St   7401 2329   9–4A
Right by Waterloo, this "cavernous" newcomer (with a calm dining mezzanine and "noisy" bar below) has had a bumpy start – the launch chef (a Ramsay protégée) left after a few months, which may account for the "confused" feedback; we don't think a rating appropriate. / www.arch-1.com; 10.30 pm; set weekday L £22 (FP).

Archduke Wine Bar SE1   £39
Concert Hall Approach, South Bank   7928 9370   2–3D
With all its "nooks and crannies", this veteran wine bar (set in "attractive" railway arches) makes a handy – if historically lacklustre – South Bank stop-off; a take-over by the Black & Blue chain in mid-2009 should improve matters – their standard menu of grills is now served (and in due course, the whole place may carry the B&B brand). / www.thearchduke.co.uk; 11 pm; closed Sat L & Sun.

The Arches NW6   £36   ❹❸❷
7 Fairhazel Gdns   7624 1867   8–2A
"A phenomenal depth of wine" – and at very "sensible prices" – makes this "friendly" Swiss Cottage bistro a "North West London secret" worth discovering; the "reasonable" food is beside the point. / 10.30 pm; no Amex.

Archipelago W1   £50   ❸❶❶
110 Whitfield St   7383 3346   2–1B
You're "not obliged to eat strange animals", if you visit this "bazaar of Far East exotica", but it's all part of the "novelty" that makes this "bonkers" Fitzrovian a big hit, especially for romance; of late, however, the cooking has seemed less "weirdly wonderful" and more "gimmicky" than before. / www.archipelago-restaurant.co.uk; 10.30 pm; closed Sat L & Sun.

The Ark W8   £50   ❹❸❸
122 Palace Gardens Ter   7229 4024   6–2B
A "squashed" Notting Hill Italian with a "cosy yet stylish" atmosphere; "the food varies" – it can be "great", but it can be "average" too. / www.ark-restaurant.com; 11 pm; closed Mon L & Sun.

Ark Fish E18 £36 ❷❷④
142 Hermon Hill 8989 5345 1–1D
"A real find in a gastronomic desert" – it's "well worth the wait" ("up to an hour") for a table at this "fantastic" South Woodford chippy. / www.arkfishrestaurant.co.uk; Tue-Thu 9.45 pm, Fri & Sat 10.15 pm, Sun 8.45 pm; closed Mon; no Amex.

Artigiano NW3 £48 ❸❷④
12a, Belsize Ter 7794 4288 8–2A
A Belsize Park spot which, on the majority view, is a "friendly" place where "real Italian food" is "beautifully presented"; the odd doubter, though, notes "problems in maintaining quality", or just finds the whole style "pretentious". / www.etruscarestaurants.com; 11 pm, Sun 10 pm; closed Mon L; set weekday L £29 (FP), set Sun L £31 (FP).

Artisan
Westbury Hotel W1 £57 ❸❸④
37 Conduit St 7629 7755 3–2C
Something of a "secret" – half way up Bond Street! – this "enjoyable" hotel dining room makes a handy destination, especially for an "unobtrusive business lunch" (or breakfast). / www.westburymayfair.com; 10.30 pm; closed Sat L & Sun.

L'Artista NW11 £30 ④④❸
917 Finchley Rd 8731 7501 1–1B
A "loud, brash, cheap 'n cheerful Italian", under the railway at Golder's Green; it can be "fun", especially with kids in tow, offering (slightly "indifferent") "pasta 'n' pizza" dishes that come in "ridiculously big portions". / midnight; no Amex.

L'Artiste Musclé W1 £38 ④④❸
1 Shepherd Mkt 7493 6150 3–4B
Looking "like a little neighbourhood spot in France", this "cramped" bistro, in Mayfair's Shepherd Market, offers "simple" fare that may be "nothing special", but is affordable "for this neck of the woods". / 10.30 pm; closed Sun L.

Arturo W2 £42 ❸❷❸
23 Connaught St 7706 3388 6–1D
"A bit off the beaten track", a "quiet" Bayswater Italian, mostly praised for its "good-value" cuisine. / www.arturorestaurant.co.uk; 10 pm, Sun 9.30 pm; closed Sat L & Sun L.

Asadal WC1 £38 ❸④④
227 High Holborn 7430 9006 2–1D
Despite an unpromising setting (under Holborn tube) and "erratic" service, this "dimly-lit" basement offers "a good if pricey introduction to Korean food". / www.asadal.co.uk; 11 pm; closed Sun L.

Asakusa NW1 £28 ❷④④
265 Eversholt St 7388 8533 8–3C
"Still going strong after all these years"; this stalwart near Euston station is "typically Japanese" – "a very basic-looking place", "full of oriental customers", it serves "fresh sushi and sashimi, plus home-cooked favourites", at "decent prices". / 11.30 pm, Sat 11 pm; D only, closed Sun; no Amex.

Asia de Cuba
St Martin's Lane Hotel WC2   £84   ④⑤❸
45 St Martin's Ln   7300 5588   4–4C
It's "still cool and buzzing", but this "loud" and "nightclubby" venue,
on the fringe of Covent Garden, seems all "style over substance"
nowadays; the "overpriced" Asian-Cuban sharing cuisine can
be "surprisingly poor", but it's the "obnoxious" service that really irks.
/ www.stmartinslane.com; midnight, Thu-Sat 12.30 am, Sun10.30 pm.

Ask! Pizza   £27   ⑤④④
Branches throughout London
"Patchy" food and service undermine the appeal of this "attractive"
pizza chain; fans still claim it as a "worthy competitor
to PizzaExpress", but its ratings now lag way behind its rival – odd, as
the two groups are under common ownership! / www.askcentral.co.uk;
most branches 11 pm, Fri & Sat 11.30 pm; some booking restrictions apply.

ASSAGGI W2   £58   ❶❶❷
39 Chepstow Pl   7792 5501   6–1B
It has a "bizarre location" – "a small, bright room over a Bayswater
pub" – but this "happy" venture is yet again rated London's
best Italian, thanks to Nino Sassu's "wonderful" but "unpretentious"
cooking, and the "entertaining and informative" service;
NB "you need to book well ahead". / 11 pm; closed Sun; no Amex.

Les Associés N8   £37   ❸❶❷
172 Park Rd   8348 8944   1–1C
"Crouch End's finest!"; this "intimate" front-room operation continues
to delight the neighbourhood with its "classic Gallic cooking" and its
"friendly and informed" service. / www.lesassocies.co.uk; 10 pm;
Tue-Sat D only, closed Mon & Sun D.

Atami SW1   £50   ❸❸④
37 Monck St   7222 2218   2–4C
This stylish and "highly proficient" Japanese corner restaurant comes
as a surprise in a "thin" part of Westminster; critics though, say that
– with its "miniature portions" and "outrageous prices" – it's only
good "if you're on a diet"! / www.atami-restaurant.com; 10.30 pm; closed
Sat L & Sun.

Atari-Ya   £16   ❶❸④
20 James St, W1   7491 1178   3–1A
31 Vivian Ave, NW4   8202 2789   1–1B NEW
"Some of the best quality sushi outside of top restaurants" –
"so cheap it makes you weep" – wins raves for this "amazing"
Marylebone take-away ("there are a couple of tables, if you're early"),
run by a leading firm of Japanese food importers; for greater comfort,
head to their new sushi bar, in Hendon. / www.atariya.co.uk;
W1 8.30 pm, NW4 10 pm; NW4 closed Mon.

L'ATELIER DE JOEL ROBUCHON WC2   £85   ❷❸❷
13-15 West St   7010 8600   4–2B
Fans hail "sublime food from the world's best chef", at the "dark"
and "sexy" Covent Garden outpost of M. Robuchon's global empire,
where "exquisite" dishes are served tapas-style on "perched" seating,
with the "magnificent drama" of an open kitchen (or more formally
upstairs); the catch? – "nosebleeding" prices. / www.joelrobuchon.com;
11 pm; no trainers; set weekday L & pre-theatre £48 (FP).

The Atlas SW6 £37 ❷❸❷
16 Seagrave Rd 7385 9129 5–3A
A "benchmark for what a London local should be" – this "chilled"
back-street boozer, near Earl's Court 2, offers a "breezy" and
"constantly changing" Mediterranean menu, while all the time
"managing to remain a pub"; "lovely, intimate garden".
/ www.theatlaspub.co.uk; 10 pm; no booking.

Atma NW3 £40 ❷❷④
106c Finchley Rd 7431 9487 8–2A
"Interesting" Indian dishes are prepared with "genuine care" at this
"quiet" and "sensibly-priced" Belsize Park "gem".
/ www.atmarestaurants.com; 11 pm; closed Mon; set weekday L £26 (FP).

Atrium SW1 £41 ④④④
4 Millbank 7233 0032 2–4C
A "light and spacious" dining room, with a "handy" position for
politicos and journos, off the atrium of Parliament's media centre;
we suspect it's always going to trade on its location, but its perennially
lacklustre standards have, of late, been somewhat on the up.
/ www.atriumrestaurant.com; 9.45 pm; closed Sat & Sun.

Aubaine £43 ④④④
4 Heddon St, W1 7440 2510 3–2C
260-262 Brompton Rd, SW3 7052 0100 5–2C
A "combo of bakery and chic café" that's tipped in particular for
a "good brunch" (and "sensational pastries"); at busy times, though,
"chaos" never seems very far away. / www.aubaine.co.uk; SW3 10 pm,
Sun 10 pm; W1 11 pm; W1 closed Sun.

Aubergine SW10 £92
11 Park Wk 7352 3449 5–3B
Even before the mid-2009 departure of William Drabble – the chef
who succeed Gordon Ramsay on this Chelsea site almost a decade
ago – this once-celebrated restaurant was drifting very badly;
its prospective performance seems so uncertain that we can't see any
point in awarding a rating. / www.auberginerestaurant.co.uk; 10.30 pm;
closed Mon, Sat L & Sun D; no jeans or trainers; set weekday L £54 (FP).

Aurora W1 £38 ❸❸❷
49 Lexington St 7494 0514 3–2D
A "cosy, cute and dimly-lit" interior and a "magical" rear courtyard
help set a romantic tone at this "sweet" Soho "gem", which also
impresses most reporters with its "consistently good" food. / Mon &
Tue 10 pm, Wed-Sun 10.30 pm; closed Sun.

Automat W1 £47 ④④❸
33 Dover St 7499 3033 3–3C
This "American-style diner", popular with Mayfair's "hedgies and
Eurotrash", continues to divide opinion – fans "love everything about
it" (especially the burgers and brunch), whereas critics think it's
a "cheesy" place which "could try harder". / www.automat-london.com;
midnight, Sun 10 pm; closed Sat D & Sun D.

L'Autre Pied W1 £49 ❷❸④
5-7 Blandford St 7486 9696 2–1A
"A worthy little sister to Pied à Terre", say fans of this year-old bistro,
who laud its "adventurous" dishes (and "fabulous-value" set menus);
the "cramped" Marylebone premises "have bad feng shui", though,
and a few critics find the whole experience simply "overhyped".
/ www.lautrepied.co.uk; 11 pm, Sun 9.30 pm.

The Avalon SW12 NEW £38 ④④❷
16 Balham Hill 8675 8613 10–2C
It's certainly been "a welcome addition" to Balham, but the success of this "beautiful" revamped pub ("with masses of garden seating") had led to a "mixed-bag" performance, not least on the service front; it can be "excruciatingly loud" too. / www.theavalonlondon.co.uk; 10.30 pm, Sun 9 pm.

L'Aventure NW8 £50 ❷❷❶
3 Blenheim Ter 7624 6232 8–3A
"Just the spot for a romantic evening"; Catherine Parisot's "consummate neighbourhood French restaurant" in St John's Wood is "everyone's favourite", with "personal" service and "authentic" cuisine (plus, on sunny days, a "leafy" terrace); be prepared, though – "Madame occasionally 'loses it' with her staff". / 11 pm; closed Sat L & Sun; set weekday L £28 (FP).

The Avenue SW1 £55 ④④④
7-9 St James's St 7321 2111 3–4D
This "bright and buzzy" '90s brasserie has long been a popular St James's business rendezvous; critics, however, view it as a "dull" and noisy "shed" with "mundane" cooking, and feel it's "in need of a relaunch". / www.theavenue-restaurant.co.uk; midnight; closed Sat L & Sun.

Awana SW3 £52 ❸④④
85 Sloane Ave 7584 8880 5–2C
Fans still say you get a "glamorous night out", and "marvellous" satay too, at this "hip" Chelsea Malaysian; standards are tumbling, though – many "ordinary and expensive" meals are recorded, and reports on service are very up-and-down. / www.awana.co.uk; Mon-Wed 11 pm, Thu-Sat 11.30 pm, Sun 10.30 pm; set weekday L £32 (FP).

Axis
One Aldwych Hotel WC2 £54 ❸❷④
1 Aldwych 7300 0300 2–2D
A "cavernous" Covent Garden basement outfit that's "never quite made it as a 'destination'"; its service is "very professional" though, and its "spacious" tables and "reliably good" food win it numerous recommendations for business (or pre-theatre). / www.onealdwych.com; 10.45 pm, Sat 11.30 pm; closed Sat L & Sun; set dinner £35 (FP).

Ba Shan W1 NEW £25 ④❸❸
24 Romilly St 7287 3266 4–3A
In sleek tea-house-style – with "tiny tables and hard stools" – this Soho newcomer inspires very positive reports for its "revolutionary" tapas-style take on Sichuanese cuisine; for such "small portions", though, prices can seem "extortionate", and critics find some dishes surprisingly "bland". / 11 pm, Fri 11.30 pm.

Babur SE23 £35 ❶❷❷
119 Brockley Rise 8291 2400 1–4D
For a "taste bud sensation", it's "worth the trip" to this "upmarket" but obscurely-located (Honor Oak Park) south London subcontinental, where the "unusual" cuisine has a huge fan club. / www.babur.info; 11.30 pm.

Babylon
Kensington Roof Gardens W8 £65 ④④❷
99 Kensington High St 7368 3993 5–1A
An 8th-floor Kensington eyrie, where "beautiful views" (of London and the greenery in the Roof Gardens below) and "blingy" décor create a "special" vibe; in other respects, however, it "doesn't hit any high spots" and is "too expensive". / www.virgin.com/roofgardens; 11 pm; closed Sun D; set weekday L £37 (FP).

Il Bacio £32 ❸❷❷
61 Stoke Newington Church St, N16 7249 3833 1–1C
178-184 Blackstock Rd, N5 7226 3339 8–1D
"Tiny, cramped and hugely popular" – these "cracking little joints", in Highbury and Stoke Newington, are "convivial" and "cheering" places, which serve up some "delicious" Sardinian fare; "authentic" pizza a speciality. / www.ilbaciohighbury.co.uk; 11 pm.

Back to Basics W1 £45 ❶❸❸
21a Foley St 7436 2181 2–1B
It may look "cramped" and "rustic", but this Fitzrovia spot is a "top-class fish restaurant", where a "huge variety" of "inventive" dishes are realised to a "truly exceptional" standard; it's "excellent value" too, and on sunny days you can eat outside. / www.backtobasics.uk.com; 10.30 pm; closed Sun.

Baker & Spice £36 ❸⑤④
54-56 Elizabeth St, SW1 7730 3033 2–4A
47 Denyer St, SW3 7589 4734 5–2D
75 Salusbury Rd, NW6 7604 3636 1–2B
20 Clifton Rd, W9 7266 1122 8–4A
"Mounds of irresistible goodies" – "superb" baked goods and "marvellous" salads – offer some reward for the "chaotic" and "overcrowded" conditions endured at these chichi deli/bakeries; the biggest problem, though, is that they're so "cripplingly expensive". / www.bakerandspice.uk.com; 7 pm, Sun 5 pm-6 pm; closed D; no Amex; no booking.

Balans £37 ⑤❸④
34 Old Compton St, W1 7439 3309 4–2A
60 Old Compton St, W1 7439 2183 4–3A
239 Old Brompton Rd, SW5 7244 8838 5–3A
214 Chiswick High Rd, W4 8742 1435 7–2A
187 Kensington High St, W8 7376 0115 5–1A
"A lazy brunch" is the best way to sample these "always-buzzing" diners (whose Soho and Earl's Court branches are gay-scene linchpins); more generally, though, the food – which "used to be great" – is horribly "formulaic" nowadays. / www.balans.co.uk; midnight-2 am; 34 Old Compton St 24 hrs; some booking restrictions apply.

Bald Faced Stag N2 £35 ❸❸❷
69 High Rd 8442 1201 1–1B
This "very good gastropub", in East Finchley, comes "highly recommended" – and not just by locals – for its "lively" atmosphere, and its "simple" but "solid" cooking. / www.thebaldfacedstagn2.co.uk; 10.30 pm, Sun 9.30 pm; no Amex.

Balfour WC1 £33 ④❷❷
75-77 Marchmont St 7713 6111 8–4C
The Italian cuisine at this "quirky" and "crowded" yearling, near Russell Square, may be "inconsistent", but it's a "genuine" place, with a "comfortable" and "buzzing" vibe. / www.balfourrestaurant.co.uk; 10 pm; no Amex; set weekday L £19 (FP).

Baltic SE1 £42 ❸④❷
74 Blackfriars Rd 7928 1111 9–4A
Boosted by the "wide range of cocktails" (and vodkas), this stylish "barn" near Southwark tube is a "fun" (and "noisy") destination, where the "modern twist on traditional Polish cuisine" is "comforting" and "surprisingly effective". / www.balticrestaurant.co.uk; 11.15 pm, Sun 10.15 pm.

Bam-Bou W1 £44 ❷❸❶
1 Percy St 7323 9130 2–1C
"A nice place to chill and be romanced"; this "dimly-lit" Fitzrovia townhouse – decorated in "chic", "French-colonial" style – not only offers a "buzzy" setting, but also "subtle" Franco-Vietnamese food of a "high standard", and "great cocktails" too. / www.bam-bou.co.uk; 11 pm; closed Sat L & Sun; booking: max 6.

The Banana Leaf Canteen SW11 £28 ❸❸❸
75-79 Battersea Rise 7228 2828 10–2C
A "hectic", "no-frills" communal canteen, in Battersea, popular for its "reliable" oriental food and "excellent value". / 11 pm; need 6+ to book; set weekday L £17 (FP).

The Banana Tree Canteen £28 ❸❸❸
237 West End Ln, NW6 7431 7808 1–1B
412-416 St John St, EC1 7278 7565 8–3D
"Prepare to queue" for these "packed" noodle canteens in West Hampstead and near Angel – "casual", "fun" pit-stops, serving "good value" pan-Asian dishes. / 11 pm, Sun 10.30 pm; booking: min 6.

Bangalore Express SE1 £32 ❸❷❷
103-107 Waterloo Rd 7021 0886 9–4A
"Vibrant flavours and novel menu ideas" add to the appeal of this "quirky and busy" Waterloo pit stop (run by the Painted Heron team); all this, plus "speedy" service and a "jolly" setting (with "gimmicky tables up ladders adding to the fun"). / www.bangaloreexpress.co.uk; 11.30 pm.

Bangkok SW7 £34 ❸❷❸
9 Bute St 7584 8529 5–2B
"I've been dining here for 30 years, and it hasn't changed a bit!"; the UK's longest-established Thai restaurant, in South Kensington, continues to please with its "freshly-made" scoff. / 11 pm; closed Sun; no Amex.

Bank Westminster
St James Court Hotel SW1 £48 ④④④
45 Buckingham Gate 7630 6644 2–4B
A "spacious" setting, "swift" service and generally "reliable" food make this large brasserie, not far from Buckingham Palace, "fine for a business meal"; critics find it a "characterless" place, but the ambience is sometimes buoyed by the "terrific" bar. / www.bankrestaurants.com; 10.45 pm; closed Sat L & Sun.

Banners N8 £35 ④④❸
21 Park Rd 8348 2930 1–1C
This "lively" boho linchpin of Crouch End life is best known as a "great spot for a long lazy breakfast", and at other times is a "fun" option for "comfort food with a Caribbean twist"; the cooking can be "indifferent", however, and "iffy" service "is all part of the charm". / 11.30 pm, Fri midnight; no Amex.

Baozi Inn WC2 £16 ❸④❸
25 Newport Ct 7287 6877 4–3B
"Excellent Sichuan-style 'small eats'" (including the *"amazing"* buns
after which the place is named), and at *"unbeatable"* prices too,
have made a big name for this *"uncomfortable"* (but characterful)
Chinatown yearling. / 10 pm, Thu-Sat 10.30 pm; no credit cards; no booking.

Bar Estrela SW8 £29 ④❷❷
111-115 South Lambeth Rd 7793 1051 10–1D
This *"buzzing"* bar is a linchpin of Lambeth's 'Little Portugal';
foodwise it's *"good for snacks"* and *"great for breakfast"*. / midnight.

Bar Italia W1 £18 ❸❸❶
22 Frith St 7437 4520 4–2A
*"Where else can you have such a good expresso, so late, while
watching Soho's low-life drifting by?"*; this *"outstanding, traditional
Italian bar"* offers *"London's best coffee"* and *"great people-
watching"* too, 24/7. / www.baritaliasoho.com; open 24 hours, Sun 3 am;
no booking.

Bar Shu W1 £38 ❷④❸
28 Frith St 7287 6688 4–3A
"Joltingly hot" dishes – *"the best Sichuan food in town"* – have made
a big name for this *"amazing"* Soho corner spot, which was closed for
much of 2009 after a fire; it should be back in business by the time
you read this. / www.bar-shu.co.uk; 11 pm.

Bar Trattoria Semplice W1 🆕 £43 ❸❸④
22-23 Woodstock St 7491 8638 3–2B
Fans tip this sparsely-furnished new Mayfair trattoria *"for a quick and
easy bite"*; it also takes flak, though, for *"indifferent service and
uneven food"* – *"you do much better, and not much more
expensively, in its parent, just a few doors away"*.
/ www.bartrattoriasemplice.com; 10.30 pm; set weekday L £28 (FP).

Barcelona Tapas £33 ④④⑤
481 Lordship Ln, SE22 8693 5111 1–4D
1 Beaufort Hs, St Botolph St, EC3 7377 5111 9–2D
24 Lime St, EC3 7929 2389 9–2D
13 Well Ct, EC4 7329 5111 9–2B
"Reasonable tapas" and *"authentic"* staff maintain a steady following
for this small Spanish group; *"the '80s décor is growing very tired"*,
though. / www.barcelona-tapas.com; 10.30 pm; all City branches closed
Sat & Sun.

Il Baretto W1 🆕 £42 ❸④⑤
43 Blandford St 7486 7340 2–1A
Arjun Waney's new Marylebone trattoria is both less ambitious and
less successful in its own terms than his other investments (Zuma,
Roka and La Petite Maison); its noisy basement setting (formerly
Giusto, RIP) is *"unappealing"*, and its cooking – *"from simple
pizza/pasta to more accomplished dishes"* – is too variable.
/ www.ilbaretto.co.uk; 10.45 pm; closed Sun.

The Barnsbury N1 £41 ❸❸❸
209-211 Liverpool Rd 7607 5519 8–2D
"One of the better gastropubs" in Islington – this *"charming"* boozer
wins consistent local praise for its *"high-quality"* food (*"if with
no fireworks"*) and *"genial"* service; *"a nice garden is an added
bonus"*. / www.thebarnsbury.co.uk; 10 pm; closed Sun D.

Barrafina W1 £42 ❶❷❷
54 Frith St 7813 8016 4–2A
"The best tapas bar outside Spain!" – the Hart brothers'
"impeccable" homage to Barcelona's 'Cal Pep' is pure genius;
"effervescent" staff serve up "exquisitely fresh and vibrant" dishes
to the lucky few (only 23 seats!) who have survived the "long queue";
"you must get there early". / www.barrafina.co.uk; 11 pm; no booking.

Basilico £29 ❸❸⑤
690 Fulham Rd, SW6 0800 028 3531 10–1B
26 Penton St, N1 0800 093 4224 8–3D
515 Finchley Rd, NW3 0800 316 2656 1–1B
175 Lavender Hill, SW11 0800 389 9770 10–2C
178 Upper Richmond Rd, SW14 0800 096 8202 10–2B
"The best delivery pizza in town" – "with lots of interesting toppings"
and "crisp bases" – wins uniform praise for this home delivery chain;
they arrive "when they say they will" too. / www.basilico.co.uk; midnight;
no booking.

The Bathhouse EC2 NEW £40
8 Bishopsgate Churchyard 7920 9207 9–2D
On the site most recently known as Ciro's Pizza Pomodoro,
this intriguing spot near Liverpool Street – built as subterranean
Victorian Turkish baths – was being relaunched as this guide went
to press; expect a bar/restaurant/music venue.
/ www.thebathhousevenue.com; 9.30 pm; closed Sat & Sun.

Bayee Village SW19 £33 ❸❷❸
24 High St 8947 3533 1–4A
A Wimbledon Village fixture, which continues to win praise for its
"good, if not cheap Chinese" fare, and its "personal" service.
/ www.bayee.co.uk; 11 pm.

Beach Blanket Babylon £52 ⑤⑤❷
45 Ledbury Rd, W11 7229 2907 6–1B
19-23 Bethnal Green Rd, E1 7749 3540 12–1C
"Let's face it, you go for the fun, not the food", to these "decadently"
decorated Gaudiesque ventures in Notting Hill and Shoreditch –
"great places to hang out", but "not to eat". / www.beachblanket.co.uk;
10 pm; W2 some booking restrictions apply Fri & Sat.

Beauberry House
Belair Park SE21 £52 ❹❸❹
Gallery Rd, Dulwich Village 8299 9788 1–4C
Few dining rooms have so "beautiful" a location as this Grade I-listed
house, by Belair Park – one of Dulwich's handful of "grown up"
eateries; its wacky French/Japanese cuisine excites little feedback,
but such as there is suggests it's still "hit-and-miss".
/ www.beauberryhouse.co.uk; 10.30 pm; closed Mon & Sun D.

Bedford & Strand WC2 £42 ❹❸❷
1a Bedford St 7836 3033 4–4D
"Well-chosen" wine and "friendly" service make for a "great vibe"
in this "crowded" hide-away, handily located off the Strand; "decent"
food too. / www.bedford-strand.com; 10 pm; closed Sat & Sun; set dinner
£27 (FP).

Bedlington Café W4 £23 ❸❷❹
24 Fauconberg Rd 8994 1965 7–2A
A long-established Thai café, lost deep in leafy Chiswick; "the food's
not outstanding, but strong on value" – "you can buy alcohol,
but most people BYO". / 10 pm; closed Sun L; no credit cards.

The Beehive W1 £36 ④❸④
126 Crawford St 7486 8037 2–1A
A Marylebone gastropub, where the Italian slant is a recipe for something of an identity crisis; its "decent" dishes, though, generally satisfy. / www.thebeehive-pub.co.uk; 10 pm; closed Sun.

Beirut Express £35 ❷④⑤
65 Old Brompton Rd, SW7 7591 0123 5–2B
112-114 Edgware Rd, W2 7724 2700 6–1D
"No-frills" and "great-value", these Lebanese pit stops offer "huge portions of tasty food". / www.maroush.com; W2 2 am; SW7 midnight.

Beiteddine SW1 £41 ❸❷⑤
8 Harriet St 7235 3969 5–1D
"Dishes just like you get in Beirut" win praise for this "comfy, slightly faded and rather cramped" spot, just off Sloane Street; "prices are low… for Knightsbridge". / www.beiteddine.com; midnight.

Bel Canto EC3 £73 ④④❷
4 Minster Ct 7444 0004 9–3D
"Brilliant opera-singing staff" lend a "unique" atmosphere to this City yearling; "look out for half-price offers", though – otherwise its Gallic cuisine can seem "a bit pricey". / www.lebelcanto.co.uk; 11.30 pm; D only, closed Mon & Sun.

Belgo £36 ④④④
50 Earlham St, WC2 7813 2233 4–2C
67 Kingsway, WC2 7242 7469 2–2D
72 Chalk Farm Rd, NW1 7267 0718 8–2B
44-48 Clapham High Rd, SW4 7720 1118 10–2D
The "superlative" choice of Belgian beer remains a highlight at these "cavernous" but "buzzy" outlets; the moules/frites menu still has fans too, but critics find this a "tired" formula, and the "ludicrously overpriced" too – set deals, such as the early-evening 'Beat the Clock', are the best bets. / www.belgo-restaurants.co.uk; most branches 10.30 pm-11.30 pm; SW4 midnight, Thu 1 am, Fri & Sat 2 am, Sun 12.30 am.

Bellamy's W1 £70 ④❸❸
18-18a Bruton Pl 7491 2727 3–2B
"You know what you'll get", at this posh Mayfair mews brasserie – an "über-smooth" welcome, "discreet" service and "clubby" fare; the package is "very, very expensive" for what it is, though, and the uninitiated may find it "underwhelming". / www.bellamysrestaurant.co.uk; 10.15 pm; closed Sat L & Sun; set weekday L £51 (FP).

Bellevue Rendez-Vous SW17 £37 ❸④❸
218 Trinity Rd 8767 5810 10–2C
As Mini Mundus (its former name), this "friendly" local, near Wandsworth Common, won praise for its "great", Gallic cuisine; this year, though, it also inspired a couple of "very poor" reports – hopefully just a wobble prior to the recent rebranding (under the same owner and chef). / www.bellevuerendezvous.com; 10.30 pm; closed Mon L.

Belvedere W8 £57 ❸❷❶
Holland Pk, off Abbotsbury Rd 7602 1238 7–1D
Set in "the prettiest park in London", this "elegant" Art Deco-styled fixture is unbeatable for a "special occasion", or for "romantic" dining (and also for a "fantastic-value Sunday lunch"); "the food is reliable and the service unquestionable, but don't expect culinary inspiration". / www.belvedererestaurant.co.uk; 10 pm; closed Sun D.

Benares W1 £70 ❷❸❸
12 Berkeley Hs, Berkeley Sq   7629 8886   3–3B
"Modern Indian cuisine at its best" still wins very high acclaim for Atul Kochar's "slick" (if slightly "dull") first-floor Mayfair premises; a few reporters this year, however, found the food "not all it's cracked up to be" – is he starting to spend too much time on TV? / www.benaresrestaurant.co.uk; 10.30 pm; no trainers; set weekday L & pre-theatre £41 (FP).

Bengal Clipper SE1 £38 ❷④④
Shad Thames   7357 9001   9–4D
Sometimes "contemptuous" service again takes the gloss off reports on this spacious, and otherwise "lovely" South Bank Indian, which offers "a very good standard of cooking"; jazz pianist some evenings. / www.bengalclipper.co.uk; 11.30 pm.

Benihana £55 ④④④
37 Sackville St, W1   7494 2525   3–3D
77 King's Rd, SW3   7376 7799   5–3D
100 Avenue Rd, NW3   7586 9508   8–2A
The one-time "novelty" of this US-based teppan-yaki chain has worn thin over the passing decades; some reporters still find its "juggling" chefs make for a "fun" night out, but too many see it as "one big gimmick" nowadays, with "mediocre" food, "gloomy" décor and "comical" prices. / www.benihana.co.uk; 10.30 pm, Sun 10 pm.

Benja W1 £45 ❷❷❸
17 Beak Street   7287 0555   3–2D
In the heart of the West End – but still often a "discovery" for reporters – this small but lavishly-furnished Soho townhouse Thai offers food that's somewhere between "good" and "excellent". / www.benjarestaurant.com; 10.45 pm; closed Sun.

Bentley's W1 £60 ❷❸❸
11-15 Swallow St   7734 4756   3–3D
A "clubby" Mayfair seafood "classic" – revamped to good effect in recent times by Richard Corrigan – where the "casual" ground-floor oyster bar is often tipped in preference to the "stuffy" first-floor restaurant; opinions differ on whether service is "slick" or just "smug". / www.bentleys.org; 10.30 pm; no jeans; booking: max 8.

Bento Cafe NW1 £30 ❷❸❸
9 Parkway   7482 3990   8–3B
By Camden Town's celebrated Jazz Café, this "fun and buzzy" pit stop offers "fantastic budget sushi", plus a "mammoth" menu of "fairly adventurous" other dishes. / bentocafe.co.uk; 10.15 pm, Fri & Sat 11 pm.

Benugo £28 ④④❷
14 Curzon St, W1   7629 6246   3–4B
23-25 Gt Portland St, W1   7631 5052   3–1C
V&A Museum, Cromwell Rd, SW7   7581 2159   5–2C
Westfield, Unit 1070 Ariel Way, W12   8746 9490   7–1C
St Pancras International, , NW1   7833 0201   8–3C
BFI Southbank, Belvedere Rd, SE1   7401 9000   2–3D
116 St John St, EC1   7253 3499   9–1A
82 City Rd, EC1   7253 1295   12–1A
*From the "beautiful tiled rooms" of the V&A to the "groovy" BFI
branch (complete with "buzzy bar"), this upmarket snack chain
certainly has "great styling"; its 'dash for growth', however, has led
to too many reports of "mediocre" food and "inefficient" service
nowadays. / www.benugo.com; most branches 4 pm; SE1 11pm,
Sun 10.30 pm; W1 & EC1 branches closed Sat & Sun; W1 & EC1 branches,
no credit cards.*

Beotys WC2 £47 ⑤④④
79 St Martin's Ln   7836 8768   4–3B
*A comfortable West End veteran liked by fans (often of decades'
standing) as a "peaceful" Theatreland "haven", rather than for its
"very unimaginative" Franco-Greek food; even some of its
staunchest supporters, though, have found it a touch "disappointing"
in recent times. / www.covent-garden.co.uk/beotys/; 11 pm; closed Sun.*

Bermondsey Kitchen SE1 £40 ④④④
194 Bermondsey St   7407 5719   9–4D
*This boho Bermondsey bistro wins tips for breakfast and as a
"decent" all-round performer; on some reports this year, however,
"it didn't live up to expectations". / www.bermondseykitchen.co.uk;
10.30 pm; closed Sun D.*

Bertorelli £40 ⑤⑤⑤
11-13 Frith St, W1   7494 3491   4–2A
19-23 Charlotte St, W1   7636 4174   2–1C
37 St Martin's Ln, WC2   7836 5837   4–4C
44a Floral St, WC2   7836 3969   4–2D
15 Mincing Ln, EC3   7283 3028   9–3D
1 Plough Pl, EC4   7842 0510   9–2A
*A "very run-of-the-mill" Italian chain, which once again inspires far
too many "absolutely horrendous" reports, featuring "dire" food and
"truly appalling" service. / www.santeonline.co.uk; 10 pm; EC3 closed
Sat & Sun; booking: W1 max 10, WC2 max 6.*

Best Mangal W14 £24 ❸❷❸
104 North End Rd   7610 1050   7–2D
*"Succulent meats barbecued in a central fire pit" provide the basis for
many "excellent" meals at this "cheap" and "buzzing" café,
near West Kensington tube; not quite everyone, though, is convinced
its "immense reputation amongst kebab connoisseurs" is entirely
justified. / www.bestmangal.com; midnight, Sat 1 am; no Amex.*

Bevis Marks EC3 £60 ❸❸❸
Bevis Marks   7283 2220   9–2D
*"Top-quality food, that happens to be kosher" is served at this useful
City lunching venue – the unusual and "beautiful conservatory-
annexe" of an ancient synagogue. / www.bevismarkstherestaurant.com;
8.30 pm; closed Fri D, Sat & Sun.*

Beyoglu NW3 £30 ❸❸④
72 Belsize Ln 7435 7733 8–2A
"An ever-reliable Turkish delight" – all reports sing the praises of this
"welcoming" and *"reasonably-priced"* Belsize Park spot.
/ www.beyoglu.co.uk; 11 pm; no Amex or Maestro.

Bianco Nero W6 £40 ❷❸❸
206-208 Hammersmith Rd 8748 0212 7–2C
A *"pleasingly weird"* find, *"opposite Hammersmith bus station"* –
thanks to its *"crisp"* monochrome design and *"quality"* cooking,
this *"classy"* Italian is managing to make quite a go of its terrible
location. / www.bianconerorestaurants.com; 10 pm; closed Sat L & Sun;
set pre theatre £26 (FP).

Bibendum SW3 £67 ❸❷❶
81 Fulham Rd 7581 5817 5–2C
"Standards are up again", at this Brompton Cross *"icon"*, whose
"stunning" setting makes a particularly *"lovely, light and airy"* lunch
location; service is *"impeccable"* too, the food is *"sensitively
prepared"*, and perusing the wine list is *"like reading Hugh Johnson's
World Atlas of Wine!"* / www.bibendum.co.uk; 11 pm, Sun 10.30 pm;
booking: max 12 at L, 10 at D.

Bibendum Oyster Bar SW3 £52 ❸❸❷
81 Fulham Rd 7589 1480 5–2C
"The freshest oysters, prawns and langoustines you'll find anywhere"
are served – often with a glass of fizz – at this elegant seafood bar,
in the *"interesting"* foyer of Chelsea's Michelin building.
/ www.bibendum.co.uk; 10.30 pm; no booking.

Big Easy SW3 £43 ④❸❷
332-334 King's Rd 7352 4071 5–3C
"In you're in a party mood", this *"loud"* and *"brash"* US-style Chelsea
dive can be *"lots of fun"*; it serves an *"extensive"* but *"expensive"*
range of *"tasty"* dishes (majoring in burgers and seafood),
in authentically *"large"* portions. / www.bigeasy.uk.com; 11.30 pm, Fri &
Sat 12.30 am.

Bincho Yakitori W1 £31 ④❷❸
16 Old Compton St 7287 9111 4–2A
This Soho yakitori (grilled skewer) restaurant seems a *"likeable"*
enough place to most reporters (*"as long as you like salt"*);
it's difficult, however, not to lament the closing of its infinitely more
handsome South Bank sibling. / www.bincho.co.uk; 11.30 pm,
Sun 10.30 pm.

Bingham TW10 £50 ❸❸❷
61-63 Petersham Rd 8940 0902 1–4A
This *"lovely"* hotel dining room, near Richmond Bridge, is a top all-
round *"special-occasion"* destination, complete with a *"magical setting
near the banks of the Thames"*; *"very good-value set lunch"* too.
/ www.thebingham.co.uk; booking: max 7 in main restaurant.

Bistro 1 £20 ④❷❸
27 Frith St, W1 7734 6204 4–3A
28 Brewer St, W1 7734 0179 3–2D
75 Beak St, W1 7287 1840 3–2D
33 Southampton St, WC2 7379 7585 4–3D
"Probably cheaper than eating at home!"; these *"friendly"*
Turkish/Mediterranean bistros offer *"unbeatable"* prices for central
London – *"just the job"* for a *"swift"* budget meal. / www.bistro1.co.uk;
midnight.

Bistro Aix N8 £43 ❸❸❷
54 Topsfield Pde, Tottenham Ln   8340 6346   8–1C
*"A hidden gem"; thanks to its "neatly-executed" food and its
"intimate" style, this "friendly French bistro" remains a big hit with
the cognoscenti of Crouch End. / www.bistroaix.co.uk; 11 pm; closed Mon,
Tue-Fri D only, Sat & Sun open L & D.*

Bistro 190
Gore Hotel SW7 £54 ❹❹❸
190 Queen's Gate   7584 6601   5–1B
*"Excellent pre-Albert Hall", it may be, but this hotel bistro is "not as
good as it used to be" (and "a bit amateurish at times"); fans find
it "attractive", though, and say it offers some "decent prix-fixe
options". / www.gorehotel.com; 11.30 pm.*

Bistrotheque E2 £45 ❸❸❷
23-27 Wadeson St   8983 7900   1–2D
*This "edgy" East Ender – a "relaxed warehouse-style" space –
is known as a "good-night-out" destination, with "a nice bar", "well-
cooked" food and an "original" cabaret; critics, though, fear it's going
"downhill" – "it's only gay-scene popularity which keeps it so busy".
/ www.bistrotheque.com; 10.30 pm; closed weekday L.*

Black & Blue £46 ❸❹❹
90-92 Wigmore St, W1   7486 1912   3–1A
105 Gloucester Rd, SW7   7244 7666   5–2B
215-217 Kensington Church St, W8   7727 0004   6–2B
205-207 Haverstock Hill, NW3   7443 7744   8–2A
1-2 Rochester Walk, SE1   7357 9922   9–4C
*It's still "a reliable place for steak" (and with "excellent" burgers too),
but this upmarket chain seems otherwise to be going backwards –
service is declining, and the ambience appears ever more "anodyne".
/ www.blackandbluerestaurant.com; most branches 11 pm, Fri & Sat
11.30 pm; no booking.*

Blah! Blah! Blah! W12 £31 ❸❸❹
78 Goldhawk Rd   8746 1337   7–1C
*A BYO veggie café, near Goldhawk Road tube, which inspires few
reports nowadays; all still applaud its "interesting" fare.
/ www.blahvegetarian.com; 10.30 pm; closed Sun; no credit cards.*

Blakes
Blakes Hotel SW7 £104 ❺❹❷
33 Roland Gdns   7370 6701   5–2B
*This once famously louche and romantic South Kensington basement
attracts little comment nowadays (and has been reported
as "very quiet"); long-time supporters may still discern something
"special" in the atmosphere, and the eye-popping prices have
an aphrodisiac quality all of their own. / www.blakeshotels.com; 11.30 pm;
closed Sun.*

BLEEDING HEART EC1 £49 ❷❷❷
Bleeding Heart Yd, Greville St   7242 8238   9–2A
*"Hidden-away down a cobbled alley", near Holborn, this "historic"
warren – comprising a tavern, bistro and restaurant – remains one
of the best-liked places in town; with its "traditional Gallic" approach,
its "very intimate" nooks and its "epic" wine list, it manages to "cover
all the bases, from business to romance". / www.bleedingheart.co.uk;
10.30 pm; closed Sun.*

Blue Elephant SW6 £52 ❸❸❶
4-6 Fulham Broadway 7385 6595 5–4A
Tropical vegetation "transports you from Fulham to Phuket", at this "Disneyesque" Thai extravaganza – one of the most "impressive" restaurant interiors in town; but while this still pleases – even "enthralls" – most reporters, neither food nor service are up to their past best standards. / www.blueelephant.com; 11.30 pm, Sun 10.30 pm; closed Sat L (except Stamford Bridge match days).

Blue Jade SW1 £31 ❸❶④
44 Hugh St 7828 0321 2–4B
A tucked-away Pimlico Thai, where "really delightful" service is the highlight; the food may be "predictable", but the overall experience is "a safe bet". / 11 pm; closed Sat L & Sun.

Bluebird SW3 £52 ⑤⑤⑤
350 King's Rd 7559 1000 5–3C
The introduction of sub-£20 prix-fixe menus (always available) has been a (rare) positive development at this "cavernous" Chelsea brasserie; it's a D&D group property, though, and too many reporters still find the food "rubbish", and "incredibly overpriced" too. / www.bluebird-restaurant.co.uk; 10 pm; set dinner £30 (FP).

Bluebird Café SW3 £35 ⑤⑤⑤
350 King's Rd 7559 1000 5–3C
"A dreadful place"; run by the D&D group, the café attached to this Chelsea landmark is simply "very overpriced and mediocre"; good people-watching at weekends, though. / www.bluebird-restaurant.co.uk; 10 pm, Sun 5 pm.

Blueprint Café
Design Museum SE1 £48 ④④❷
28 Shad Thames, Butler's Wharf 7378 7031 9–4D
A "stunning" location, with "outstanding" views of the Thames and Tower Bridge is, as ever, the draw to this "bright" and "airy" South Bank dining room; in the best D&D (fka Conran) group tradition, however, the food is "no better than average". / www.blueprintcafe.co.uk; 10.45 pm; closed Sun D.

Bob Bob Ricard W1 £52 ⑤④❸
1 Upper James St 3145 1000 3–2D
"What is the point?"; this "glamorous", "20s"-style Soho newcomer (on the site of Circus, RIP) "looks amazing", but too often seems "gimmicky and gauche"; being "stupidly overpriced" is the main show-stopper, but the "bizarre" menu, "ordinary" results and "not-great" service don't help. / www.bobbobricard.com; 1 am.

Bocca Di Lupo W1 NEW £39 ❷❷❷
12 Archer St 7734 2223 3–2D
"Dazzling" Italian dishes – "regionally identified", and served "in 'tasting' or 'full' portions" – have made this "vibey" and "fantastically friendly" Soho newcomer a truly "exciting addition to London dining"; "the best seats are at the chef's counter". / www.boccadilupo.com; 11 pm; booking: max 10.

Bodean's   £36   ④④④
10 Poland St, W1   7287 7575   3–1D
Fulham Broadway, SW6   7610 0440   5–4A
57 Westbourne Grove, W2   7727 9503   6–1C
169 Clapham High St, SW4   7622 4248   10–2D
16 Byward St, EC3   7488 3883   9–3D
*For a "proper barbecue", these "meaty-licious" dives – majoring
in ribs, burgers, and pulled pork – aim to "recreate an American rib
shack" ("complete with live US sport" on the TV); the food "isn't
as good as back home", though, and "has gone of the boil"
significantly as the group has expanded.* / www.bodeansbbq.com; 11 pm,
Sun 10.30 pm; EC3 10 pm; EC3 closed Sun.

Boiled Egg & Soldiers SW11   £24   ④④④
63 Northcote Rd   7223 4894   10–2C
*"If you can stand the kids", this yummy-mummy Battersea café
is often tipped for "the best breakfasts"; it's "pricey", though,
and "shows every sign of resting on its laurels".* / L & afternoon tea only;
no Mastercard or Amex; no booking.

Boisdale SW1   £60   ④④❷
13-15 Eccleston St   7730 6922   2–4B
*"All kilt and no bagpipes!"; Ranald Macdonald's tartan-themed
Belgravian still wins praise for its "clubby" ("male") atmosphere,
"excellent" jazz, "extensive" whiskies and "wonderful" cigar terrace;
"service can be a let-down", though, and the "meaty" Scottish fare
is "pricey" and seems increasingly "poor".* / www.boisdale.co.uk;
11.30 pm; closed Sat D & Sun.

Boisdale of Bishopsgate EC2   £50   ❸④❸
202 Bishopsgate, Swedeland Ct   7283 1763   9–2D
*"Business clients love the tartan" of this Scottish-themed City bar –
its basement restaurant seems to be producing rather better
"carnivorous" fare nowadays than the Belgravia original.*
/ www.boisdale.co.uk; 9 pm; closed Sat & Sun.

The Bolingbroke SW11 NEW   £37   ❸❸❸
174 Northcote Rd   7228 4040   10–2C
*"Helpful" staff help create a "chilled" atmosphere at this popular
new Battersea gastropub (on the site of Nikson's, RIP), which serves
scoff that's "well-cooked and reasonably-priced"; at weekends,
"be prepared for lots of yummy mummies and their kids".*
/ www.renaissancepubs.co.uk; 10.30 pm, Sun 9 pm.

Bombay Bicycle Club   £36   ④④④
128 Holland Park Ave, W11   7727 7335   6–2A
3a Downshire Hill, NW3   7435 3544   8–2A
95 Nightingale Ln, SW12   8673 6217   10–2C
*"Plummeting downhill since the change of ownership" – this "old-
favourite" Indian chain "has lost its way" over the past year,
with rising complaints about so-so service, "decidedly average" food
and "stingy" portions.* / www.thebombaybicycleclub.co.uk; 11 pm,
Sun 10.30 pm.

Bombay Brasserie SW7   £73   ❸④④
Courtfield Close, Gloucester Rd   7370 4040   5–2B
*After its "tragic" refurbishment ("'70s ballroom-meets-Novotel"),
this large South Kensington Indian looks unlikely to regain its former
"favourite" status any time soon; unless you go for the "excellent-
value Sunday buffet", it can seem "grossly overpriced".*
/ www.bombaybrasserielondon.com; 11.30 pm; set weekday L £44 (FP).

Bombay Palace W2 £44 **❶❶⑤**
50 Connaught St 7723 8855 6–1D
"Wonderfully fresh" and "subtly-spiced" Indian cooking
(in "traditional" style) makes this Bayswater veteran a big "favourite"
for its large fan club; service is "charming" too, but the setting is a
"lost cause". / www.bombay-palace.co.uk; 11.30 pm.

Bonds
Threadneedles Hotel EC2 £55 **❸❸❸**
5 Threadneedle St 7657 8088 9–2C
This "delightfully calm" venue – a former banking hall in the heart
of the City – really "understands its niche", and offers "competent"
cuisine that's "perfect for business… so long as it's on expenses";
service, though, "can lag". / www.theetoncollection.com/restaurants/bonds/;
10 pm; closed Sat & Sun; set weekday L & dinner £25 (FP).

Bord'Eaux
Grosvenor House Hotel W1 £58 **❸❸⑤**
Park Ln 7399 8460 3–3A
"Impressive" in scale but "soulless" in character, this Mayfair
brasserie has sometimes been reported "quiet" – a shame, as the
Gallic fare, if "rather dear", is of a "high standard".
/ www.bord-eaux.com; 10.30 pm, 11 pm Fri & Sat.

Il Bordello E1 £38 **❷❷❷**
81 Wapping High St 7481 9950 11–1A
"A miracle for Wapping" – this "bustling" and "squeezed-in" Italian
has long been a firm favourite, thanks to its "huge portions" of "fresh
and vibrant" fare (pizzas are "particularly excellent"); "the challenge
is getting in". / 11 pm; closed Sat L.

La Bota N8 £22 **❸❸❷**
31 Broadway Pde 8340 3082 1–1C
A "firm-favourite" Crouch End tapas bar and restaurant, praised for
its "very good" food, and at "bargain" prices too. / www.labota.co.uk;
11 pm, Fri & Sat 11.30 pm; no Amex.

The Botanist SW1 £48 **④⑤④**
7 Sloane Sq 7730 0077 5–2D
"Seemingly aimed at the Euroset", the Martin brothers' "hectic"
Sloane Square brasserie yearling is certainly "very buzzy"; you do get
"rammed in" though, to enjoy "unremarkable" and "overpriced" food,
"sloppily" served. / www.thebotanistonsloanesquare.com; 10.30 pm.

La Bottega £12 **❸❹④**
25 Eccleston St, SW1 7730 2730 2–4B
65 Lower Sloane St, SW1 7730 8844 5–2D
14 Gloucester Rd, SW7 7581 6980 5–1B **NEW**
"Almost like real paninotecas!" – these "good and authentic" Chelsea,
Belgravia and, most recently, South Kensington cafés are getting a bit
of a name locally for "absolutely the best coffee and Italian pastries".
/ www.labottega65.com; Lower Sloane St 6.30 pm, Sat 6 pm, Sun 5 pm;
Eccleston St 6.30 pm; SW7 8 pm; Eccleston St closed Sun; no booking.

La Bouchée SW7 £47 **❸❸❷**
56 Old Brompton Rd 7589 1929 5–2B
It may be "squashed", but this "effortlessly French" bistro, near South
Kensington tube, has "stood the test of time"; it's a "cosy, candlelit
and romantic" place, which serves "reliable", "classic" fare.
/ www.boudinblanc.co.uk; 11 pm, Sat 11.30 pm; set weekday L & dinner
£28 (FP).

Le Bouchon Bordelais SW11 £44 ④④④
5-9 Battersea Rise   7738 0307   10–2C
A "popular" and "noisy" Gallic local, in Battersea, known for its
"decent", classic dishes (including an "excellent châteaubriand");
"it sometimes lets itself down" though, with "uninspiring" cooking.
/ www.lebouchon.co.uk; 11 pm; closed Mon L & Tue L; set always available
£25 (FP).

Le Bouchon Breton E1 £45 ④❸④
8 Horner Sq   08000 191704   12–2C
Newly-opened above Spitalfields Market, this "cavernous" space has
had a "classy" fit-out as an "old-fashioned brasserie", and its
"attentive" (if slightly "haphazard") staff serve up some "well-
executed" Gallic fare; shame it "costs so much" though, and can
seemingly "struggle for trade". / www.lebouchon.co.uk; 11 pm; closed
Mon D, Sat L & Sun D.

Boudin Blanc W1 £54 ❷❸❶
5 Trebeck St   7499 3292   3–4B
"Just the kind of place you expect to find in Paris"; this "charming"
candlelit favourite, "tucked-away" in Shepherd Market, offers some
"great classic dishes" (albeit with an occasional dose of "attitude");
"perfect" outside tables in summer. / www.boudinblanc.co.uk; 11 pm;
set weekday L & dinner £28 (FP).

Boulevard WC2 £37 ⑤⑤⑤
40 Wellington St   7240 2992   4–3D
New owners (Med Kitchen) "have ruined everything that was good"
about this Covent Garden brasserie; for such a touristy location, it was
once a "safe bet" – too often nowadays, it seems a "complete and
utter disgrace". / www.boulevardbrasserie.co.uk; Mon-Thu 11 pm, Fri & Sat
11.30 pm, Sun 10.30 pm.

The Boundary E2 £50 ❸❸❷
2-4 Boundary St   7729 1051   12–1B
Sir Terence Conran's "glamorous but cosy" Gallic newcomer, in a
"lavishly decorated" Shoreditch basement, inspires a kaleidoscope
of verdicts, from "faultless all round" to "disappointing" – the middle
view is that it's "pleasant overall, but a bit too pricey".
/ www.theboundary.co.uk; 10.30 pm; closed Mon L & Sun D.

The Bountiful Cow WC1 £40 ❸④④
51 Eagle St   7404 0200   2–1D
"Steaks the size of plates, and burgers so big your eyes pop out" –
"properly done" too – win a big thumbs-up for this small "non-gastro"
pub, "on a back street near Holborn". / www.thebountifulcow.co.uk;
10 pm; closed Sun D.

Bowler Bar & Grill SW3 £50 ❸❸❸
2a Pond Pl   7589 5876   5–2C
A "sound" Chelsea steakhouse with a "good vibe"; it must be good,
as it's seeing out the recession in one of London's most notorious
'graveyard' sites! / www.bowlerbarandgrill.co.uk; 11.30 pm; D only,
closed Sun.

Boxwood Café
The Berkeley SW1 £62 ④❸❸
Wilton Pl   7235 1010   5–1D
Fans of Gordon Ramsay's "luxurious" (but "slightly claustrophobic")
Knightsbridge basement 'café' find it "a brilliant concept",
with "personable" service and a "casual" style; "for the price",
though, doubters feel it's "nothing special at all".
/ www.gordonramsay.com/boxwoodcafe; 11 pm; booking: max 8.

Bradley's NW3 £48 ④④④
25 Winchester Rd 7722 3457 8–2A
A Swiss Cottage stalwart that's of particular note for its "very decent, pre-Hampstead-Theatre supper" – fans say it's a "high-quality" local generally, but reports are rather up-and-down. / www.bradleysnw3.co.uk; 11 pm; closed Sun D; set weekday L & pre-theatre £27 (FP).

Brady's SW18 £26 ❸❷❸
513 Old York Rd 8877 9599 10–2B
The owners contribute a "personal touch" to this basic chippy/fish bistro, in Wandsworth; it has long had a name for "quality" fish 'n' chips ("battered or grilled"), plus "the best mushy peas" and "decent puds". / www.bradysfish.co.uk; 10.30 pm; closed Mon L & Sun; no Amex; no booking.

La Brasserie SW3 £48 ④④④
272 Brompton Rd 7581 3089 5–2C
This age-old "coin de Paris", near Brompton Cross, is perhaps most "authentic" in its "grumpy" attitude to service; the food is "average", but this remains a "great spot for breakfast" nonetheless. / www.labrasserielondon.co.uk; 11 pm; no booking, Sat L & Sun L.

Brasserie James SW12 £39 ❸❷❸
47 Balham Hill 8772 0057 10–2C
"Very favourable impressions" are reported of this year-old brasserie, near Clapham South tube – it combines "a good buzz" and "accommodating" staff with "good and varied French cooking at reasonable prices". / www.brasseriejames.com; 10 pm; set weekday L £25 (FP).

Brasserie Roux
Sofitel St James SW1 £60 ④④④
8 Pall Mall 7968 2900 2–3C
With its "ideal West End location" and "excellent-value" set menus, this "dramatic" (but "rather soulless") chamber can be "excellent pre-theatre" or "for a business lunch"; service is "patchy", though, and some "expect more of the Rouxs" than the "nothing-special" cuisine on offer here. / www.sofitelstjames.com; 10.45 pm; set pre-theatre £26 (FP), set weekday L £32 (FP).

Brasserie St Jacques SW1 £47 ④④⑤
33 St James's St 7839 1007 3–4C
Starry backers have brought "no particular distinction" to this airy but strangely "dull" Gallic brasserie yearling, in St James's; on the plus side, the absence of custom can make it "quite relaxing" (and, if you can't get a table at the Wolseley, you can usually get one here!) / www.brasseriestjacques.co.uk; 11 pm, Sun 10 pm; closed Sun; no jeans or trainers.

Brick Lane Beigel Bake E1 £6 ❶④⑤
159 Brick Ln 7729 0616 12–1C
"There's no better bagel either side of the Atlantic!" than at this 24/7 East End legend, where there's "always an eclectic mix of people queuing, especially after midnight"; most popular fillings: salt beef ("incredible"), or smoked salmon ("extraordinary"). / open 24 hours; no credit cards; no booking.

The Brickhouse E1 £35 ④❸❷
152c, Brick Ln   7247 0005   12–2C
With its "great entertainment" and bed-filled bar, this East End venue
is tipped by its small fanclub as "a great place for a fab night out",
with food that's "surprisingly good" by the standards of such places.
/ www.thebrickhouse.co.uk.

The Bridge SW13 £37 ④④❸
204 Castelnau   8563 9811   7–2C
Fans of this north Barnes gastroboozer, which has a "nice garden",
say it "does the job", and is "worth crossing Hammersmith Bridge
for"; "the food's declined" since it opened, though, and service can
be "indifferent". / www.thebridgeinbarnes.co.uk; 10.30 pm.

Brilliant UB2 £35 ❷❷④
72-76 Western Rd   8574 1928   1–3A
Bollywood on the TV helps enliven the atmosphere at this large
(and somewhat "odd and bright") Indian veteran, lost deep in the
Southall suburbs; it's worth the trek if you're looking for a curry that's
"the real McCoy". / www.brilliantrestaurant.com; 11.30 pm, Fri & Sat
midnight; closed Mon, Sat L & Sun L; booking: weekends only.

Brinkley's SW10 £44 ④④❸
47 Hollywood Rd   7351 1683   5–3B
John Brinkley's Chelsea back street haunt is perhaps the key Sloane
("and ex-Sloane") rendezvous de nos jours – a "fun" place with
"inexpensive" wine (not as cheap as it used to be, though) and
"pretty" garden; food and service, however, are "fading" badly.
/ www.brinkleys.com; 11 pm; closed weekday L.

Brinkley's Kitchen SW17 NEW £35 ④④❸
35 Bellevue Rd   8672 5888   10–2C
"At last this 'difficult' location has found a formula that seems
to work!" – John Brinkley's annexation of the former Amici (RIP) site,
overlooking Wandsworth Common, has generally been welcomed,
but sceptics observe that "the good-value wine only partially
compensates for the unimaginative food". / www.brinkleys.com.

La Brocca NW6 £32 ❸❸❷
273 West End Ln   7433 1989   1–1B
This West Hampstead "gem" – a "crowded", candlelit cellar beneath
a bar – has a "huge neighbourhood following" and is "always
buzzing"; aside from its "great" pizza 'n' pasta, though, dishes can
seem "pricey" and "not that well cooked". / www.labrocca.co.uk; Sun-Thu
10.30 pm, Fri & Sat 11 pm; booking: max 8.

Brompton Bar & Grill SW3 NEW £39 ④❷❷
243 Brompton Rd   7589 8005   5–2C
Rather mixed reports on this "buzzy" Knightsbridge successor to the
Brasserie St Quentin (RIP); wines are notably "reasonably priced",
but views on the "straightforward" cuisine differ widely, balancing out
somewhere round "decent, but unexciting".
/ www.bromptonbarandgrill.com; 11 pm, Sun 10 pm.

Brompton Quarter Café SW3 £43 ④⑤④
223-225 Brompton Rd   7225 2107   5–2C
Not far from Harrods, this bright corner café is, say fans,
"an excellent spot for a light lunch" (or "for a coffee and a cake");
service is sometimes "abysmal", though, and critics can find the place
"insanely overpriced". / www.bromptonquartercafe.com; 10.30 pm.

Brouge £22 ④❷❸

241 Hampton Rd, TW2   8977 2698   1–4A **NEW**

5 Hill St, TW9   8332 0055   1–4A **NEW**

*In Twickenham, and, more recently, in Richmond, a proto-chain
of Belgian bistros, with the moules 'n' beers emphasis you'd expect;
early days reports (few) are broadly positive, with particular praise for
the "very friendly service". / www.brouge.co.uk; TW2 10 pm;
TW9 10.30 pm; no Amex; set always available £19 (FP).*

The Brown Dog SW13 £40 ❸❸❷

28 Cross St   8392 2200   10–1A

*A "fabulous", "cosy" atmosphere – plus a cute garden – has made
quite a name for this little pub, in the chichi back streets of Barnes's
'Little Chelsea'; "welcoming" service and enjoyable gastropub fare
complete the formula. / www.thebrowndog.co.uk; 10 pm.*

Browns £38 ④④④

47 Maddox St, W1   7491 4565   3–2C

82-84 St Martin's Ln, WC2   7497 5050   4–3B

9 Islington Grn, N1   7226 2555   8–3D

Butler's Wharf, SE1   7378 1700   9–4D

Hertsmere Rd, E14   7987 9777   11–1C

8 Old Jewry, EC2   7606 6677   9–2C

*The "buzzy" branches of this "middle-of-the-road" brasserie group
can make it a "useful" stand-by, especially "for groups"; they've
"really gone off the boil" in recent years, though, with "chain-style"
service and "mass-produced" food. / www.browns-restaurants.co.uk;
most branches 10 pm-11 pm; EC2 closed Sat & Sun; W1 closed Sun D.*

Brula TW1 £43 ❷⓿⓿

43 Crown Rd   8892 0602   1–4A

*This "quintessential" corner bistro, in St Margaret's, is "just the sort
of place anyone would like to have on their street"; a number
of reports speak of "recent improvements"… but it was already very
good! / www.brula.co.uk; 10 pm; closed Sun D; set always available £26 (FP).*

Brunello

Baglioni Hotel SW7 £70 ④❷❸

60 Hyde Park Gate   7368 5900   5–1B

*The Italian food can be "very good", but this self-conscious
Kensington design hotel has a very small following among reporters;
if you don't mind "hilarious" prices, though, check out the "extensive
Italian wine list" . / www.baglionihotellondon.com; 11 pm.*

Buchan's SW11 £41 ❸❷❸

62-64 Battersea Bridge Rd   7228 0888   5–4C

*A well-established, Scottish-themed wine bar, just over Battersea
Bridge; it inspires the odd middling report, but for its loyal fans it's
a "firm favourite". / www.buchansrestaurant.co.uk; 10.45 pm; set weekday
L £26 (FP), set Sun L £29 (FP).*

Buddha Bar WC2 £50 ⑤⑤❸

8 Victoria Embankment   3371 7777   2–2D

*This "style-over-substance" sibling of the famous Parisian hang-out
has failed to make waves in its first year of operation; yes, its "dimly-
lit" setting, near the Savoy, is "atmospheric", but – given the
"clueless" service and "appalling" oriental food – the prices are
"shocking". / www.buddhabar-london.com; 12.30 am; no jeans or trainers.*

Buen Ayre E8 £42 ❷❸❸
50 Broadway Mkt   7275 9900   1–2D
*"Deepest Hackney masquerades convincingly as Buenos Aires",
at this "cracking" 'parillada' (grill restaurant), which serves up "huge"
and "perfectly-cooked" steaks at "bargain" prices.
/ www.buenayre.co.uk; 10.30 pm; closed weekday L.*

Buenos Aires SE3 £40 ❸❷❷
17 Royal Pde   8318 5333   1–4D
*"Amazing steaks" – and in Blackheath too! – make this Argentinean
"oasis" a rare find locally; it also offers "simple but good-quality
wines" and, by night, the outside tables have "lovely views over the
heath". / www.buenosairesltd.com; 10.30 pm; no Amex.*

The Builders Arms SW3 £39 ❹❹❷
13 Britten St   7349 9040   5–2C
*The "charming interior" of this Chelsea boozer helps give it a "great
ambience"; in other respects it's "steady" but unexciting – yes, it's
a Geronimo Inn. / www.geronimo-inns.co.uk; 10 pm, Sat 11 pm, Sun 9 pm;
no booking.*

The Bull N6 £45 ❹❹❹
13 North Hill   0845 456 5033   1–1C
*A smart Highgate gastropub that's "satisfactory all-round, but not
really worth the prices charged". / www.inthebull.biz; 10.30 pm; closed
Mon; set weekday L £24 (FP).*

Bull & Last NW5 NEW £41 ❶❷❷
168 Highgate Rd   7267 3641   8–1B
*"A true gastropub"; this "cracking" Kentish Town newcomer –
with cooking "way beyond what you expect of a pub", and at very
"decent" prices too – has been the best all-round opening of the year;
the only real downside is that it can get "very noisy".
/ www.thebullandlast.co.uk; 10 pm; no Amex.*

Bumpkin £38 ❸❸❸
102 Old Brompton Rd, SW7   7341 0802   5–2B
209 Westbourne Park Rd, W11   7243 9818   6–1B
*This faux-"rustic" duo put in disparate performances; the Notting Hill
original offers "hearty British grub" in "gorgeous" and "relaxed"
surroundings, but its South Kensington spin-off too often seems
"arrogant", "ordinary" and "overpriced". / www.bumpkinuk.com; 11 pm.*

Buona Sera £33 ❹❸❷
289a King's Rd, SW3   7352 8827   5–3C
22 Northcote Rd, SW11   7228 9925   10–2C
*This "crammed" Battersea Italian has – thanks to its "tasty and
plentiful pasta and pizza" – been a top cheap 'n' cheerful local
destination for over 20 years; its lesser-known Chelsea offshoot has
"unusual" double-decker seating, but is more "haphazard". / midnight;
WC2 11.30 pm, Sun 10 pm; SW3 closed Mon L.*

Busaba Eathai £29 ❷❸❷
106-110 Wardour St, W1   7255 8686   3–2D
8-13 Bird St, W1   7518 8080   3–1A
22 Store St, WC1   7299 7900   2–1C
*"Much better than Wagamama"; these "always-buzzing" communal
Thais, stylishly "decked out with dark wood", serve up "fantastic",
"fresh" and "fragrant" food (in particular "addictive calamari")
at "canteen prices"; arrive early to avoid the "crazy" queue. / 11 pm,
Fri & Sat 11.30 pm, Sun 10 pm; W1 no booking; WC1 booking: min 10.*

Butcher & Grill £44 ④④④
39-41 Parkgate Rd, SW11   7924 3999   5–4C
33 High St, SW19   8944 8269   10–2B
"Just not good"; these "novel" and potentially "useful" outfits – grill rooms with butchers shops attached – inspire too many reports of "lumpen" and "overpriced" food, and "inattentive" service. / www.thebutcherandgrill.com; 11 pm; SW11 closed Sun D; SW19 closed Mon.

Butcher's Hook SW6 £38 ❸❷❷
477 Fulham Rd   7385 4654   5–4A
This "always-friendly" gastropub, by Stamford Bridge, wins nothing but praise for its "innovative food" and "great wine"… and "anywhere serving puy lentils opposite a footie ground deserves respect"! / www.thebutchershook.co.uk; 10.30 pm; no Amex.

Butlers Wharf Chop House SE1 £46 ⑤④④
36e Shad Thames   7403 3403   9–4D
"An amazing view of Tower Bridge" boosts the appeal of this D&D-group bar/restaurant, especially for business visitors; the too many reporters who have experienced "dreadful" British food and/or a "poor" atmosphere, though, simply want to know: "how does it still exist?" / www.chophouse.co.uk; 10.45 pm.

La Buvette TW9 £38 ❸❷❸
6 Church Walk   8940 6264   1–4A
"Hidden-away in the heart of Richmond", in a churchyard, this "lovely" and "good-value" bistro (sibling to St Margaret's Brula) is a "solid" Gallic performer, with "first-class" service. / www.labuvette.co.uk; 10 pm; set weekday L £25 (FP), set Sun L £27 (FP).

Byron £27 ❸❸❸
Westfield, Ariel Way, W12   8743 7755   7–1C **NEW**
222 Kensington High St, W8   7361 1717   5–1A
"Making mincemeat of the opposition!"; this expanding chain of upscale, "very buzzy" diners – owned by the same people as PizzaExpress – offers a "good all-round experience", not least "succulent" burgers and "utterly delicious" shakes. / www.byronhamburgers.com; 11 pm, Fri & Sat 11.30 pm, Sun 10.30 pm; W12 8 pm, Thu & Fri 9 pm, Sun 5 pm; W12 closed Sun D; no booking Sat & Sun L, W12 no booking.

C&R Cafe £28 ❷❸④
3-4 Rupert Ct, W1   7434 1128   4–3A
52 Westbourne Grove, W2   7221 7979   6–1B
"It's well worth queuing for one of the cramped tables", say fans of this "hidden-away" Chinatown "gem" – a "proper, full-on, authentic Malaysian eating experience" offering "some of the best-value in the area"; the Bayswater sibling attracts limited attention. / 11 pm.

The Cabin SW6 £39 ❷❷❷
125 Dawes Rd   7385 8936   10–1B
In deepest Fulham – a bar/diner with an enthusiastic local following for its "great steaks", burgers and grills (and good brunches too). / www.thecabinbarandgrill.co.uk; 10.30 pm; D only, ex Sun open L & D; no Amex.

The Cadogan Arms SW3 **NEW** £37 ❸❷❸
298 Kings Rd   7352 6500   5–3C
From the Martin brothers (of Gun fame), this new Chelsea gastroboozer offers a rather elegant take on pub fare, and an early-days reporter already found it "lively". / www.thecadoganarmschelsea.com; 11 pm, Sun 10.30 pm.

Café 209 SW6 £23 ④❷❶
209 Munster Rd 7385 3625 10–1B
Proprietress Joy "remains hilarious", at this "shabby" and "crammed-in" BYO Thai in deepest Fulham; "you go for her cheeriness, and the good-value food". / 10.30 pm; D only, closed Sun, closed Dec; no Amex.

Le Café Anglais
Whiteley's W2 £52 ❸④❸
8 Porchester Gdns 7221 1415 6–1C
Rowley Leigh's huge and "bright" Art Deco-style brasserie seems surprisingly "classy" for somewhere atop the Whiteleys shopping mall, in Bayswater; its "extensive" menu is generally "well executed" (especially the "remarkable hors d'oeuvres"), but service can be "haphazard". / www.lecafeanglais.co.uk; 11.30 pm, Sun 10.30 pm.

Café Bohème W1 £42 ④④❷
13 Old Compton St 7734 0623 4–2A
"So useful" – this "open-all-hours" bar/brasserie, "in the heart of Soho", remains a "loud", "always-busy" linchpin of the area; no-one seems to mind much that the service is "stretched", or the food "uneven". / www.cafeboheme.co.uk; 3 am, Sun 12 pm; booking: max 12.

Café des Amis WC2 £46 ④④④
11-14 Hanover Pl 7379 3444 4–2D
"Run-of-the-mill" cooking reduces this Covent Garden veteran – cutely located in a lane by the Opera House – to "tourist-trap" status nowadays; curiously, however, the "superb" cellar bar – with its "chatty" staff, "excellent" cheese and "reasonably-priced" wine – remains well worth seeking out. / www.cafedesamis.co.uk; 11.30 pm; closed Sun D; set weekday L & pre-theatre £29 (FP).

Café du Jardin WC2 £44 ④❸❸
28 Wellington St 7836 8769 4–3D
A few steps from the Royal Opera House, this "dependably buzzing fixture" makes an "excellent pre-theatre venue" (or for lunch, or post-theatre), with "swift" service and "good but unspectacular" food. / www.lecafedujardin.com; Midnight, Sun 11 pm; set pre theatre £29 (FP).

Café du Marché EC1 £48 ❷❷❶
22 Charterhouse Sq 7608 1609 9–1B
"You could be in France", at this "supremely consistent" stalwart, "tucked-away down an alley", near Smithfield Market; with its "excellent" rustic cooking, and its "fantastic" service, it suits both business or romance; "cool jazz piano" in the evenings. / www.cafedumarche.co.uk; 10 pm; closed Sat L & Sun; no Amex.

Café Emm W1 £28 ④④❸
17 Frith St 7437 0723 4–2A
"Imagine Café Rouge, but good!" – this "cheap 'n' cheerful" Soho bistro is "worth the wait, even if there's a queue". / www.cafeemm.com; 10.30 pm, Fri-Sat 11.30 pm; no Amex.

Café España W1 £23 ❸❷❷
63 Old Compton St 7494 1271 4–3A
In the seedy heart of Soho, a "friendly", "relaxed" and "fun" tapas bar, that's "always packed", thanks not least to the "bargain" prices. / midnight, Sun 11 pm; no Amex; booking at L and after 10 pm only.

Café in the Crypt
St Martin's in the Fields WC2 £24 ④④❷
Duncannon St 7766 1158 2–2C
"For a cheap eat in an expensive bit of town", you could do worse than the "good buffet" in the "atmospheric" Trafalgar Square crypt; it recently re-opened after a major facelift. / www.smitf.org; Sun 6 pm, Mon-Tue 8 pm, Wed-Sat 9 pm; no Amex; no booking.

Café Japan NW11 £30 ❶❶❸
626 Finchley Rd 8455 6854 1–1B
"Fantastic" sushi – "fit for a connoisseur" – comes at prices that are "a steal" at this "very friendly" but "basic" Japanese stalwart, opposite Golder's Green station. / www.cafejapan.co.uk; 10 pm; closed Mon & Tue; no Amex.

Café Laville W2 £29 ④❸❷
453 Edgware Rd 7706 2620 8–4A
Cutely perched over the canal, this Maida Vale café is "a perfect stop for a pot of tea" (or for breakfast); as a more serious dining venue, however, it "needs to get its act together". / 11 pm, Sun 10 pm; no Amex; set weekday L £19 (FP).

Café Med NW8 £38 ④④④
21 Loudon Rd 7625 1222 8–3A
"On a nice day, sit on the terrace", at this pub-like fixture (allied with Med Kitchen), which is tipped as a "cheap 'n' cheerful" St John's Wood stand-by; quality "varies", though, with some meals "substandard". / 11 pm.

Café Pacifico WC2 £34 ④❸❷
5 Langley St 7379 7728 4–2C
Despite its "tourist-trap location", this "cramped" and "crazy" Covent Garden cantina is hailed by fans as a "surprisingly good Mexican"; as ever, though, it leaves the occasional reporter "very disappointed". / www.cafepacifico-laperla.com; 11.45 pm.

Café Rouge £32 ⑤④④
Branches throughout London
"Why hasn't this woeful chain gone bust yet?" – these fake French joints do have fans, especially for breakfast, but attract far too many reports of "dire" food and "uninterested" service. / www.caferouge.co.uk; 11 pm, Sun 10.30 pm; set weekday L £19 (FP).

Café Spice Namaste E1 £40 ❷❷❸
16 Prescot St 7488 9242 11–1A
"Cyrus Todiwala's innovative approach always yields some culinary surprises", at this "cheerful" and "slightly off-beat" stalwart on the eastern fringes of the City; service is notably "efficient and well-informed". / www.cafespice.co.uk; 10.30 pm; closed Sat L & Sun.

Caffè Caldesi W1 £51 ❸④④
118 Marylebone Ln 7487 0751 2–1A
The "informal" nearby offshoot of the former Marylebone Italian of the same name pleases most reporters with its "excellent antipasti", its "simple but delectable pasta", and so on; prices are high, though, and the room is only "pleasant enough". / www.caldesi.com; 10.30 pm; closed Sun.

Caffè Nero £13 ④❸❸
Branches throughout London
*"It has the best chain coffee by miles", say fans
of "the most authentically Italian, and least corporate" of the major
multiples; everything else, however, is merely "fine". / most branches
7 pm; City branches earlier; most City branches closed all or part of weekend;
some branches no credit cards; no booking.*

Caffé Vergnano £10 ❸④❸
62 Charing Cross Rd, WC2   7240 8587   4–3B
Royal Festival Hall, SE1   7921 9339   2–3D
*Cappuccinos like "big frothy cups of heaven", and "dense, rich and
almost chewy" espressos offer the "closest you get to the genuine
Italian experience", say fans of this "tiny" outfit in WC2; SE1 is a full
restaurant operation, by the Royal Festival Hall, which attracts little
feedback (formula price £42). / www.caffevergnano.com; SE1 midnight;
WC2 8 pm, Fri & Sat midnight; no Amex.*

La Cage Imaginaire NW3 £40 ④❸❷
16 Flask Walk   7794 6674   8–1A
*This old-fashioned Gallic veteran, in a quiet Hampstead lane, couldn't
have a cuter location; it can seem "a little uninspired", but is still
"pleasant" overall. / www.lecageimaginaire.co.uk; 11 pm.*

Cambio de Tercio SW5 £48 ❷❷❷
163 Old Brompton Rd   7244 8970   5–2B
*A "vibrant" setting, "daring" tapas and an "encyclopaedic" Spanish
wine list win continuing acclaim for this Earl's Court bar; satisfaction
slipped a bit this year, though, with occasional reports of "indifferent"
service and food that "sometimes missed its mark".
/ www.cambiodetercio.co.uk; 11.30 pm.*

Camden Brasserie NW1 £41 ④❸④
9-11 Jamestown Rd   7482 2114   8–3B
*Since its heyday (a few years ago, and in a different location),
this "welcoming" but anodyne Camden Town institution has given
an ongoing performance that's somewhere round "OK-ish".
/ www.camdenbrasserie.co.uk; 11 pm.*

Camino N1 £40 ④④❷
3 Varnishers Yd, Regent Quarter   7841 7331   8–3C
*Adjacent to the hell which is King's Cross – but "feeling a world away,
in a quiet courtyard" – this "lively" Spanish bar/restaurant
is something of an oasis; reports on its tapas still vary, however,
from "superb" to "never above average". / www.camino.uk.com; 11 pm.*

Canela £26 ❸❷❷
1 Newburgh St, W1   7494 9980   3–2D
33 Earlham St, WC2   7240 6926   4–2C
*In Covent Garden and near Carnaby Street, these "charmingly laid-
back" Portuguese cafés are worth knowing about for their "good-
value" scoff; "great Brazilian music" too. / www.canelacafe.com;
10.30 pm, Thu-Sat 11 pm, Sun 8 pm; WC2 no booking.*

Canta Napoli W4 NEW £35 ❸❸④
9 Devonshire Rd   8994 5225   7–2A
*"Simpler" than its predecessor, Vino Rosso (RIP), this Chiswick
newcomer offers "tasty" and "reasonably-priced" Neapolitan fare,
not least "great pizza". / www.cantanapoli.co.uk; 10.30 pm.*

Canteen £37 ④④④
55 Baker St, W1   686 1122   2–1A **NEW**
Royal Festival Hall, SE1   0845 686 1122   2–3D
Crispin Pl, Old Spitalf'ds Mkt, E1   0845 686 1122   12–2B
*"Super-straightforward" British grub served in a "cool" setting
is clearly a "wonderful concept", so it's a shame that this particular
attempt at it appears to be "heading down the pan" – the cooking
is "lacklustre", staff too often seem "bored" (or like "headless
chickens"), and the ambience can be "dull". / www.canteen.co.uk;
11 pm; no booking weekend L.*

Cantina del Ponte SE1 £41 ⑤⑤④
Butler's Wharf Building, 36c Shad Thames   7403 5403   9–4D
*Near Tower Bridge, this D&D (fka Conran) group Italian benefits
from "lovely views of the Thames"; that's "all it has going for it",
though – otherwise, it's "mediocre in all respects", not least the
"bland and very uninspiring food". / www.cantina.co.uk; 11 pm,
Sun 10 pm; set weekday L £26 (FP).*

Cantina Italia N1 £35 ❸❸❸
19 Canonbury Ln   7226 9791   8–2D
*"Popular, cheap and cheerful", this Islington Italian is liked for its
"fabulous" pizza and "interesting" Sicilian wines. / 11 pm, Fri & Sat
11.30 pm; closed weekday L; no Amex.*

Cantina Vinopolis
Vinopolis SE1 £50 ④④④
1 Bank End   7940 8333   9–3C
*Set in "lovely" vaults, this South Bank museum of wine's in-house
eatery has – as you might hope – a wine list that's "almost a bible"
(with many options by the glass); fans feel the food's "very good" too,
but critics complain of "disappointing" cooking, a "bland" interior and
"collapsing" standards generally. / www.cantinavinopolis.com; 10.30 pm;
closed Sun D.*

Cape Town Fish Market W1 £46 ④④④
5 & 6 Argyll St   7437 1143   3–1C
*Near Oxford Circus, this "odd" culinary concept – wherein South
Africa meets Asia, especially Japan – inspires bizarrely opposing
views; fans find it an "amazing" place, serving up "lovely fish" and
"delightful sushi", whereas critics just decry a "tourist trap",
with "plastic food, poor service and no atmosphere". / www.ctfm.com;
11 pm, Fri-Sat 11.30 pm.*

THE CAPITAL RESTAURANT
CAPITAL HOTEL SW3 £88 ❶❷❸
22-24 Basil St   7589 5171   5–1D
*In culinary terms, this "hidden gem", by Harrods, has for many years
been one of London's great Gallic dining rooms, thanks to the
unstinting efforts of chef Eric Chavot; as this guide was going to press,
however, news emerged of his departure. / www.capitalhotel.co.uk;
10 pm; no jeans or trainers; set weekday L £55 (FP).*

Caponata NW1 **NEW** £32 ❸❷❸
3-7 Delancey St   7387 5959   8–3B
*"A bright addition to Camden Town", this new venture on the former
Café Delancey (RIP) site is consistently praised by early-days reviewers
for its "good" and "well-priced" Sicilian fare; there's a pricier
restaurant upstairs… and an adjoining music venue too! / Rated
on Editors' visit; www.caponatacamden.co.uk; 10.30 pm, Sun 10 pm.*

LE CAPRICE SW1 £56 **②⓪⓪**
Arlington Hs, Arlington St 7629 2239 3–4C
This super-"smooth" '80s-style brasserie, behind the Ritz, remains the
epitome of "effortless" sophistication, drawing a perennially
"glamorous" crowd with its "utterly reliable" ("but not fancy")
formula. / www.caprice-holdings.co.uk; midnight, Sun 11 pm.

Caraffini SW1 £44 **❸⓪❸**
61-63 Lower Sloane St 7259 0235 5–2D
"Waiters who've been there for years" treat all guests "as regulars"
at this "busy" Italian, near Sloane Square; foodwise it's pretty
"reliable", but – especially on the ambience front – "some of the
'heart' has gone out of it in recent times". / www.caraffini.co.uk;
11.30 pm; closed Sun.

Cafe Caramel SW1 £34 **④④❸**
77 Wilton Rd 7233 8298 2–4B
"Perfect if you're nursing a hang-over", this "cramped" Pimlico
café/diner is of particular note as a "great-value" breakfast stop.
/ 11 pm; closed Mon D & Sun D.

Caravaggio EC3 £52 **④④④**
107-112 Leadenhall St 7626 6206 9–2D
Fans of this large City Italian of long standing say it's a "reliable" spot
for business – the food is only "middle-of-the-road", though,
and "doesn't match the prices". / www.etruscarestaurants.com; 10 pm;
closed Sat & Sun.

Carluccio's Caffè £34 **④④④**
Branches throughout London
"Spin has triumphed over substance", at this "bustling" but curiously
"passionless" Italian chain, where the cooking has "really gone
downhill" in recent years; if you must go, "stick to a coffee and
a pastry". / www.carluccios.com; most branches 11 pm, Sun 10.30 pm;
no booking weekday L.

Carnevale EC1 £36 **❸②④**
135 Whitecross St 7250 3452 12–2A
"Out of the way, but well worth hunting out!" – this "friendly and
cosy" veggie, near the Barbican, doesn't inspire many reports
nowadays, but still serves up some "imaginative" and "delicious" fare.
/ www.carnevalerestaurant.co.uk; 11 pm; closed Sat L & Sun; no Amex.

Carpaccio's SW3 £51 **⑤④❸**
4 Sydney St 7352 3433 5–2C
"It's the atmosphere that counts", at this "lively" Chelsea Italian –
for what it is, though, it is notably "overpriced".
/ www.carpacciorestaurant.co.uk; 11.30 pm, Sun 10.30 pm.

The Carpenter's Arms W6 £40 **❸❸❸**
91 Black Lion Ln 8741 8386 7–2B
A "varied" menu and "interesting" wine list are among the attractions
of this "comfy" gastropub (with "nice garden"), "tucked-away" in a
"quiet" Hammersmith backwater; there's a slight feeling, however,
that – perhaps through no fault of its own – it's been "overhyped".
/ 10 pm, Sun 9.30 pm.

Casa Brindisa SW7 **NEW** £34 **❸❸❸**
7-9 Exhibition Rd 7590 0008 5–2C
Right by South Kensington tube, this "buzzy" (but "slightly sterile")
new tapas bar makes a handy venue for some "tasty" dishes; by a
clear margin, however, it's "not as good as the Borough Market
original". / www.casabrindisa.com; closed Sun D.

Le Cassoulet CR2 £45 ❸❸④
18 Selsdon Rd 8633 1818 10–2D
In "unpromising" South Croydon, Malcolm John's "very creditable"
bistro "oasis" – with its menu of Gallic "classics" – has been a major
"breath of fresh air"; the occasional reporter, however, speaks
of repeatedly poor experiences. / www.lecassoulet.com; 10.30 pm.

Castello SE16 £27 ❸④❸
192-196 Jamaica Rd 7064 4631 11–2A
"Not quite as good as when the previous owner was in charge",
but this family-friendly Bermondsey pizzeria still wins praise for its
"good pizza" and "great value". / 11 pm; closed Mon, Sat L & Sun.

Catch
Andaz Hotel EC2 £69 ④④④
40 Liverpool St 7618 7200 9–2D
Fans of this quite "classy"-looking City venue (deep in an hotel
by Liverpool Street) praise its "very good fish"; the food often
"misses", though, and other potential drawbacks include "mediocre"
service, and noise-pollution from the adjoining bar.
/ www.andazdining.com; 10.15 pm; closed Sat & Sun.

Cây Tre EC1 £30 ❸④⑤
301 Old St 7729 8662 12–1A
"Tasty food reminiscent of Vietnam" has made a big name for this
"busy" oriental, near Hoxton Square; "it's becoming a victim of its
own success", though, and the "packed" interior could "use a make-
over". / www.vietnamesekitchen.co.uk; 11 pm, Fri-Sat 11.30 pm,
Sun 10.30 pm.

Cecconi's W1 £50 ❸❸❷
5a Burlington Gdns 7434 1500 3–3C
From breakfast on, Nick Jones's "smart" and "buzzy" Italian
brasserie is a hub for Mayfair's "beau monde" (from "schmoozing
PRs" to "hedge fund types"); the food is undoubtedly "pricey", but it's
also "consistently good". / www.cecconis.co.uk; 1am, Sun midnight.

Cellar Gascon EC1 £35 ❸❸❸
59 West Smithfield Rd 7600 7561 9–2B
"There's always a decent glass of wine to be had", at this Smithfield
budget spin-off from the nearby Club Gascon; it likewise features
"unusual" tapas, but overall it's "not a patch on big brother".
/ www.cellargascon.com; midnight; closed Sat & Sun.

Centrepoint Sushi WC2 £26 ❷❸④
20-21 St Giles High St 7240 6147 4–1B
You'd easily miss this small café, above an oriental supermarket
by Centre Point; its "good-value, fresh sushi" is, however, well worth
seeking out. / www.cpfs.co.uk; 10.30 pm; closed Sun; no Amex.

Le Cercle SW1 £46 ❶❷❷
1 Wilbraham Pl 7901 9999 5–2D
"Exquisitely-presented, tiny French tapas" have carved a major
reputation for this "dramatic" and "elegant" basement "gem",
near Sloane Square – a sibling to Club Gascon; shoppers, don't miss
the "terrific-value lunch"! / www.lecercle.co.uk; 11 pm; closed Mon & Sun.

Cha Cha Moon £20 ④❸❸
15-21 Ganton St, W1   7297 9800   3–2C
Whiteleys, 151 Queensway, W2   7792 0088   6–1C **NEW**
For a "cheap" and "casual" Chinese fix (mostly noodles),
many reporters love this duo of strikingly-designed and lively
canteens, from Wagamama-creator Alan Yau (and the queue can
be "mad"); the dishes, though, are rather "samey".
/ www.chachamoon.com; 11 pm, Fri & Sat 11.30 pm, Sun 10.30 pm.

Chakalaka £36 ❸❸④
1-4 Barley Mow Pas, W4   8995 4725   7–2A **NEW**
136 Upper Richmond Rd, SW15   8789 5696   10–2B
"You won't find better zebra in London" than at this South African-
themed duo (now in Chiswick as well as Putney), which specialise
in exotic grills; "take away the SA theme", however, and what
remains is arguably "nothing special". / www.chakalakarestaurant.com;
10.45 pm; SW15 closed weekday L.

Chamberlain's EC3 £54 ❸④④
23-25 Leadenhall Mkt   7648 8690   9–2D
In the heart of Leadenhall Market (with some pleasant semi-al fresco
tables), a seafood restaurant popular for informal City lunches;
the food is "pretty good" but, unsurprisingly, "expensive for what
it is". / www.chamberlains.org; 9.30 pm; closed Sat & Sun.

Chamomile NW3 £22 ❸❷❸
45 England's Ln   7586 4580   8–2B
"They take pride in what they do", at this "charming" Belsize Park
café, which serves "huge" breakfasts, "locally made" cakes,
and "almost-gourmet" lunches. / 6 pm; L only; no Amex.

Champor-Champor SE1 £43 ❷❷❶
62 Weston St   7403 4600   9–4C
"Out of the way, but worth finding!" – this "unique" venue, hidden-
away near London Bridge, has "a style all of its own", and offers
"poetically inventive" Malay-fusion cuisine in an "eccentric" and
"magical" setting; perhaps in the nature of the thing, however,
the occasional doubter "just can't see it". / www.champor-champor.com;
10.15 pm; D only, closed Sun.

The Chancery EC4 £48 ❷❷④
9 Cursitor St   7831 4000   9–2A
It may look "low-key", but this "minimalist" legal-land destination can
be "perfect for a business lunch or dinner", thanks to its "original"
cuisine and the generally "efficient" (but occasionally "slow") service.
/ www.thechancery.co.uk; 10.30 pm; closed Sat & Sun.

Chapters SE3 £39 ❸❷❸
43-45 Montpelier Vale   8333 2666   1–4D
"A more modern bistro feel" ("noisier" too) now characterises this
relaunched Blackheath destination, formerly known as Chapter Two;
it still offers food that's "always good, and sometimes excellent".
/ www.chaptersrestaurants.com; 10.30 pm, Fri-Sat 11 pm.

Le Chardon £39 ④④❸
65 Lordship Ln, SE22   8299 1921   1–4D
32 Abbeville Rd, SW4   8673 9300   10–2D
"A lovely restoration of an ex-butcher's shop" provides a cute setting
for the East Dulwich original of this Gallic duo (also with a presence
in Clapham); fans applaud "good bistro fare", but results can also
be "rather average". / www.lechardon.co.uk; 11 pm.

Charles Lamb N1 £33 ❸❸❷
16 Elia St   7837 5040   8–3D
A "fun" and "always-buzzing" pub, in the back streets behind Angel;
the owners may be French, but the cooking is "interesting"… and
British – expect "a very good, traditional Sunday lunch (and nice beer
too!"). / www.thecharleslambpub.com; 9.30 pm; closed Mon L, Tue L & Sun D;
no booking.

Charlotte's Place W5 £45 ❸❷❸
16 St Matthew's Rd   8567 7541   1–3A
"A comfortable setting overlooking Ealing Common" helps make this
very "passable" bistro the area's top eatery; fans hail the quality of its
"classic" fare too, but not all reporters are convinced.
/ www.charlottes.co.uk; 10 pm; set weekday L £29 (FP).

The Chelsea Brasserie
Sloane Square Hotel SW1 £46 ⑤⑤④
7-12 Sloane Sq   7881 5999   5–2D
An "unpretentious" brasserie, on Sloane Square, sometimes praised
for its "relaxed" style; it rarely looks busy, though, and too many
reporters find its performance "utterly inept".
/ www.chelsea-brasserie.co.uk; 10.30 pm; no Amex.

Chelsea Bun Diner SW10 £24 ❸❸④
9a Lamont Rd   7352 3635   5–3B
"You won't need to eat again all day", if you try one of the
"enormous range of English, French and American breakfasts"
on offer at this "upmarket greasy spoon", at World's End; BYO.
/ www.chelseabun.co.uk; 6 pm; L only; no Amex; no booking, Sat & Sun.

The Chelsea Kitchen SW10 🆕 £23 ④❸❸
451 Fulham Rd   3055 0088   5–3B
Named after a still sadly-missed King's Road '50s-relic,
this "very basic" new bistro, now at the 'other' end of Chelsea,
is owned by the same family as the original; even in this swanky part
of town, its budget charms seem to have found an instant market.
/ www.chelseakitchen.com; 11 pm.

Cheyne Walk Brasserie SW3 £63 ④④❷
50 Cheyne Walk   7376 8787   5–3C
This "glamorous Gallic brasserie" features a large wood-burning grill,
and benefits from a "casually elegant" Chelsea setting (and a
"sprinkling of celebrity buzz" too); it's arguably "overpriced", though,
and standards have "slipped" of late. / www.cheynewalkbrasserie.com;
10.30 pm; closed Mon L & Sun D; set weekday L £35 (FP).

CHEZ BRUCE SW17 £58 ❶❶❷
2 Bellevue Rd   8672 0114   10–2C
"In a business fuelled by hype, exaggeration and celebrity", Bruce
Poole's "perfect neighbourhood place", by Wandsworth Common,
"quietly 'delivers' every time"; for the fifth year it is London's Favourite
Restaurant, thanks to its "thoughtful" staff, its "refined" yet "unfussy"
cuisine and its "lovely" (if "cramped") setting; "exceptional" wine too.
/ www.chezbruce.co.uk; 10.30 pm; booking: max 6 at D; set Sun L £44 (FP).

Chez Gérard £42 ⑤⑤④
Thistle Hotel, 101 Buck' Palace Rd, SW1 7868 6249 2–4B
31 Dover St, W1 7499 8171 3–3C
36-40 Rupert St, W1 7287 8989 4–3A
8 Charlotte St, W1 7636 4975 2–1C
119 Chancery Ln, WC2 7405 0290 2–2D
45 Opera Ter, Covent Garden, WC2 7379 0666 4–3D
9 Belvedere Rd, SE1 7202 8470 2–3D
64 Bishopsgate, EC2 7588 1200 9–2D
14 Trinity Sq, EC3 7480 5500 9–3D
1 Watling St, EC4 7213 0540 9–2B
"Yuck" food – "the steak was like a carpet tile" – and "shocking"
service are ever-present risks at this "unimpressive" steak/frites chain;
especially for business, though, some reporters still see it as
a "passable" option, and the branch above Covent Garden market
certainly has an "amazing" location. / www.chezgerard.co.uk;
10 pm-11.30 pm; City branches closed all or part of weekend; some booking
restrictions apply.

Chez Kristof W6 £42 ④④④
111 Hammersmith Grove 8741 1177 7–1C
"Promises much, but frequently fails to deliver" – sadly, an oft-heard
complaint of late about this "cramped" but quite "glamorous"
Hammersmith local; an optimist, however, suggests that a new chef
has "improved" the rustic Gallic fare "enormously".
/ www.chezkristof.co.uk; 11 pm, Sun 10 pm.

Chez Liline N4 £36 ❶❷⑤
101 Stroud Green Rd 7263 6550 8–1D
Don't be put off by the "outdated" looks of this Finsbury Park
"hidden gem"; chef Sylvain Hong (recently back at the stove) puts
"an exotic Mauritian twist" on his "superb, inventive and original"
dishes – some of the best fish in London. / ww.chezliline.com; 11 pm;
closed Mon; set weekday L £22 (FP).

Chez Lindsay TW10 £37 ❸❷❸
11 Hill Rise 8948 7473 1–4A
"Long a welcome refuge", near Richmond Bridge – this "authentically
Breton" bistro has "a very loyal local following", thanks to its "terrific"
service and its "great crêpes"; the cider and seafood can be pretty
good too. / www.chezlindsay.co.uk; 11 pm; no Amex.

Chez Marcelle W14 £27 ❶④④
34 Blythe Rd 7603 3241 7–1D
"Charming, control-freak Marcelle" personally oversees this Olympia
institution, so service can sometimes be "slow" as a result; even so,
it's an "indisputably brilliant" destination, with "proper, home-cooked
Lebanese food" – a recent "IKEA-style" refit has "dragged the décor
into the '90s" too! / 10 pm; closed Mon, Tue-Thu D only,Fri-Sun open L & D;
no credit cards.

Chez Patrick W8 £43 ❷❶❸
7 Stratford Rd 7937 6388 5–2A
"Patrick, the charming and amusing owner" adds life to this Gallic
venture in a quiet Kensington mews; a small but enthusiastic fan club
praises its "simple but exquisite" fish and seafood.
/ www.chezpatrickinlondon.co.uk; 11 pm; closed Sun D.

Chi Noodle & Wine Bar EC4 £24 ❷❷❸
5 New Bridge St 7353 2409 9–2A
In the City, this "fabulous, family-run noodle bar" wins consistent applause for its "reliable" and "speedy" (but "relaxed") lunching possibilities. / www.chinoodle.com; 10.30 pm; closed Sat & Sun.

Chicago Rib Shack SW1 £41 ⑤⑤④
145 Knightsbridge 7591 4664 5–1D
Fans find "nostalgic" charms in the resurrection of this "cheerful" Knightsbridge institution, praising its "decent" ribs and "excellent" Mississippi Mud Pie; the atmosphere of "enforced fun" is not for everyone, though, and critics say the setting's "ghastly" and the food "vile". / www.thechicagoribshack.co.uk; 11 pm.

Chilango £12 ❸❸④
27 Upper St, N1 7704 2123 8–3D NEW
142 Fleet St, EC4 128 505 9–2A NEW
"Top burritos" are the highlight of the "fresh Mexican fare" on offer at this "quick" and "friendly" new mini-chain, whose "good prices" recommend it to most (if not quite all) reporters. / www.chilango.co.uk; EC4 9 pm; N1 10 pm, Fri & Sat midnight; EC4 closed Sat & Sun; no booking.

Chimes SW1 £29 ④❸❸
26 Churton St 7821 7456 2–4B
An "unchanging" Pimlico pie house, whose formula of "reliable roasts and pies, plus good cider" still has a following; it can, however, seem rather "ordinary". / www.chimes-of-pimlico.co.uk; 10.15 pm, Sun 9.15 pm.

China Tang
Dorchester Hotel W1 £75 ④④④
53 Park Ln 7629 9988 3–3A
"Silly prices" take the gloss off David Tang's "sumptuous and breathtaking" '30s-Shanghai-style Mayfair basement, and the "average" food and "dismissive" service don't help either – leave out the glitter-factor, and this place can feel like "an overpriced theme park for people with too much money". / www.thedorchesterhotel.com; 11.30 pm; set weekday L £37 (FP).

The Chinese Experience W1 £29 ❸❸⑤
118-120 Shaftesbury Ave 7437 0377 4–3A
"Dim sum all day" is part of a "creative" approach that makes this "friendly" Chinatown café a "dependable" choice for a "fast" meal (and an "excellent-value" one too); "bland and downmarket décor" is the only real "let-down". / www.chineseexperience.com; 11 pm, Fri & Sat 11.30 pm.

The Chippy W1 NEW £19 ❸❸❸
38 Poland St 7434 1933 3–1D
"A fish and chip shop, not a gastro-chippy" – the look may be contemporary, but this pleasant Soho newcomer simply 'does what it says on the can'. / 9 pm, Sun 6 pm; closed Sun D.

Chisou W1 £38 ❷❷④
4 Princes St 7629 3931 3–1C
It may look "plain", but this Japanese café, near Oxford Circus, "impresses" reporters with its "slick" service of "super fresh food" – a "reliable blend of conservative and innovative dishes" (not least "fantastic" sushi and sashimi). / www.chisou.co.uk; 10.30 pm; closed Sun.

Cho-San SW15 £39 ❷⓿❸
292 Upper Richmond Rd   8788 9626   10–2A
*"Utterly delightful family service" adds to the "really authentic" spirit
– "just like being in Tokyo" – of this Putney Japanese; it serves
up "excellent sushi and sashimi" and "good home cooking",
at "wonderful value-for-money prices". / 10.30 pm; closed Mon; no Amex.*

Chop'd £12 ❷❸④
52 Curzon St, W1   7495 1014   3–3B
335 High Holborn, WC1   7242 8095   2–1D
St Pancras International, NW1   7837 1603   8–3C
Unit 1 34 The North Colonnade, E14   3229 0087   11–1C
2 Horner Sq, Old Spitalfields Mkt, E1   7247 8757   12–2B
1 Leadenhall Mkt, EC3   7626 3706   9–2D
*"Top-quality" salads – "both ready-made, and to order", and with
"interesting extras" – win nothing but praise for these "healthy" pit
stops. / www.chopd.co.uk; 6 pm; no Amex.*

Chor Bizarre W1 £43 ❷❸❷
16 Albemarle St   7629 9802   3–3C
*"Extravagant" décor helps create a "fun" atmosphere at this "quirky"
Mayfair Indian; given its "interesting" and "well-executed" cuisine,
it's perhaps surprising that it doesn't have a wider following.
/ www.chorbizarre.com; 11.30 pm; closed Sun L.*

Chowki W1 £28 ④⑤⑤
2-3 Denman St   7439 1330   3–2D
*This once-excellent Soho Indian has "gone right off" in recent years
(and its menu, once notable for changing monthly, now changes only
quarterly) – "it's such a shame to see a beacon of interesting, well-
executed food become just another run-of-the-mill West End refuelling
joint". / www.chowki.com; 11.30 pm, Sun 10.30 pm.*

Choys SW3 £37 ④❷④
172 King's Rd   7352 9085   5–3C
*This "welcoming" Chelsea Chinese is certainly a survivor – it opened
in 1952 – and it still makes a "reliable" and "efficient" stand-by
today; the formula, though, can seem "bland" by current standards.
/ midnight.*

Christopher's WC2 £55 ④④❸
18 Wellington St   7240 4222   4–3D
*A "beautiful" dining room – reached up a sweeping staircase – is the
highlight of this grand Covent Garden American; its surf 'n' turf menu
is generally rather "formulaic", and it is as a "lovely brunch spot" that
the place receives the most whole-hearted commendations.
/ www.christophersgrill.com; 11 pm, Sat-Sun 11.30 pm; booking: max 12;
set pre theatre £32 (FP).*

Chuen Cheng Ku W1 £32 ❸❸❸
17 Wardour St   7437 1398   4–3A
*"The trolleys keep on coming", during the "terrific" lunchtime dim
sum sessions, at this "huge and bustling" Chinatown landmark –
a "fun", "cheap", and "filling" experience, and "great for kids" too.
/ www.chuenchengku.co.uk; 11.45 pm.*

Churchill Arms W8 £22 ❷④❷
119 Kensington Church St   7792 1246   6–2B
*Thai "scoff" as "cheap-as-chips" makes this "life-affirming" annexe
to a pub near Notting Hill Gate a true "perennial favourite";
"overcrowding is rife", however, and service "quick but unsmiling" –
"expect to be rushed". / 10 pm; closed Sun D.*

Chutney SW18 £26 ❷❶❸
11 Alma Rd 8870 4588 10–2B
"Wonderful food, cooked with care" makes this "cosy" Wandsworth local "a perfect place for a simple curry". / www.chutneyrestaurant.co.uk; 11.30 pm; D only.

Chutney Mary SW10 £52 ❷❷❷
535 King's Rd 7351 3113 5–4B
With its "beautiful, subtle and aromatic" cuisine and its "strikingly stylish" décor, this Chelsea-fringe pioneer still offers a "package which takes some beating" – almost twenty years on, this is still "one of the best Indians in London". / www.realindianfood.com; 11.30 pm, Sun 10.30 pm; closed weekday L; booking: max 12.

Chutneys NW1 £28 ❸❸④
124 Drummond St 7388 0604 8–4C
An "amazing-value" buffet (lunch and all Sunday) has long been the main draw to this "stalwart" veggie café, in Euston's 'Little India'. / www.chutneyseuston.com; 11 pm; no Amex; need 5+ to book.

Ciao Bella WC1 £31 ④❷❶
86-90 Lamb's Conduit St 7242 4119 2–1D
This "crammed" and "bustling" Bloomsbury stalwart is, for fans, everything a "happy", "old-school" Italian should be, and "unbelievable value" too; some reporters, though, sense that the always-"routine" cooking has seemed positively "churned out" of late. / www.ciaobellarestaurant.co.uk; 11.30 pm, Sun 10.30 pm.

Cibo W14 £44 ④❷④
3 Russell Gdns 7371 6271 7–1D
It's hard to avoid the impression that this once-fashionable Olympia back street Italian "has lost its way"; die-hard fans still extol its "charming" service and quality cooking – to critics, though, "it's not a 'destination' any more" ("and not really a decent neighbourhood restaurant either"). / www.ciborestaurant.net; 11 pm; closed Sun D.

Cicada EC1 £38 ❸❷❸
132-136 St John St 7608 1550 9–1B
Will Ricker's ever-"buzzy" Shoreditch hang-out has shown amazing staying power; there's the odd concern that it's "losing momentum", but more in the way of praise for its "light and tasty" Pan-Asian fare, and staff who "try hard". / www.rickerrestaurants.com; 11 pm; closed Sat L & Sun.

Cigala WC1 £44 ❸❷④
54 Lamb's Conduit St 7405 1717 2–1D
"Substantial and tasty" Spanish dishes, "a good choice of wines" and "welcoming" service all won praise this year for this "useful" Bloomsbury corner spot, which has improved standards all round in recent times. / www.cigala.co.uk; 10.45 pm, Sun 9.30 pm.

THE CINNAMON CLUB SW1 £62 ❷❸❷
Old Westminster Library, Great Smith St 7222 2555 2–4C
Westminster's old Library provides the "palatial" home for London's grandest "nouvelle Indian"; even more impressive, though, is its "stunning" and "delicate" cuisine – a "clever but unpretentious" take on traditional dishes. / www.cinnamonclub.com; 10.45 pm; closed Sun; no trainers; set weekday L & dinner £41 (FP).

Cinnamon Kitchen EC2   £52   ❶❷❸
9 Devonshire Sq   7626 5000   9–2D
"A real treat in the City"; the Cinnamon Club's lofty new "Manhattan-style" offshoot, near Liverpool Street, looks set to rival its impressive sibling, thanks to its "magical" Indian tapas dishes, its "glamorous" décor and its overall "attention to detail". / www.cinnamon-kitchen.com; 10.30 pm, Sun 10 pm; set weekday L £32 (FP).

Cipriani W1   £75   ⑤⑤④
25 Davies Street   7399 0500   3–2B
"Rude, arrogant, self-centred…", and that's just the customers!; this "grossly self-important" Mayfair Italian serves up "bland" ("worst since Spaghetti House in 1970") and "overpriced" fare to a "hilarious" crowd of "wannabe-hedgies and has-been celebs", at prices – inevitably – that "only fools would pay". / www.cipriani.com; 11.45 pm.

City Café
City Inn Westminster SW1   £41   ④④④
30 John Islip St   7932 4600   2–4C
"Handy for Tate Britain and Westminster", this "surprisingly good hotel restaurant" offers "well-executed" dishes – particularly the simpler items – from a "limited" menu; good buffet-style carvery on Sundays. / www.citycafe.co.uk; 11 pm.

City Miyama EC4   £48   ❷④⑤
17 Godliman St   7489 1937   9–3B
"Shame about the knackered décor", at this age-old City Japanese – service is "wonderful" and the sushi bar "simply outstanding". / www.miyama.co.uk; 9.30 pm; closed Sat D & Sun; set dinner £29 (FP).

The Clarence SW12   £32   ❸❷❸
90-92 Balham High Rd   8772 1155   10–2C
An unpretentious and consistently crowd-pleasing Balham boozer, where "amazing burgers" are the culinary highlight. / www.clarencebalham.com; midnight, Fri & Sat 1 am.

Clarke's W8   £56   ❷❷❸
124 Kensington Church St   7221 9225   6–2B
While fans of Sally Clarke's Kensington stalwart say its Californian-inspired cuisine is consistently "excellent", critics feel it has not been as good "since they stopped the no-choice dinner" (which was a few years ago); views on the ambience differ too – it's "romantic" or "staid", to taste. / www.sallyclarke.com; 10 pm; closed Sun; booking: max 14.

The Clerkenwell Dining Room EC1   £52   ❸❸❸
69-73 St John St   7253 9000   9–1B
"Conveniently located for the City", this "hype-free" Smithfield venture serves up food that's "intelligent" and "well-prepared". / www.theclerkenwell.com; 11 pm; closed Sat L & Sun.

Clifton E1   £22   ❷❸❸
1 Whitechapel Rd   7377 5533   9–2D
"It hasn't failed me yet!" – this "deservedly busy" Brick Lane Bangladeshi offers a "nicely varied regional menu", and "pleasant" service too. / www.cliftonrestaurant.com; midnight, Sat & Sun 1am.

The Clissold Arms N2 £42 ④❸❸
Fortis Grn 8444 4224 1–1C
This Muswell Hill yearling is often hailed as "a fantastic addition" to an area with "a dearth of good pubs"; on the downside, however, the décor is "very plain", and the food's "variable" and "not cheap". / 10 pm, Sun 9 pm; no Amex.

Clos Maggiore WC2 £45 ❷①①
33 King St 7379 9696 4–3C
An "oasis" amidst Covent Garden's tourist tat that's beginning to make quite a name for itself – this "magical" restaurant is of special note for its "leafy" and "romantic" conservatory, and also its "mind-boggling" (2000+ bins) wine list; amazingly, the food is "very competent" too, and service "impeccable". / www.closmaggiore.com; 10.45 pm, Sat 11.15 pm, Sun 10 pm; closed Sat L; set dinner £30 (FP).

Club Gascon EC1 £62 ❷❷❸
57 West Smithfield 7796 0600 9–2B
With its "strongly flavoured and imaginative" tapas from SW France and the Basque country, this foie-gras-fixated Smithfield fixture remains on "brilliant" form; "unusual and well-chosen" regional wines add much further interest. / www.clubgascon.com; 10 pm, Fri & Sat 10.30 pm; closed Sat L & Sun.

Coach & Horses EC1 £38 ❸❸④
26-28 Ray St 7278 8990 9–1A
A "decent" Clerkenwell gastropub, offering "interesting" food ("from quite a short menu"), and "reasonably-priced" wines. / www.thecoachandhorses.com; 11 pm; closed Sat L & Sun D.

Coast NW1 NEW £40
108 Parkway 7267 9555 8–3B
Billing itself as 'a breath of crisp Cornish air in the heart of Camden' – this simple, new café, puts a strong (but not exclusive) emphasis on fish; we didn't have time to visit it before we went to press, but early reviews include more good than bad. / www.coastdining.co.uk; 11 pm.

Cochonnet W9 £33 ❸❷❷
1 Lauderdale Pde 7289 0393 1–2B
"Great pizza and a surprisingly extensive wine list" – the two highpoints at this "buzzy" Maida Vale "local", which is "good for families" too. / www.cochonnet.co.uk; midnight.

Cock Tavern EC1 £25 ❸④④
Smithfield Mkt 7248 2918 9–2A
"As you might expect in the middle of Smithfield meat market", this cellar pub offers the "best English breakfast going"… but not much else. / L only, closed Sat & Sun.

Cocoon W1 £55 ❸④❷
65 Regent St 7494 7600 3–3D
The "Austin Powers-fantasy" décor and "very nice cocktails" are the main reasons to seek out this "chic" and "fun" bar/restaurant, looking down on Regent Street; "good" pan-Asian food is "a bonus", but arguably weighs in rather "overpriced". / www.cocoon-restaurants.com; 1 am, Sat 3 am; closed Sat L & Sun.

The Collection SW3   £67   ⑤④④
264 Brompton Rd   7225 1212   5–2C
Approached via a catwalk, a large and Eurotrashy Brompton Cross
bar (with mezzanine restaurant), that's "so full of beautiful people
you forget about the food" – probably no bad thing.
/ www.the-collection.co.uk; midnight; D only, closed Sun.

La Collina NW1   £39   ❸❸④
17 Princess Rd   7483 0192   8–3B
"Unusual" Piedmontese cooking helps create "an all-round good
experience" at this Primrose Hill local, which benefits from a "lovely
decked area at the back". / 11 pm; closed weekday L.

Le Colombier SW3   £48   ❸❶❷
145 Dovehouse St   7351 1155   5–2C
"A wonderful feeling of France", "delicious classic fare",
and "exemplary" service help win high acclaim for this "smart but
pricey" bistro, by Chelsea Square. / www.lecolombier-sw3.co.uk; 10.30 pm,
Sun 10 pm.

Commander W2   £46   ④④④
47 Hereford Rd   7229 1503   6–1B
A grand, vaguely Americanised Bayswater pub-conversion (plus deli);
fans say it offers a "pleasant" gastropub-style experience, but critics
find it a "pointless" place with "clueless" service and "uninteresting"
food. / www.commanderrooms.co.uk; 10 pm, Sun 9.30 pm; no Amex.

Como Lario SW1   £43   ❸❸❷
18-22 Holbein Pl   7730 2954   5–2D
Not much changes, at this "cramped" and "old-fashioned" trattoria,
just off Sloane Square, with its "always-reliable" food, its "friendly"
("slightly shambolic") service and a general "hustle and bustle".
/ www.comolario.uk.com; 11.30 pm, Sun 10 pm; set Sun L £31 (FP).

Comptoir Gascon EC1   £46   ❷❸❷
63 Charterhouse St   7608 0851   9–1A
"Genuinely like a really good bistro in France", this "cute" but
"cramped" Smithfield spin-off from nearby Club Gascon offers
"robust food with minimal fuss", at "sensible prices"; by day, they do
"wonderful coffee" and "perfect pastries". / www.comptoirgascon.com;
10 pm, Thu & Fri 11 pm; closed Mon & Sun.

Comptoir Libanais   £13   ❸❸❸
65 Wigmore St, W1   7935 1110   3–1A **NEW**
Westfield, Ariel Way, W12   8811 2222   7–1C **NEW**
26 London St, W2   6–1D **NEW**
An embryonic Lebanese chain that wins praise for its "tasty" fare and
"cool" design; on the downside, it's "pricey", though, and service can
be "chaotic". / www.lecomptoir.co.uk; W12 9 pm, Thu & Fri 10 pm,
Sun 6 pm; W1 9.30 pm; W12 closed Sun D; no Amex; no bookings.

Il Convivio SW1   £55   ❷❶❸
143 Ebury St   7730 4099   2–4A
Something of a "hidden gem"; this "bright and airy" Belgravia Italian
continues to win all-round acclaim for its "really accomplished"
cooking and "gracious" service. / www.etruscarestaurants.com; 10.45 pm;
closed Sun.

Coq d'Argent EC2 £58 ④❸❸
I Poultry 7395 5000 9–2C
With its "fantastic" terraces and roof gardens, this "unique" 6th-floor
D&D-group operation in the City is never going to be a budget
destination, but improved food and service have made it better value
of late; though it's mainly a business venue, of course, it can
be "surprisingly busy" at weekends too. / www.coqdargent.co.uk; 9.45 pm;
closed Sat L & Sun D.

Cork & Bottle WC2 £33 ⑤④❷
44-46 Cranbourn St 7734 7807 4–3B
"In the wasteland of Leicester Square", this "old-favourite" cellar wine
bar has long been a "cosy" oasis; the food may rarely be better than
"so-so", but it's not really the point – it's "all about Don Hewitson's
beautiful and carefully-chosen wine list". / www.corkandbottle.net;
11.30 pm; no booking after 6.30 pm.

Corrigan's Mayfair W1 NEW £60 ❸❷❸
28 Upper Grosvenor St 7499 9943 3–3A
Shame the amiable Richard Corrigan's smart Mayfair newcomer was
so "hyped" by his many friends in the media; some reporters
do indeed find "outstanding" results from his "rustic" British menu,
but others are "hugely disappointed" – given the build-up – to find
no "wow-factor" at all. / www.corrigansmayfair.com; 11 pm; set Sun L
£44 (FP).

Costa's Fish Restaurant W8 £23 ❸❸⑤
18 Hillgate St 7727 4310 6–2B
An "old-established" chippy, near Notting Hill Gate, where the fish
comes with "excellent light batter" and "good chips". / 10 pm; closed
Mon & Sun; no credit cards.

Costa's Grill W8 £23 ④❸④
12-14 Hillgate St 7229 3794 6–2B
A "cheap 'n' cheerful" Greek taverna, serving up "simple dishes with
quirky humour"; results may be "ordinary", but "prices are
modest for just off Notting Hill Gate". / www.costasgrill.com; 10.30 pm;
closed Sun (closed 3 weeks in Aug).

Côte £35 ④❸④
124-126 Wardour St, W1 7287 9280 3–1D
17-21 Tavistock St, WC2 7379 9991 4–3D NEW
47 Kensington Ct, W8 7938 4147 5–1A NEW
8 High St, SW19 8947 7100 10–2B
For "basic food at reasonable prices", some reporters tip this
expanding Gallic bistro chain (backed by Ivy-owner Richard Caring,
and run by the team who created Strada); it's already becoming
"standardised and boring", though – soon be in the rogues' gallery
alongside Café Rouge? / www.cote-restaurants.co.uk; 11 pm.

Cottons £38 ④❸❸
55 Chalk Farm Rd, NW1 7485 8388 8–2B
70 Exmouth Mkt, EC1 7833 3332 9–1A
The "West Indian comfort food" isn't bad, but the cocktails are the
biggest draw to these "fun" Caribbean Rhum Shacks.
/ www.cottons-restaurant.co.uk; EC1 10.30 pm, Fri-Sat 11 pm; NW1 midnight,
Fri & Sat 1 am; NW1 closed Mon-Fri L; EC1 closed Sat D; deposit required for
bookings over 7.

FSA

The Cow W2 £49 ❷④❷
89 Westbourne Park Rd 7221 0021 6–1B
*Tom Conran's "hip" faux-Irish pub is a Notting Hillbilly classic
(even though it's actually in Bayswater); downstairs, in the "packed"
bar, they serve "first-class" seafood and Guinness – upstairs, there's
a "cosy" room, where the style is more "gastronomic".
/ www.thecowlondon.co.uk; 10.30 pm; closed weekday L; no Amex.*

Crazy Bear W1 £56 ❸❸❶
26-28 Whitfield St 7631 0088 2–1C
*With its "really sexy bar" and "cool" upstairs dining room,
this Fitzrovia spot is "definitely a place to impress a date", and the
Thai/Chinese food is "excellent" too (if progressively seeming rather
"pricey" for what it is); don't under any circumstances miss the
"most bizarre" loos. / www.crazybeargroup.co.uk; 10.30 pm; closed
Sat L & Sun; no shorts.*

Crazy Homies W2 £38 ❷④❷
125 Westbourne Park Rd 7727 6771 6–1B
*Tom Conran's "cramped" and "noisy" – but "thoroughly enjoyable" –
Bayswater hang-out has "quite a rough and authentic Mexican feel";
its "unfancy" and "affordable" scoff generally pleases, but the
"slow and forgetful" service does not. / www.crazyhomieslondon.co.uk;
closed weekday L; no Amex.*

Criterion W1 £55 ④❷❷
224 Piccadilly 7930 0488 3–3D
*Mercifully, "the most beautiful restaurant in London" –
in extraordinary neo-Byzantine style – changed hands in the summer
of 2009; it's now rather smarter and more comfortable than before,
and offers an all-things-to-all-men menu that's not inexpensive,
but reasonably well realised. / www.criterionrestaurant.com; 11pm,
Sun 10.30; set weekday L & dinner £34 (FP).*

Cruse 9 N1 £40 ❸④④
62-63 Halliford St 7354 8099 8–2D
*"It deserves to succeed!", say local fans of this slightly "sterile" new-
build yearling, at the north End of Islington; service may be "erratic",
but the food is "interesting" (and desserts can be "memorable").
/ www.cruse9.com; 10 pm, Sun 9 pm.*

Crussh £14 ❸❸④
1 Curzon St, W1 7629 2554 3–3B
BBC Media Village, Wood Ln, W12 8746 7916 6–2A
27 Kensington High St, W8 7376 9786 5–1A
One Canada Sq, E14 7513 0076 11–1C
Unit 21 Jubilee Pl, E14 7519 6427 11–1C
48 Cornhill, EC3 7626 2175 9–2C
6 Farringdon St, EC4 7489 5916 9–2A
*"Addictive" soups, "imaginative" salads and "delicious" smoothies
again win praise for these "healthy" pit-stops; service is "personable"
too. / www.crussh.com; 8 pm, varies on weekends; many branches closed all
or part of weekend; no credit cards in many branches.*

Cumberland Arms W14 £35 ❸❷❸
29 North End Rd 7371 6806 7–2D
*"No frills and no faults!"; "in the Olympia gastro-wilderness",
this "buzzing" gastropub is a "much needed" amenity, praised for its
"unpretentious" style and food that's "more interesting than average".
/ www.thecumberlandarmspub.co.uk; 10 pm.*

Curve
London Marriott W' India Quay E14   £58   ④④⑤
52 Hertsmere Rd   7517 2808   11–1C
At its best, this Canary Wharf dining room still transcends its "dull" décor, thanks to its "fantastic" dishes (with fish straight from New Billingsgate); it's "gone downhill" this year, though, and one former fan notes: "it used to be good value, but now they scrimp on everything". / www.marriothotel.co.uk; 10.30 pm, Sun 10 pm; closed Sat L & Sun L.

Cyprus Mangal SW1   £25   ❷❸④
45 Warwick Way   7828 5940   2–4B
"Leave at home any inhibitions about kebabs", if you visit this "fine charcoal grill" behind a Pimlico take-away; its "cheerful" staff dish up "the highest-quality Turkish grilled meat dishes", at "great-value" prices. / Sun-Thu midnight, Fri & Sat 1 am; no Amex.

The Czechoslovak Restaurant NW6   £29   ❸④④
74 West End Ln   7372 1193   1–1B
Looking for "delicious goulash, heavenly dumplings and superb draft Czech beers"? – head for this quirky West Hampstead émigrés' club, whose other attractions include "authentic" style and "modest" prices. / www.czechoslovak-restaurant.co.uk; 10 pm; closed Mon, Tue-Fri D only, Sat & Sun open L & D; no credit cards.

D Sum 2 EC4   £40   ④⑤⑤
14 Paternoster Row   7248 2288   9–2B
"Great dim sum" helps make this modern bar a "good place for lunch", near St Paul's; critics find prices too high though, and say service needs to up its act. / www.dsum2.com; 11 pm; closed Sat L & Sun D.

Da Mario SW7   £35   ④④❸
15 Gloucester Rd   7584 9078   5–1B
A "lively" and "characterful" South Kensington Italian, long known as "the best place for a pre-Albert Hall pizza" (and "great with children too"); "try to stay on the ground floor". / www.damario.co.uk; 11.30 pm.

Dalchini SW19   £31   ❸❷❸
147 Arthur Rd   8947 5966   10–2B
"Great Indian/Chinese fusion fare" wins nothing but praise for this "cheerful" Wimbledon Park fixture; NB "go upstairs". / www.dalchini.co.uk; 10.30 pm, Fri & Sat 11 pm; no Amex.

Dans le Noir EC1   £59   ⑤❸❷
29 Clerkenwell Grn   7253 1100   9–1A
"A theme park, but a fascinating one"; this "bizarre" Clerkenwell venture – where, served by blind staff, you eat "in total darkness" – is surprisingly often found to be "an even more extraordinary experience than it sounds"; the food, however, is "abysmal". / www.danslenoir.com; 9.30 pm; D only.

Daphne NW1   £31   ❸❶❷
83 Bayham St   7267 7322   8–3C
"You're made very welcome" at this "homely" taverna of long standing, in Camden Town, which benefits from a "lovely roof terrace for the summer"; the "good-value" food – featuring some "well-cooked" fish – is a "cut above" most Greek places too. / 11.30 pm; closed Sun; no Amex.

Daphne's SW3 £48 ❸❷❷
112 Draycott Ave 7589 4257 5–2C
For "a gossipy ladies' lunch" or "an intimate tête-à-tête",
this "warm and inviting" Chelsea Italian perfectly fits the bill; staff
"don't chase you to turn the table" and the cooking is "better than
it was when the place was at its most fashionable" (in the days of the
late Princess of Wales). / www.daphnes-restaurant.co.uk; 11.30 pm,
Sun 10.30 pm; booking: max 12; set weekday L & dinner £29 (FP).

Daquise SW7 £30 ❹❸❹
20 Thurloe St 7589 6117 5–2C
This "unchanging, old friend" – a post-war Polish bistro – may look
"tired", but it still offers "filling" fare at prices that are "cheap",
especially for somewhere right by South Kensington tube; handy for
post-museums tea and cakes too. / 11 pm; no Amex.

The Dartmouth Arms SE23 £35 ❸❷❸
7 Dartmouth Rd 8488 3117 1–4D
This Forest Hill local – "a very nice gastropub in an area with
relatively few attractive offerings" – serves a "small but interesting"
menu. / www.thedartmoutharms.com; 10.30 pm; no Amex.

Daylesford Organic £40 ❹❹❹
Bamford & Sons, 31 Sloane Sq, SW1 7881 8020 5–2D
44B Pimlico Rd, SW1 7881 8060 5–2D
208-212 Westbourne Grove, W11 7313 8060 6–1B NEW
"Yummy mummies galore" descend on Lady ('JCB') Bamford's
buzzing deli/cafés, in Pimlico and, now, Notting Hill, particularly for
the "great breakfasts"; more ambitious dishes can be "inconsistent"
though, and foes deride these places as "pretentious" and
"overpriced". / www.daylesfordorganic.com; Sloane Sq 5.30 pm,
Wed 6.30 pm, Sun 4.30 pm; Pimlico Rd 7 pm, Sun 3.30 pm; W11 10 pm,
Sun 4.30 pm; closed Sun D; Sloane Sq L only; Sloane Sq no booking;
W11 no booking L.

De Cecco SW6 £39 ❸❸❸
189 New King's Rd 7736 1145 10–1B
This convivial Fulham Italian has long been an "uncomplicated and
reliable" local favourite; service is a wild card, though – sometimes
outstanding, sometimes "uninterested". / www.dececcorestaurant.com;
11 pm; closed Sun D.

Dean Street Townhouse
& Dining Room W1 NEW
Dean St 4–2A
From Nick Jones's ever-trendy Soho House group, a new hotel and
members' club, to open in late-2009; expect the restaurant (open to
all) to become a place of the moment, even if precedent suggests
that the food will be no better than middle-of-the-road.

Defune W1 £35 ❶❶❹
34 George St 7935 8311 3–1A
The "Habitat-style" interior of this stalwart Marylebone Japanese has
"little atmosphere" (and prices which are "through the roof"),
but "it doesn't matter" – the sushi and sashimi are "just perfect",
and service "flawless" too. / 10.30 pm.

Dehesa W1 £40 ❷❷❶
25 Ganton St   7494 4170   3–2C
*With its "casual and elegant" style, "unbeatable central location"
(off Carnaby Street) and "fabulous" Italian/Spanish tapas,
this "bustling", if "slightly cramped", yearling may soon be even
better-known that its brilliant elder brother, Salt Yard.*
/ www.dehesa.co.uk; 11 pm; closed Sun D; no booking.

Del'Aziz £33 ④④❷
24-32 Vanston Pl, SW6   7386 0086   5–4A
Westfield, Ariel Way, W12   8740 0666   7–1C
Swiss Cottage Leis' C'tre, Adelaide Rd, NW3   7586 3338   8–2A
11 Bermondsey Sq, SE1   7407 2991   9–4D
5 Canvey St, SE1   7633 0033   9–3B
*"Moroccan staples" feature alongside more conventional fare, such as
burgers, at this expanding small chain, whose attractions include
"unusual" breakfast fry-ups and "brilliant" cakes (not to mention
"occasional belly dancing"); "painfully slow" service can be a problem.*
*/ www.delaziz.co.uk; SW6 10.30 pm; NW3 9.30 pm; SE1 11 pm;
W12 10.45 pm, Sun 9.45 pm; SE1 11 pm.*

Delfino W1 £36 ❷❸④
121 Mount St   7499 1256   3–3B
*"Magnifico!" – this "cut-above" Mayfair pizzeria offers "proper"
pizza (and other "rustic" dishes) at "good-value" prices.*
/ www.finos.co.uk; 11 pm; closed Sat L & Sun.

La Delizia Limbara SW3 £30 ❸❸❷
63-65 Chelsea Manor St   7376 4111   5–3C
*"Squashed but fun", this Chelsea back street joint is a "classic"
neighbourhood "haunt" specialising in "excellent pizza" (plus pastas
and salads); it offers "great value" too, in a bit of town not packed
with bargains. / 11 pm; no Amex.*

The Depot SW14 £40 ④④❷
Tideway Yd, Mortlake High St   8878 9462   10–1A
*Thanks to the "lovely, lovely" views ("if you bag a window table"),
there's "always a buzz" at this Thames-side stalwart, near Barnes
Bridge; the food, though, is generally "not overly exciting".*
/ www.depotbrasserie.co.uk; 11 pm, Sun 10.30 pm.

Le Deuxième WC2 £48 ④④④
65a Long Acre   7379 0033   4–2D
*A "convenient" Covent Garden location, near the Opera House,
makes this "smart" venue "undeniably handy pre/post-theatre", or for
a business lunch; it's "cramped", though, and suffers from "very,
very average" cuisine. / www.ledeuxieme.com; midnight, Sun 11 pm;
set weekday L & pre-theatre £30 (FP).*

Devonshire House W4 £39 ⑤⑤⑤
126 Devonshire Rd   7592 7962   7–2A
*When Gordon Ramsay talked about taking British pub food 'to a new
level', most people didn't realise he was proposing the sort of "barren,
cheerless and disappointing" experience too often reported at this
Chiswick gastroboozer (it was much better before he bought it!)*
*/ www.gordonramsay.com/thedevonshire/; 10.30, Sun 9 pm; Mon-Thu D only,
Fri-Sun open L & D.*

Devonshire Terrace EC2 £40 ❸❸❸
Devonshire Sq 7256 3233 9–2D
In "a calm development off busy Bishopsgate", this large, year-old bar/brasserie is proving a "good-quality business restaurant", offering "courteous" service, and "decent execution of a not particularly adventurous menu". / www.devonshireterrace.co.uk/; midnight; closed Sat & Sun.

Dexters £31 ❹❹❸
20 Bellevue Rd, SW17 8767 1858 10–2C
36-38 Abbeville Rd, SW4 8772 6646 10–2D
"For a kiddy brunch", some reporters do tip the burgers and so on at this low-key diner duo (whose nicer branch overlooks Wandsworth Common); too many reports, though, describe the food as "dismal". / www.tootsiesrestaurants.com; 11 pm, Sun 10.30 pm.

dim T £29 ❹❹❸
56-62 Wilton Rd, SW1 7834 0507 2–4B
32 Charlotte St, W1 7637 1122 2–1C
154-156 Gloucester Rd, SW7 7370 0070 5–2B
1 Hampstead Ln, N6 8340 8800 8–1B
3 Heath St, NW3 7435 0024 8–2A
Tooley St, SE1 7403 7000 9–4C
"Losing its novelty factor", this "lively" Pan-Asian chain can still offer a "very pleasant experience"… so long as you don't mind its increasingly "incompetent" service and "very average" food; NB SE1 has "spectacular views of Tower Bridge". / www.dimt.co.uk; most branches 11 pm, Sun 10.30pm.

Diner £30 ❹❺❸
18 Ganton St, W1 7287 8962 3–2C
64-66 Chamberlayne Rd, NW10 8968 9033 1–2B
2 Jamestown Rd, NW1 7485 5223 8–3B
128 Curtain Rd, EC2 7729 4452 12–1B
These "classic" diners sharply divide opinions; fans applaud "the most convincing American-style burgers in town", "great pancakes" and "shakes to die for" – critics, meanwhile, pan "terrible" quality, "unjustified" prices and "poor" service. / www.thedinershoreditch.com; midnight; W1 & NW1 Sun 11.30 pm; EC2 Sun & Mon 10.30 pm; booking: max 10.

Dinings W1 £34 ❶❷❹
22 Harcourt St 7723 0666 8–4A
"A cheaper, tiny Nobu!"; Tomanari Chiba's "hard-to-find" two-year-old – in a "stark" Marylebone bunker – actually achieves even higher survey ratings than his former employers, thanks to his "divine" sushi (and "awesome" other dishes too); "book well ahead". / 10.30 pm; closed Sat L & Sun L.

Dish Dash SW12 £28 ❹❹❸
11-13 Bedford Hill 8673 5555 10–2C
"You cram in like sardines", at this "always-busy" Balham Persian; not every reporter likes it, but fans say the food's "great". / www.dish-dash.com; 11 pm.

Diwana Bhel-Poori House NW1 £22 ❸❺❺
121-123 Drummond St 7387 5556 8–4C
It's the "wonderful lunchtime buffet" – "a trencherman's dream" – which most excites visitors to this "staple" '60s veggie canteen, in Little India; well, it certainly isn't the décor or service; BYO. / 11 pm, Sun 10 pm; need 10+ to book; set weekday L £13 (FP).

Dockmaster's House E14 NEW   £49   ❸❷❸
1 Hertsmere Rd   7345 0345   11–1C
A "magnificent" Georgian house with a "jaw-dropping" conservatory
addition, provides the "lovely" (if slightly "businessy") setting for this
ambitious Indian newcomer; unusually for the environs of Canary
Wharf, the "delicate and well thought-out" cuisine "lives up to the
location". / www.dockmastershouse.com; 11.30 pm; closed Sun; set always
available £37 (FP).

Dolada W1   £65   ❹❹❹
13 Albermarle St   7409 1011   3–3C
A new Italian, which is not much more than a relaunch of Mosaico
(RIP) which preceded it in this Mayfair basement site;
very modest survey feedback tends to confirm our view that it's
notably overpriced, but it seems to have a local business following
nonetheless. / www.dolada.co.uk; 10.30 pm; closed Sat L & Sun.

$ EC1   £39   ❹❸❷
2 Exmouth Mkt   7278 0077   9–1A
Stick to the "great cocktails" and "good burgers", and you won't
go far wrong at this "dark and cosy" Farringdon bar/diner – "perfect
for a girls' night out, or lunch with your better half".
/ www.dollargrills.com; 11 pm, Fri & Sat 11.30 pm, Sun 10pm.

The Don EC4   £47   ❷❷❷
20 St Swithin's Ln   7626 2606   9–3C
"The best business restaurant in the City" – combining an "airy and
civilised" upstairs, with an informal and "atmospheric" cellar –
is quietly tucked-away near Bank; the cooking is "good verging
on very good", backed up by a "cracking" wine list and "slick"
service. / www.thedonrestaurant.com; 10 pm; closed Sat & Sun; no trainers.

don Fernando's TW9   £33   ❸❷❸
27f The Quadrant   8948 6447   1–4A
A large and "bright" tapas bar, right by Richmond Station – it is
perennially praised for its "enjoyable" dishes and "speedy" service,
and its "fun" and "easy-going" atmosphere. / www.donfernado.co.uk;
11 pm; no Amex; no booking.

Don Pepe NW8   £35   ❸❷❸
99 Frampton St   7262 3834   8–4A
"Dated, but generally in a good way", London's oldest tapas bar,
near Lord's, is a jolly place, with "lovely" staff, and "dependable" and
"good-value" grub. / 11.30 pm; closed Sun; set always available, weekday
L & dinner £22 (FP).

Donna Margherita SW11   £37   ❷❷❸
183 Lavender Hill   7228 2660   10–2C
"A great neighbourhood Italian", in Battersea, which serves
up "fabulous thin crust pizzas" (plus "interesting daily specials"),
and a "warm and friendly welcome every time".
/ www.donna-margherita.com; 10.30 pm, Sat 11 pm; closed Mon,
Tue-Fri D only, Sat & Sun open L & D.

Donzoko W1   £37   ❷❹❹
15 Kingly St   7734 1974   3–2C
"A voluminous menu is freshly prepared", at this "bustling" Japanese
'izakaya', on the fringe of Soho; service, though, is "iffy". / 10 pm;
closed Sat L & Sun.

Dorchester Grill
Dorchester Hotel W1 £83 ④❸④
53 Park Ln 7629 8888 3–3A
"Try to close your eyes" to the "tartan-riot" décor of this "bizarre"-looking Mayfair grill room; in fact, it's best to keep them closed all the way through until the "huge bill" arrives – given the "average" cooking, it can seem just as "hideous"! / www.thedorchester.com; 11 pm, Sun 10.30 pm; no trainers.

Dotori N4 NEW £24 ❸❷④
3 Stroud Green Rd 7263 3562 8–1D
It may have an "unprepossessing" location, near Finsbury Park, but this "tiny" newcomer is of note for serving "some excellent Korean and Japanese food", and at "bargain prices" too. / 11 pm; closed Mon; no booking.

Dover Street Restaurant & Bar W1 £47 ⑤④④
8-10 Dover St 7491 7509 3–3C
A long-established Mayfair dive, whose main appeal is its "interesting" music (to which you can dance) – the food is incidental and "overpriced". / www.doverstreet.co.uk; 2 am; D only, closed Sun; no trainers.

Dragon Castle SE17 £30 ❶❷❷
114 Walworth Rd 7277 3388 1–3C
"Worth a trip to Elephant & Castle" – this huge and "stylishly-decorated" Chinese is again hitting the "fabulous" standards which made it such a big hit when it opened two years ago; the top attraction is "dim sum better than anything in Chinatown", but the main menu is "wonderful" too. / www.dragoncastle.eu; 11 pm, Fri 11.30 pm, Sun 10.30 pm.

The Drapers Arms N1 NEW £33 ④❸❷
44 Barnsbury St 7619 0348 8–3D
"Back, and triumphantly so!", say fans of this "beautiful" Georgian boozer, hidden-away in Islington, which was recently relaunched; we count ourselves among the early-days sceptics, though, who feel that realisation of the "no-nonsense" menu "needs work". / www.thedrapersarms.com; 11 pm.

The Drunken Monkey E1 £27 ❷❷❸
222 Shoreditch High St 7392 9606 12–1B
"Very fresh-tasting" dim sum "at bargain prices" maintains the appeal of this "fun" Shoreditch boozer; as the evening wears on, "a DJ adds to the vibe", and "you may need to shout to be heard". / www.thedrunkenmonkey.co.uk; midnight, Sun 11 pm; closed Sat L.

The Duke of Cambridge N1 £42 ④④❸
30 St Peter's St 7359 3066 1–2C
This "committed" organic gastroboozer, in Islington, pleases its many fans with its "chilled" style and "tasty" fare; critics say prices are "a little OTT", though, for food that's "nothing special". / www.dukeorganic.co.uk; 10.30 pm, Sun 10 pm; no Amex.

Duke Of Sussex W4 £35 ❸❸❸
75 South Pde 8742 8801 7–1A
"An interesting menu" – "typical staples served with flair, plus Spanish-influenced dishes" – adds character to this "beautiful" restoration of a Victorian boozer on the Chiswick/Acton borders; "good garden" too. / midnight, Sun 11 pm; closed Mon L; no Amex.

The Duke of Wellington W1 £41 ❷❷❷
94a, Crawford St   7723 2790   3–3A
A "fine" make-over of a Marylebone inn wins acclaim for this
"cramped" and "buzzy" yearling, whose cooking is "as good as you're
likely to get in a pub which still looks like a pub".
/ www.thedukew1.co.uk; 10 pm, Sun 9 pm; Booking: max 25 in restaurant.

Duke on the Green SW6 £38 ④④④
235 New King's Rd   7736 2777   10–1B
On the south edge of Parson's Green, this "buzzing" pub still wins
praise for its "feel-good" style, and its "tasty" food; quality "dropped
off a bit this year", though, with the odd "terrible" experience
recorded. / www.dukeonthegreen.co.uk; midnight, Sun 11.30 pm.

The Duke's Head SW15 £34 ④❷❶
8 Lower Richmond Rd   8788 2552   10–1B
"The most amazing views of the Thames" are the highlight attraction
of this "airy" dining room, which is located in a "pleasantly
traditional" (but "child-friendly") landmark boozer, near Putney
Bridge. / www.dukesheadputney.co.uk; 11 pm, Fri & Sat midnight.

E&O W11 £45 ❶❸❶
14 Blenheim Cr   7229 5454   6–1A
"Beautiful people enjoy beautiful food", at Will Ricker's "sexy", softly-
lit and always "buzzing" Notting Hill hang-out, where the
"imaginative" cuisine of "Asian-fusion tapas" is as "awesome"
as ever. / www.rickerrestaurants.com; 11 pm, Sun 10.30 pm; booking: max 6.

The Eagle EC1 £25 ❸④❷
159 Farringdon Rd   7837 1353   9–1A
"The original, and still the best", claims a fan of this "ever-lively"
Farringdon gastropub (London's first, 1992); that's overdoing it a bit
nowadays, but the Mediterranean food is still "consistently good"
(and getting a seat is still a "free-for-all"). / 10.30 pm; closed Sun D;
no Amex; no booking.

Eagle Bar Diner W1 £31 ❸④❸
3-5 Rathbone Pl   7637 1418   4–1A
A "fun" joint, just off Oxford Street, with "great burgers" and
"the best shakes", plus a busy bar with delicious cocktails; service,
though, is sometimes "oblivious". / www.eaglebardiner.com; Mon-Wed
11 pm, Thu-Sat 1 am; closed Sun D; no Amex; need 6+ to book.

Ealing Park Tavern W5 £38 ❸❸❸
222 South Ealing Rd   8758 1879   1–3A
A "congenial" west London gastroboozer, still hailed by some
reporters as offering "the best food in Ealing" (and from
an "interesting" and "diverse" menu) – standards, though,
have slipped a bit under the new régime. / www.ealingparktavern.com;
10 pm, Sun 9 pm; booking: max 10.

Earl Spencer SW18 £37 ❸❸❷
260-262 Merton Rd   8870 9244   10–2B
A "beacon" in the "sea of mediocrity" that is Southfields – this large
gastropub inspires impressively consistent praise for its "top-class"
food and its "unpretentious" but "atmospheric" style.
/ www.theearlspencer.co.uk; 10 pm, Sun 9.30 pm; no booking.

The East Hill SW18 £38 ❸❸❷
21 Alma Rd 8874 1833 10–2B
One of the stronger members of the Geronimo Inns group, this "lovely" Wandsworth gastroboozer is a "buzzy" place, where the grub is sometimes "very good". / www.geronimo-inns.co.uk; 10 pm, Thu-Sat 10.30 pm, Sun 9 pm.

The East Room EC2 NEW £45 ❸❷❶
2a, Tabernacle St 847876 12–2A
The "chilled" dining room of a private club (open to non-members), just off Finsbury Square, featuring "awesome" funky décor (plus terrace), and "an interesting wine romp around the New World"; the "simple" food pleases too, but has rather a supporting role. / www.thstrm.com; 11 pm; closed Sat L & Sun D.

The Easton WC1 £32 ❸❸❸
22 Easton St 7278 7608 9–1A
"Enormous and very tasty meals" again win praise for this laid-back Aussie-run gastropub, near Exmouth Market. / 10 pm; no Amex.

Eastside Inn EC1 NEW £43 ❹❷❹
40 St John St 7490 9230 9–1B
"Stunning" or "bizarre"? – first-week reports of Bjorn van der Horst's brave Smithfield newcomer (part bistro/part fine dining) were all over the show; our own view – from the cheaper seats – was that the food is good but pricey for what it is, and that the overall experience doesn't quite hang together. / www.esilondon.com; 10 pm; closed Mon, Sat L & Sun; no trainers.

Eat £11 ❹❸❹
Branches throughout London
Fans say it "outshines Pret", but this "reliable" sandwiches-and-more chain still lags the market leader's overall ratings; "superb soup" is a menu highlight. / www.eat.co.uk; 4 pm-8 pm; most City branches closed all or part of weekend; no credit cards; no booking.

Eat & Two Veg W1 £33 ❺❹❺
50 Marylebone High St 7258 8595 2–1A
"How can you get hummus wrong?"; this "huge" diner-style veggie is an "interesting" concept, but results are far too "average and unexciting" – it's no great surprise that the former Muswell Hill offshoot is no more. / www.eatandtwoveg.com; 10.30 pm, Sun 10 pm.

The Ebury SW1 £45 ❹❸❷
11 Pimlico Rd 7730 6784 5–2D
The food at this "cool" Pimlico bar/restaurant (which saw the renovation of its upstairs dining room in 2009) is sometimes "very good" nowadays, if still not invariably so; it's a perennially "busy" place, though, and service can be "slow". / www.theebury.co.uk; 10.30 pm, Sun 10 pm.

Ebury Wine Bar SW1 £41 ❹❹❸
139 Ebury St 7730 5447 2–4A
A "cosy" and "unchanging" Belgravia veteran, with a "well-researched" wine list; its cooking is "reliable" enough, but there remains a feeling that the place is "overpriced" and in "gentle decline". / www.eburywinebar.co.uk; 10.15 pm; closed Sun L.

Eco SW4 £29 ❸④❸
162 Clapham High St 7978 1108 10–2D
"Still churning out great pizzas" – this *"very crowded"* and *"noisy"* Clapham joint *"has been going for over a decade, and with good reason"*. / www.ecorestaurants.com; 11 pm, Fri & Sat 11.30 pm.

Ed's Easy Diner £23 ❸❸❷
12 Moor St, W1 7434 4439 4–2A
Trocadero, 19 Rupert St, W1 7287 1951 3–3D
"For an impromptu burger and milkshake", these *"bustling"* Happy Days-style diners still really hit the spot. / www.edseasydiner.co.uk; Rupert St 10 pm, Wed 10.30 pm, Thu 11 pm, Fri & Sat midnight; Moor St midnight, Sun 11 pm; no Amex; Moor St no booking.

Edera W11 £47 ❸❸④
148 Holland Park Ave 7221 6090 6–2A
An upscale Holland Park *"neighbourhood"* Italian, which attracts praise for its *"authentic"* Sardinian cuisine; the décor *"needs refreshing"* though, and prices can seem *"uncompetitive"*. / 11 pm.

Edokko WC1 £42 ❷❷❸
50 Red Lion St 7242 3490 2–1D
"No prizes for décor", at this rickety *"slice of Japan"*, off Holborn, but – for *"really good and authentic sushi"* – it can be *"outstanding"*. / 10 pm, Sat 9.30 pm; closed Sat L & Sun.

Efes £32 ❸❸④
1) 80 Gt Titchfield St, W1 7636 1953 2–1B
2) 175-177 Gt Portland St, W1 7436 0600 2–1B
Who cares if they've *"not changed in 20 years"*? – *"if you like cheap and basic meat dishes"*, these *"faded"* but *"amazing"* Turkish *"time warps"*, in Marylebone, can still be *"just the ticket"* (especially *"in a group"*). / Gt Titchfield St midnight; Gt Portland St 1 am, Fri & Sat 3 am.

Eight Over Eight SW3 £45 ❷❸❷
392 King's Rd 7349 9934 5–3B
A *"fun"* and *"happening"* Chelsea scene which serves up some *"prime people-watching"*, to go with an *"utterly delicious"* menu of Asian-fusion tapas. / www.rickerrestaurants.com; 11 pm, Sun 10.30 pm; closed Sun L.

Ekachai £26 ❸④④
14 Woodstock St, W1 7629 2988 3–1B **NEW**
Southside Shopping Cntr, SW18 8871 3888 10–2B
9-10 The Arcade, Liverpool St, EC2 7626 1155 9–2D
"For a quick, inexpensive, City lunch" of *"punchy"* noodles and curries, the EC2 original of this Chinese/Malaysian group remains *"just the job"*; its year-old Wandsworth offshoot wins similar praise *"for a swift post-cinema meal"* (and there's now also an offshoot near Oxford Street). / www.ekachai.net; 10 pm; SW18 Fri & Sat 10.30 pm; EC2 closed Sat & Sun; min credit card payment £10; booking: min 3, no booking L.

Electric Brasserie W11 £39 ❸❸❷
191 Portobello Rd 7908 9696 6–1A
For weekend brunch, *"it's a scrum waiting for a table"*, at this *"fast-paced"* Notting Hill hang-out; the attraction? – *"classic, comfort food"* served to a *"super-trendy"* crowd. / www.the-electric.co.uk; 10.45 pm.

Elena's L'Etoile W1 £51 ⑤④❸
30 Charlotte St 7636 7189 2–1C
*"Old-style glamour and eccentricity" still help make a "favourite"
of this "very traditional" Gallic restaurant, in Fitzrovia; the food has
"really slipped", though, and the service "declines" when the
"wonderful Elena" is not there.* / www.elenasletoile.co.uk; 10.30 pm; closed
Sat L & Sun.

Elephant Royale
Locke's Wharf E14 £39 ❸❷❸
Westferry Rd 7987 7999 11–2C
*"Hidden-away" at the tip of the Isle of Dogs – with super river views
from its terrace – this glitzily-decorated but well-run Thai wins praise
for its "quality" cooking; it can seem "expensive", though, unless you
go for the "excellent-value Sunday buffet".* / www.elephantroyale.com;
11.30 pm, Fri & Sat midnight, Sun 11 pm.

Elistano SW3 £42 ❸❷❸
25-27 Elystan St 7584 5248 5–2C
*This long-established Chelsea back street Italian has been
transformed by the appointment of a new chef – "for a local
restaurant, it offers great food and service"; pizzas (a new option)
win particular praise.* / www.elistano.com; 10.30 pm; closed Sun D.

The Elk in the Woods N1 £38 ④❸❸
39 Camden Pas 7226 3535 8–3D
*"Tucked-away off Upper Street", this "interesting" Islington hang-out
serves a "comfort food" menu whose forte is a "perfect breakfast";
some reporters, though, feel standards are suffering as the place
"tries too hard to be to trendy".* / www.the-elk-in-the-woods.co.uk; 10.30 pm;
no Amex.

Emile's SW15 £37 ❷⓿❸
96 Felsham Rd 8789 3323 10–2B
*Emile Fahy's "photographic memory for guests" helps draw much
repeat custom to this "busy" bistro favourite, in the back streets
of Putney; the menu offers "something for everyone" too
(plus "superb" wines), at notably "competitive" prices.*
/ www.emilesrestaurant.co.uk; 11 pm; D only, closed Sun; no Amex.

Emni N1 £37 ❸❸④
353 Upper St 7226 1166 8–3D
*"One of Upper Street's better offerings" – a "much above-average"
Islington Indian that puts "a modern twist on classic dishes".*
/ www.emnirestaurant.com; 11 pm, Fri midnight; Mon-Thu D only, Fri-Sun open
L & D.

The Empress of India E9 £41 ④❸❸
130 Lauriston Rd 8533 5123 1–2D
*This Victoria Park gastropub – a sibling to the famous Gun – offers
"good" food in a "pleasant" setting; it has its critics, though, who say
it "sounds better than it really is".* / www.theempressofindia.com; 9.30 pm.

The Engineer NW1 £43 ❸④❷
65 Gloucester Ave 7722 0950 8–3B
*Despite ups and downs over the years, this "relaxed" gastropub
linchpin of Primrose Hill life "remains a favourite", thanks to its
"lovely" garden and "cosy" interior, and food that's "consistently
good"; it's "a bit pricey", though, and service can be "sporadic".*
/ www.the-engineer.com; 11 pm, Sun 10.30 pm; no Amex.

Enoteca Turi SW15 £50 ❷❷❸
28 Putney High St 8785 4449 10–2B
"Glorious" Italian cooking is but one of the attractions of the Turi
family's "fabulous" and "friendly" stalwart, near Putney Bridge;
top billing goes to the wine list – "an epic journey through the regions
of Italy", with "gems at all price levels". / www.enotecaturi.com; 11 pm;
closed Sun; set weekday L £30 (FP).

The Enterprise SW3 £45 ❸❸❷
35 Walton St 7584 3148 5–2C
A "warmly atmospheric Knightsbridge bar/restaurant" – in a former
pub – where "a good crowd of locals" enjoys a "well-executed" menu;
it's not a big place, however, and "the no-bookings policy can be hard
to swallow". / www.theenterprise.co.uk; 10.30 pm, Sun 10 pm; no booking,
except weekday L.

Eriki NW3 £37 ❶❶❸
4-6 Northways Pde, Finchley Rd 7722 0606 8–2A
The location is "unexciting" and the décor "ordinary", but this Swiss
Cottage Indian has won a formidable following, thanks to its
"fantastic" service and its "sensational" cuisine – "better than
Benares, and half the price!" / www.eriki.co.uk; 10.30 pm; closed Sat L.

Esarn Kheaw W12 £27 ❶❸④
314 Uxbridge Rd 8743 8930 7–1B
It certainly looks "unpromising", but this small Shepherd's Bush
"treasure" has long offered "gorgeous", "simple" and "spicy" dishes
that rank "among the very best Thai food in London"; "a little TLC
on the décor", though, would do no harm. / www.esarnkheaw.co.uk;
11 pm; closed Sat L & Sun L; no Amex.

Esca SW4 £25 ❸❸❸
160a, Clapham High St 7622 2288 10–2D
A "friendly" Italian deli, near Clapham Common tube, which hits the
spot "for a filling lunch"; have a cake for pudding! / www.escauk.com;
9 pm; no Amex.

L'Escargot W1 £52 ❸❷❷
48 Greek St 7437 2679 4–2A
Standards at this "elegant retreat in the middle of frantic Soho"
dipped a fraction this year – most reporters still praise its "romantic"
style and "excellent" Gallic cuisine, but some meals were
"forgettable" or "insipid"; the upstairs Picasso Room was being
revamped as this guide was going to press, but no further details
were available. / www.whitestarline.org.uk; 11.30 pm; closed Sat L & Sun;
set always available £34 (FP).

Essenza W11 £52 ❷❷❷
210 Kensington Park Rd 7792 1066 6–1A
Oddly little commented-on, given its fashionable Notting Hill location,
this small Italian restaurant is nevertheless unanimously hailed as a
"high-quality" destination, offering "great value for money".
/ www.essenza.co.uk; 11.30 pm; set weekday L £31 (FP).

The Establishment £40 ❸❸❸
45-47 Parson's Green Ln, SW6 7384 2418 10–1B
35-37 Battersea Rise, SW11 7228 9400 10–2C **NEW**
A Parson's Green bar, recently joined by a new Battersea sibling;
they can be "loud" places, but win all-round praise for their "friendly"
attitude and "really good" food. / www.theestablishment.com;
SW6 10.30 pm, Sun 9.30 pm; SW11 midnight, Mon 11 pm, Sun 10.30 pm;
SW11 Mon-Fri D only.

L'Etranger SW7 £52 ❸❸❸
36 Gloucester Rd 7584 1118 5–1B
Go for the "high-quality oriental menu" ("not the French fare"), if you visit this stylish and rather "different" fusion-restaurant, in South Kensington; the undoubted star attraction, however, is the "never-ending" (and "very pricey") wine list. / www.etranger.co.uk; 11 pm; closed Sat L; set weekday L £33 (FP).

Ev Restaurant, Bar & Deli SE1 £29 ④④❷
97-99 Isabella St 7620 6191 9–4A
A "lovely, leafy outside area" is a great boon at this "lively" Tas-group restaurant, intriguingly housed under railway arches, near Southwark tube, which offers "inexpensive" Turkish fare. / www.tasrestaurant.com; 11.30 pm.

Everest Inn SE3 £30 ❸❸❸
41 Montpelier Vale 8852 7872 1–4D
Now in a new site, closer to the heath, this recently-expanded Blackheath Nepalese continues to win praise for its "above-average" cooking and "pleasant" service. / www.everestinn.co.uk; 11.30 pm, Fri & Sat midnight.

Eyre Brothers EC2 £50 ❸❷❸
70 Leonard St 7613 5346 12–1B
A "serious Hispanic menu" of "rich" and "authentic" dishes inspires continued applause for this "unusual" Shoreditch hang-out, where the "urban" décor "just misses being drab"; "professional" service helps win the place quite a business following. / www.eyrebrothers.co.uk; 10.45 pm; closed Sat L & Sun.

Fabrizio EC1 £38 ❷❷④
30 Saint Cross St 7430 1503 9–1A
"It's a gem – shout it from the rooftops!"; fans of this "obscurely-located" (and "under-reviewed") Farringdon café say it's "well worth a trip" for its "charming" service and its "exceptional" Sicilian food. / www.fabriziorestaurant.co.uk; 10 pm; closed Sat L & Sun.

Fairuz W1 £41 ❸❸④
3 Blandford St 7486 8108 2–1A
A Marylebone Lebanese that's become a "staple" for some reporters, thanks to its "genuine" dishes and its "friendly" service. / www.fairuz.uk.com; 11 pm, Sun 10.30 pm.

Fakhreldine W1 £54 ④④④
85 Piccadilly 7493 3424 3–4C
It may have "great views" over Green Park, but it's hard to recommend this first-floor contemporary-look Lebanese, near the Ritz – the food can seem "dull" and "pricey", and service "brusque" and "impatient"; see also 1001 Nights. / www.fakhreldine.co.uk; midnight, Sun 11 pm.

Il Falconiere SW7 £38 ④❷⑤
84 Old Brompton Rd 7589 2401 5–2B
It looks a bit "drab" nowadays, but this "very traditional" South Kensington trattoria retains a fair following for its "value-for-money" set meals. / www.ilfalconiere.co.uk; 11.30 pm; closed Sun; set weekday L £24 (FP).

La Famiglia SW10 £47 ④❸❸
7 Langton St   7351 0761   5–3B
It's still "packed" – and the garden is "wonderful in summer" –
but this long-established "Chelsea-set" trattoria has started to look
a little "past its best" of late, and prices for its rather variable cuisine
can seem "out of proportion". / www.lafamiglia.co.uk; 11.45 pm.

The Farm SW6 £40 ④④❸
18 Farm Ln   7381 3331   5–3A
In a rather "strange" back street location near Fulham Broadway,
a much-modernised bistro/boozer – "worth finding", if you're in the
area, but "not especially memorable". / www.thefarmfulham.co.uk;
10.30 pm, Sun 10 pm; closed for L Mon-Thu & Sun D.

El Faro E14 £40 ❶❶❸
3 Turnberry Quay   7987 5511   11–2C
"Some of the best Spanish food in London!" – "not just tapas" either
– makes it worth tackling the "awkward" location of this
"very friendly" outfit, near Crossharbour DLR; it has a waterside
position which "comes into its own in summer". / www.el-faro.co.uk;
11 pm; closed Sun D.

The Fat Badger W10 £41 ❸❷④
310 Portobello Rd   8969 4500   6–1A
A couple of years after its (overhyped) opening, this North Kensington
gastropub has settled into a surprisingly "charming" early middle age,
and most reporters find its food "really enjoyable".
/ www.thefatbadger.com; 10 pm, Fri-Sat 10.30 pm, Sun 9 pm.

Fat Boy's £27 ④❸❸
33 Haven Grn, W5   8998 5868   1–2A
201 Upper Richmond Rd, SW14   8876 0644   1–4A **NEW**
431-433 Richmond Rd, TW1   8892 7657   1–4A
68 High St, TW8   8569 8481   1–3A
10a-10b Edensor Rd, W4   8994 8089   10–1A
The "family-friendly" East Sheen branch has proved a good addition
to this small Thai chain, praised by most – if not quite all – reporters
for its "good-value" and "always-reliable" scoff; at breakfast and
lunch, a standard British caff menu is served. / www.fatboysthai.co.uk;
11 pm.

Faulkner's E8 £30 ❷❷❸
424-426 Kingsland Rd   7254 6152   1–1D
"Unbeatable" fish 'n' chips in "vast" portions wins continued acclaim
from (most) reporters on this celebrated Dalston veteran. / 10 pm;
no Amex; need 8+ to book.

The Fellow N1 **NEW** £38 ❸④❸
24 York Way   7833 4395   8–3C
"Just opposite King's Cross station", this "bustling" new "gastropub-
style" bistro feels "just like what the area needs"; service, though,
"has degenerated since opening". / www.thefellow.co.uk; 10 pm; closed
Sun D.

Feng Sushi   £30   ④④④
26 Elizabeth St, SW1   7730 0033   2–4A
218 Fulham Rd, SW10   7795 1900   5–3B
101 Notting Hill Gate, W11   7727 1123   6–2B
21 Kensington Church St, W8   7937 7927   5–1A
1 Adelaide St, NW3   7483 2929   8–2B
13 Stoney St, SE1   7407 8744   9–4C
Royal Festival Hall, SE1   7261 0001   2–3D
"Basic" but "reliable" sushi still wins praise for these simple cafés; survey feedback, however, tends to confirm the fears of those who say they've "slipped somewhat". / www.fengsushi.co.uk; 10 pm, Thu-Sat 11 pm.

The Fentiman Arms SW8   £34   ④❸❷
64 Fentiman Rd   7793 9796   10–1D
"Expansive outdoor areas" are a big plus-point at this "lively" Lambeth gastropub, where the cooking is "serviceable, but not really very memorable". / www.geronimo-inns.co.uk; 10 pm, Fri-Sat 10.30 pm, Sun 8 pm.

Fernandez & Wells   £25   ❶❷❷
43 Lexington St, W1   7734 1546   3–2D
73 Beak St, W1   7287 8124   3–2D
"Proof that a sandwich can be a memorable event!"; these "coolly utilitarian" cafés dispense "simple" but "decadent" snacks, plus "juices like nectar" and "coffee like no other"; "fab wine" too (Lexington). / www.fernandezandwells.com; Lexington St 10 pm; Beak St 6 pm.

Ffiona's W8   £45   ❸❷❶
51 Kensington Church St   7937 4152   5–1A
"The food's OK", at this "cosy" candlelit Kensington bistro, "but you really go for the atmosphere and to chat with Ffiona"; fall out with la patronne, though – it can happen – and the party's over! / www.ffionas.com; 11 pm, Sun 10 pm; D only, closed Mon; no Amex.

Fifteen Dining Room N1   £85   ④④④
15 Westland Pl   0871 330 1515   12–1A
Jamie Oliver's charitable Hoxton Italian remains "way overpriced, 'cos of his name"; fans do say "the expense is worth it", citing "passionate food and service", but critics just find it just "too pricey for cooking by trainees", especially given the "dingy" and "soulless" basement setting. / www.fifteenrestaurant.net; 9.30 pm; booking: max 6.

Fifteen Trattoria N1   £46   ④④❸
15 Westland Pl   0871 330 1515   12–1A
Fans love the "great pasta" and other simple dishes on offer at the "casual" ground floor of Jamie Oliver's Hoxton Italian, although critics just want to know how this "bad" and "overpriced" place survives; all, however, agree that breakfast is "the meal they get right". / www.fifteen.net; 10 pm; booking: max 12.

**The Fifth Floor Café
Harvey Nichols SW1**   £46   ④④④
109-125 Knightsbridge   7823 1839   5–1D
"The most delicious teas", and a "perfect cappuccino" too, figure in reports on this top-floor Knightsbridge café; otherwise, it inspires little in the way of excitement, and strikes critics as "not offering good value for money". / www.harveynichols.com; 11 pm, Sun 5 pm; closed Sun D; no booking at L; set dinner £30 (FP).

The Fifth Floor Restaurant
Harvey Nichols SW1   £63   ④④④
109-125 Knightsbridge   7235 5250   5–1D
It was really quite a place in its day, but this dining room above the famous Knightsbridge store often just strikes reporters as "strange" nowadays; it does, however, benefit from a "good-value set menu" (available lunch and dinner, Mon-Fri), and a "really superb choice of wines". / www.harveynichols.com; 11 pm; closed Sun D.

54 Farringdon Road EC1   £35   ❷❷④
54 Farringdon Rd   7336 0603   9–1A
An "out-of-the-way" Farringdon yearling which offers a slightly "strange" mix of Malay and European cuisine; the former is particularly "delicious", though, and service is notably "efficient". / www.54farringdon.com; 11 pm; closed Sat L & Sun.

Fig N1   £46   ❷❶❷
169 Hemingford Rd   7609 3009   8–3D
It may be "hidden-away in the leafy streets of Barnsbury", but this tiny "one-off" has won a big fan club with its "original", "Nordic-influenced" food, its "sweet" service, and its "casual" and "romantic" ambience. / www.fig-restaurant.co.uk; 10.15 pm, Sun 9 pm; D only, closed Sun-Tue.

La Figa E14   £36   ❷❷❸
45 Narrow St   7790 0077   11–1B
"Pizza and pasta in enormous portions" – and "sunny" service too – "draw in crowds" to this "well-run" Docklands Italian; it can get "loud". / 11 pm, Sun 10.30 pm.

Fine Burger Company   £31   ④④④
330 Upper St, N1   7359 3026   8–3D
O2 Centre, Finchley Rd, NW3   7433 0700   8–2A
Fans may say it still "lives up to its name", but there are too many reports of "a drop-off in standards" at this basic chain for it just to be coincidence. / www.fineburger.co.uk; most branches 10 pm-11 pm.

Fino W1   £52   ❷❷❷
33 Charlotte St   7813 8010   2–1C
"Impressive" tapas and a "terrific Spanish wine list" win continued acclaim for the Hart brothers' "always-buzzing" Fitzrovia venture, which manages to be "stylish, despite being in a basement". / www.finorestaurant.com; 10.30 pm; closed Sat L & Sun; booking: max 12.

Fire & Stone   £30   ❸④❷
31-32 Maiden Ln, WC2   712550   4–3D
Westfield, Ariel Way, W12   0844 371 2550   7–1C **NEW**
"Unorthodox" pizzas – "to suit all tastes, no matter how bizarre" – usually turn out "tasty" enough at these "trendy" joints (a Westfield spin-off having recently joined the large and "funky"-looking Covent Garden original); service, though, can be "amnesiac". / www.fireandstone.com; WC2 11 pm; W12 11 pm, Sat & Sun 11.30 pm.

The Fire Stables SW19   £41   ④④❸
27-29 Church Rd   8946 3197   10–2B
When it first opened, this "lovely relaxing gastropub local" was exactly what Wimbledon needed; nowadays, it's just "expensive, and not particularly good". / www.firestableswimbledon.co.uk; 10.30 pm, Sun 10 pm; booking: max 8, Sat & Sun.

Firezza £29 ❷❸④
12 All Saints Rd, W11 7221 0020 6–1B
48 Chiswick High Rd, W4 8994 9494 7–2B
276 St Paul's Rd, N1 7359 7400 8–2D
40 Lavender Hill, SW11 7223 5535 10–1C
205 Garrett Ln, SW18 8870 7070 10–2B
"Find me a better pizza delivery service!"; these "brilliant" take-ways — "they're not places to eat in" — win many raves for their "fantastic bases and delicious toppings". / www.firezza.com; 11 pm, Fri & Sat midnight; N1 closed Sun; no Amex.

First Floor W11 £42 ④❷❶
186 Portobello Rd 7243 0072 6–1A
If you're looking for "boho-chic" Notting Hill style, you won't do better than this "very dependable" and "romantic" local fixture (which features an "amazing" and "different'" party room). / www.firstfloorportobello.co.uk; 11 pm; closed Mon & Sun D.

Fish Central EC1 £27 ❸❷❸
149-155 Central St 7253 4970 12–1A
"Popular with cabbies, so it must be good value", this "dingy" — but "packed and jolly" — East Ender is "part chippy, part serious fish restaurant". / www.fishcentral.co.uk; 10.30 pm, Fri & Sat 11 pm; closed Sun; no Amex.

Fish Club £32 ❷❷④
189 St John's Hill, SW11 7978 7115 10–2C
57 Clapham High St, SW4 7720 5853 10–2D
"Making fish 'n' chips a gourmet treat"; these "relaxed" Clapham and Battersea concepts are a "brilliant reinvention of the chippy for the 21st century", with everything "cooked in varying styles, to order"; "for such sophisticated food", though, the eat-in space can seem a little "primitive". / www.thefishclub.com; 10 pm, Sun 9 pm; SW4 closed Mon L, SW11 closed Mon.

Fish Hook W4 £47 ❷❸④
6-8 Elliott Rd 8742 0766 7–2A
"Fantastically fresh fish and seafood" is cooked "with confidence and flair", at Michael Nadra's very "tightly-packed" Chiswick fixture (where the top deal is the "brilliant-value set lunch"); service, however — which is generally "charming" — can sometimes be a "let-down". / www.fishhook.co.uk; 10.30 pm, Sun 10 pm; set weekday L £28 (FP).

Fish in a Tie SW11 £28 ④❷❷
105 Falcon Rd 7924 1913 10–1C
"A great, fun place to go with a group of mates" – this "noisy" Battersea bistro in fact "serves more meat than fish", and at prices which are "a veritable bargain". / midnight; no Amex; set weekday L £16 (FP).

Fish Shop EC1 £44 ❸④④
360-362 St John's St 7837 1199 8–3D
"A great place for a bite to eat pre/post-Sadlers Wells"; the fish dishes are "very enjoyable", but service can be iffy. / www.thefishshop.net; 11 pm; closed Mon & Sun D; set pre theatre £29 (FP).

fish! SE1 £41 ④④④
Cathedral St 7407 3803 9–4C
By Borough Market, this impressive-looking glass shed remains popular for "lovely, simply-cooked fish"; dishes are "fairly basic", though, and critics find the service "disjointed" and the ambience "clattery". / www.fishkitchen.com; 11pm, Sun 10.30 pm.

Fishworks £44 ❸④④
7-9 Swallow St, W1   7734 5813   3–3D
89 Marylebone High St, W1   7935 9796   2–1A
*"For spanking fresh fish cooked just how you like it",
this café/fishmonger chain still has much to commend it (the demise
of many of its branches notwithstanding); prices remain "high",
however, and interiors are "cramped" and "functional".*
/ www.fishworks.co.uk; 10.30pm-11.30 pm.

5 Cavendish Square W1 £66 ⑤⑤⑤
5 Cavendish Sq   7079 5000   3–1C
*"Only go for the décor", to this showy bar/club/restaurant, in a
massive Marylebone townhouse – it may be strong on "grandeur",
but service is "lacklustre", and the food "isn't worth half what they
charge for it".* / www.no5ltd.com; 10 pm; closed Sat L & Sun D; no trainers;
set weekday L £39 (FP).

Five Hot Chillies HA0 £23 ❷❷⑤
875 Harrow Rd   8908 5900   1–1A
*"Freshly-cooked" curries and kebabs at "fantastic prices" make
it worth braving the trip to this "very friendly", if grotty-looking,
Sudbury Indian, on a busy highway; "BYO makes it even better
value".* / 11.30 pm; no Amex.

500 N19 NEW £33 ❷❷④
782 Holloway Rd   7272 3406   8–1C
*"There is life in Archway!"; this "brave" and "simply-furnished"
Sicilian newcomer has brought "a real spark of Mediterranean
warmth" to this unpicturesque corner of the capital; be warned,
though – "you'll need to book on any night of the week".*
/ www.500restaurant.co.uk; 10 pm; closed Mon & Sun L.

Flâneur EC1 £42 ④❸④
41 Farringdon Rd   7404 4422   9–1A
*Some reporters find it "fun" to eat amidst the produce on display
at this trendy Farringdon deli/diner; not everyone agrees, though,
and the food can be a mite "variable".* / www.flaneur.com; 10 pm;
closed Sun.

The Flask N6 £34 ❸④❶
77 Highgate West Hill   8348 7346   1–1C
*A "superb" location – "quietly set in Highgate village with nice outside
seating" – ensures this lovely old inn is always "busy"; the food
is "varied" and "fresh", but ultimately a bit beside the point.* / 10 pm.

Flat White W1 £9 ❶❶❷
17 Berwick St   7734 0370   3–2D
*Coffee that's "so good it's illegal" is the – really – big deal at this
"pokey" Kiwi-run bar, in a seamy part of Soho.* / www.flat-white.co.uk;
L only; no credit cards.

Floridita W1 £52 ⑤⑤❷
100 Wardour St   7314 4000   3–2D
*Some "fantastic" evenings are spent at this massive, Cuban-themed
cocktails 'n' music venue in the heart of Soho; nothing to do with the
food, though, which can be "so disappointing".*
/ www.floriditalondon.com; 2 am, Fri & Sat 3 am; D only, closed Mon & Sun.

Foliage
Mandarin Oriental SW1 £87 ❸❷❸
66 Knightsbridge 7201 3723 5–1D
*With its "majestic views" (from the window tables) and "comfortable"
interior, this park-side dining room put in a very decent showing
under Chris Staines – his mid-2009 resignation, in anticipation
of Heston Blumenthal's arrival at the hotel in 2010, doesn't augur
particularly well for the restaurant's final months.*
*/ www.mandarinoriental.com; 10.15 pm; booking: max 6; set weekday L
£52 (FP).*

Food for Thought WC2 £17 ❷④④
31 Neal St 7836 0239 4–2C
*The setting may be "rustic" and the chairs may be "wobbly", but this
Covent Garden basement veggie is usually "insanely crowded" – well,
there aren't many places where "you can buy an interesting and
substantial lunch for well under a tenner"; BYO. / 8 pm, Sun 5 pm;
no credit cards; no booking.*

Footstool
St Johns SW1 £41 ④④❸
St John's, Smith Sq 7222 2779 2–4C
*Even under new management, this characterful crypt (beneath
a Westminster church that's nowadays a concert hall) can still offer
up the occasional dish that's "as tough as old boots"; for fans, though,
the place remains "ideal before a performance". / www.sjss.org.uk;
L only (ex concert evenings), closed Sat & Sun; no Amex.*

The Forge WC2 £47 ④❸❸
14 Garrick St 7379 1531 4–3C
*A "comfy" Gallic spot, handily-sited in Covent Garden which can
be "great for a pre-theatre dinner", or for "a business lunch"; as a
serious dining destination, though, its standards tend to "average".
/ www.theforgerestaurant.co.uk; midnight; set weekday L & pre-theatre
£30 (FP).*

Forman's E3 NEW £47
Stour Rd, Fish Island 8525 2365 1–1D
*If you want to see the Olympic Stadium in construction, this lofty
dining room – part of acclaimed smoked salmon producer, H Forman
& Son's new-build smokery on the River Lea – is the place to be;
it's nigh on impossible to find, but early reports – too few for a rating
– are positive; all-English wine list. / www.formans.co.uk; 11.30 pm;
Sun-Wed closed D.*

(Fountain)
Fortnum & Mason W1 £50 ④❸❸
181 Piccadilly 7734 8040 3–3D
*For a "delightful, quintessentially British breakfast", "ladies' lunch"
or afternoon tea, the buttery at the grand "old-money" St James's
grocery store offers "a quieter alternative to The Wolseley"... and
one that's "improved since the recent make-over"; see also 1707.
/ www.fortnumandmason.co.uk; 10.45 pm; closed Sun D; no booking at L.*

Four O Nine SW9 £46 ❷❸❷
409 Clapham Rd 7737 0722 10–1D
*Entered "speakeasy-style", this "serene oasis" (above a Clapham pub)
makes a "romantic" find, and one where the cooking is "above
expectations"; of late, however, standards – particularly on the
service front – have become more variable. / www.fouronine.co.uk;
10.30 pm; D only, ex Sun open L & D.*

Four Regions TW9 £36 ❸❷④
102-104 Kew Rd 8940 9044 1–4A
The food is "not gourmet, but plainly good", at this "old-favourite" neighbourhood Chinese; its "handy pre-Richmond Theatre" too. / 11.30 pm.

The Four Seasons W2 £27 ❷⑤⑤
84 Queensway 7229 4320 6–1C
"The best crispy duck in the world" has long won renown for this "crowded" Bayswater veteran; it's a bit of "slum", though, and staff are "dismissive" going-on "rude" – "you should hear what they say about the customers in Cantonese!" / 11 pm; no Amex.

The Fox EC2 £37 ❸④❸
28 Paul St 7729 5708 12–1B
A dining room above a trendy but "real" Shoreditch pub, which offers "good" traditional food and a nice pint; "now open for Sunday lunch!" / www.thefoxpublichouse.com; 10 pm; closed Sat L & Sun D; no Amex.

The Fox & Hounds SW11 £37 ❷❷❷
66 Latchmere Rd 7924 5483 10–1C
"Battersea's number one"; this "brilliant" and "unfailing" gastropub attracts many compliments for its "inventive food" and "exceptional value". / www.thefoxandhoundspub.co.uk; 10 pm; closed Mon L, Tue, Wed & Thu.

The Fox and Anchor EC1 £37 ❸❷❶
115 Charterhouse St 7250 1300 9–1B
A "beautiful refurbishment" last year widened the appeal of this "wonderful" Victorian pub, in Smithfield; it still does its famous "gut-busting breakfasts, washed down with a pint of Guinness", but its "generous" (and not especially 'gastro') British cuisine makes a visit worthwhile at any time. / www.foxandanchor.co.uk; 10 pm; closed Sun.

The Fox Reformed N16 £34 ⑤④❸
176 Stoke Newington Church St 7254 5975 1–1C
It's the "great atmosphere" and "tiny walled garden" that inspire affection for this long-established Stoke Newington wine bar; the menu – "practically as old as the venue!" – is very much an incidental attraction. / www.fox-reformed.co.uk; 10.30 pm; closed weekday L.

Foxtrot Oscar SW3 £40 ⑤⑤⑤
79 Royal Hospital Rd 7352 4448 5–3D
"Oh dear, bring back the old FO!"; Gordon Ramsay's "drab" revamp of this long-standing Chelsea bistro "fails on so many levels"... not least the "woeful" food; note restricted opening hours. / www.gordonramsay.com/foxtrotoscar/; 10 pm; closed Mon, Tue, Wed L & Thu L.

Franco Manca SW9 £14 ❶❸❸
Unit 4 Market Row 7738 3021 10–2D
"If this isn't the best in England, tell me where is, and quickly!"; "hidden-away" in the heart of Brixton Market, this "taste of Naples" serves "simply perfect pizza" – "I've never tasted anything like it!" – at "extraordinary-value" prices. / www.francomanca.com; L only, closed Sun; no Amex.

Franco's SW1 £55 ④❸④
61 Jermyn St 7499 2211 3–3C
Fans of the Hambro family's "refined" St James's Italian say its cooking "will never win awards for cutting-edge cuisine, but is surprisingly good"; critics, however, feel the place "lacks soul" and gives a performance that's "OK" but rather "limp".
/ www.francoslondon.com; 11 pm, Fri & Sat midnight; closed Sun.

Frankie's Italian Bar & Grill £39 ⑤⑤⑤
3 Yeomans Row, SW3 7590 9999 5–2C
68 Chiswick High Rd, W4 8987 9988 7–2B
263 Putney Bridge Rd, SW15 8780 3366 10–2B
"They don't know what they're trying to achieve", at MPW and Franco Dettori's supposedly glamorous pizza chain; its glitter-ball décor – "disco-meets-Moroccan brothel" – is "impressive but lacks charm", staff are "uninterested", and the food is "let down by basic errors". / www.frankiesitalianbarandgrill.com; 11 pm; SW15 9.45 pm; W4 closed Mon-Fri L.

Franklins SE22 £38 ❸④❸
157 Lordship Ln 8299 9598 1–4D
A "consistently good" Dulwich local, whose "flavoursome" fare pleases almost all who comment on it; it is now bereft of its Kennington sibling. / www.franklinsrestaurant.com; 10.30 pm.

Frantoio SW10 £43 ❸❶❷
397 King's Rd 7352 4146 5–3B
"You can always be sure of a good reception", at this "brilliant local Italian" in World's End, which serves "traditional" food in a "genuine" style. / 11.15 pm.

Fratelli la Bufala NW3 £35 ④④④
45a South End Rd 7435 7814 8–2A
The somewhat "eccentric" service doesn't always hit the right note, but this "popular" Belsize Park spot serves "consistently good" pizzas (and pasta too); other fare, though, can be "ordinary". / 11 pm; closed Mon L; no Amex.

Frederick's N1 £50 ④❸❷
106 Camden Pas 7359 2888 8–3D
"Especially on a summer evening", this Islington veteran – with its "beautiful" conservatory – has a real "special-occasion" feel; its food, however, often "lacks imagination" nowadays, and service can be "slow". / www.fredericks.co.uk; 11 pm; closed Sun; no Amex; set weekday L & pre-theatre £32 (FP).

Freemasons Arms NW3 £38 ④④❸
32 Downshire Hill 7433 6811 8–2A
"A wonderful setting near Hampstead Heath", "the biggest beer garden around" and a "very agreeable conservatory" help make this "very buzzy" gastropub quite a success; the food, though, is "formulaic". / www.freemasonsarms.com; 10 pm.

French House W1 £48 ❸❸❷
49 Dean St 7437 2477 4–3A
The "Bohemian" charm of this "tiny" and "cramped" room over a famous Soho pub can make it feel like a "great discovery"; it dishes up a "limited" menu of "bistro basics", "with honesty, if not flair". / www.frenchhousesoho.com; 11 pm; closed Sun; booking: max 8.

Fresco W2 £16 ❷⓿❸
25 Westbourne Grove   7221 2355   6–1C
"The best juices" are the star turn at this *"efficient"* Lebanese pit
stop in Bayswater, which is also acclaimed for its *"fantastic-value
mezze"* and falafel wraps that are a *"must"*. / www.frescojuices.co.uk;
11 pm.

Friends SW10 £42 ❹❸❸
6 Hollywood Rd   7376 3890   5–3B
This Chelsea pizzeria inspired mixed views this year; most reporters
still rate it highly, but one or two former fans say it's *"gone downhill
significantly"* of late. / 11 pm; closed weekday L; no Amex.

La Fromagerie Café W1 £28 ❷❸❷
2-6 Moxon St   7935 0341   3–1A
"Beautiful" cheese isn't the sole attraction of eating in at Patricia
Michaelson's fabled Marylebone store – it also does *"excellent"*
salads and *"great breakfasts and brunches"*; recent expansion of the
dining area seems to have improved standards generally.
/ www.lafromagerie.co.uk; 7.30 pm, Sat 7 pm, Sun 6 pm; L only; no booking.

The Frontline Club W2 £42 ❹❸❷
13 Norfolk Pl   7479 8960   6–1D
"Photo-journalism on the walls" provides a *"catalyst to conversation"*
at this *"buzzy and stylish"* media hang-out – one of the few half-
decent places in Paddington; pity the food's *"utterly random"*,
but Malcolm Gluck's *"quirky"* and *"incredible-value"* wine list offers
much consolation. / www.frontlineclub.com; 11 pm; closed Sat L & Sun D;
set always available £24 (FP).

Fryer's Delight WC1 £10 ❸❸⓿
19 Theobald's Rd   7405 4114   2–1D
A *"classic old-school chippy"*, in Holborn, always of note for its
"mouth-wateringly fresh fish 'n' chips". / 11 pm; closed Sun; no credit
cards; no booking.

Fujiyama SW9 £23 ❸❸❸
5-7 Vining St   7737 2369   10–2D
"For honest, fast, fun Japanese", try this *"bustling"* Brixton café,
where *"efficient"* staff serve a *"good and reasonably-priced"* menu
of ramen, curries, sushi and so on. / www.newfujiyama.com; 11 pm, Fri &
Sat midnight.

Fung Shing WC2 £36 ❷❸⑤
15 Lisle St   7437 1539   4–3A
This Chinatown *"stalwart"* may be *"shabby"*, but its cooking – while
"not edgy, fusion or new" – is *"more sophisticated than most"*;
highlights include *"gorgeous seafood"* and *"superb specials"*.
/ www.fungshing.co.uk; 11.15 pm.

Furnace N1 £31 ❸❸❸
1 Rufus St   7613 0598   12–1B
"Very authentic, thin crust, Italian-style pizzas", at *"good-value"*
prices, help ensure this *"friendly"* outfit, just off Hoxton Square,
is *"always busy"*. / www.hoxtonfurnace.com; 11 pm; closed Sat L & Sun;
no Amex.

Fuzzy's Grub £13 ❷❷④
6 Crown Pas, SW1 7925 2791 3–4D
96 Tooley St, SE1 7089 7590 9–4D
15 Basinghall St, Unit 1 Mason's Ave, EC2 7726 6771 9–2C
56-57 Cornhill, EC3 7621 0444 9–2C
58 Houndsditch, EC3 7929 1400 9–2D
10 Well Ct, EC4 7236 8400 9–2B
22 Carter Ln, EC4 7248 9795 9–2B
62 Fleet St, EC4 7583 6060 9–2A
"A complete roast dinner in a sandwich!" – that's the proposition that
makes this (largely) take-away small chain "heaven" for traditionalists;
brace yourself for "interminable queues at peak times".
/ www.fuzzysgrub.com; 3.30 pm-5 pm; no Amex; no booking.

Gaby's WC2 £26 ❸❸④
30 Charing Cross Rd 7836 4233 4–3B
There's "nothing better" than a falafel or a salt-beef sandwich from
this "bustling", if "slightly grotty", deli/take-way, by Leicester Square
tube – an "unchanging" and "very cheap and cheerful" option, in the
heart of Theatreland. / midnight, Sun 10 pm; no credit cards.

Gail's Bread £25 ❷❸❸
138 Portobello Rd, W11 7460 0766 6–1B
64 Hampstead High St, NW3 7794 5700 8–1A
5 Circus Rd, NW8 7722 0983 8–3A **NEW**
"Out-of-the-ordinary" sandwiches, soups, salads and cakes win
acclaim for these "bustling and cheerful" contemporary-style
café/bakeries; "not cheap, but they don't stint on portions".
/ www.gailsbread.co.uk; W11 8 pm; NW3 9 pm; no booking.

Galicia W10 £30 ④④❷
323 Portobello Rd 8969 3539 6–1A
"A genuinely Spanish feel" enlivens this "buzzing" North Kensington
veteran; views on the tapas vary, but prices are low, and a visit here
is "never dull". / 11.30 pm; closed Mon; set Sun L £20 (FP).

Gallery Mess
Saatchi Gallery SW3 **NEW** £35 ④④❸
Duke Of Yorks HQ, Kings Rd 7730 8135 5–2D
Fans of this large, bright Chelsea café (which has an impressive
terrace overlooking a former parade ground) say it's a "promising"
newcomer with "simple, clean-tasting" dishes; early-days reports,
however, are up-and-down. / www.saatchi-gallery.co.uk; 9 pm.

Gallipoli £25 ❸❸❷
102 Upper St, N1 7359 0630 8–3D
107 Upper St, N1 7226 5333 8–3D
120 Upper St, N1 7359 1578 8–3D
"Don't go if you want a quiet night!"; these "boisterous" Turkish
bistros, in the heart of Islington, are always "crowded", thanks to their
"jolly" style and their "cracking-value" mezze; "it doesn't matter
which one you go to". / www.cafegallipoli.com; 11 pm, Fri & Sat midnight;
107 Upper St closed Mon.

Galvin at Windows
Park Lane London Hilton Hotel W1   £75   ❸❸❷
22 Park Ln, 28th Floor   7208 4021   3–4A
"Not just trading on its fantastic views", this 28th-floor Mayfair eyrie
also – to the surprise of some reporters – offers "rather good" food;
needless to say, though, you don't get anything like the same value
you would in the Galvin brothers' Marylebone HQ.
/ www.galvinatwindows.com; 11 pm; closed Sat L & Sun D; no trainers;
set weekday L £42 (FP).

GALVIN BISTROT DE LUXE W1   £45   ❶❶❷
66 Baker St   7935 4007   2–1A
"It would do Paris proud!"; the Galvin brothers' "smart" and
"very professional" Marylebone bistro has achieved an astonishing
following, and "never disappoints" with its "perfect" bourgeois cuisine;
"superb" wines too, many 'en carafe'. / www.galvinrestaurants.com;
10.30 pm, Sun 9. 30 pm; set dinner £29 (FP).

Galvin La Chapelle E1 NEW
35 Spital Sq   12–2B
The Galvin brothers have yet to put a foot seriously wrong, so there
are high hopes for this ambitious conversion of a Spitalfields chapel,
set to open in late-2009; it will include a range of dining options,
and a bar.

Ganapati SE15   £29   ❷❷❷
38 Holly Grove   7277 2928   1–4C
"Far from the usual Identikit Indian", this "communal" but "lovely"
Peckham diner is "worth a trek", thanks to its "genuine", "ever-
changing" and "spice-scented" south Indian cuisine.
/ www.ganapatirestaurant.com; 10.45 pm; closed Mon; no Amex.

Garbo's W1   £41   ❹❸❹
42 Crawford St   7262 6582   2–1A
A cramped but "friendly" Swedish "old favourite", in Marylebone,
liked for its "homely" style and "hearty" food (including a huge
lunchtime buffet); "it's variable, but the good days compensate for the
bad…" / 10.30 pm; closed Sat L & Sun D; set weekday L £25 (FP), set Sun L
£28 (FP).

Garrison SE1   £43   ❸❸❶
99-101 Bermondsey St   7089 9355   9–4D
This "happening" gastropub, near Bermondsey Antiques Market,
remains extremely popular, thanks to the "cosy" and "laid-back" style
of its "eclectically decorated" (and slightly "crushed") interior; "lovely"
food – including "great" brunch fare – completes the formula.
/ www.thegarrison.co.uk; 10 pm, Sun 9.30 pm.

Garufa N5 NEW   £36   ❸❹❸
104 Highbury Pk   7226 0070   8–1D
"Great Argentinean steaks and brunches" have helped makes this
"cosy and buzzing" Highbury newcomer a big local hit; reports are
not entirely consistent, though, and "OTT charges for side dishes" are
a source of some complaint. / www.garufa.co.uk; 10.30 pm.

Gastro SW4   £38   ❹❺❷
67 Venn St   7627 0222   10–2D
The "authentically French" nature of this "shabby-chic" Clapham
bistro features in practically all reports; the staff are "less surly in the
mornings"… perhaps explaining the particular popularity as a
breakfast destination. / midnight; no Amex; set weekday L £25 (FP).

FSA

The Gate W6 £39 ❷❷④
51 Queen Caroline St 8748 6932 7–2C
"They do amazing things with vegetables", at this "church hall"-style Hammersmith stalwart, long regarded as one of London's top meat-free destinations… although reports of some "heavy" meals of late signal a slight drift in overall satisfaction; pleasant summer terrace. / www.thegate.tv; 10.45 pm; closed Sat L & Sun.

Gaucho £50 ❸❸❸
25 Swallow St, W1 7734 4040 3–3D
125 Chancery Ln, WC2 7242 7727 2–1D
89 Sloane Ave, SW3 7584 9901 5–2C
64 Heath St, NW3 7431 8222 8–1A
02 Centre, Peninsular Sq, SE10 8858 7711 11–2D
2 Moore London, Riverside, SE1 7407 5222 9–4D
Tow Path, TW10 8948 4030 1–4A
29 Westferry Circus, E14 7987 9494 11–1B
93A, Charterhouse St, EC1 7490 1676 9–1B
5 Finsbury Ave, Broadgate, EC2 7256 6877 12–2B
1 Bell Inn Yd, EC3 7626 5180 9–2C
A "carnivore-heaven" menu and "stonking" wine list make these stylish Argentineans easily – among the chains – "the best steakhouses in town", and "perfect for business"; ratings slipped this year, though, amid gripes that prices are getting "a bit steep". / www.gauchorestaurants.co.uk; 11 pm, Fri & Sat 11.30 pm; EC3 & EC2 closed Sat & Sun; WC2 closed Sun.

El Gaucho £40 ❸❸❸
Chelsea Farmers' Mkt, Sydney St, SW3 7376 8514 5–3C
30 Old Brompton Rd, SW7 7584 8999 5–2B
"For a consistently good steak, and smiley service", fans still tip these basic grills in South Kensington and in a shack in Chelsea's Farmer's Market; they attracted few and somewhat mixed reports this year, though. / www.elgaucho.co.uk; SW3 9 pm; SW7 11.30 pm.

LE GAVROCHE W1 £112 ❷④❷
43 Upper Brook St 7408 0881 3–2A
Michel Roux's "clubby" Mayfair "old-stager" offers a "marvellous" and "indulgent" mix of "heavenly" ("so rich"!) "classic" cuisine, "exemplary" service and "mind-blowing" wine; even fans can find the formula "dated", though, and prices – apart from the "godsend" of a set lunch – are "flabbergasting". / www.le-gavroche.co.uk; 10.45 pm; closed Sat L & Sun; jacket required; set weekday L £75 (FP).

Gay Hussar W1 £39 ④❸❷
2 Greek St 7437 0973 4–2A
Even fans of this "red-velvet" Soho "classic" say it relies rather too much on its "Hungarian charm" nowadays – the clientele of Socialist intelligentsia for which it was once famous has largely been replaced "by tourists, who don't mind the dreadful food". / www.gayhussar.co.uk; 10.45 pm; closed Sun.

The Gaylord E14 £25 ❸④④
141 Manchester Rd 7538 0393 11–2D
A "reliable" Isle of Dogs Indian, which retains an ardent local fan club – "I sometimes try to go elsewhere, but the curries always bring me back". / www.gaylordrestaurant.co.uk; midnight.

Gaylord W1 £36 ❸④–
79-81 Mortimer St 7580 3615 2–1B
A "good standard" of cooking wins consistent praise for this Fitzrovia
outpost of an international Indian chain; after our survey had closed,
its décor received a much-needed revamp, so no ambience rating
is appropriate. / www.gaylordlondon.com; 11.30 pm, Sun 11 pm.

Gazette £35 ④❸❸
79 Riverside Plaza, Chatfield Rd, SW11 7223 0999 10–1C
1 Ramsden Rd, SW12 8772 1232 10–2C
"What a French brasserie should be", say fans of this "classic" Gallic
duo, of which the hidden-away branch near Wandsworth Bridge
is much the better-known; sceptics, however, say the food is "nothing
to write home about". / www.gazettebrasserie.co.uk; 11 pm.

Geale's W8 £37 ❸❸④
2 Farmer St 7727 7528 6–2B
"Set back from the hustle of Notting Hill Gate", this "old haunt" –
resurrected a few years ago – offers "great fish 'n' chips in a slightly
upmarket environment"; it is, however, "more expensive and less
atmospheric" than of yore; (an offshoot is rumoured to be opening
on the former Tom's Place site, in Chelsea, some time in late-2009).
/ www.geales.com; 10.30 pm; closed Mon L.

Geeta NW6 £18 ❷❷⑤
57-59 Willesden Ln 7624 1713 1–1B
The staff, including the eponymous Geeta, are "always friendly",
at this decrepit-looking Kilburn veteran; most reports applaud
"outstanding" home-cooked south Indian dishes at "extraordinarily
low prices"; BYO. / 11 pm; no Amex.

Gem N1 £24 ❸❷❸
265 Upper St 7359 0405 8–2D
"Good value is rare on Upper Street", but this "welcoming" and
"homely" Islington restaurant "lives up to its name", providing "filling"
and "delicious" Kurdish mezze and grills at "very reasonable prices".
/ www.gemrestaurant.org.uk; 10 pm, Fri & Sat midnight, Sun 10.30 pm.

George & Vulture EC3 £39 ⑤④❷
3 Castle Ct 7626 9710 9–3C
An "authentically Dickensian" City chophouse, with a "brilliant old-
fashioned interior"; shame the food is sometimes likened to "slop",
and "hugely overpriced" too. / L only, closed Sat & Sun.

Getti £48 ④④④
16-17 Jermyn St, SW1 7734 7334 3–3D
42 Marylebone High St, W1 7486 3753 2–1A
Even a reporter praising "surprisingly good" cooking at this West End
Italian chain concedes there's "nothing to make it stand out from the
crowd", but its prominently-located branches can be "handy pre-
theatre". / www.getti.com; 10.45 pm; SW1 closed Sun.

The Giaconda Dining Room WC2 £35 ❷❶④
9 Denmark St 7240 3334 4–1A
In a "dingy" road in the shadow of Centre Point, Aussie chef Paul
Merrony's "jammed" café "feels like a real find" (... unless you've read
all the newspaper reviews, that is); its "lovely" staff serve up "proper"
bistro dishes at "incredibly good-value" prices. / www.giacondadining.com;
9.45 pm; closed Sat & Sun.

Il Giardino SW3 £44 ❸④❷
119 Sydney St 7352 2718 5–3C
A Chelsea townhouse Italian yearling that's made few ripples; with its "beautiful" garden and "intimate" interior, it echoes its predecessor Dan's (long RIP)... as do the rather "inconsistent" standards.
/ www.ilgiardinorestaurant.co.uk; 11 pm; no jeans or trainers.

Gilgamesh NW1 £50 ④⑤❷
The Stables, Camden Mkt, Chalk Farm Rd 7428 4922 8–2B
"Lavish" and "amazing" carved-wood décor on a huge scale helps create an "incredible" setting, at this "cavernous" Camden Town "behemoth"; nothing else matches up to it, though – the "soulless" oriental food comes at "bloated" prices, and service can be "abysmal". / www.gilgameshbar.com; midnight; no trainers.

Gilmour's SW10 NEW £40 ④❸❷
9 Park Walk 7349 6800 5–3B
"Civilised comfort eating for the credit crunch era" – the proposition at this "posh" but "jovial" Chelsea newcomer; in the Christopher Gilmour tradition, though, the cooking is sometimes "a little disappointing". / www.gilmoursparkwalk.co.uk; 10.30 pm; set always available £30 (FP).

Giraffe £34 ④❸❸
6-8 Blandford St, W1 7935 2333 2–1A
19-21 The Brunswick Centre, WC1 7812 1336 8–4C
270 Chiswick High Rd, W4 8995 2100 7–2A
7 Kensington High St, W8 7938 1221 5–1A
29-31 Essex Rd, N1 7359 5999 8–3D
46 Rosslyn Hill, NW3 7435 0343 8–2A
Royal Festival Hall, Riverside, SE1 7928 2004 2–3D
27 Battersea Rise, SW11 7223 0933 10–2C
1 Crispin Pl, E1 3116 2000 12–2B
"So kid-friendly it's scary!"; this "buzzing" chain majors in "lovely, laid-back brunches" – its "adventurous" world-food menu is otherwise very "hit-and-miss". / www.giraffe.net; 10.45 pm, Sun 10.30pm; no booking, Sat & Sun 9am-5pm.

Glaisters SW10 £37 ④④❸
4 Hollywood Rd 7352 0352 5–3B
A "relaxed", if slightly "lacklustre", Chelsea bistro stalwart, where the food is somewhere between "perfectly good" and "in need of an overhaul"; "on a sunny day, the back garden makes a visit worthwhile". / www.glaisters.co.uk; 11.30 pm; closed Sun D.

The Glasshouse TW9 £57 ❶❶❸
14 Station Pde 8940 6777 1–3A
"Not quite as good as Chez Bruce... but nearly!" – the Kew sibling of London's Favourite Restaurant similarly offers "beautiful" cooking, "perfectly pitched" service, "spectacular" cheese and "interesting" wine in an "understated" (and "rather cramped") setting.
/ www.glasshouserestaurant.co.uk; 10.30 pm.

Golden Dragon W1 £28 ❸④❸
28-29 Gerrard St 7734 2763 4–3A
"A safe bet for Chinatown"; this "big, bright and bustling" main drag fixture offers "efficient" (sometimes "too quick") service and a well-executed "classic" menu – notably "very good dim sum". / 11 pm, Fri & Sat 11.30 pm, Sun 10.20 pm.

Golden Hind W1 £20 ❶❶❸
73 Marylebone Ln 7486 3644 2–1A
"Head and shoulders, the best chippy in central London" –
this "tiny and bustling" Marylebone café boasts not just "perfect fish
'n' chips" but also "delightful" service; BYO. / 10 pm; closed Sat L & Sun.

Goldfish NW3 £39 ❷❷❸
82 Hampstead High St 7794 6666 8–2A
"Interesting and delicious new-wave Chinese food" again wins more-
than-local acclaim for this "cramped but charming" two-year-old,
"bang in the middle of Hampstead". / www.goldfish-restaurant.co.uk;
10.30 pm, Sat & Sun 11 pm; no Amex.

Good Earth £52 ❸❸④
233 Brompton Rd, SW3 7584 3658 5–2C
143-145 The Broadway, NW7 8959 7011 1–1B
The food is "consistently good", but prices are increasingly "hard to
justify", at these "upscale" Chinese restaurants, whose branch near
Harrods has been in business for over 25 years.
/ www.goodearthgroup.co.uk; 11 pm, Sun 10.45 pm.

Goodman W1 NEW £53 ❷❷④
26 Maddox St 7499 3776 3–2C
Bizarrely, it's Russian money which is behind "the closest thing to a
NY steakhouse London has to offer" – a "relentlessly masculine"
(but very welcoming) Mayfair newcomer serving "a wide selection"
of "superb" USDA (and other) cuts. / www.goodmanrestaurants.com;
11 pm; closed Sun; set weekday L £29 (FP).

Gopal's of Soho W1 £28 ❸❷④
12 Bateman St 7434 1621 4–2A
"The West End lacks decent 'standard' curry houses" – this "packed"
Soho stalwart is "probably the best". / www.gopalsofsoho.co.uk; 11.30 pm.

GORDON RAMSAY SW3 £115 ❸❸❸
68-69 Royal Hospital Rd 7352 4441 5–3D
"Professional, but lacking soul"; esteem for GR's Chelsea
HQ "went down faster than the stock market" this year; prices seem
ever more "stratospheric", but there's a growing feeling that this
is just "not a 3-Michelin-star experience" – the expected
"excitement" too often is absent… just like the man himself!
/ www.gordonramsay.com; 11 pm; closed Sat & Sun; no jeans or trainers;
booking: max 8; set weekday L £65 (FP).

Gordon Ramsay at Claridge's
Claridge's Hotel W1 £93 ④❸❸
55 Brook St 7499 0099 3–2B
"Claridges deserves better", say critics of this potentially "lovely" Art
Deco Mayfair dining room; true, its (dwindling) fan club still says it's
"first-class", but too often the food's found to be "not worth all
(or any) of the hype", and to come at "outrageous" prices too.
/ www.gordonramsay.com; 11 pm; no jeans or trainers; booking: max 8;
set weekday L £48 (FP).

Gordon's Wine Bar WC2 £24 ⑤❸❶
47 Villiers St 7930 1408 4–4D
"Dark", "dusty" and "Dickensian", this cellar wine bar,
by Embankment tube, is just "unbeatable" for ambience, and the
wine (and cheese) is pretty good too – otherwise, fare is "basic";
large, leafy terrace (recently enlarged), with barbecue.
/ www.gordonswinebar.com; 11 pm, Sun 10 pm; no booking.

The Goring Hotel SW1 £68 ❸⓿⓿
15 Beeston Pl 7396 9000 2–4B
"The perfect place to take a great aunt", this "wonderfully old-fashioned" and very English family-run hotel is "a haven of calm", near Victoria; with its "splendid, airy dining room" and "discreet" service, it's also great for business (and, inevitably, does an "unbeatable breakfast"). / www.goringhotel.com; 10 pm; closed Sat L; set weekday L £48 (FP).

Gourmet Burger Kitchen £22 ❸④④
15 Frith St, W1 7494 9533 4–2A
13-14 Maiden Ln, WC2 7240 9617 4–4D
163-165 Earl's Court Rd, SW5 7373 3184 5–2A
49 Fulham Broadway, SW6 7381 4242 5–4A
107 Old Brompton Rd, SW7 7581 8942 5–2B
160 Portobello Rd, W11 7243 6597 6–1B
50 Westbourne Grove, W2 7243 4344 6–1B
131 Chiswick High Rd, W4 8995 4548 7–2A
200 Haverstock Hill, NW3 7443 5335 8–2A
44 Northcote Rd, SW11 7228 3309 10–2C
333 Putney Bridge Rd, SW15 8789 1199 10–2B
84 Clapham High St, SW4 7627 5367 10–2D
Condor Hs, St Paul's Churchyard, EC4 7248 9199 9–2B
"Britain's best burger chain" offers "the most amazing range of incredible-quality options", as well as "crispy" fries and "decadent" shakes; "you only go for the food", though – service can be "slow", and the "cramped", "cafeteria-style" interiors "don't encourage you to linger". / www.gbkinfo.com; 10.45 pm; EC4 10 pm; SW19 11 pm, Sun 10 pm; no booking.

Gourmet Pizza Company £29 ④④❷
Gabriels Wharf, 56 Upper Ground, SE1 7928 3188 9–3A
18 Mackenzie Walk, E14 7345 9192 11–1C
A small chain, whose funky pizzas offer a "good alternative to PizzaExpress"; the SE1 branch has nice outside tables and a "great river view". / www.gourmetpizzacompany.co.uk; E14 10.30pm; SE1 10.45pm; E14 closed Sat & Sun; booking: E14 min 6, SE1 min 7.

Gourmet San E2 £15 ⓿④⑤
261 Bethnal Green Rd 7613 1366 12–1D
"Don't be fooled by appearances" – the décor may be "terrible", but the quality of the "authentic" cuisine at this "brusque" East End Sichuanese "dive" is "amazing"; "expect to queue".
/ www.oldplace.co.uk; 11 pm; D only.

Gow's EC2 £45 ❸❸④
81 Old Broad St 7920 9645 9–2C
A "reliable" basement operation that's "well-suited for business in the current financial climate" – its "semi-plush" décor may be "bog-standard", and its fish dishes sometimes "mediocre", but the package comes at reasonable prices, by City standards. / www.ballsbrothers.co.uk; 9.30 pm; closed Sat & Sun; booking: max 10.

The Gowlett SE15 £28 ❷❷❷
62 Gowlett Rd 7635 7048 1–4C
"Unexpectedly good", "paper-thin" pizza is the particular draw to this "great little pub", in Peckham; "great ales" too.
/ www.thegowlett.com; 10.30 pm, Sun 9 pm.

Goya SW1 £34 ④❸④
34 Lupus St 7976 5309 2–4C
A "reliable" and "fairly-priced" tapas bar that's "nothing exceptional",
but makes a "useful discovery" in a part of Pimlico with relatively few
other options. / www.goyarestaurant.co.uk; 11.30 pm.

Gran Paradiso SW1 £40 ④❷❸
52 Wilton Rd 7828 5818 2–4B
The "predictable" charms of this "time warp" trattoria have
recommended it to Pimlico politicos (and others) since time
immemorial; "always-friendly" staff are key to the formula. / 10.45 pm;
closed Sat L & Sun.

The Grapes E14 £39 ❸❸❷
76 Narrow St 7987 4396 11–1B
"Fantastic river views" boost the appeal of this "quaint, historical
pub", in Docklands; however, it also serves "excellent seafood" in its
"wonderful, atmospheric upstairs dining room" (plus a "good Sunday
roast" in the bar). / 9.30 pm; closed Sat L & Sun D.

Great Eastern Dining Room EC2 £40 ❸❸❷
54-56 Great Eastern St 7613 4545 12–1B
Will Ricker's Shoreditch "old-timer" (by the standards of the area)
remains a "buzzy" hang-out, serving "well-presented" pan-Asian
dishes and "brilliant" cocktails; it drew more flak this year, though,
for its "limited" menu, and for "overpricing".
/ www.rickerrestaurants.com; 10.30 pm; closed Sat L & Sun.

Great Nepalese NW1 £25 ❸❸⑤
48 Eversholt St 7388 6737 8–3C
The décor may be "awful", but this "friendly" stalwart, by Euston
station, is still "worth a visit"… not for the standard Indian dishes
(which tend to "average"), but for the "fantastic" Nepalese specials.
/ www.great-nepalese.co.uk; 11.30 pm; closed Sun.

Great Queen Street WC2 £38 ❷❸❸
32 Great Queen St 7242 0622 4–1D
"Real genius in combining simple ingredients" – to create "robust"
and "seasonal" British menus – has won a vast following for this
"buzzy" Covent Garden two-year-old; however, its "mock-frugal" style
– "serving wine in tumblers", for example – irritates quite a few
reporters. / 10.15 pm; closed Mon L & Sun D; no Amex.

Green & Blue SE22 £25 ④❸❸
38 Lordship Ln 8693 9250 1–4D
"Mind-blowingly esoteric, value-for-money wines" inspire rave reports
on this East Dulwich shop; its café does "great deli-food"
to accompany them, or you have the option of paying 'chippage' –
for a per-capita charge, you can bring your own food!
/ www.greenandbluewines.com; 11 pm, Fri & Sat midnight, Sun 10.30 pm;
no Amex.

Green & Red Bar & Cantina E1 £39 ❸④❷
51 Bethnal Green Rd 7749 9670 12–1C
"Always a fun night out", say fans of this "trendy" Mexican hang-out,
near Brick Lane, which boasts a massive array of tequilas;
the "simple, fresh food" can be "excellent" too, but can also seem
"a little beside the point". / www.greenred.co.uk; 11 pm, Sun 10 pm; closed
Sat & Sun L.

Green Chilli W6 £30 ❸❷④
220 King St 8748 0111 7–2B
It's "not much to look at", but this Hammersmith Indian offers
an "excellent wide-ranging menu" of "high-quality curries" –
"particularly good vegetarian choices, but plenty for meat-eaters too".
/ www.greenchillilrestaurant.co.uk; 11.30 pm.

The Green Olive W9 £44 ❸❷❸
5 Warwick Pl 7289 2469 8–4A
It attracts relatively little feedback nowadays, but this "casual" Maida
Vale spot is still praised by its loyal fans as a "fantastic neighbourhood
Italian". / 10 pm; D only, ex Fri & Sat open L & D, closed Sun; booking:
max 20.

Green's £62 ❸❷❸
36 Duke St, SW1 7930 4566 3–3D
14 Cornhill, EC3 9–2C **NEW**
"If you want the whole Bertie Wooster experience", try Simon Parker
Bowles's "clubby" St James's "classic", which is a haven for "pin-
striped elderly gentlemen"; "excellent fish" is the highlight of the
"traditional" and "pricey" British fare; a City offshoot opens around
the publication date of this guide. / www.greens.org.uk; SW1 11 pm;
SW1 closed Sun (May-Sep).

The Greenhouse W1 £90 ❸❷❷
27a Hays Mews 7499 3331 3–3B
Now rivalling many better-known names, Marlon Abela's "discreet"
Mayfair veteran is a "professional" operation, where Antonin Bonnet's
"intricate and beautifully-executed" cooking is teamed up with
"attentive" service and a "lovely" setting; the stand-out feature,
however, is a wine list "like War & Peace".
/ www.greenhouserestaurant.co.uk; 10.30 pm; closed Sat L & Sun; booking:
max 10.

Greig's W1 £50 ❸❸④
26 Bruton Pl 7629 5613 3–2B
Just off Bond Street, an upmarket steakhouse of long standing, which
perennially divides opinions between those who say it's an "efficient"
place with "great" grills, and those who just find it "disappointing".
/ www.greigs.com; 11.30 pm; set weekday L £27 (FP).

Grenadier SW1 £42 ❸❸❶
18 Wilton Row 7235 3074 5–1D
A wonderful "olde worlde" pub, hidden-away in one of London's
most picturesque mews, in Belgravia; its small dining room received
few reports this year, but all of them complimentary; in the bar,
the classic snack is a sausage and a Bloody Mary. / 9.30 pm,
Sun 7.30 pm.

Ground W4 £26 ❷❸④
219-221 Chiswick High Rd 8747 9113 7–2A
"Amazing burgers, with toppings both classic and unusual" still win
a big fan club for this simple Chiswick outfit; its stellar ratings
declined this year, however – ambience can be "lacklustre", and the
food now "only narrowly beats the nearby GBK".
/ www.groundrestaurants.com; 10.30 pm.

Grumbles SW1 £35 ④❷❸
35 Churton St 7834 0149 2–4B
This "great Pimlico stalwart" may look "dated", but it can still be a
"useful find" – "staff are welcoming", and the food is "enjoyable" and
"very reasonably priced". / www.grumblesrestaurant.co.uk; 10.45 pm;
set dinner £23 (FP).

The Guinea Grill W1 £56 ❷❸❸
30 Bruton Pl 7499 1210 3–3B
This "old-school" grill room, behind a Mayfair pub, may be
"cramped" and "expensive", but it's "good at what it does" –
"traditional British food", of the nature of "quality steaks" and
"legendary pies". / www.theguinea.co.uk; 10.30 pm; closed Sat L & Sun;
booking: max 10.

The Gun E14 £43 ❸❸❷
27 Coldharbour 7515 5222 11–1C
"A breath of fresh air, compared to the 'corporate' ventures
of Canary Wharf", this "charming" and renowned Thames-side pub
(with "great views of the O2") is especially good in summer
(when attractions include a "Portuguese BBQ"); service can be "slow".
/ www.thegundocklands.com; 10.30 pm, Sun 9.30 pm.

Gung-Ho NW6 £34 ❸❷❷
328-332 West End Ln 7794 1444 1–1B
"A favourite for years", this "exemplary local Chinese",
in West Hampstead, offers an appealing combination of "smart"
décor, "genuinely warm" service and "above-average" cooking.
/ www.stir-fry.co.uk; 11.30 pm; no Amex.

Haandi SW3 £35 ❷❸④
7 Cheval Pl 7823 7373 5–1C
Hidden-away in a mews, just five minutes' walk from Harrods,
this surprisingly "authentic" Indian is well worth knowing about for its
"consistent" and "well-spiced" cuisine. / www.haandi-restaurants.com;
11 pm, Fri-Sat 11.30 pm.

Haché £28 ❷❸❷
329-331 Fulham Rd, SW10 7823 3515 5–3B
24 Inverness St, NW1 7485 9100 8–3B
"A cut-above GBK and Byron" – this "classy" (if "crowded") bistro-
style mini-chain scores highly with reporters for its "wonderfully
inventive" burgers (which are "properly cooked to order").
/ www.hacheburgers.com; 10.30 pm, Sun 10 pm.

HAKKASAN W1 £74 ❷❸❶
8 Hanway Pl 7927 7000 4–1A
"Hands down 'the daddy' of London's Chinese restaurants!" –
this "so glam" West End basement's "sleek" looks and the
"mouthwatering" quality of its cuisine have held up surprisingly well
since founder Alan Yau sold out; prices remain "extortionate", though
– for a 'value-visit', try weekend dim sum. / www.hakkasan.com;
11.30 pm, Thu-Sat 12.30 am.

Halepi W2 £40 ④❷❸
18 Leinster Ter 7262 1070 6–2C
An age-old Bayswater taverna, serving "consistently hearty" fare –
it offers "all the buzz of a Greek holiday without the sun and sea!"
/ www.halepi.co.uk; midnight.

Hamburger Union £20 ④④④
25 Dean St, W1 7437 6004 4–2A
64 Tottenham Court Rd, W1 7636 0011 2–1C
4-6 Garrick St, WC2 7379 0412 4–3C
Irving St (off Leicester Sq), WC2 7839 8100 4–4B
341 Upper St, N1 7359 4436 8–3D
"For a quick juicy burger", this "functional" chain fits the bill nicely;
it's "not as good as it was", though, with ratings now falling behind
arch-rival GBK. / 10.30 pm; W1 11 pm; no booking, except N1 upstairs
room Fri & Sat.

Hammersmith Café W6   £18   ④④⑤
1a Studland St   8748 2839   7–2B
*"It looks terrible, but it's great", say fans of this scruffy greasy spoon,
which moonlights as a BYO Thai with "rock-bottom" prices.*
/ 10.30 pm; closed Sun; no Amex; set weekday L £11 (FP).

Haozhan W1   £37   ❶❷④
8 Gerrard St   7434 3838   4–3A
*This "stark" oriental yearling – with standards generally a "cut above"
the Chinatown norm – is carving a strong reputation for "exciting"
and "unusually creative" Chinese cuisine; service is atypically
"friendly" too. / www.haozhan.co.uk; 11.30 pm, Fri & Sat midnight,
Sun 11 pm.*

Harbour City W1   £29   ❷❸④
46 Gerrard St   7439 7859   4–3B
*"Always humming" at lunchtime, this Chinatown stalwart has
a particular, and deserved, reputation for "great-value" dim sum.
/ 11.30 pm, Fri & Sat midnight, Sun 10.*

Hard Rock Café W1   £42   ④④❷
150 Old Park Ln   7629 0382   3–4B
*"It's old, but we love it"; the original Mayfair branch of this worldwide
chain may be "tired" and "touristy" nowadays, but can still
"pleasantly surprise" with its "bubbly" ("unsurprisingly noisy")
atmosphere and OK burgers. / www.hardrock.com; midnight; need 10+
to book.*

Hardy's Brasserie W1   £40   ④❷❸
53 Dorset St   7935 5929   2–1A
*An "always-welcoming" Marylebone fixture, liked for its solid cooking
and its "diverse" and "properly-priced" wine list.
/ www.hardysbrasserie.co.uk; 10.30 pm; closed Sat & Sun.*

Hare & Tortoise   £26   ❸④④
15-17 Brunswick Sq, WC1   7278 4945   2–1D
373 Kensington High St, W14   7603 8887   7–1D
38 Haven Grn, W5   8610 7066   1–2A
296-298 Upper Richmond Rd, SW15   8394 7666   10–2B
*"Ample helpings" of "enjoyable" dishes from a "wide selection
of oriental cuisines" lead to "good-value" experiences at these "fast"
and "clattery" canteens; "if it weren't for the permanent queues,
I'd eat here all the time". / www.hareandtortoise-restaurants.co.uk;
10.45 pm, Fri & Sat 11.15 pm; EC4 9.30 pm; W14 no bookings.*

Harlem W2   £39   ④④❸
78 Westbourne Grove   7985 0900   6–1B
*"Delicious" and "very American" breakfasts win fans for this
"very NYC-style" Bayswater spot, and it's "good for evening drinks"
too; it can seem "a little expensive", though, and service is "dodgy".
/ www.harlemsoulfood.com; midnight, Wed-Sat 2.30 am, Sun 10 pm.*

Harrison's SW12   £39   ④④④
15-19 Bedford Hill   8675 6900   10–2C
*Fans applaud the "lovely" (if "noisy") atmosphere at Sam Harrison's
relaunch of the former Balham Bar & Grill, also praising its
"fantastic" cocktails and "juicy burgers"; critics are put off, though,
by "unremarkable" food and "patchy" service.
/ www.harrisonsbalham.co.uk; 10.30 pm, Sun 10 pm.*

Harry Morgan's NW8 £33 ④④④
31 St John's Wood High St 7722 1869 8–3A
"You won't leave hungry", from this "traditional" (but recently revamped) Jewish deli in St John's Wood; fans extol its "huge bowls of chicken soup" and "the best salt beef", but others rate the staple fare as "no better than OK". / www.harryms.co.uk; 10 pm.

Harwood Arms SW6 £39 ❷❸❷
Walham Grove 7386 1847 5–3A
"Amazing game" ("cooked in exemplary style") is the highlight of the "seriously good" cooking at this backstreet Fulham local – "well and truly re-born under Brett Graham and Mike Robinson", it has quickly emerged as "one of the best gastropubs in town". / www.harwoodarms.com; 9.30 pm, Fri & Sat 10 pm, Sun 9 pm.

The Hat & Feathers EC1 £43 ④④④
2 Clerkenwell Rd 7490 2244 9–1B
A Clerkenwell gastropub that attracts relatively few reports, perhaps because praise often comes with a 'catch': "accomplished cooking, but miserly portions…", "decent, but too focussed on turnover…", or "reasonable food, but not worth a diversion". / www.hatandfeathers.com; 10 pm; closed Sat L & Sun; no Amex.

The Havelock Tavern W14 £37 ❷⑤❸
57 Masbro Rd 7603 5374 7–1C
"It's always hard getting a table", at this "buzzing" backstreet Olympia local, long known as one of west London's best gastropubs; though still "good", however, its "straightforward" food is "not what it was" a few years ago, but some things are constant – the "haughty" service is "as bad as ever". / www.thehavelocktavern.co.uk; 10 pm, Sun 9.30 pm; no Amex; no booking.

The Haven N20 £42 ❸❸❸
1363 High Rd 8445 7419 1–1B
"Book well in advance", for this "jolly" and "good-value" Whetstone local, whose "consistently reliable" food has long made it the brightest spark for miles around; it draws the odd accusation, however, of "a rush to turn tables". / www.haven-bistro.co.uk; 11 pm; no Amex; set weekday L £26 (FP).

Hawksmoor E1 £52 ❸④④
157 Commercial St 7247 7392 12–2C
Even critics of this "trendy Spitalfields steakhouse" acknowledge its "mind-blowingly delicious" steaks and "superb" cocktails; given the "ordinary" décor and average service, however, the package can seem "insanely overpriced". / www.thehawksmoor.com; 10.30 pm; closed Sat L & Sun.

Haz £32 ❸❸❸
9 Cutler St, E1 7929 7923 9–2D
6 Mincing Ln, EC3 7929 3173 9–3D
These big and "buzzing" Turkish operations, in the City, continue to deliver "tasty" fare at "reasonable" prices; on the downside, they tend to be rather "noisy", and service can be "flaky". / www.hazrestaurant.co.uk; 11.30 pm.

Hazuki WC2 £33 ❸❷④
43 Chandos Pl 7240 2530 4–4C
"A welcome option near Trafalgar Square" – this "cramped" Japanese place has "fast and helpful" service, and offers "good value for money". / www.hazukilondon.co.uk; 10.30 pm, Sun 9.30 pm; closed Sat L & Sun L.

Hélène Darroze
The Connaught Hotel W1   £102   ⑤④❸
Carlos Pl   7499 7070   3–3B

"Oh dear!"; with its "over-elaborate", "unbalanced" and "massively overpriced" cuisine, this outpost of the famous Parisienne chef has had a "dreadful" first year in its "plush" Mayfair home; service is "pretentious" and "haphazard" too – no wonder Michelin rushed to give the place a star! / www.the-connaught.co.uk; 10.30 pm; closed Mon, Sat & Sun; jacket & tie; set weekday L £48 (FP).

Hellenik W1   £36   ❷⓪❸
30 Thayer St   7935 1257   2–1A

"Unchanging, reliable, extremely friendly" – this *"civilised"* Greek taverna maintains the virtues that first made it popular long before Marylebone became the trendy place it is today; *"I always go back every 20 years, with no complaints!"* / 10.45 pm; closed Sun; no Amex.

Henry J Beans SW3   £36   ④④❸
195-197 King's Rd   7352 9255   5–3C

In the heart of Chelsea, a large and formulaic American diner, which we list because it boasts one of the largest gardens in town. / www.henryjbeans.com; 10 pm.

Hereford Road W2   £40   ❷❸❸
3 Hereford Rd   7727 1144   6–1B

Tom Pemberton's *"thoughtful"* and *"deliciously simple"* British food is winning ever greater acclaim for this Bayswater yearling; the *"minimal"* interior can seem *"underwhelming"*, but most reporters find it *"pleasant"* enough (the best seats being the booths at the front). / www.herefordroad.org; 10.30 pm, Sun 10 pm.

Hibiscus W1   £85   ❸❸④
29 Maddox St   7629 2999   3–2C

Claude Bosi's original Ludlow venture was so dazzling that it's hard not to feel *"mildly let down"* by its Mayfair reincarnation; the *"elaborate"* cuisine here shows *"some flair"* but too often *"creates no excitement"*, and the *"oh-so-safe"* décor lends a pretty *"soulless"* air... all of which makes Michelin's award to it of two stars somewhat baffling! / www.hibiscusrestaurant.co.uk; 10 pm; closed Mon, Sat D & Sun; set weekday L £39 (FP).

High Road Brasserie W4   £48   ④④❸
162-166 Chiswick High Rd   8742 7474   7–2A

It's too *"posy"* for some tastes, but the Soho House group's *"noisy"* Chiswick outpost is certainly *"very popular"*, not least with the glitterati of west London; the food is only *"average"*, though, and service can get *"stretched"*. / www.highroadhouse.co.uk; 11 pm, Fri & Sat midnight, Sun 10 pm; set weekday L £24 (FP).

High Timber EC4 NEW   £51   ❸❷❸
8 High Timber   7248 1777   9–3B

"Ask for a tour" of the *"fabulous cellar"* (full of South African wines) if you visit this City newcomer (by the 'Wobbly Bridge'); *"great"* Thames views, *"amicable"* service and *"unpretentious"* food (*"mostly grills"*) make it a *"safe business bet"*. / www.hightimber.com; 10 pm; closed Sun.

Hilliard EC4 £27 **❶❷❸**
26a Tudor St 7353 8150 9–3A
A major "cut above your average casual City eatery" –
this "cramped" diner, by the Temple, uses "superb" ingredients
to produce "imaginative" sandwiches, salads and so on;
it's "not cheap", but well "worth it". / www.hilliardfood.co.uk; 6 pm; closed
Sat & Sun; no booking.

Hix Oyster & Chop House EC1 £48 **❸❹❹**
35-37 Greenhill Rents, Cowcross St 7017 1930 9–1A
"What's the fuss?" – too many reporters feel Mark Hix's "bustling"
Farringdon yearling has been "over-hyped"; realisation of its
"carnivore's delight" British menu is typically "solid"
("not spectacular"), the "cold" room often seems "overcrowded",
and service (though "improved" of late) is easily "flustered" too.
/ www.restaurantsetcltd.com; 11 pm; closed Sat L.

Hokkien Chan EC2 £41 **❸❸❹**
85 London Wall 7628 5772 9–2C
A "noisy" City basement Thai that "suffers from its location";
the food's "good", though. / www.orientalrestaurantgroup.co.uk; 10.30 pm;
closed Sat & Sun.

Hole in the Wall W4 £39 **❸❸❸**
12 Sutton Lane North 8742 7185 7–2A
A "lovely garden" is a high-point at this attractive gastropub, tucked-
away in a cute backstreet south of Turnham Green; locals say that –
with its "friendly" staff and "great pub food" – it's "under-rated".
/ 9.45 pm, Sun 9.15 pm; no Amex.

Holly Bush NW3 £36 **❹❹❶**
22 Holly Mount 7435 2892 8–1A
"Hidden-away in the back streets of Hampstead", a "superior old-
style pub", with lots of "nooks and crannies", offering "decent" but
"basic" fare. / www.hollybushpub.com; 10 pm, Sun 9 pm; no Amex.

Holy Cow SW11 £20 **❷❸❸**
166 Battersea Pk Rd 7498 2000 10–1C
"I pity those outside Battersea!", say fans of this "addictive and
exciting local-delivery Indian" (one of the few such outfits we list);
service slows on weekend nights. / www.holycowfineindianfood.com; 11 pm,
Sun 10.30 pm; D only; no Amex.

Homage
Waldorf Hilton WC2 £66 **❹❹❹**
22 Aldwych 7759 4080 2–2D
Shame this "beautiful" and "ornate" – but rather hidden-away –
Covent Garden dining room (once a ballroom) has never really 'taken
off'… probably because it's "quite pricey" and "just not good enough,
considering". / www.homagerestaurant.co.uk; 10.30 pm; closed
Sat L & Sun L; set weekday L & dinner £39 (FP).

The Horseshoe NW3 £37 **❸❹❸**
28 Heath St 7431 7206 8–2A
It has an "odd layout", but this "above-average" gastropub is "one of
the better places to eat in Hampstead"; "if you like beer, there's
a good microbrewery too". / www.thehorseshoehampstead.com; 10 pm;
no Amex.

Hot Stuff SW8 £22 **❶❷❷**
19 Wilcox Rd 7720 1480 10–1D
"Appearances aren't everything"; this "shoe-box-sized" BYO caff, in a "dodgy-looking" Vauxhall street, "does not offer fine dining", but its "spicy and delicious" curries are "unbelievably cheap", and its "gregarious" service adds to the "welcoming" vibe.
/ www.eathotstuff.com; 10 pm; closed Sun; no Amex.

The House N1 £46 **❹❹❸**
63-69 Canonbury Rd 7704 7410 8–2D
It has a "real buzz", but this Canonbury hang-out is "getting a bit expensive for a gastropub", especially as standards "can wobble alarmingly" – "the food is often tasty and well-executed, but at worst it's slapdash and ineptly delivered". / www.inthehouse.biz; 10.30 pm, Sun 9.30 pm; closed Mon L.

Hoxton Apprentice N1 £36 **❹❸❸**
16 Hoxton Sq 7749 2828 12–1B
A trendily-located training-venue for the disadvantaged; for most reporters, its "variable" standards are compensated for by "good-value" prices, "charming" service and an "enticing", if "basic", setting. / www.hoxtonapprentice.com; 11 pm; no Amex; set brunch £22 (FP).

The Hoxton Grille EC2 £41
81 Great Eastern St 7739 9111 12–1B
This "oddly-located" eating place – part of the "combined reception/bar/kitchen/restaurant area" of a "hip" Hoxton hotel – was acquired by the Soho House group in mid-2009; it now boasts an all day 'American diner' menu and décor to match, but given all the recent changes, we've left it unrated. / 11 pm.

Hudson's SW15 £34 **❺❹❷**
113 Lower Richmond Rd 8785 4522 10–1A
It's still "a winner for breakfast", but "otherwise don't bother" with this Putney bistro, which "used to be good", but regularly suffers nowadays from "terrible" food and "uninterested" service. / 10 pm, Sun 9 pm; no Visa.

Hummus Bros £16 **❸❸❸**
88 Wardour St, W1 7734 1311 3–2D
36-67 Southampton Row, WC1 7404 7079 2–1D
"I didn't know I could get so excited about hummus!"; these "unflashy" joints make "a great stopping-off point" for a snack that's "simple", "appetising", "cheap", "quick" and "healthy".
/ www.hbros.co.uk; 10 pm, Thu-Sat 11 pm; WC1 9 pm; WC1 closed Sat & Sun; no booking.

Hunan SW1 £48 **❶❷❹**
51 Pimlico Rd 7730 5712 5–2D
"Let Mr Peng order for you!" – "the food never stops coming" – and you'll enjoy an "utterly joyful" banquet at this "unparalleled" Pimlico stalwart; shame, though, that what's now – for cuisine – the survey's highest-rated Chinese is rather "cramped" and "claustrophobic". / www.hunanlondon.com; 11 pm; closed Sun.

Huong-Viet
An Viet House N1   £21   ❷⑤④
12-14 Englefield Rd   7249 0877   1–1C
*"Hardly renovated since its days as public baths", this Vietnamese
community hall in De Beauvoir Town converts at night into
an "always-packed" canteen; "don't go in a hurry" – service is "often
slow" – but you can have a "great, cheap BYO night out".*
/ www.huongviet.co.uk; 11 pm; closed Sun; no Amex.

Hush W1   £55   ④⑤④
8 Lancashire Ct   7659 1500   3–2B
*"Located in a very cute courtyard", this trendy Mayfair bar/brasserie
benefits, on sunny days, from some very good al fresco tables;
the "pricey" food is only "average" though, and service can
be "snotty" and "haphazard".* / www.hush.co.uk; 10.30 pm; closed Sun;
booking: max 12.

Ibérica W1 NEW   £40   ❷❸❸
195 Great Portland St   7636 8650   2–1B
*"Heavenly tapas" has won early-days plaudits for this "airy",
contemporary newcomer, in the "soulless" environs of Great Portland
Street tube; there's also a pricier upstairs, 'Caleya Ibérica'.*
/ www.ibericalondon.co.uk; midnight; no Amex.

Ikeda W1   £75   ❶❷⑤
30 Brook St   7629 2730   3–2B
*"My Japanese friend tells me this is the best sushi in London!";
this little-known Mayfair veteran has long been acclaimed for its
"excellent" and "authentic" – "albeit expensive" – food; service
is "engaging" too, but the setting is "austere".* / 10.30 pm; closed
Sat L & Sun.

Imli W1   £29   ❸❸❸
167-169 Wardour St   7287 4243   3–1D
*A "lively" Soho canteen, "worth knowing about" for its "interesting
twist on Indian cuisine", presented "street-food" (tapas) style.*
/ www.imli.co.uk; 11 pm, Sat 11.30 pm, Sun 10 pm.

Imperial China WC2   £35   ❸❸❸
25a Lisle St   7734 3388   4–3B
*"A rather nicer-looking-than-usual Chinese" hidden-away
in Chinatown; "very good dim sum" is the star of its "reliable" cuisine.*
/ www.imperial-china.co.uk; 11.30 pm.

Imperial City EC3   £41   ❸❷❷
Royal Exchange, Cornhill   7626 3437   9–2C
*"Smart" cellars beneath the Royal Exchange provide an "impressive"
and "slightly different" location for this City Chinese; sceptics say the
food is "fairly standard", but most reporters praise its "high quality".*
/ www.orientalrestaurantgroup.co.uk; 11 pm; closed Sat & Sun.

Inaho W2   £33   ❶⑤④
4 Hereford Rd   7221 8495   6–1B
*Thanks to sushi that's amongst "the best in town", you "have to
excuse the unbelievably bad service" at this tiny, "living room"-style
Bayswater shack (where "you almost sit on top of your neighbour").*
/ 11 pm; closed Sat L & Sun; no Amex or Maestro.

Inamo W1 £34 ④❷⓪
134-136 Wardour St 7851 7051 3–1D
"Yes, it's a gimmick" – "interactive" tables for ordering and
entertainment – but, even if the Asian-fusion fare is "nothing special",
reporters like this "fun" Soho yearling; "if your date's boring, you can
always play battleships…" / www.inamo-restaurant.com; midnight.

Incognico WC2 £54 ④❸④
117 Shaftesbury Ave 7836 8866 4–2B
This "fabulously-located" Theatreland brasserie inspires bizarrely
divergent views – reports on its pre-/post-show and lunch deals say
the food's "well-executed" and "great value", but diners à la carte
tend to find a place with "absolutely nothing to recommend it"!
/ www.incognico.com; 11 pm; closed Sun.

L'Incontro SW1 £60
87 Pimlico Rd 7730 6327 5–2D
An upmarket Pimlico Italian of long standing that rebranded briefly
as 'Mauro for Santini' this year; in its new guise it inspired few reports
and stood accused of mediocre "wannabe" standards – same as ever,
then? / www.lincontro-restaurant.com; 11 pm; closed Mon L, Sat L & Sun;
set weekday L £34 (FP).

Indali Lounge W1 NEW £33 ❸②❸
50 Baker St 7224 2232 2–1A
"Spicy" but "healthy" cooking – "with no cream, butter or ghee" –
helps make this large, style-conscious new bar/restaurant, near Baker
Street, an "interesting addition" to the subcontinental scene.
/ www.indalilounge.com; 11.30 pm; closed Sat L.

India Club
Strand Continental Hotel WC2 £23 ④④⑤
143 Strand 7836 0650 2–2D
This "relic from a bygone age" – a "grim" BYO canteen on the
first floor of an Aldwych hotel – seems to be losing some of its quirky
appeal; fans still love its "very authentic, home-style Indian food",
but sceptics can see only an "over-rated" "dive", with "very little going
for it". / 10.50 pm; no credit cards; booking: max 6.

Indian Ocean SW17 £26 ❷⓪❸
216 Trinity Rd 8672 7740 10–2C
"Busy every night", this "high-quality" Wandsworth operation remains
a model local curry house. / 11.30 pm.

Indian Rasoi N2 £31 ❷❸❸
7 Denmark Ter 8883 9093 1–1B
"A blast of fresh air"; this "smart" (but "crowded") Muswell Hill
Indian wins rave recommendations from across north London for its
"exquisite", "light" and "innovative" cuisine. / www.indian-rasoi.co.uk;
11 pm.

Indian Zing W6 £38 ⓪⓪❸
236 King St 8748 5959 7–2B
"Out-zinging its rivals!"; Manoj Vasaikar's "cracking" modern Indian
cuisine is building an impressive reputation for his "buzzy" but
"unpretentious" establishment, "in a dreary stretch
of Hammersmith"; service is notably "caring" and "professional" too.
/ www.indianzing.co.uk; 10.30 pm.

Indigo
One Aldwych WC2 £57 ❸❷❸
1 Aldwych 7300 0400 2–2D
The "relaxing" mezzanine dining room of this trendy Covent Garden-fringe hotel makes a "great place for business" – its "reliable" cuisine (improved again this year) also has its fans for brunch, and pre-theatre. / www.onealdwych.com; 11.15 pm; set pre theatre £30 (FP).

The Inn at Kew Gardens
Kew Gardens Hotel TW9 £35 ④❷④
292 Sandycombe Ln 8940 2220 1–4A
A "nicely revamped" pub, a short walk from Kew Gardens tube; it doesn't inspire many reports, but all speak in terms of "good food" and "reasonable prices". / www.theinnatkewgardens.com; 10 pm.

Inn the Park SW1 £46 ⑤⑤❸
St James's Pk 7451 9999 2–3C
Fan say the "heavenly" setting of Oliver Peyton's architecturally-striking concession in St James's Park makes its British food "taste better than it is" – that's just as well, as it's sometimes "awful", and it can come with "diabolical" service too... and all at "exorbitant" prices! / www.innthepark.com; 8.30 pm.

Inshoku SE1 £26 ❸④⑤
23-24 Lower Marsh 7928 2311 9–4A
"Good-value set lunches" make this "cheerful and pretty cheap" Japanese, in a grungy street behind Waterloo, a "favourite lunchtime spot" for some reporters; service, however, can be "slow". / 10.30 pm; closed Sat L & Sun; set weekday L £12 (FP).

Inside SE10 £43 ❷❷④
19 Greenwich South St 8265 5060 1–3D
"By far the best food in Greenwich" ("not a demanding accolade, admittedly") is to be had at this "good-value" local; even fans, though, may feel that the interior "could do with a bit of an upgrade". / www.insiderestaurant.co.uk; 10.30 pm, Fri-Sat 11pm; closed Mon & Sun D; set weekday L £25 (FP).

Isarn N1 £35 ❷❶❸
119 Upper St 7424 5153 8–3D
"Islington's best Thai" is "a great local", with an "intimate" modern interior; it demonstrates "real attention to customer service", and its dishes are usually "beautifully presented". / www.isarn.co.uk; 11 pm.

Ishbilia SW1 £42 ❷❷④
9 William St 7235 7788 5–1D
A short walk from Harrods, this authentic Lebanese provides "attentive" service and "very good" food. / www.ishbilia.com; 11.30 pm.

Isola del Sole SW15 £38 ❸❶❷
16 Lacy Rd 8785 9962 10–2B
"Earthy" and "slightly unusual" cuisine and "obliging" service win local praise for this "cramped" and "buzzy" Putney Sardinian. / www.isoladelsole.co.uk; 10.30 pm; closed Sun; no Amex; set weekday L £17 (FP).

Itsu £28 ❸❸④

1 Hanover Sq, W1   7491 9799   3–2C
103 Wardour St, W1   7479 4790   3–2D
118 Draycott Ave, SW3   7590 2400   5–2C
28a Jubilee Pl, E14   7512 9650   11–1C
Level 2, Cabot Place East, E14   7512 5790   11–1C

"Hearty soups", "dependable sushi" and "healthy salads" constitute the "above-average fast food" on offer at these "stylish" conveyor-cafés; drifting survey feedback, however, supports those who say "standards are slipping". / www.itsu.co.uk; 11 pm; E14 10 pm; Cabot Pl closed Sun; no booking.

THE IVY WC2 £60   ④❷❷

1 West St   7836 4751   4–3B

It's "not as starry, now the celebs have been siphoned off by the Ivy Club, next door", but this infamously hard-to-book Theatrelander is as "buzzy" as ever, and – for fans – still "consistently fantastic"; doubters, though, find realisation of the menu of "comfort" fare increasingly "ordinary". / www.the-ivy.co.uk; midnight; booking: max 6.

Izgara N3 £29   ❸❸④

11 Hendon Lane   8371 8282   1–1B

"Wonderful grills" maintain this East Finchley café/take-away's position as "the best Turkish local in the area" ("and there are many nowadays"). / www.izgararestaurant.net; midnight; no Amex.

Jade Garden W1 £28   ❸④❸

15 Wardour St   7437 5065   4–3A

"A Chinatown old-favourite" that still "does all the dim sum classics well" (and at "absurdly low" prices too); even a fan, though, says he "wouldn't go in the evening". / www.londonjadegarden.co.uk; 11 pm.

Jamie's Italian E14 NEW £35

Churchill Place Mall   11–1C

After a series of successful openings elsewhere, Jamie Oliver's Italian chain is set to reach the capital – well, Canary Wharf, anyway – around the publication date of this guide; a flagship branch follows in Covent Garden in mid-2010. / www.jamiesitalian.com.

Jenny Lo's Tea House SW1 £27   ❷❷❸

14 Eccleston St   7259 0399   2–4B

"Staff are always warm and welcoming", at this "jam-packed" and "canteen-like" Belgravia fixture, which serves "zingy" and "comforting" noodle dishes at "great-value" prices. / www.jennylo.co.uk; 10 pm; closed Sat L & Sun; no credit cards; no booking.

Jin Kichi NW3 £38   ❶❷⑤

73 Heath St   7794 6158   8–1A

"Great" value, "lovely" people, "lousy" décor – that's the "unchanging" formula for the success of this "cosy" and "crowded" Hampstead Japanese; sushi and sashimi are "excellent", but "the yakitori (skewer) bar is the place to be". / www.jinkichi.com; 11 pm, Sun 10 pm; closed Mon, Tue-Fri D only, Sat & Sun open L & D.

Joanna's SE19 £36   ❸❷❷

56 Westow Hill   8670 4052   1–4D

"A nice surprise in Crystal Palace" – this "brasserie-style", neighbourhood favourite offers "homely" cooking, "professional" service and a "lovely", "buzzy" atmosphere. / www.joannas.uk.com; 11 pm.

Joe Allen WC2 £42 ④❸❶
13 Exeter St 7836 0651 4–3D
A "famous haunt" that's "long traded on the incredible atmosphere
of its virtually unmarked, dim and cavernous, basement location",
just off the Strand; "pre- or post-theatre, it's the place to be",
but foodwise only the "secret burger" (famously "off-menu") can
really be recommended. / www.joeallen.co.uk; 12.45 am, Sun 11.45 pm;
booking: max 10 Fri & Sat; set pre theatre £28 (FP).

Joe's Brasserie SW6 £37 ❸❸❷
130 Wandsworth Bridge Rd 7731 7835 10–1B
"You wouldn't go specifically for the food", but this stalwart Sands
End brasserie "has got 'being a local' down to a tee" – it offers
"wine at great prices", and some "very adequate" fodder to go with
it. / www.brinkleys.com; 11 pm, Sat 11.30 pm, Sun 10.30 pm.

Jom Makan SW1 £27 ⑤④④
5-7 Pall Mall East 7925 2402 2–2C
"Despite its excellent central location", off Trafalgar Square,
this "minimalist" Malaysian "fails to shine"; at its best, it's a "useful"
stand-by, offering "simple" food at "good prices"; sadly, though,
results are sometimes just "ghastly". / www.jommakan.co.uk; 11 pm,
Sun 10 pm; no Amex.

Joy King Lau WC2 £27 ❷❸④
3 Leicester St 7437 1132 4–3A
A Chinatown "old favourite" that "may not be the snazziest place",
but which offers "most reliable" cooking at "thrifty" prices; "truly
authentic dim sum" completes a winning package. / 11.30 pm.

Julie's W11 £56 ④④❶
135 Portland Rd 7229 8331 6–2A
With its "amazing" labyrinthine layout and lavish décor, this Holland
Park veteran has a "magical" ambience, especially "for romantic
trysts"; in other respects, it "lost the plot" a long time ago, but, a
recent refurbishment has coincided with some "improvement" across
the board. / www.juliesrestaurant.com; 11 pm.

The Junction Tavern NW5 £35 ❸❷❷
101 Fortess Rd 7485 9400 8–2B
An "always-buzzy" and "friendly" Kentish Town gastroboozer, where
the menu is "interesting" and "well-realised". / www.junctiontavern.co.uk;
10.30 pm; no Amex.

Just Falafs £16 ❸❸④
155 Wardour St, W1 7734 1914 3–1D
27b Covent Garden Piazza, WC2 7240 3838 4–3D
"For a quick bite", these simple café/take-outs are "tasty, healthy and
cheap"; the Covent Garden branch has a brilliant location, in the
Market. / www.justfalafs.com; 8 pm; W1 Fri 9 pm; W1 closed Sun.

Just St James SW1 £55 ⑤⑤⑤
12 St James's St 7976 2222 3–4D
How does this vast venture, in a former St James's banking hall,
keep going? – it generates a tiny volume of reports... many to the
effect that this "potentially splendid" location is "spoilt by a dull menu
and truly dreadful service". / www.juststjames.com; 10.45 pm; closed Sun;
set always available £31 (FP).

K10 EC2 £31 ❸④④
20 Copthall Ave   7562 8510   9–2C
As "a reliable stop for conveyor-sushi", this "noisy and bustling" City
basement "puts many others of the same ilk to shame".
/ www.k10.net; L only, closed Sat & Sun; no booking.

Kai Mayfair W1 £80 ❸④④
65 South Audley St   7493 8988   3–3A
Did that new Michelin star go straight to the head of this "über-posh"
but "anodyne" Mayfair Chinese?; fans still say its cuisine's "beyond
compare", but critics – for whom the food's "average" – now focus
on its "outrageous" prices. / www.kaimayfair.com; 10.45 pm,
Sun 10.15 pm; set weekday L £51 (FP).

Kaifeng NW4 £50 ❸❸④
51 Church Rd   8203 7888   1–1B
A kosher Chinese that's long been a Harrow fixture; even fans think
it's "expensive", but they say its "wonderful" cooking "does it proud".
/ www.kaifeng.co.uk; 10.30 pm; closed Fri & Sat.

kare kare SW5 £34 ❸❷④
152 Old Brompton Rd   7373 0024   5–2B
"It's still better than the Noor Jahan or the Star", say fans of this low-
key South Kensington Indian – they vaunt its "very good curry",
and say it has "nicer service" than its more famous neighbours.
/ www.karekare.co.uk; 11 pm; closed L Mon - Wed.

Karma W14 £28 ❸❷④
44 Blythe Rd   7602 9333   7–1D
"Defy the off-the-beaten-track location!", say fans of this tucked-away
Olympia spot, who applaud its "different twist" on Indian cuisine,
and its "good value" too. / www.k-a-r-m-a.co.uk; 11.30 pm; no Amex.

Kastner & Ovens WC2 £10 ❶❷–
52 Floral St   7836 2700   4–2D
We don't usually list take-aways, but this "hidden gem", beside the
Royal Opera House, is of real note for its "brilliant lunch boxes" –
"a bit more expensive than Pret, but worth every penny". / L only,
closed Sat & Sun; no credit cards; no booking.

Kastoori SW17 £28 ❶❷④
188 Upper Tooting Rd   8767 7027   10–2C
"Puris like little taste bombs" are amongst the "amazingly delicious"
Gujarati/East African dishes that have made this extremely "friendly",
family-run Tooting stalwart something of a south London legend…
"even if the outside does look rather grungy".
/ www.kastoorirestaurant.com; 10.30 pm; closed Mon L & Tue L; no Amex
or Maestro; booking: max 12.

Kazan £38 ❷❸❸
93-94 Wilton Rd, SW1   7233 7100   2–4B
34-36 Houndsditch, EC3   7626 2222   9–2D
"Good-quality Middle Eastern/Turkish cuisine" makes these "really
lively" Pimlico and City "stand-bys" consistently popular – the former
location, in a still surprisingly 'thin' part of inner London, is "a great
find". / www.kazan-restaurant.com; 10.45 pm; EC3 closed Sun.

Keelung WC2 🆕 £26 ❸❸❸
6 Lisle St   7734 8128   4–3A
Quite chic by Chinatown standards, a summer-2009 Taiwanese
newcomer that makes a congenial place for a pre-theatre bite;
seafood – for which a confusing special menu is offered – is a
speciality. / Rated on Editors' visit; 11 pm, Thu-Sat 11.30 pm; no Amex.

Ken Lo's Memories SW1   £55   ❷❷❸
65-69 Ebury St   7730 7734   2–4B
"Consistency is the key", for the many long-term fans of this veteran Belgravia Chinese, for whom "it's not the cheapest, but it is the best" – of late, however, the odd disappointment has been reported. / www.londonfinedininggroup.com; 11 pm; closed Sun L.

Ken Lo's Memories of China W8   £50   ❷❸④
353 Kensington High St   7603 6951   7–1D
This "Premier League" Kensington oriental was back on better form this year; for a "smart Chinese", though, the food strikes some reporters as "good rather than special", and prices are "quite steep". / www.memories-of-china.co.uk; 11 pm.

Kennington Tandoori SE11   £28   ❸❷❸
313 Kennington Rd   7735 9247   1–3C
"Very popular with local yuppies and MPs", this "reliable" curry house has achieved a wide following for its "light and fresh-tasting" fare. / www.kenningtontandoori.com; midnight.

Kensington Place W8   £40   ④❸④
201-209 Kensington Church St   7727 3184   6–2B
"Come back Rowley Leigh!" – this once-famous Kensington 'goldfish bowl' has "gone very downhill" since joining the D&D group a couple of years ago; "they've slashed prices" of late, however, and a new chef is said to have "sharpened up" the cooking. / www.danddlondon.com; 10 pm.

Kensington Square Kitchen W8   £27   ❸❷❸
9 Kensington Sq   7938 2598   5–1A
A "cute" café, "hidden-away at the corner of a leafy Kensington square", serving "light" and "fresh" fare; "fantastic breakfasts" are a highlight. / www.kensingtonsquarekitchen.co.uk; 5 pm, Sun 4 pm.

The Kensington Wine Rooms W8 NEW   £37   ④④❷
127-129 Kensington Church St   7727 8142   6–2B
"An exceptional wine selection by the glass" (from an 'Enomatic' machine) is the special draw to this new wine bar, near Notting Hill Gate – "a real locals' place", it offers food that's somewhere between "OK" and "good". / www.greatwinesbytheglass.com; 11 pm, Sun 10.30 pm.

(Brew House)
Kenwood House NW3   £24   ④④❷
Hampstead Heath   8341 5384   8–1A
For "a pit stop after a walk on Hampstead Heath", this self-service café can be "lovely" – especially if you sit in the delightful garden on a sunny day; stick to simple fare, though – the more complicated stuff can be "terrible". / www.companyofcooks.com; 6 pm (summer), 4 pm (winter); no Amex.

Kenza EC2   £52   ④④❷
10 Devonshire Sq   7929 5533   9–2D
"Hidden-away in a City basement", this lavishly-decorated Moroccan yearling is one of the few 'party-style' restaurants in that part of town; while the food is "perfectly decent", however, prices are "exorbitant". / www.kenza-restaurant.com; 10 pm, Thu-Fri 11 pm, Sat 11.30 pm; closed Sun; set weekday L £31 (FP).

Kettners W1   £47   ④④⑤
29 Romilly St   7734 6112   4–2A
*"What have they done?"; redevelopment has "ripped the soul" out
of this "once-lovely" Soho "old-timer" (originally founded in 1863
by the former chef to Napoleon III), to create a bizarrely-conceived
"apology" for a café/bistro. / www.kettners.com; midnight, Sun 9 pm;
need 7+ to book.*

Kew Grill TW9   £48   ④④❸
10b Kew Grn   8948 4433   1–3A
*This "always-buzzy" and tightly-packed venture is the sole London
survivor of Antony Worrall Thompson's grill chain; it still inspires
reports of "delectable", if "expensive" fare, but some reporters also
find it simply "disappointing". / www.awtonline.co.uk; 10.30 pm, Fri - Sat
11.30pm, Sun 10 pm; closed Mon L; set weekday L £27 (FP).*

Khan's W2   £20   ❷❸❸
13-15 Westbourne Grove   7727 5420   6–1C
*For a "filling" curry at "bargain" prices, this cavernous Bayswater
canteen has long been a "reliable" destination; no alcohol.
/ www.khansrestaurant.com; 11.45 pm.*

Khan's of Kensington SW7   £34   ❸②④
3 Harrington Rd   7584 4114   5–2B
*A long-established Indian, by South Kensington tube, that's invariably
hailed as a "convenient", "reliable" and "good-value" destination.
/ www.khansofkensington.co.uk; 11 pm, Fri & Sat 11.30 pm.*

Khoai   £24   ❸❸⑤
362 Ballards Ln, N12   8445 2039   1–1B
6 Topsfield Pde, N8   8341 2120   1–1C
*A duo of "cheap 'n' cheerful" Vietnamese cafés – in Crouch End and
North Finchley – hailed for their "very fresh" and "reliable" fare;
they're "always busy". / 11.30 pm; N12 closed Mon; no booking Fri & Sat
after 7.30 pm.*

Kiasu W2   £28   ❸④⑤
48 Queensway   7727 8810   6–2C
*"Great-value Malaysian food" has helped make quite a name for this
"cheap 'n' cheerful" Bayswater "pit stop"; the quality of the dishes
"varies", though, leaving the occasional reporter wondering: "what's
the fuss?" / www.kiasu.co.uk; 11 pm; no Amex or Maestro.*

Kiku W1   £60   ❷❸⑤
17 Half Moon St   7499 4208   3–4B
*"Great-quality" Japanese cooking at "relatively affordable prices" wins
consistent praise for this "rather sterile" and "canteen-like" fixture;
the set lunch is – by Mayfair standards – a "bargain".
/ www.kikurestaurant.co.uk; 10.15 pm; closed Sun L; set weekday L £27 (FP).*

Kings Road
Steakhouse & Grill SW3 NEW   £40
386 King's Rd   7351 9997   5–3B
*The former Chelsea site of Jimmy's (RIP) was relaunched in mid-2009
as a steakhouse, seemingly inspired by the supposed success of MPW
Steakhouse & Grill (with which it shares an owner); we didn't have
the opportunity to visit before this guide went to press.
/ www.kingsroadsteakhouseandgrill.com; 11 pm, Sun 10 pm.*

Kipferl EC1 £26 ❸❷❸
70 Long Ln 7796 2229 9–1B
"A great range of unusual, authentic Austrian dishes" (including "Sachertorte made the traditional way") makes it worth seeking out this "intimate" (11-seat) Smithfield café; be warned, though – they "desperately need more space". / www.kipferl.co.uk; L only, closed Sun; no Amex.

Knaypa W6 £35 ❹❷❹
268 King St 8563 2887 7–2B
A year-old shop conversion, near Ravenscourt Park tube; the Polish fare is "a bit variable, but when it's good, it's very good and authentic". / www.theknaypa.co.uk; 10.30 pm.

Koba W1 £44 ❸❷❹
11 Rathbone St 7580 8825 2–1C
"Having your food cooked right in front of you makes for a sociable experience" – and also a "consistently high quality" one – at this "ever-friendly" Korean barbecue, in Fitzrovia; "lots of ex-pat regulars testify to its authenticity". / www.koba-london.com; 11 pm; closed Sun L; set weekday L £24 (FP).

Kolossi Grill EC1 £24 ❹❸❸
56-60 Rosebery Ave 7278 5758 9–1A
"The food gets rougher and readier as time passes", at this '60s taverna in Clerkenwell; staff remain "competent", though, and the place still has a certain "cheap 'n' cheerful" charm. / www.kolossigrill.com; 11 pm; closed Sat L & Sun.

Konditor & Cook £20 ❷❸❹
Curzon Soho, 99 Shaftesbury Ave, W1 7292 1684 4–3A
46 Gray's Inn Rd, WC1 7404 6300 9–1A
30 St Mary Axe, EC3 0845 262 3030 9–2D
"Dangerously delicious" cakes and "outstanding pâtisserie" – plus "a varied menu of hot dishes, soups and tartlets" – inspire ongoing raves for these (generally) "tiny" café/take-aways. / www.konditorandcook.com; W1 11 pm, Sun 10.30 pm; Cornwall Rd & Stoney St SE1 6 pm; WC1 7 pm; WC1 & EC3 closed Sat & Sun; Cornwall Rd & Stoney St closed Sun; no booking.

Konstam WC1 £45 ❷❸❸
2 Acton St 7833 5040 8–3D
Oliver Rowe's "brave", eco-conscious pub-conversion, near King's Cross, remains a "really interesting" destination – working with "a narrow range of local ingredients" (sourced from in/around the M25) inspires some notably "inventive" cooking. / www.konstam.co.uk; 10.30 pm; closed Sat L & Sun D.

Kovalam NW6 £26 ❸❷❹
12 Willesden Ln 7625 4761 1–2B
"Very tasty" south Indian food and "charming" service again won praise from most (if not quite all) reporters on this hidden-away Kilburn spot. / www.kovalamrestaurant.co.uk; 11.15 pm, Fri & Sat 11.45 pm; no Amex.

Kulu Kulu £26 ❸❹❺
76 Brewer St, W1 7734 7316 3–2D
51-53 Shelton St, WC2 7240 5687 4–2C
39 Thurloe Pl, SW7 7589 2225 5–2C
"High turnover means the food is always fresh", at these "divey-looking" conveyor-sushi cafés; they're still "authentic", "quick" and "cheap", but standards are "run-of-the-mill" compared to what they used to be. / 10 pm; SW7 10.30 pm; closed Sun; no Amex; no booking.

Kurumaya EC4 £31 ❶❷❷
76-77 Watling St   7236 0236   9–2B
"Excellent sushi and sashimi" – some of the best-value Japanese food
in the Square Mile – make this *"reasonably-priced"* Kaiten-Zushi
outfit, near Mansion House, well worth seeking out.
/ www.kurumaya.co.uk; 9.30 pm; closed Sat & Sun.

L-Restaurant & Bar W8 £40 ❸❷④
2 Abingdon Rd   7795 6969   5–1A
"Truly welcoming" service helps win fans for this offbeat Kensington
spot, whose Spanish *"tapas-and-more"* menu is *"enjoyable"* and
"a bit different"; if you're considering a visit, look out for a 50%-off
deal, to which they seem rather prone. / www.l-restaurant.co.uk;
10.30 pm, Sun 10 pm; closed Mon L; set dinner £20 (FP), set pre-theatre
£25 (FP).

The Ladbroke Arms W11 £43 ❷④❷
54 Ladbroke Rd   7727 6648   6–2B
"If only all pub grub was as good" as the *"interesting"*, *"seasonal"*
fare on offer at this hugely popular Notting Hill boozer; it's not all
good news, though – *"on a sunny day, don't even think about trying
to bag one of the tables outside!"* / www.capitalpubcompany.com;
9.30 pm; no booking after 7.30 pm.

Ladurée £64 ④④④
Harrods, 87-135 Brompton Rd, SW1   7730 1234   5–1D
71-72 Burlington Arc, Piccadilly, W1   7491 9155   3–3C
"Opulent and pricey, but a great treat"; the Knightsbridge spin-off
from the legendary Parisian tearoom offers their hallmark *"divine"*
macaroons, alongside *"fabulous"* (*"if fabulously expensive"*) snacks,
cakes and teas; (macaroons and coffee only in Piccadilly).
/ www.laduree.com; SW1 7.45 pm, Sun 5.45 pm; W1 7 pm, Sun 5 pm;
W1 no booking, SW1 no booking 3 pm-6 pm.

Lahore Kebab House E1 £22 ❶④④
2-4 Umberston St   7488 2551   11–1A
"Ridiculous queues" advertise the *"addictive"* appeal of this *"stupidly
cheap"* East End *"institution"*, which *"vies with New Tayyabs"* to offer
"the best kebabs this side of Karachi"; *"no décor"*; BYO.
/ www.lahore-kebabhouse.com; midnight; need 8+ to book.

Lamberts SW12 £45 ❶❶❷
2 Station Pde   8675 2233   10–2C
"Stunning value" wins acclaim for this Balham *"gem"*, which offers
an *"interesting, seasonally-changing menu"* and *"professional, friendly
service"*; it's tempting to see it as *"an alternative to Chez Bruce"*,
but cognoscenti caution that its aims (and prices) are less lofty.
/ www.lambertsrestaurant.com; 10.30 pm, Sun 9 pm; closed Mon,
Tue-Fri L & Sun D; no Amex.

The Landau
The Langham W1 £75 ❷❷❷
1c, Portland Pl   7965 0165   2–1B
Thanks to Andrew Turner's *"exquisite"* cuisine – largely served
'grazing'-style – this grand and *"elegant"* dining room, not far from
Oxford Circus, is emerging as a real success-story (and one of the few
top hotel restaurants of which Londoners can be at all proud).
/ www.thelandau.com; 10 pm; closed Sat L & Sun D; no trainers.

(Winter Garden)
The Landmark NW1 £79 ④④❷
222 Marylebone Rd 7631 8000 8–4A
A "giant glasshouse" of an atrium – "like you might find in Dubai!" –
provides a "spectacular" setting at this Marylebone hotel; it has its
fans, especially for afternoon tea or "champagne brunch",
but "for the quite ordinary food, prices are stratospheric".
/ www.landmarklondon.co.uk; 10.30 pm; no trainers; booking: max 12.

Langan's Bistro W1 £38 ④④④
26 Devonshire St 7935 4531 2–1A
"Charmingly old-fashioned" and "discreet", or "pretty unimpressive"
(even "laughable")? – both schools of thought are well represented
in reports on this "cramped" Marylebone fixture.
/ www.langansrestaurants.co.uk; 11 pm; closed Sat L & Sun.

Langan's Brasserie W1 £51 ⑤④❷
Stratton St 7491 8822 3–3C
"It still has that buzz", but this "fun" Mayfair veteran "let itself go"
years ago, and the food is "stuck in the '80s"; "for a casual, business
lunch", though, the place still has its fans.
/ www.langansrestaurants.co.uk; 11.30 pm; closed Sun.

Langan's Coq d'Or Bar & Grill SW5 £46 ④④④
254-260 Old Brompton Rd 7259 2599 5–3A
This Earl's Court "staple" sometimes seems "empty" nowadays; it can
be "a useful stand-by" and has "great outside tables", but a number
of former fans have found it "not up to its usual standard" of late.
/ www.langansrestaurants.co.uk; 11 pm, Sun 10 pm.

The Lansdowne NW1 £38 ❸④❸
90 Gloucester Ave 7483 0409 8–3B
This "amiable" but "noisy" Primrose Hill gastroboozer still pleases the
crowds, in particular with its "superb" and "crisp" pizzas; those who
live in fear of "north London trendies" (and their kids), however,
should steer well clear of weekend lunchtimes.
/ www.thelansdownepub.co.uk; 10 pm; no Amex.

La Lanterna SE1 £38 ❸❷❸
6-8 Mill St 7252 2420 11–2A
"Big portions at reasonable prices" and a "lovely courtyard for
summer evenings" help create a "memorable" experience for fans
of this "friendly" Italian, just over Tower Bridge.
/ www.pizzerialalanterna.co.uk; 11 pm; closed Sat L.

The Larder EC1 £43 ④④④
91-93 St John St 7608 1558 9–1A
A two-part Clerkenwell operation, of which one section is a
bakery/take-away serving "door-step" sandwiches; the "massive",
woody brasserie wins some praise for its "good" and "hearty" fare,
but critics find it just too "unmemorable". / www.thelarderrestaurant.com;
10.30 pm; closed Sat L & Sun.

Latium W1 £48 ❶❶❸
21 Berners St 7323 9123 3–1D
Thanks to Maurizio Morelli's "magnificent" cooking, and the "classy"
service too, this "hidden gem", just north of Oxford Street, is now
seriously in contention as "London's finest Italian"; only the décor,
perhaps, "could do with a little dressing up".
/ www.latiumrestaurant.com; 10.30 pm, Fri-Sat 11pm; closed Sat L & Sun.

Latymers W6 £28 ❷④⑤
157 Hammersmith Rd 8741 2507 7–2C
It's "nothing to look at", but this "cheap 'n' cheerful" canteen at the
rear of a huge Hammersmith gin palace serves Thai scoff that's
"great, simple and reliable". / 10 pm; closed Sun D; no Amex; no booking
at L.

Launceston Place W8 £72 ❷❷❸
1a Launceston Pl 7937 6912 5–1B
"Stylish" cuisine and "charming" staff underpin a "wonderful
transformation" of this "delightful" Kensington townhouse "gem",
which was relaunched a year or so ago by the D&D group;
it's "much more expensive" than it was, though, and its style can
strike long-term fans as "pretentious". / www.danddlondon.com; 11 pm;
closed Mon L; set weekday L £57 (FP).

THE LEDBURY W11 £75 ❶❶❷
127 Ledbury Rd 7792 9090 6–1B
Nowadays thoroughly "top-tier" – this "consistently outstanding"
Notting Hill "all-rounder" offers "rising star" Brett Graham's
"flawless" and "adventurous" cuisine, in a "comfortable" and
"relaxed" setting. / www.theledbury.com; 10.30 pm; set weekday L £44 (FP).

Lemonia NW1 £37 ④❷❶
89 Regent's Park Rd 7586 7454 8–3B
A "huge", "vibrant" and "bustling" Primrose Hill taverna, where long-
term fans find "the owner Tony and his staff are like old friends";
nowadays, however, the place "trades on its reputation", serving
"basic" scoff that's "mediocre and overpriced". / 11.30 pm; closed
Sat L & Sun D; no Amex; set weekday L £19 (FP), set dinner £24 (FP).

Lena EC2 NEW £46 ④④④
66 Great Eastern St 7739 5714 12–1B
A style-conscious Shoreditch Italian newcomer (on the site once called
Savarone, RIP); arguably "the décor justfies the prices", but early-days
reports suggest that standards otherwise do not.
/ www.lenarestaurant.com; 11 pm.

Leon £20 ❸❸❸
275 Regent St, W1 7495 1514 3–1C
35-36 Gt Marlborough St, W1 7437 5280 3–2C
73-76 The Strand, WC2 7240 3070 4–4D
7 Canvey St, SE1 7620 0035 9–4B
Cabot Place West, E14 7719 6200 11–1C
3 Crispin Pl, E1 7247 4369 12–2B
12 Ludgate Circus, EC4 7489 1580 9–2A
86 Cannon St, EC4 7623 9699 9–3C
"A breath of fresh air in the world of fast food"; this "quirky" chain
is "not quite as nice as when it started", but fans still recommend its
"healthy, hearty and honest" dishes as "a great alternative to a
sarnie". / www.leonrestaurants.co.uk; 10 pm; W1 8.45 pm; E14 8 pm;
EC4 closed Sun; W1 closed Sat & Sun; no booking L.

Leong's Legends W1 £26 ❸⑤❸
4 Macclesfield St 7287 0288 4–3A
"Fresh" and "authentic" Taiwanese food ("a nice change from
Cantonese") and "interesting", "opium-den" décor make a winning
combination for this Chinatown spot – "no wonder it's popular";
service, though, is "a lottery". / 11 pm, Sat 11.30 pm; no Amex;
no booking.

Levant W1 £49 ④④❶
Jason Ct, 76 Wigmore St 7224 1111 3–1A
"Was the money we paid for the belly dancers, not the chefs?" –
this *"souk-like"* Marylebone hang-out may have a *"lovely, dark and
romantic"* vibe (and *"great cocktails"* too), but its *"expensive"*
Lebanese fare is sometimes *"awful"*. / www.levant.co.uk; 11.30 pm.

The Light House SW19 £45 ❸④④
75-77 Ridgway 8944 6338 10–2B
"Wimbledon's best bet" for quality cuisine – this airy outfit realises
"an ever-changing" menu with *"the odd flash of inspiration"*.
/ www.lighthousewimbledon.com; 10.30 pm, Fri-Sat 10.45 pm; closed Sun D;
set weekday L £27 (FP).

The Lighthouse SW11 £32 ❷❷❷
441 Battersea Park Rd 7223 7721 10–1C
"A good place in a not especially lovely area" – this Battersea
gastropub has many local fans, thanks to its *"well constructed"* dishes
and its *"really nice"* beer garden. / 10 pm, Sun 9 pm.

Lisboa Pâtisserie W10 £6 ❷④❸
57 Golborne Rd 8968 5242 6–1A
A *"happy"* and *"bustling"* North Kensington café, known for its
"unbeatable Portuguese custard tarts" and *"great coffee"*. / 7.30 pm;
L & early evening only; no booking.

Little Bay £27 ④❷❷
228 Belsize Rd, NW6 7372 4699 1–2B
228 York Rd, SW11 7223 4080 10–2B
171 Farringdon Rd, EC1 7278 1234 9–1A
"Zany" décor and *"consistent tasty food"* at *"how-do-they-do-it"*
prices makes this budget bistro chain one of *"the best bargains
in London"*. / www.little-bay.co.uk; 11 pm; no Amex, NW6 no credit cards.

Little Italy W1 £53 ④❸❸
21 Frith St 7734 4737 4–2A
"You can have a great night out" – complete with *"dancing and
flowing champagne"* – at this louche Soho Italian (which *"turns into
a club later on"*); doubters, though, just find it *"overpriced"* and
"disappointing". / www.littleitalysoho.co.uk; 4 am, Sun 11.30 pm.

The Little Square W1 £40 ④④❸
3 Shepherd Mkt 7355 2101 3–4B
"A great location", *"in the heart of Shepherd Market"*, is key to the
appeal of this *"cramped"* corner bistro – the food *"doesn't match
up"*. / 11 pm.

Livebait £46 ④⑤⑤
21 Wellington St, WC2 7836 7161 4–3D
43 The Cut, SE1 7928 7211 9–4A
This *"cold"* white-tiled chain (*"like eating in a public loo"*) has totally
"lost its spark", and seems increasingly to suffer from a *"production-
line"* mentality; curiously, the *"unfussy"* fish dishes – *"uninspired but
decent enough"* – are its best feature. / www.santeonline.co.uk; 11 pm;
SE1 Sun 9 pm; WC2 Sun 7.30 pm.

LMNT E8 £30 ④❸❶
316 Queensbridge Rd 7249 6727 1–2D
"With its crazy decor, and its cheap 'n' cheerful food", this *"OTT"*
temple of *"high Egyptian kitsch"*, in Dalston *"has all the makings of a
great party night out"*; *"call ahead to book one of the tree houses!"*
/ www.lmnt.co.uk; 10.45 pm; no Amex.

Lobster Pot SE11 £50 ❷❷❷
3 Kennington Ln 7582 5556 1–3C
"Wacky" design (with "taped seagull noises") and "crazy" staff set
a French-surreal tone at this "strange" but "fun" stalwart, in a
"dubious"-looking bit of Kennington; its traditional Gallic fish and
seafood dishes are "first-class" too. / www.lobsterpotrestaurant.co.uk;
10.30 pm; closed Mon & Sun; booking: max 8.

Locanda Locatelli
Churchill InterCont'l W1 £62 ❸❷❸
8 Seymour St 7935 9088 2–2A
Giorgio Locatelli's low-lit and "sophisticated" Marylebone dining room
is, for its army of fans, "still the best Italian in London"; opinion,
however, is becoming ever more divided, and for a growing number
of sceptics "the only wow is the size of the bill!"
/ www.locandalocatelli.com; 11 pm, Fri & Sat 11.30 pm; booking: max 8.

Locanda Ottomezzo W8 £69 ④❷④
2-4 Thackeray St 7937 2200 5–1B
According to its fans, this "low-lit" Kensington Italian is a
"neighbourhood" sort of place, offering "lovely" food – even they can
find it "a little expensive", though, and critics feel prices are plain
"outrageous". / www.locandaottoemezzo.co.uk; 10.30 pm, Fri & Sat
10.45 pm; closed Sat L & Sun.

Loch Fyne £38 ④④④
2-4 Catherine St, WC2 7240 4999 2–2D
175 Hampton Rd, TW2 8255 6222 1–4A
"Superb" oysters are a menu highlight at this middle-of-the-road,
fish 'n' seafood chain; standards are typically "only good in parts",
however, and ratings slid across the board this year. / www.lochfyne.com;
10 pm; WC2 11 pm; set weekday L £20 (FP).

The Lock Dining Bar N17 £38 ❷❷❷
Heron Hs, Hale Wharf, Ferry Ln 8885 2829 1–1C
This Tottenham three-year-old, at the foot of an obscurely-located
office block, is not easy to find; the pay-off, however, is "great food
at reasonable prices", especially the "truly unbelievable credit-crunch
menus". / www.thelockrestaurant.com; 10 pm; closed Mon, Sat L & Sun D;
no Amex; set weekday L & dinner £22 (FP).

Lola & Simón W6 £34 ❸❸❸
278 King St 8563 0300 7–2B
By day, this Hammersmith yearling is a "neighbourhood café" that
suits a "lazy" brunch, or a coffee and a cake; by night, though,
"the candles come out" and a "short, well-executed" menu (including
"Argentinean steaks") is served. / www.lolaandsimon.co.uk; 10 pm; closed
Mon; no Amex.

Lola Rojo £29 ❷❷❸
140 Wandsworth Bridge Rd, SW6 7371 8396 10–1B
78 Northcote Rd, SW11 7350 2262 10–2C
"Pushing the tapas envelope!"; these modern Spaniards put
"a fantastic spin on traditional dishes" both at the "lively" Clapham
original, and its "relaxed" new outpost in deepest Fulham.
/ www.lolarojo.net; SW11 11.30 pm; SW6 11 pm; SW6 Mon-Fri D only.

The Lord Palmerston NW5 £38 ⑤④④
33 Dartmouth Park Hill 7485 1578 8–1B
It's potentially a "very nice gastropub", but this Dartmouth Park
operation, now owned by Geronimo Inns, "continues its downwards
slide". / www.geronimo-inns.co.uk; 10 pm; no booking.

Lots Road SW10 £37 ❸❸❸
114 Lots Rd   7352 6645   5–4B
If you find yourself anywhere in the vicinity of "the gastronomic wasteland of Chelsea Harbour", this is a very "decent" corner gastropub that's worth seeking out. / www.lotsroadpub.com; 10 pm, Sun 9.30 pm.

Lotus Chinese Floating Restaurant E14 £36 ❸❸❷
38 Limeharbour   7515 6445   11–2C
The "unusual setting" – a floating barge with "great Canary Wharf views" – helps win praise for this large, Isle of Dogs oriental, but it's also tipped for its "good food" (especially "weekend dim sum"). / www.lotusfloating.co.uk; 10.30 pm.

Lower East E14 NEW £48 ❸④④
Unit 1, 28 Westferry Circus   7536 2862   11–1B
Very bare and chain-like, this darkly-furnished new Canary Wharf grill restaurant nonetheless has a pleasant waterside position (and good al fresco tables); the brutally short and simple menu was well-realised on our early-days visit, but – given the general feel of the place – prices seemed high. / Rated on Editors' Visit; www.lowereast.co.uk; 10.30 pm.

Luc's Brasserie EC3 £46 ④④④
17-22 Leadenhall Mkt   7621 0666   9–2D
This City bistro, charmingly located on the first floor of Leadenhall Market, sometimes pleases reporters with its "reasonably-priced", meat-heavy Gallic staples; feedback is inconsistent, though, and, given the location, very modest in volume. / www.lucsbrasserie.com; 9 pm; closed Sat & Sun; set dinner £30 (FP).

Luciano SW1 £61 ⑤⑤⑤
72-73 St James's St   7408 1440   3–4D
Like so many MPW restaurants, this St James's Italian can be "bitterly disappointing"; for business, its "spacious" and "comfortable" setting has it attractions, but many critics just deride this as a "barn-like" and "massively overpriced" place, with "dreary" food and "laughably bad" service. / www.lucianorestaurant.co.uk; 10.30 pm; closed Sun; set dinner £31 (FP).

Lucio SW3 £60 ❸⓪❸
257 Fulham Rd   7823 3007   5–3B
"Back on form this year", this "nicely chilled" Chelsea spot is again – for its small fan club – "one of London best Italians", with "impeccable" service and food that's "always good"; look out for the "particularly good-value" lunch deal. / 11 pm; set weekday L £34 (FP).

Lucky Seven W2 £30 ❷❸❶
127 Westbourne Park Rd   7727 6771   6–1B
You have to share booths, at Tom Conran's "really funky", "retro Americana" diner, on the fringes of Notting Hill, but it's worth it for the "awesome" burgers and "tasty" shakes. / www.tomconranrestaurants.com; 11 pm; no Amex; no booking.

Luna Rossa W11 £38 ④⑤❸
192 Kensington Park Rd   7229 0482   6–1A
Fans of this "very busy" Notting Hill Italian proclaim it to be a "high-tempo" hang-out, serving "delicious pizza"; service can be "awfully slow" though, and critics just find the food "disappointing". / www.madeinitalygroup.co.uk; 11.30 pm; closed Mon L.

Lutyens EC4 NEW   £48   ❸❷❸
85 Fleet St   7583 8385   9–2A
For the first time since the launch of Harden's almost 20 years ago,
Sir Terence Conran has launched a restaurant we personally like! –
a grand and comfortable (almost too pretty) Gallic brasserie,
with conscientious service and Gallic favourites done to a tee; with its
ultra-handy 'midtown' location it's set to become a major
City/business hit. / Rated on Editors' visit; www.lutyens-restaurant.com;
midnight; closed Sat & Sun.

The Luxe E1 NEW
109 Commercial St   12–2C
Not that far from his existing operation, Smiths of Smithfield,
this long-awaited opening by John Torode (also of MasterChef fame)
is expected around the publication date of this guide; as we go to
press, the information available boils down to four buzzwords:
'bar, restaurant, music, art'... so now we know. / www.theluxe.co.uk.

Ma Cuisine   £36   ❹❸❹
6 Whitton Rd, TW1   8607 9849   1–4A
9 Station Approach, TW9   8332 1923   1–3A
With their "check tablecloths" and "OK" cooking, John McClements'
"pastiche" bistros can make handy, "basic" stand-bys; oddly,
the Twickenham original is not as good as the Kew spin-off, and the
best branch – a new one in Barnes – recently closed (to become
Le Provence). / 10 pm, Fri & Sat 10.30 pm.

Ma Goa SW15   £34   ❷0❷
244 Upper Richmond Rd   8780 1767   10–2B
"Extremely interesting" Goan "home cooking", with notably "friendly
and professional" service, wins huge support – from Putney and
beyond – for this impressive family-run restaurant. / www.ma-goa.com;
11 pm, Sun 10 pm; closed Mon, Tue–Sat D only, Sun open L & D.

Made in Italy SW3   £34   ❷❹❷
249 King's Rd   7352 1880   5–3C
This popular Chelsea hang-out is usually "busy", and – thanks to the
"sometimes disastrous" service – occasionally "chaotic"; it's a "fun"
place, though, and its "great pizza saves the day"; "super terrace for
sunny weather" too. / www.madeinitalyrestaurant.co.uk; 11.30 pm,
Sun 10.30 pm; closed weekday L; no Amex.

Madhu's UB1   £36   00❸
39 South Rd   8574 1897   1–3A
"Well worth the schlepp to Southall"; this "consistent" high-achiever
is again acclaimed for its "impeccable" service, its "deliciously
different" (Kenyan-influenced) Indian food and its "bargain prices".
/ www.madhusonline.com; 11.30 pm; closed Tue, Sat L & Sun L.

Madsen SW7 NEW   £38   ❹❹⑤
20 Old Brompton Rd   7225 2772   5–2B
An "interesting" Scandinavian menu adds to the promise of this
"IKEA-esque" Danish newcomer; while fans see it as "a good
addition" to South Kensington, though, some reporters are
"disappointed" by its "high prices" and "lack of atmosphere".
/ www.madsenrestaurant.com; 10 pm, Mon & Sun 9.30 pm, Fri 11 pm;
set weekday L £20 (FP).

Magdalen SE1 £48 ❷❷❸
152 Tooley St 7403 1342 9–4D
"Thoughtful" British cooking "bursting with flavour" underpins the lofty reputation of this foodie "haven", near the London Assembly building. / www.magdalenrestaurant.co.uk; 10 pm; closed Sat L & Sun.

Maggie Jones's W8 £46 ❹❸❶
6 Old Court Pl 7937 6462 5–1A
"On a cold winter lunchtime", this "dark", rustic-style Kensington veteran is an "ideal" retreat from the world (especially for romance); for fans, its "old-fashioned comfort" food "never fails", but sceptics just find it "mediocre" nowadays. / 11.30 pm, Sun 10.30 pm.

Magic Wok W2 £29 ❷❸❹
100 Queensway 7792 9767 6–2C
A "friendly", "authentic" and "no-nonsense" Bayswater Chinese, where the menu is "vast", but the food is both "surprisingly reliable" and "good value"; "great roast duck", and "good seafood" are highlights. / 11 pm.

Maison Bertaux W1 £11 ❷❸❶
28 Greek St 7437 6007 4–2A
A "lovely" – if ever so slightly "mad" – Soho institution (established 1871), London's oldest pâtisserie is still worth seeking out for its "marvellous cakes and croissants". / 11 pm, Sun 8 pm; no credit cards; no booking.

Malabar W8 £36 ❸❷❹
27 Uxbridge St 7727 8800 6–2B
*"Tucked-away off Notting Hill Gate", this "neighbourhood Indian-with-a-twist" has long been a "very civilised" favourite, with "welcoming" staff and "stylish" curries; it's drifting, though, and the food can sometimes seem rather "bland" nowadays.
/ www.malabar-restaurant.co.uk; 11.15 pm, Sun 10.30 pm.*

Malabar Junction WC1 £36 ❸❸❸
107 Gt Russell St 7580 5230 2–1C
The "unpromising exterior" of this Bloomsbury spot conceals a "sunny and relaxed" conservatory, and fans say its "enjoyable" South Indian food is "a breath of fresh air"; of late, however, there's also been the occasional disappointment. / www.malabarjunction.com; 11 pm.

Malmaison Brasserie EC1 £49 ❸❷❸
18-21 Charterhouse St 7012 3700 9–1B
It's often "overlooked", but this stylish Smithfield basement is typically "greatly enjoyed" by reporters, not least for food that's "well above average for an hotel". / www.malmaison.com; 10 pm, Sat & Sun 10.30 pm; closed Sat L.

La Mancha SW15 £39 ❹❹❹
32 Putney High St 8780 1022 10–2B
Especially "for a large group", this well-established Putney venue has a "brilliant" atmosphere, and its "serviceable" tapas offer "good value for money". / www.lamancha.co.uk; 11 pm; need 6+ to book; set weekday L £23 (FP).

Mandalay W2 £25 ❷❶⑤
444 Edgware Rd 7258 3696 8–4A
"A warm welcome from the Ally family" happily offsets the "dive" atmosphere of this "café-style" joint, north of Edgware Road tube; its "simple and different" Burmese dishes can offer "excellent value" too. / www.mandalayway.com; 11 pm; closed Sun; set weekday L £12 (FP).

Mandarin Kitchen W2 £34 ❶④⑤
14-16 Queensway   7727 9012   6–2C
"Lobster noodles in a class of their own" are the highpoint of the
"amazing Chinese seafood" on offer at this "consistently fantastic"
Bayswater spot; service is "cursory", though, and the interior
"dismal". / 11.30 pm.

Mangal Ocakbasi E8 £22 ❶③④
10 Arcola St   7275 8981   1–1C
"Mountains of food for the money" – "succulent" meat, with "fresh"
salads – offer "incredible" value-for-money, at this "basic" and
"crammed-to-the-gills" Dalston Turk, whose front room
is "dominated" by a "gigantic" charcoal grill; BYO. / www.mangal1.com;
midnight; no credit cards.

Mango & Silk SW14 £29 ❸②❸
199 Upper Richmond Rd   8876 6220   1–4A
"Udit Sarkhel is back!", say fans of this Sheen yearling, hailing its
"welcoming" style and its "innovative" Indian cuisine; the new site
is "smaller and noisier than its Southfields predecessor", however,
and the cooking can seem "disappointing in comparison".
/ www.mangoandsilk.co.uk/; 10 pm, Fri & Sat 10.30 pm; closed weekday L.

Mango Room NW1 £37 ❸②②
10-12 Kentish Town Rd   7482 5065   8–3B
A "moodily-lit" and "chilled" Caribbean hang-out, in the heart
of Camden Town, where "informative" staff serve up some "eclectic
and delicious" food. / www.mangoroom.co.uk; 11 pm.

Mango Tree SW1 £50 ❸③④
46 Grosvenor Pl   7823 1888   2–4B
It's a bit of a "barn", but this "busy" Belgravia Thai has many fans for
its "very good" food; critics say it's "nothing out of the ordinary",
though, and "expensive, unless you've got a 'deal'".
/ www.mangotree.org.uk; 11 pm, Thu-Sat 11.30 pm.

Mango Tree SE1 £29 ❷④④
5-6 Cromwell Buildings, Red Cross Way   7407 0333   9–4C
"Lovely" and "different" Indian dishes again win praise for this
"cramped" Borough Market venture, which "looks more like a bistro
than a curry house". / www.justmangotree.co.uk; 11 pm.

Manicomio £47 ④④④
85 Duke of York Sq, SW3   7730 3366   5–2D
6 Gutter Ln, EC2   7726 5010   9–2B
Oddly-mixed locations – near Sloane Square, and close to the Bank
of England – make it hard to generalise about this Italian duo; they're
both "popular", if rather "formulaic", places, with "average" food and
pleasant al fresco tables. / www.manicomio.co.uk; SW3 10.30 pm,
Sun 10 pm; EC2 10.30 pm; EC2 closed Sat & Sun.

Manna NW3 £41 ④④④
4 Erskine Rd   7722 8028   8–3B
Fans of this veteran Primrose Hill veggie (the UK's oldest) say it's
"a winner", thanks to its "delicious, seasonal food"; critics, though,
couldn't disagree more, and say it's busy "despite the appalling
cooking". / www.mannav.com; 11 pm; closed Mon L; no Amex.

Mao Tai SW6 £50 ❷❷❷
58 New King's Rd 7731 2520 10–1B
"Much hipper and livelier than most Chinese places" – this evergreen Parson's Green veteran (which is more pan-Asian really) wins continued praise for its "really lovely" cuisine; it's "not cheap" though. / www.maotai.co.uk; 11.30 pm; D only, ex Sun open L & D.

Marco
Stamford Bridge SW6 £58 ⑤④⑤
Fulham Rd 7915 2929 5–4A
Even the odd fan of MPW's Gallic yearling at Stamford Bridge feels it "trades on his name"; it started off well enough, but the few reports it attracts after a year in business tend to suggest it's a "gloomy" place that's "trying to be extremely clever"… but "failing miserably". / www.marcorestaurant.co.uk; 10.30 pm; D only, closed Mon & Sun.

Marco Pierre White Steakhouse & Grill
East India House E1 NEW £52 ④④⑤
109-117 Middlesex St 7247 5050 9–2D
MPW-branding is often more of a warning than a lure, and so it has proved on the relaunch of this City-fringe basement that was Lanes (RIP) – the food is often "dreadful", and it comes at inflated prices too. / www.mpwsteakhouseandgrill.com; 10 pm; closed Sun.

MARCUS WAREING
THE BERKELEY SW1 £115 ❶❶❷
Wilton Pl 7235 1200 5–1D
"London's No. 1!" – "Marcus has not just stepped out of Ramsay's shadow but now eclipsed him", thanks to the "meticulous" and "subtle" cuisine served up by "gracious and unobtrusive" staff at this "absolutely superb" Knightsbridge dining room; the wine list is a veritable "tome" too. / www.the-berkeley.co.uk; 10.30 pm; closed Sat L & Sun; no jeans or trainers; booking: max 10; set weekday L £98 (FP).

Marine Ices NW3 £29 ④❷❷
8 Haverstock Hill 7482 9003 8–2B
"An endless list of ice creams" turns everyone into a kid again at this "true stalwart" – of 80 years standing! – in Chalk Farm; among other dishes, the pizza can be "pretty good" but some others are really "average". / www.marineices.co.uk; 11 pm; closed Mon; no Amex.

Market NW1 £40 ❷❸❸
43 Parkway 7267 9700 8–3B
"The problem is that you want to eat everything on the menu!"; this year-old Camden Town "hit" is a bistro anyone would like in their neighbourhood, offering "hearty" and "honest" British dishes at "very competitive" prices. / www.marketrestaurant.co.uk; 10.30 pm; closed Sun D.

Maroush £39 ❸④④
I) 21 Edgware Rd, W2 7723 0773 6–1D
II) 38 Beauchamp Pl, SW3 7581 5434 5–1C
III) 62 Seymour St, W1 7724 5024 2–2A
IV) 68 Edgware Rd, W2 7724 9339 6–1D
V) 3-4 Vere St, W1 7493 3030 3–1B
'Garden') 1 Connaught St, W2 7262 0222 6–1D
London's foremost Lebanese chain is best-known for its "hugely busy" café/takeaways (at I, II and V) which serve "quality mezzes" and "the best shawarma in town" into the wee hours; service can be "sketchy", though, particularly in the quieter and plusher restaurants. / www.maroush.com; 12.30 am-5 am.

The Marquess Tavern N1 £40 ❸④❸
32 Canonbury St 7354 2975 8–2D
A "sympathetically restored" Victorian boozer, on an impressive scale,
in leafy Canonbury, serving a "short and seasonal" menu of "solid
and dependable" dishes. / www.marquesstavern.com; 10 pm; closed
weekday L; set dinner £27 (FP).

Masala Zone £27 ④❸❸
9 Marshall St, W1 7287 9966 3–2D
48 Floral St, WC2 7379 0101 4–2D
147 Earl's Court Rd, SW5 7373 0220 5–2A
583 Fulham Rd, SW6 5–4A
71-75 Bishop's Bridge Rd, W2 7221 0055 6–1C
80 Upper St, N1 7359 3399 8–3D
25 Parkway, NW1 7267 4422 8–3B
"Not your bog-standard Indian" – this "fun" street-food chain
continues to win support for its "changing menu of fresh dishes"
at "great prices"; critics, though, find the food "satisfying rather than
exciting". / www.realindianfood.com; 11 pm, Sun 10.30 pm; no Amex;
booking: min 10.

The Mason's Arms SW8 £40 ❸❷❸
169 Battersea Park Rd 7622 2007 10–1C
"In the shadow of Battersea Power Station", this "crowded"'
gastropub "can be very good"; even a fan, though, notes that it "isn't
very consistent". / www.london-gastros.co.uk; 10 pm.

Masters Super Fish SE1 £24 ❷❷④
191 Waterloo Rd 7928 6924 9–4A
"You can't get a table", such is the press of "stoutly-built cab drivers",
at this "superb chippy" near Waterloo; "nuff said!" / 10.30 pm; closed
Mon L & Sun; no Amex; no booking Fri D.

Matsuba TW9 £43 ❸④④
10 Red Lion St 8605 3513 1–4A
"A good selection of sushi" is a highpoint at this Japanese "staple",
a couple of minutes' walk from Richmond town-centre. / 11 pm;
closed Sun.

Matsuri £65 ❸❸⑤
15 Bury St, SW1 7839 1101 3–3D
Mid City Place, 71 High Holborn, WC1 7430 1970 2–1D
"The teppan yaki is great theatre", and realised to "a very high
standard", at this "good but expensive" Japanese duo, in St James's
and Holborn, also known for their "perfect" sushi; however, they're
"not the most exciting-looking places"... / www.matsuri-restaurant.com;
SW1 10.30 pm; WC1 10 pm; WC1 closed Sun.

Maxwell's WC2 £38 ④④❸
8-9 James St 7836 0303 4–2D
To think, this vast Covent Garden burger parlour used to be
something of a 'destination' – it attracts very little commentary
nowadays, but its "lively" charms still have the occasional fan,
and "kids love it". / www.maxwells.co.uk; midnight.

MAZE W1 £65 ❷❷❸
10-13 Grosvenor Sq 7107 0000 3–2A
Jason Atherton's "pioneering", tapas-inspired approach still "wows"
visitors to this "minimalist" Ramsay-group Mayfair dining room;
"microscopic" portions twinned with "astronomical" prices, however,
contribute to the impression of a slight "loss of sparkle" of late.
/ www.gordonramsay.com/maze; 10.30 pm.

maze Grill W1 £75 ❸④④
10-13 Grosvenor Sq 7107 0000 3–2A
*After a good start, this "beige" and "clinical" Ramsay-group Mayfair
steakhouse has "gone down fast" in its first full year – the food seems
increasingly "underwhelming" and "overpriced", and service is too
often by the "Keystone Kops". / www.gordonramsay.com; 10.30 pm;
no trainers.*

**The Meat & Wine Co
Westfield W12 NEW** £42 ⑤④④
Unit 1026 Ariel Way 8749 5914 7–1C
*By the entrance to Westfield, this glitzily "impressive" steakhouse
yearling has still inspired only a few reports, but some of them very
negative – "in eight years of living in London, I've never felt so ripped
off", for example. / www.themeatandwineco.com; 11.30 pm, Sun 10.30 pm;
no Maestro.*

Medcalf EC1 £42 ❸❸❸
40 Exmouth Mkt 7833 3533 9–1A
*"An uncomplicated place for lunch, dinner, or drinks" – this "cool"
bar/restaurant offers "good and solid traditional food" in a "lively"
Clerkenwell setting. / www.medcalfbar.co.uk; 10 pm, Fri & Sat 10.30 pm;
closed Sun D; no Amex.*

Mediterraneo W11 £47 ④④④
37 Kensington Park Rd 7792 3131 6–1A
*This "lively" Notting Hill linchpin has "definitely slipped" over the
last few years – prices for the "very average" Italian food can seem
"very ambitious" nowadays. / www.mediterraneo-restaurant.co.uk;
11.30 pm; booking: max 10.*

Mekong SW1 £27 ④❸❸
46 Churton St 7630 9568 2–4B
*For "tasty Vietnamese fare at very competitive prices" this "cheerful"
Pimlico veteran still usually hits the spot, even if it can feel "a bit
tired". / 11.30 pm.*

Mela £33 ❸❸❸
152-156 Shaftesbury Ave, WC2 7836 8635 4–2B
136-140 Herne Hill, SE24 7738 5500 10–2D
*With their "innovative" menus, "chatty" service, and "excellent-value
meal deals" – plus a "convenient" location (WC2) – these "modern
Indians" still make "useful" options; since the early days, however,
"some decline" is evident. / www.melarestaurant.co.uk; 11.30 pm.*

Melati W1 £34 ④❷④
21 Gt Windmill St 7437 2745 3–2D
*"Huge and good portions" of "hot and spicy" scoff maintain the loyal
fan club of this crowded Indo-Malaysian veteran, not far from
Piccadilly Circus. / 11.30 pm.*

Mem & Laz N1 £27 ④④❸
8 Theberton St 7704 9089 8–3D
*This "bustling" side street establishment, near Angel, makes
"an excellent Islington stand-by"; it offers "reliable" nosh, from a
"varied" Mediterranean/Turkish menu, at "reasonable" prices.
/ www.memlaz.com; 11.30 pm.*

Memories of India SW7 £33 ❸❸④
18 Gloucester Rd 7581 3734 5–1B
*For a "no-nonsense" Indian meal, this long-established, but little-
known South Kensington curry house still fits the bill.
/ www.memoriesofindia.co.uk; 11.30 pm.*

Memsaheb on Thames E14 £27 ❸❸❷
65/67 Amsterdam Rd 7538 3008 11–2D
"A notch above a standard curry house", this Isle of Dogs fixture also
offers service for whom *"nothing is too much trouble"*; Thames-views
too. / www.memsaheb.uk.com; 11.30 pm; closed Sat L.

Menier Chocolate Factory SE1 £37 ⑤❹❸
51-53 Southwark St 7407 4411 9–4B
Dining at this *"interesting"* Southwark playhouse is certainly *"handy
if you're going to the theatre"*, and some *"good-value"* deals are
available; of late, however, the food has seemed notably *"ordinary"*.
/ www.menierchocolatefactory.com; 11 pm; closed Mon & Sun D;
set weekday L £24 (FP).

The Mercer EC2 £46 ❸❸❸
34 Threadneedle St 7628 0001 9–2C
This *"buzzy"* brasserie – in a lofty former banking hall – has been
a *"useful"* addition to the Square Mile; it's a *"reliable"* place, even if
the overall formula is rather *"standard"*. / www.themercer.co.uk; 9.30 pm;
closed Sat & Sun.

Le Mercury N1 £25 ❹❸❶
140a Upper St 7354 4088 8–2D
"For frugal romance", it's impossible to beat this *"lively"* bistro,
near Islington's Almeida Theatre; its basic scoff is *"not high fashion"*,
but *"astonishingly cheap"* – *"I feel like I'm 20 again… and so do the
prices!"* / www.lemercury.co.uk; 1 am, Sun 11.30 pm.

Meson don Felipe SE1 £30 ❹❹❷
53 The Cut 7928 3237 9–4A
This *"old-faithful"* tapas bar, near the Old Vic, is always *"rammed"*
with fans, thanks to its *"noisy"* and *"convivial"* style (with flamenco
guitarist) and its *"interesting"* vino; this *"ain't no Barrafina"*, though,
and the *"basic"* tapas are *"not that exciting"*. / 11 pm; closed Sun;
no Amex; no booking after 8 pm.

Mestizo NW1 £36 ❸❹❹
103 Hampstead Rd 7387 4064 8–4C
This *"dodgily-located"* Mexican, near Warren Street tube, divides
opinion; fans say it's a *"buzzy"* venue, with *"wonderful"* cocktails and
"authentic" dishes – critics that it's *"a bit pricey"* and *"average"*,
with *"the worst service"*. / www.mestizomx.com; 11.30 pm.

Met Su Yan NW11 £41 ❹❸❸
134 Golders Green Rd 8458 8088 1–1B
A Chinese restaurant, in the heart of Golder's Green; fans say the
food's *"authentic, even if it is kosher"* – critics that it's *"passable,
but not the real thing"* (and *"a bit expensive"* too).
/ www.metsuyan.co.uk; 11 pm; closed Fri & Sat.

Le Metro SW3 £43 ❹❹❹
28 Basil St 7591 1213 5–1D
"Great for 'time out' from shopping at Harrods!" – this basement bar
offers *"OK"* food, plus *"good wines and champagnes by the glass"*.
/ www.lemetro.co.uk; 9.30 pm; closed Sun D; need 5+ to book.

Metrogusto N1 £46 ④❸❸
13 Theberton St 7226 9400 8–3D
*"Mouthwatering wines" – and "the staff's guidance on them" –
are the star turn at this "quirky" Islington Italian; the "basic" food
plays second fiddle , and the "friendly" service can be "slow", making
the overall package "disappointing" for some reporters.*
/ www.metrogusto.co.uk; 10.30 pm, Fri & Sat 11 pm, Sun 10 pm;
Mon-Fri D only; booking: max 8, Sat & Sun; set brunch £24 (FP).

Mews of Mayfair W1 £52 ❸④❸
10-11 Lancashire Ct, New Bond St 7518 9388 3–2B
*This "crowded", style-conscious venue sits above a bar in a cute alley,
off Bond Street; fans say it's a "cool place", with "reliable" cooking –
others that service is "slow" and the food "too pricey".*
/ www.mewsofmayfair.com; 11 pm; closed Sun; booking: max 8; set weekday L
£33 (FP).

Mezzanine
Royal National Theatre SE1 £40 ⑤④④
Southbank Centre, Belvedere Rd 7452 3600 2–3D
*"It's a pity they don't do more for their captive audience" – the RNT's
in-house restaurant is certainly "handy", but the food can
be "alarmingly variable".* / www.nationaltheatre.org.uk; 11 pm; closed
Mon L, Fri L & Sun.

Michael Moore W1 £57 ❸②④
19 Blandford St 7224 1898 2–1A
*"Amusing service" adds to the appeal of Mr Moore's "very cramped"
Marylebone venture; his "high-quality" and "quite unusual" cuisine
has made the place a "long-term favourite" for some reporters, but it
seemed "not as good" this year (and attracted particular gripes about
"tiny portions at big prices").* / www.michaelmoorerestaurant.com;
10.30 pm; closed Sat L & Sun; set weekday L £33 (FP).

Mildred's W1 £32 ❷❸❷
45 Lexington St 7494 1634 3–2D
*"London's best veggie" serves "imaginative" and "wholesome" dishes
at a "funky", "diner-style" Soho site, which – though "squashed" and
"noisy", and frequently "with a queue" – is usually "loads of fun".*
/ www.mildreds.co.uk; 11 pm; closed Sun; no booking.

Min Jiang
The Royal Garden Hotel W8 £55 ❷❶❶
2-24 Kensington High St 7361 1988 5–1A
*"Memorable" Peking duck (the house speciality, ordered in advance),
"superb" dim sum and "extremely helpful" service are just three
highlights of this "terrific", tenth-floor Chinese yearling – all the more
remarkable for a room with "stupendous" views (over Kensington
Gardens)!* / www.minjiang.co.uk; 10 pm; set weekday L £33 (FP).

Mint Leaf £60 ④④④
Suffolk Pl, Haymarket, SW1 7930 9020 2–2C
Angel Ct, Lothbury, EC2 76000 992 9–2C
*A "stylish" Indian restaurant duo that suffer from being "painfully
pricey" – the West End branch nearly gets away with it, thanks to its
"wonderful", "dark-hued" décor and its "inventive" dishes, but the
"exceptionally small" portions and "over-attentive" service of the
loungier City offshoot seem harder to forgive.*
/ www.mintleafrestaurant.com; SW1 11 pm, Sun 10.30 pm; EC2 11 pm;
SW1 closed Sat & Sun D; EC2 closed Sat & Sun.

Mirch Masala £27 ❶④⑤
171-173 The Broadway, UB1 8867 9222 1–3A
3 Hammersmith Rd, W14 6702 4555 7–1D
1416 London Rd, SW16 8679 1828 10–2C
213 Upper Tooting Rd, SW17 8767 8638 10–2D
111 Commercial Rd, E1 7247 9992 12–2D
*"Don't be put off by the plastic table tops and strip-lighting!"; you get
"stunning" subcontinental scoff – and "at ridiculously low prices" too
– at these "tatty" but "bustling" Pakistani canteens; (NB. W14
actually trades as Mirin Masala, but it's essentially identical).
/ www.mirchmasalarestaurant.co.uk; midnight.*

Misato W1 £26 ❷⑤⑤
11 Wardour St 7734 0808 4–3A
*"A brilliant find for ultra cheap and tasty Japanese fare near Leicester
Square"… "if you can get past the queue of Japanese people",
that is; "you don't go for the ambience". / 10.30 pm; no credit cards.*

Missouri Angel EC3 £56 ④④⑤
14 Cross Wall 7481 8422 9–3D
*"An oasis in the Tower Hill wasteland" – this American restaurant
serves some "decent" steaks in particular, but the "inflated" prices
seem to reflect the absence of local competition. / www.missourigrill.com;
10.30 pm; closed Sat & Sun.*

Mitsukoshi SW1 £50 ❷❸⑤
Dorland Hs, 14-20 Lower Regent St 7930 0317 3–3D
*"The sushi bar is still the best (and most undiscovered) in town",
say aficionados of this "most reliable" and "true" Japanese, in an
ultra-drab department store basement, near Piccadilly Circus.
/ www.mitsukoshi-restaurant.co.uk; 10 pm; set weekday L £28 (FP).*

Miyama W1 £63 ❸❸⑤
38 Clarges St 7499 2443 3–4B
*The setting is "soulless" and "dingy", but they treat their food
"with respect" at this long-established Japanese; by "Mayfair
standards", it's "reasonably priced" too. / www.miyama.co.uk; 10.15 pm;
closed Sat L & Sun.*

The Modern Pantry EC1 £42 ❸❸❸
47-48 St Johns Sq 7553 9210 9–1A
*With its "strikingly unusual" fusion menu, Anna Hansen's "bright"
newcomer ("upstairs dining room, downstairs noisier café") divides
reporters; most say its "clean and elegant" cuisine makes it a "great
addition to Clerkenwell" – others wonder: "did I eat in the same
place all the critics praised?". / www.themodernpantry.co.uk.*

Mogul SE10 £29 ❸❸④
10 Greenwich Church St 8858 1500 1–3D
*A "cheap, cheerful and reliable" Greenwich Indian; "go for a table
in the cavernous downstairs for the best ambience".
/ www.mogulindian.co.uk; 11.30 pm.*

Mohsen W14 £27 ❸❸⑤
152 Warwick Rd 7602 9888 7–1D
*Grungily-sited opposite Kensington's Homebase, this "busy" Persian
spot has quite a name for its "delicious" kebabs and rice; a BYO
policy adds to its budget appeal. / midnight; no credit cards.*

Momo W1 £59 ④⑤❷
25 Heddon St 7434 4040 3–2C
Mourad Mazoouz's "sophisticatedly kitsch" Moroccan is a
"wonderfully atmospheric" fashionista hang-out, just off Regent
Street; given the sometimes "tasteless" food, and the "rude and
pushy" service, however, the prices too often seem "seriously
unnecessary". / www.momoresto.com; 11 pm; closed Sun L; set weekday L
£36 (FP).

Mon Plaisir WC2 £54 ④④❸
19-21 Monmouth St 7836 7243 4–2B
"Standards have plummeted", at this "little piece of Paris" that's
occupied a Covent Garden corner for over half a century;
for romance, though, its "cosy", traditional charms still weave their
spell, and lunch and pre-theatre menus still offer "good value".
/ www.monplaisir.co.uk; 11.15 pm; closed Sat L & Sun; set pre-theatre £19
(FP), set weekday L £31 (FP).

Mona Lisa SW10 £24 ④❷❸
417 King's Rd 7376 5447 5–3B
"What a mix" of people you get, at this "old-fashioned, genuine
greasy spoon", at the far end of Chelsea; it offers "a simple menu,
brilliantly executed, at a fabulously low cost". / 11 pm, Sun 5.30 pm;
closed Sun D; no Amex.

Monkey & Me W1 £25 ❷❷④
114 Crawford St 7486 0400 2–1A
Surprisingly little commented-on, this small Marylebone restaurant
serves "fresh and authentic" Thai food; the premises are set
to double in size some time during the currency of this guide, so they
must be doing something right.

Monmouth Coffee Company £10 ❶❷❷
27 Monmouth St, WC2 7379 3516 4–2B
2 Park St, SE1 7645 3585 9–4C
"The best coffee in London, undoubtedly" – that's the draw to this
"charming" Borough Market café (where "filling" Saturday breakfasts
of bread, jam and pastries are something of an institution); Covent
Garden is retail/coffee only. / www.monmouthcoffee.co.uk; 6 pm-6.30 pm;
closed Sun; no Amex; no booking.

Montpeliano SW7 £64 ④④④
13 Montpelier St 7589 0032 5–1C
A veteran Italian that's undoubtedly "handy" for Harrods shoppers;
it's "far too expensive for what it offers", though, often striking the
uninitiated as "dull" and "tired". / midnight, Sun 11 pm.

Monty's £29 ❸❸④
692 Fulham Rd, SW6 0872 148 1291 10–1B
54 Northfield Ave, W13 8567 6281 1–2A
1 The Mall, W5 8567 8122 1–2A
11 High St, W5 8579 4646 1–3A
224 South Ealing Rd, W5 8560 2619 1–3A
As Ealing locals are aware, branches of this Nepalese 'chain' are
"not all owned by the same people" – all offer a "consistent" curry,
though, with South Ealing Road top on points.

More SE1 [NEW] £38
104 Tooley St 7403 0635 9–4D
This new, all-day South Bank café/bar/restaurant opened to press acclaim for its appealing style and zesty, affordable fare; go now, though, before co-owner Theodore Kyriakou cashes out and it goes down the tubes – the pattern at his previous start-ups (Livebait and The Real Greek). / www.moretooleystreet.com; 11 pm; closed Sun D.

The Morgan Arms E3 £41 ❸④❸
43 Morgan St 8980 6389 1–2D
In default of much in the way of local competition, this Bow boozer remains "very popular locally"; the food is generally "reliable", but the "junk shop furniture makes comfort a lottery". / www.geronimo-inns.co.uk; 10 pm, Sun 9 pm; closed Sun D; booking: max 10.

Morgan M N7 £64 ❶❷❸
489 Liverpool Rd 7609 3560 8–2D
Morgan Meunier's "clever, intricate and delicious" Gallic cuisine – among London's very best – is "an inspiration", and well justifies a trip to his "out-of-the-way" pub-conversion in an "unsalubrious" bit of Holloway; the interior is rather "sober", but it is "warmed up by the personality of the staff". / www.morganm.com; 9 pm; closed Mon, Tue L, Sat L & Sun D; no Amex; booking: max 6; set weekday L £39 (FP).

MORO EC1 £46 ❶❷❷
34-36 Exmouth Mkt 7833 8336 9–1A
"Punishing acoustics" aside, it's "really hard to fault" this "exceptional" Farringdon favourite, where "smiling" staff perennially serve up "surprising" and "mouthwatering" Spanish/Moorish dishes; "unusual" wines and "superb sherries" too. / www.moro.co.uk; 10.30 pm; closed Sun.

Mosaica
The Chocolate Factory N22 £40 ❷❷❷
Unit C005, Clarendon Rd 8889 2400 1–1C
Hidden-away in an "unpromising" location behind a factory, this Wood Green "gem" is "a real find", thanks to its "novel" setting and "very friendly" service; "interesting" and "affordable" cooking too. / www.mosaicarestaurants.com; 9.30 pm; closed Mon, Sat L & Sun D; no Amex.

Motcombs SW1 £45 ④④④
26 Motcomb St 7235 6382 5–1D
"Well-located on a Belgravia corner" (since long before the area became fashionable), this "reliable" wine bar attracts a nicely louche crowd with its "pleasant, old-fashioned food"; unsurprisingly, though, it can seem "expensive for what it is". / www.motcombs.co.uk; 11 pm; closed Sun D.

Moti Mahal WC2 £47 ❷❷❸
45 Gt Queen St 7240 9329 4–2D
"An unexpected delight!"; this "classy" contemporary Indian, in Covent Garden, can make a "great discovery" for first-timers, thanks not least to its "thoughtful" and "extremely original" cuisine. / www.motimahal-uk.com; 11.30 pm, Sat & Sun 11.15 pm; closed Sat L & Sun L.

Mr Chow SW1 £70 ❸④④
151 Knightsbridge 7589 7347 5–1D
This once mega-fashionable '60s-style Chinese inspires few reports nowadays; fans still rate it highly, but "all-round disappointment" is far from unknown. / www.mrchow.com; midnight.

Mr Kong WC2 £30 ❸❷❸
21 Lisle St 7437 7341 4–3A
This celebrated Chinatown "old-timer" is an "affable" place by the standards of the area, and looks "vastly improved" since last year's post-fire refurb; "specials and regional Chinese dishes are best". / www.mrkongrestaurant.com; 2.45 am, Sun 1.45 am.

Mr Wing SW5 £45 ❸❷❶
242-244 Old Brompton Rd 7370 4450 5–2A
A setting in a "supremely kitsch basement" (complete with "fish tanks, and jazz") helps make this "fun" Earl's Court veteran something of "a long-term favourite" for parties and romance; "impeccably friendly" service and "classy" Chinese cooking play honourable supporting roles. / www.mrwing.com; midnight.

Mrs Marengos W1 NEW £15 ❷❷④
53 Lexington St 7287 2544 3–2D
Really good pâtisserie is hard to find in London, so we welcome this small Soho café, where the home-made gâteaux, in particular, really are exceptional. / Rated on Editors' visit; www.mrsmarengos.co.uk; L only, closed Sun; no Amex; no booking.

Mugen EC4 £43 ❸❷④
26 King William St 7929 7879 9–3C
For "a swift and reasonably-priced" City lunch, this "everyday" Japanese, by London Bridge, hits the spot, thanks not least to its "fresh" and "good-value" fare. / 10.30 pm; closed Sat & Sun.

Mulberry Street W2 £38 ④④❸
84 Westbourne Grove 7313 6789 6–1B
"TVs with football and cartoons makes for low-stress family outings" to this US sports bar-style Bayswater spot; the size of its "whopping", 20' pizzas is "amazing" ("never order by the slice"), but a few reporters find their quality "not particularly good". / www.mulberrystreet.co.uk; midnight, Sun 11 pm.

Murano W1 £77 ❷❶❸
20-22 Queen St 7592 1222 3–3B
"Well done Angela!"; Ms Hartnett's cooking – "simple Italian dishes beautifully executed" – has proved notably "more self-assured" in this elegant new Ramsay-group Mayfair dining room than it was at The Connaught; the setting itself can seem a bit "soulless", but "fabulous" service contributes to a "charming" overall impression nonetheless. / www.gordonramsay.com/murano; 10 pm; closed Sun.

Nahm
Halkin Hotel SW1 £82 ④④⑤
5 Halkin St 7333 1234 2–3A
Fans of David Thompson's Belgravia Thai continue to argue that its "stunning" cuisine is "London's best" of its type; it's also "unbelievably pricey", though, and to sample it you have to endure "patronising" service in a "dead" dining room that's "very obviously part of an hotel". / www.nahm.como.bz; 10.30 pm; closed Sat L & Sun L.

Namo E9 £32 ❸❸❸
178 Victoria Park Rd 8533 0639 12–1D
"The owner really makes everything work", at this "crowded" Hackney Vietnamese; it draws "every young Guardian-reading family for miles around" with its "fresh" and "well-priced" food. / www.namo.co.uk; 11 pm; closed Mon, Tue L, Wed L & Thu L; no Amex.

Nancy Lam's Enak Enak SW11 £41 ❸❸❸
56 Lavender Hill 7924 3148 10–1C
Despite la patronne's TV celebrity, there's thin survey feedback on this unpretentious Battersea Thai – as usual, it suggests that the food is "tasty, if a little overpriced". / www.nancylam.com; 10.30 pm; D only, closed Sun.

Nando's £22 ④④❸
Branches throughout London
For "bearably healthy" fast food (though "sometimes it's not that fast"), this Portuguese peri-peri chicken chain wins praise for its "simple" and "spicy" formula and its "chirpy" staff; "children often like it" too. / www.nandos.co.uk; 11.30 pm; no Amex; no booking.

Napket £15 ④④❷
5 Vigo St, W1 7734 4387 3–3D
6 Brook St, W1 7495 8562 3–2B
61 Piccadilly, W1 7493 4704 3–3C **NEW**
342 King's Rd, SW3 7352 9832 5–3C
34 Royal Exchange, EC3 7621 1831 9–2C
"For a bit of glamour at lunch", fans tip these "upmarket cafés", whose "quirky" décor "is a welcome change from Pret and so on"; but while some reports say the food's "expensive but good", others find it "unimpressive" or "pretentious"; a more ambitious (and pricier) flagship recently opened on Piccadilly. / www.napket.com; 7 pm; W1 11 pm; Brook St closed Sun; EC3 closed Sat & Sun; W1 no Amex; no bookings.

Napulé SW6 £37 ❸④❸
585 Fulham Rd 7381 1122 5–4A
"A proper Mediterranean atmosphere" and "great" Neapolitan pizza (sold by the metre) are highlights at this "crowded" basement, "tucked-away" off Fulham Broadway. / 11.30 pm, Sun 10.30 pm; closed weekday L; no Amex.

The Narrow E14 £42 ④④❸
44 Narrow St 7592 7950 11–1B
"Fabulously-located" on the river, at Wapping, this "textbook" gastropub is by far the best of Gordon Ramsay's stabs at the concept … which is to say that, overall, reporters rate it "solid" (but certainly no more). / www.gordonramsay.com; 10 pm.

The National Dining Rooms
National Gallery WC2 £50 ⑤⑤④
Sainsbury Wing, Trafalgar Sq 7747 2525 2–2C
"With a name like this, I expected a dining experience our nation could be proud of", but Oliver Peyton's "very crowded" venue, overlooking Trafalgar Square, is too often just an all-round "disappointment". / www.thenationaldiningrooms.co.uk; 7.15 pm; Thu-Tue closed D.

National Gallery Café
National Gallery WC2 £45 ⑤⑤④
East Wing, Trafalgar Sq 7747 5942 4–4B
This grand and traditionally-styled Trafalgar Square café (no view) is sometimes tipped in preference to the 'Dining Rooms' in the Sainsbury Wing; sadly, however, both are classic Oliver Peyton establishments – the food is "not very good", and service too often "a struggle". / www.thenationaldiningrooms.co.uk; 11 pm, Sun 6 pm.

Nautilus NW6 £32 **❶❷⑤**
27-29 Fortune Green Rd   7435 2532   1–1B
*"The rumours are true: it's the best chippy in London!" –
this "cheerful" kosher West Hampstead veteran provides "massive
portions of fresh fish", "perfectly cooked" in matzo meal; opinions
differ, though, on whether its "old-fashioned" interior is "fun"
or "dire". / 10 pm; closed Sun; no Amex.*

Navarro's W1 £34 **❸④❷**
67 Charlotte St   7637 7713   2–1C
*Perhaps central London's top destination for "proper" ("old-school")
tapas, this "beautifully-tiled" Fitzrovia veteran is a "cheerful"
destination that's popular with most reporters; service, though,
can occasionally let the side down. / www.navarros.co.uk; 10 pm; closed
Sat L & Sun.*

Nazmins SW18 £28 **❷❸④**
398 Garratt Ln   8944 1463   10–2B
*Earlsfield residents love this "really decent" Indian veteran – "I know
many people who return here long after moving away from the area".
/ www.nazmins.com; midnight.*

New China Boulevard SW18 £35 **❸④④**
1 The Boulevard, Smugglers Way   8871 3881   10–2B
*"Tables overlooking the river are best", at this large two-floor
operation, in a modern development near Wandsworth Bridge;
its Chinese fare "can be variable", but it's generally "OK", especially
dim sum. / www.chinaboulevard.com; 11 pm.*

New Culture Revolution £24 **④④④**
305 King's Rd, SW3   7352 9281   5–3C
157-159 Notting Hill Gate, W11   7313 9688   6–2B
42 Duncan St, N1   7833 9083   8–3D
*"Hard to beat for a quick and tasty meal", these "useful stand-bys"
offer "good Chinese noodle dishes"; "no atmosphere" though.
/ www.newculturerevolution.co.uk; 10.30 pm; booking: min 4 preferable.*

New Mayflower W1 £30 **❷⑤⑤**
68-70 Shaftesbury Ave   7734 9207   4–3A
*"Don't expect a relaxing meal", at this "rudely efficient" Chinatown
veteran, which is particularly of note as a late-night destination;
its cooking, though, is "more authentic" than most, and comes
in "huge portions". / 4 am; D only; no Amex.*

New Tayyabs E1 £25 **❶④❷**
83 Fieldgate St   7247 9543   9–2D
*"The best Pakistani cooking this side of Lahore" (particularly
"lamb chops to die for") comes at "ludicrously cheap" prices at this
BYO East Ender – a "hectic" sort of place, with "long queues" and
"slightly surly service". / www.tayyabs.co.uk; 11.30 pm.*

New World W1 £30 **④④④**
1 Gerrard Pl   7734 0396   4–3A
*"They're still wheeling around the trollies for dim sum", at this
"huge and brightly lit" oriental, which has long been a "bustling"
Chinatown landmark. / 11.45 pm, Sun 11 pm; no booking, Sun L.*

Nicole's W1 £60 ④❸❸
158 New Bond St   7499 8408   3–3C
Nothing about it is bargain-basement, but this subterranean Mayfair fashion store café has a consistently supportive – but ever-smaller – fan club among reporters. / www.nicolefarhi.com; 5.30 pm; L & afternoon tea only, closed Sun.

1901
Andaz Hotel EC2 £55 ❸❷❷
40 Liverpool St   7618 7000   9–2D
"Much better than when it was called Aurora", this "grand" and "beautiful" dining room is now one of the City's best destinations for "a leisurely business lunch", thanks not least to its "efficient" service and "delicious" cooking (and elegant presentation too). / www.andazdining.com; 10 pm; closed Sat D & Sun; booking: max 8.

No.20
Sanctum Soho W1 NEW £42 ④④⑤
20 Warwick St   7292 6102   3–2D
A bizarrely "amateurish"-feeling dining room, in a curiously under-powered new boutique hotel, on the fringe of Soho – all very odd, as backer Mark Fuller usually injects at least a bit of sex-appeal. / www.sanctumsoho.com; 11.30 pm, Sun 10.30 pm.

Nobu
Metropolitan Hotel W1 £88 ❷④④
Old Park Ln   7447 4747   3–4A
The "vibrant" Japanese-fusion dishes "still rock", at this Mayfair legend, and they are still, sadly, as "ridiculously overpriced" as ever; the place is arguably "not hip any more"... which seems to working to its advantage – service is less "snooty" than of old, and the atmosphere less "frantic and noisy". / www.noburestaurants.com; 10.15 pm, Fri & Sat 11 pm, Sun 9.30 pm; booking: max 12.

Nobu Berkeley W1 £88 ❸④❸
15-16 Berkeley St   7290 9222   3–3C
More "showy" and "fun" than its Park Lane sibling, this younger (in all respects) of the Nobus is a "vibrant" destination above a happening bar; its Japanese-fusion fare can be "divine", but it's "ludicrously expensive", and service is too often "snobbish" and "unenthusiastic". / www.noburestaurants.com; 11.45 pm, Thu-Sat 12.45 am, Sun 9.45 pm; closed Sat L & Sun L.

Noodle Noodle £24 ❸④⑤
18 Buckingham Palace Rd, SW1   7931 9911   2–4B
Vauxhall Bridge Rd, SW1   7630 1778   2–4B
"If you're in a rush near Victoria", this "reasonably-priced" duo of canteens – with their "prompt" service and "great noodles" – are "the places to go". / www.noodle-noodle.co.uk; 10.30 pm; Buckingham Palace Rd closed Sun.

Noor Jahan £35 ❷❷❸
2a Bina Gdns, SW5   7373 6522   5–2B
26 Sussex Pl, W2   7402 2332   6–1D
This "straightforward" but "slightly upmarket" South Kensington stalwart has long been a key destination for a "reliable" curry, with "fast" ("brusque") service; the "cosy" Bayswater offshoot is similarly "dependable". / 11.30 pm.

Nordic Bakery W1 £13 ❸❷❸
14a, Golden Sq 3230 1077 3–2D
*"One of the best places for a coffee and a cake in central London",
this "spacious" bakery – just three minutes' walk from Piccadilly
Circus – is also of note for its "mouthwatering selection
of Scandinavian snacks". / www.nordicbakery.com; 8 pm, Sat 7 pm,
Sun 6 pm; closed Sat D & Sun; no Amex; no booking.*

The Norfolk Arms WC1 £35 ❹❹❸
28 Leigh St 7388 3937 8–4C
*A "tapas pub" may sounds like a "bizarre combination" but fans
of this Bloomsbury boozer say it "really does work"; sceptics, however,
feel the place – service in particular – has "lost some of its initial
enthusiasm". / www.norfolkarms.co.uk; 10.15 pm; closed Mon L & Tue L.*

North China W3 £30 ❷❶❸
305 Uxbridge Rd 8992 9183 7–1A
*"Dingy Acton's best kept secret"; this "friendly, family-run Chinese"
is "always full of locals", thanks to its "surprisingly good" cooking that
"beats many more expensive places". / www.northchina.co.uk; 11 pm,
Fri & Sat midnight.*

The North London Tavern NW6 £39 ❸❸❸
375 Kilburn High Rd 7625 6634 1–2B
*Kilburn locals prize this popular two-year-old; it's still "a real pub",
and it serves "consistent" food – "without fuss", and "at a fair price".
/ www.realpubs.co.uk; 10.30 pm; closed Mon L; no Amex.*

North Sea Fish WC1 £29 ❷❷❹
7-8 Leigh St 7387 5892 8–4C
*It's a bit "basic" and "faded", but this Bloomsbury institution remains
"one of the best chippies around", certainly in the centre of town.
/ www.northseafishrestaurant.co.uk; 10.30 pm; closed Sun; no Amex.*

Northbank EC4 £44 ❹❹❸
1 Paul's Walk 7329 9299 9–3B
*With its "stunning views" of Tate Modern across the river, this year-
old operation certainly has a "great" Thames-side location (and a
"perfect summer terrace" too); realisation of the West Country-
sourced menu is only "fair", though, and service can be a touch
"erratic". / www.northbankrestaurant.com; 10.30 pm; set weekday
L, dinner & pre-theatre £28 (FP).*

Noto Kikuya EC3 NEW £36
78-79 Leadenhall St 7929 0089 9–2D
*This recent newcomer replaced a branch of the newly defunct
Singapura chain; early reports (few) say its "good-value" sushi and
other Japanese fare make it "an excellent budget option by the
standards of the City". / 10 pm; closed Sat & Sun.*

Notting Hill Brasserie W11 £61 ❸❸❷
92 Kensington Park Rd 7229 4481 6–2B
*This "stylish" townhouse-restaurant – it's not a brasserie – has a
"smart" and "convivial" atmosphere (regularly pepped up with live
jazz) which particularly suits romance or a celebration; the food
is "delicious" too, but standards generally have drifted a bit of late.
/ www.nottinghillbrasserie.co.uk; 11 pm; set weekday L £37 (FP).*

Noura £44 ❸❷❸
122 Jermyn St, SW1   7839 2020   3–3D
16 Hobart Pl, SW1   7235 9444   2–4B
2 William St, SW1   7235 5900   5–1D
16 Curzon St, W1   7495 1050   3–4B
This "cool" but "welcoming" chain won more positive feedback this
year, and nothing but praise for the "consistent quality" of its
Lebanese fare. / www.noura.co.uk; 11.30 pm.

Nozomi SW3 £72 ④⑤④
15 Beauchamp Pl   7838 1500   5–1C
An allegedly glamorous Knightsbridge Japanese, which attracts hardly
any survey feedback... all to the effect that it's "arrogant", "tasteless"
and "disappointing"; someone must like it, though, as a new sushi bar
extension is set to open in late-2009. / www.nozomi.co.uk; 11.30 pm;
D only, closed Sun.

Number One Café W10 £20 ❶④④
1 Dalgarno Gdns   8968 0558   6–1A
"You'd never stumble across it by chance", but this BYO North
Kensington Thai is "always really busy", thanks to its "authentic" food
and "unbeatable value". / www.numberonecafe.tk; 10.30 pm; closed Sun L.

Number Twelve WC1 £45 ❸❷⑤
12 Upper Woburn Pl   7693 5425   8–4C
Fans of this "calm" Italian dining room, in Bloomsbury, say its
"interesting seasonal dishes" (with a Sicilian twist) make it a
"surprisingly enjoyable" destination; not everyone's convinced, though,
and the "airport lounge" décor certainly doesn't help.
/ www.numbertwelverestaurant.co.uk; 10.15 pm; closed Mon, Sat L & Sun.

Numero Uno SW11 £41 ❷❶❶
139 Northcote Rd   7978 5837   10–2C
"The very definition of a local Italian" – this "jolly", family-run
Battersea linchpin is a "fabulous" old-timer, serving "authentic" food
with "bags of charm". / 11.30 pm; no Amex.

Nuovi Sapori SW6 £38 ❸❷④
295 New King's Rd   7736 3363   10–1B
"You're made to feel very welcome", at this "great local Italian",
in Fulham; the food is "good" (if slightly "hit and miss"), but the
ambience can be something of a "let-down". / 11 pm; closed Sun.

Nusa Kitchen £8 ❷④⑤
9 Old St, EC1   7253 3135   9–1B
2 Adam's Ct, EC2   7628 1149   9–2C
"Expect to queue" for the "imaginative", "wholesome" and
"inexpensive" soups (plus salads and cakes) on offer at these ace pit
stops – "other soup just doesn't taste the same when you've tried
theirs!" / www.nusakitchen.co.uk; 4 pm; Sat & Sun; no booking.

O'Zon TW1 £26 ❸❶④
33-35 London Rd   8891 3611   1–4A
A downtown Twickenham oriental, offering a "huge choice"
of "consistently good" food, and "smiling" service too. / 11 pm.

The Oak W2 £42 ❷❸❶
137 Westbourne Park Rd   7221 3355   6–1B
"Terrific" atmosphere and "fantastic" wood-oven pizza make this
former boozer an "all-time favourite" for many Notting Hillbillies;
"you can't book, but wait in the comfy bar upstairs".
/ www.theoaklondon.com; 10.30 pm, Sun 10 pm; closed weekday L;
no booking.

Odette's NW1 £55 ❸④④
130 Regent's Park Rd   7586 8569   8–3B
This Primrose Hill landmark – once a famously romantic destination –
often just seems "pretentious" nowadays; it doesn't help that its
current décor can strike old friends as simply "horrid", or that
realisation of Bryn Williams's "high-class" cuisine is a "mixed bag" –
"sometimes fantastic, sometimes quite poor".
/ www.odettesprimrosehill.com; 10.30 pm; closed Mon & Sun D; set weekday
L £33 (FP), set Sun L £43 (FP).

Odin's W1 £54 ❸❶❶
27 Devonshire St   7935 7296   2–1A
"Feelings of well-being" pervade visits to this "old-fashioned and
elegant" Marylebone veteran (which displays the "fine art collection"
of the late Peter Langan); "very friendly" staff of long standing serve
up "surprisingly good" fare in "traditional" style. / www.langansrestaurants.co.uk; 11 pm; closed Sat L & Sun; booking: max 12.

Okawari £22 ❸❷❸
16 Lisle St, WC2   7287 6262   4–3A NEW
13 Bond St, W5   8566 0466   1–3A
In Ealing, and now Chinatown, a duo of "reliable", "cheap 'n'
cheerful" Japanese cafés with a small but vocal fan club,
most especially for their "great-value set lunch for under a fiver".
/ www.okawari.co.uk; W5 11 pm, Fri & Sat 11.30 pm; WC2 11 pm,
Sun 10.30 pm.

The Old Bull & Bush NW3 £33 ④❸❷
North End Rd   8905 5456   8–1A
"A good location by the Hampstead Heath Extension", "nice outside
tables", "handy parking", "friendly" staff and an "attractive" interior
all add to the appeal of the pub immortalised by a well-known '20s
Cockney song; perhaps inevitably, the food can seem "formulaic".
/ www.thebullandbush.co.uk; 9.30 pm.

Old Parr's Head W14 £18 ❸❸❸
120 Blythe Rd   7371 4561   7–1C
A "friendly" Olympia boozer, where the "simple" Thai fare on offer
is "delicious" and "cheap". / www.theoldparrshead.com; 10 pm, Sat & Sun
10.30 pm; no Amex.

Ye Olde Cheshire Cheese EC4 £30 ④❸❶
145 Fleet St   7353 6170   9–2A
To follow "in the steps of centuries of men of letters" (and tourists
too), visit this "venerable" inn, just off Fleet Street; the English stodge
is generally "edible". / 9.30 pm; closed Sun D; no booking, Sat & Sun.

Oliveto SW1 £49 ❶❸④
49 Elizabeth St   7730 0074   2–4A
"Like being in Italy!"; "wonderful thin-crust pizzas" justify the trip
to this "loud and bustling" Belgravia Sardinian; book.
/ www.olivorestaurants.com; 11 pm, Sun 10.30 pm; booking: max 7 at D.

Olivo SW1 £47 ❷❸④
21 Eccleston St 7730 2505 2–4B
"Fine" Sardinian cooking has long made this "buzzy" Belgravian
a popular destination, and fans say a visit to its "cramped" and
"basic" premises is "always a joy"; slipping ratings, however, support
those who feel "value is declining" here. / www.olivorestaurants.com;
11 pm, Sun 10.30 pm; closed Sat L & Sun L.

Olivomare SW1 £49 ❷❸❸
10 Lower Belgrave St 7730 9022 2–4B
"Brilliant Sardinian seafood" is served at this Belgravia two-year-old
(the "fishy sibling to nearby Olivo"); its "very white" décor, though –
"like a '70s-style moonscape" – can feel rather "cold".
/ www.olivorestaurants.com; 11 pm; closed Sun; booking: max 12.

Olley's SE24 £35 ❷❸④
65-67 Norwood Rd 8671 8259 10–2D
"South London's finest fish 'n' chips" is, say fans, to be found at this
"dynamic" Brockwell Park venture – a "high-quality chippy with
an eccentrically-decorated restaurant attached". / www.olleys.info;
10.30 pm; closed Mon.

Olympus Fish N3 £26 ❸❷⑤
140-144 Ballards Ln 8371 8666 1–1B
This Finchley café "never fails to impress" with its "always fresh" fish
'n' chips ("standard" or "char-grilled"), in "generous portions";
"you don't go for the ambience", though. / 11 pm; closed Mon;
set weekday L £14 (FP).

1 Blossom Street E1 £46 ❸④④
1 Blossom St 345 1723 12–2B
This "tricky-to-find" Spitalfields Italian is a "pleasant-enough"
destination, but attracts only a trickle of reports; it's "worth a trip
in summer", though, "if just for the walled garden". / 9 pm; closed
Sat & Sun.

1 Lombard Street EC3 £75 ❸❸④
1 Lombard St 7929 6611 9–3C
"They've tried hard during the downturn", and the ratings at this
"echoey" and "always-crowded" former City banking hall staged
a recovery this year – "solid" cooking and the incredibly "convenient"
location make it a "reliable" destination for a business lunch.
/ www.1lombardstreet.com; 10 pm; closed Sat & Sun.

1001 Nights W1 NEW £45 ④❸❸
85 Piccadilly 7629 4440 3–4C
Almost opposite the Ritz, an offshoot of long-established Mayfair
Lebanese Fakhreldine (on the floor above), which is already gathering
more of a crowd than its predecessor Diverso (RIP) ever did; though
it's decorated in dark nightclub style, we think it's of most interest for
its (relatively) reasonably priced daytime menus. / www.1001rest.com;
midnight.

One-O-One
Sheraton Park Tower SW1 £76 ❶❷④
101 Knightsbridge 7290 7101 5–1D
Pascal Proyart's "exquisite" seafood cuisine – available in "novel"
tapas-style, or more conventionally – has established this
Knightsbridge dining room as simply "the country's best fish
restaurant"; it's a real shame about the "frigid" décor.
/ www.oneoonerestaurant.com; 10 pm; booking: max 6; set weekday L
£41 (FP).

The Only Running Footman W1 £38 ❸❸❸
5 Charles St 7499 2988 3–3B
"Keep up the good work", say fans of this unpretentious gastropub, where "decent" food comes at "reasonable prices" (especially for "the heart of Mayfair"); there's a "buzzy downstairs, and a calmer bit upstairs". / www.themeredithgroup.co.uk; 10.30 pm.

Ooze £32 ④④❸
62 Goodge St, W1 7436 9444 2–1B
Westfield, Ariel Way, W12 8749 1904 7–1C NEW
"Satisfying risotto in somewhat Spartan surroundings" – that's the "tasty" formula that makes this small chain a "good stand-by". / www.ooze.biz; W1 11 pm; W12 9 pm, Thu & Fri 10 pm, Sun 6 pm; W1 closed Sun; W12 closed Sun D; W12 no booking.

The Orange SW1 NEW
37-39 Pimlico Rd 5–2D
The latest venture from Cubitt House, of Thomas Cubitt and Pantechnicon fame – a new gastropub on the site overlooking Orange Square (once known as Pimlico Green) that was for many years a pioneering microbrewery (The Orange Brewery). / www.theorange.co.uk.

Orange Tree N20 £37 ④⑤④
7 Totteridge Ln 8343 7031 1–1B
Reports on this Totteridge fixture divide pretty much 50/50 – fans say it's a "lovely", "buzzy" and "friendly" place, albeit one where the food is a bit incidental… but doubters insist that it's just "overpriced" and "disappointing". / www.theorangetreetotteridge.co.uk; 10 pm, Sun 9 pm.

L'Oranger SW1 £85 ④④④
5 St James's St 7839 3774 3–4D
This St James's restaurant may look "elegant", but it's very much "resting on its laurels" nowadays, with too many visitors finding it "hushed", "clinical" and "smug"; the Gallic cuisine is still sometimes "very refined", but prices are "alarming". / www.loranger.co.uk; 10.30 pm; closed Sat L & Sun; no jeans or trainers; booking: max 8; set weekday L £50 (FP).

Oriel SW1 £36 ⑤④❸
50-51 Sloane Sq 7730 2804 5–2D
With its unbeatable Sloane Square location, this authentic-looking Gallic brasserie is "always buzzing", and it certainly offers "great people-watching"; the food, however, "has no zing at all" – quelle surprise!, it's under the same ownership as… Café Rouge! / www.tragusholdings.com; 11 pm, Sun 10.30 pm; no booking.

Origin Asia TW9 £36 ❷❷④
100 Kew Rd 8948 0509 1–4A
A "contemporary Indian" in Richmond, where the "original take on traditional dishes" is "significantly above-average". / www.originasia.co.uk; 11 pm; set weekday L £23 (FP).

Original Tajines W1 £32 ❸❷❸
7a Dorset St 7935 1545 2–1A
"A rather special little Moroccan", tucked-away in Marylebone, where "charming" staff serve "delicious" tagines, in a "quite cramped" but cosy room. / www.original-tagines.com; 11 pm; no Amex.

Orrery W1 £72 ❷❷❸
55 Marylebone High St   7616 8000   2–1A
"The best 'Conran'" (as D&D was formerly called) – the group's
"high-calibre" Marylebone flagship offers "gorgeous" Gallic cuisine,
"immaculate" service and "wonderful" wine; the first-floor site may
be "corridor-like", but is "airy" and "calm", and has "lovely views over
a churchyard". / www.orreryrestaurant.co.uk; 10.30 pm, Fri-Sat 11 pm;
set always available £44 (FP).

Orso WC2 £50 ④❸④
27 Wellington St   7240 5269   4–3D
This "old-friend" Covent Garden Italian is once again in decline; while
fans still say it's a "bustling" and "reliable" pre/post-theatre stand-by,
with "welcoming" staff, critics just see a place that's "gloomy" and
"unexciting". / www.orsorestaurant.co.uk; midnight; set dinner £30 (FP), set
brunch £33 (FP).

Oscar
Charlotte Street Hotel W1 £58 ④④❸
15 Charlotte St   7806 2000   2–1C
A "temple for ad-land executives", this "impressive"-looking Fitzrovia
hotel bar/restaurant is the place to go "to do a deal" – if you're not
part of that scene, however, you may just find the food "average" and
"expensive". / www.charlottestreethotel.com; 10.45 pm, Sun 9.45 pm; closed
Sun L.

Oslo Court NW8 £52 ❷❶❷
Charlbert St, off Prince Albert Rd   7722 8795   8–3A
Who cares if it's a "'70s time warp", patronised mainly by geriatric
north Londoners? – this St John's Wood "perennial" is "hard not
to love", given its "outstanding" service, décor that's "so bad it's
good", and a menu "so retro" it provides "the perfect antidote
to poncy food". / 11 pm; closed Sun; no jeans or trainers.

Osteria Appennino EC2 £38 ❷❸④
3-5 Devonshire Row   7247 4472   9–2D
"Down a sidestreet near Liverpool Street station", this "cramped and
buzzing", family-run Italian serves "good fresh food at reasonable
prices". / 10.30 pm; closed Sat & Sun.

Osteria Basilico W11 £43 ❸④❷
29 Kensington Park Rd   7727 9957   6–1A
This "old friend", in Notting Hill, is always "crowded" and "noisy"
("you have to book"), thanks to its "homely" pasta, "great pizza"
and other "hearty" fare; "they can rush you", though, and "the food
isn't as good as it was". / www.osteriabasilico.co.uk; 11.30 pm,
Sun 10.30 pm; no booking, Sat L.

Osteria Dell'Angolo SW1 NEW £42 ❸⓪⑤
47 Marsham St   3268 1077   2–4C
After a "shaky start", this new Westminster Italian is winning plaudits
for its "elegant" cuisine (including "extraordinary pasta") and
"faultless" service; the fantastically "dull" décor, though, is a "major
disappointment". / www.osteriadellangolo.co.uk; 10.30 pm; closed
Sat L & Sun; booking: max 20.

Osteria dell'Arancio SW10 £46 ④④④
383 King's Rd 7349 8111 5–3B
*"Italian wine heaven" – this "relaxed" World's End trattoria offers
a "vast selection" of "excellent and unusual" vintages; the food,
however, seems on the "expensive" side, especially as results can
be "hit-and-miss". / www.osteriadellarancio.co.uk; 11 pm; closed
Mon L & Tue L.*

Osteria Emilia NW3 £38 ❸❸④
85b, Fleet Rd 7433 3317 8–2A
*"At last, a half-decent restaurant in Hampstead!", say fans of this
"crowded" year-old Italian (on the site that was for many years
Zamoyski, long RIP); doubters, though, fear it's "over-rated". / 10 pm;
closed Mon & Sun.*

Ottolenghi £43 ❶❸④
13 Motcomb St, SW1 7823 2707 5–1D
63 Ledbury Rd, W11 7727 1121 6–1B
1 Holland St, W8 7937 0003 5–1A
287 Upper St, N1 7288 1454 8–2D
*"Everything looks so pretty", at these "casual", communal café/delis,
and the food "tastes even better than it looks" – the "unbelievably
sublime cakes", the "incredible salads", and the "amazing brunch
food" too; the seating, though, is "not super-comfy".
/ www.ottolenghi.co.uk; 10.15 pm; W8 & W11 8 pm, Sat 7 pm, Sun 6 pm;
N1 closed Sun D; Holland St takeaway only; W11 & SW1 no booking,
N1 booking for D only.*

**(Brasserie)
Oxo Tower SE1** £62 ⑤⑤❸
Barge House St 7803 3888 9–3A
*"Superb views and live jazz add to the buzzy ambience", in the
"jammed-in" top-floor brasserie of this South Bank landmark; to enjoy
it, though, you too often endure "shoddy" service and sometimes
"flavour-free" food. / www.harveynichols.com; 11 pm, Sun 10 pm.*

**(Restaurant)
Oxo Tower SE1** £74 ⑤⑤④
Barge House St 7803 3888 9–3A
*"A dreary and expensive tourist trap"… "if only the cooking was
as good as the view"… "how do they get away with it year after
year?" – situation normal, then, at this "outrageously pricey" 8th-floor
South Bank landmark, which (as ever) is judged "a total rip-off".
/ www.harveynichols.com; 11 pm, Sun 10 pm.*

Ozer W1 £35 ④❸❸
5 Langham Pl 7323 0505 3–1C
*A "spacious" and "convivial" venture, near Broadcasting House, that's
reinvented itself of late – it now offers a "something-for-everyone"
menu including black cod, game… even fish 'n' chips, alongside the
former Turkish fare; results aren't bad either. / www.sofra.co.uk; 11 pm;
set always available £20 (FP).*

Pacific Oriental EC2 £45 ④④④
52 Threadneedle St 704 4060 9–2C
*A "cavernous" but usually "buzzy" former banking hall – now a
bar/brasserie/restaurant – that offers "good oriental food for a City
lunch"; in the bigger picture, though, standards might be said to be
"lacklustre". / www.orientalrestaurantgroup.co.uk; 10.30 pm; closed
Sat & Sun; no trainers.*

The Paddyfield SW12 £21 ❸❸⑤
Bedford Hill   8772 1145   10–2C
A "small and hectic", "canteen-style" Balham Thai; it offers
"very good" food at "cheap" prices, plus "the added incentive
of BYO". / 10.30 pm, Sat & Sun 11 pm; D only; no credit cards.

Il Pagliaccio SW6 £33 ④❸❷
182-184 Wandsworth Bridge Rd   7371 5253   10–1B
"Beware child-haters!" – this "cheap 'n' cheerful" Italian (specialising
in pizza) offers a "massively bambino-friendly" experience; by night
it's (even) more raucous, complete with "singing waiters".
/ www.paggs.co.uk; midnight; no Amex.

Le Pain Quotidien £33 ④④❸
Branches throughout London
"Bread to die for" and "the best bowls of coffee" help make these
"faux-rustic" Belgian cafés – part of an international chain – popular
places to hang out, particularly for breakfast; sadly, though, they're
becoming "so overpriced". / www.painquotidien.com; 7 pm-10 pm;
no booking at some branches, especially at weekends.

The Painted Heron SW10 £46 ❶❷❸
112 Cheyne Walk   7351 5232   5–3B
"Simply amazing", "eclectic" and "refined" Indian cuisine makes
it well worth seeking out this "hard-to-find" – and rather "unexciting"-
looking – spot, off Chelsea Embankment. / www.thepaintedheron.com;
11 pm; closed Sat L & Sun.

The Palm SW1 NEW £75 ④❸④
1 Pont St   7201 0710   5–1D
If you "stick to the set lunch menu", you can get "very good value"
at this swanky new Belgravia outpost of a major US steakhouse chain
(once the site of Drones, RIP); otherwise, it's "extremely expensive",
and, on our early-days visit, we couldn't quite see the justification.
/ www.thepalm.com; 11 pm, Sun 9 pm; closed Mon L; set weekday L £33 (FP).

The Palmerston SE22 £43 ❷❸❸
91 Lordship Ln   8693 1629   1–4D
"Everything you'd want from your local, and well worth the trip if it
isn't!" – this "top gastropub", down East Dulwich way, offers "fine"
and "seasonal" British cooking "without pretence".
/ www.thepalmerston.net; 10 pm, Sun 9.30 pm; no Amex; set weekday L
£26 (FP).

La Pampa Grill £42 ❸④④
4 Northcote Rd, SW11   7924 1167   10–2C
60 Battersea Rise, SW11   7924 4774   10–2C
"A simple formula with guaranteed results"; you get "excellent
steaks" in "lots of varieties" – but "not much else" – at this duo
of "unpretentious" Battersea Argentineans. / 10.30 pm, Fri & Sat
11.30 pm; D only; Battersea Rise closed Sun & Mon; no Amex.

The Pantechnicon SW1 £50 ❸❷❷
10 Motcomb St   7730 6074   5–1D
"Being in Belgravia, it's a bit grand", but this "friendly" gastroboozer –
complete with "beautiful furniture and leather seats" – has been
"a really welcome addition" to the area, thanks not least to its
"very decent posh pub food". / www.thepantechnicon.com; 11 pm.

Paolina Café WCI £18 ❸❸⑤
181 Kings Cross Rd   7278 8176   8–3D
"Judge it by what's on your plate, not how it looks!"; fans of this "tiny" BYO Thai café, by King's Cross, say its "fantastic" food helps them overlook its "shockingly shabby" interior. / 10 pm; closed Sat L & Sun; no credit cards.

Papillon SW3 £54 ❸❸❸
96 Draycott Ave   7225 2555   5–2C
Sorren Jessen's Chelsea brasserie is a "civilised" sort of place with "smart" Belle Epoque styling, "authentic" French cuisine, and an "extensive" wine list – overall, however, performance is "sound", rather than anything more. / www.papillonchelsea.co.uk; midnight, Sat & Sun 10 pm; set dinner £35 (FP).

Pappa Ciccia £28 ❷❷❷
105-107 Munster Rd, SW6   7384 1884   10–1B
41 Fulham High St, SW6   7736 0900   10–1B
90 Lower Richmond Rd, SW15   8789 9040   10–1A
"Delicious" pizza, a "fun" atmosphere and "good" staff win all-round praise for this small Fulham/Putney chain; at the SW6 branches (only), you can BYO for modest corkage. / www.pappaciccia.com; 11 pm, Sat & Sun 11.30 pm; SW6 no credit cards.

Paradise by Way of Kensal Green W10 £40 ❷❷❶
19 Kilburn Ln   8969 0098   1–2B
It's well off the beaten track, but this vast and "impressive" operation (spiritually part of Notting Hill) is "hard to get into at peak times"; the food can be "excellent", but it's the "brilliant interior and real buzz" that makes it "one of the best gastropubs in town". / www.theparadise.co.uk; 10.30 pm, Sun 8 pm; closed weekday L & Sat D; set weekday L £25 (FP).

Paradiso Olivelli £32 ④④④
9 St Christopher's Pl, W1   7486 3196   3–1A
35 Store St, WC1   7255 2554   2–1C
61 The Cut, SE1   7261 1221   9–4A
Another mixed performance this year from these Italian stand-bys; fans find them "useful" places serving "more-than-adequate" pizza and other "simple" fare – critics just say "never again". / www.ristoranteparadiso.co.uk; midnight; WC1 closed Sun.

El Parador NW1 £31 ❷❷❷
245 Eversholt St   7387 2789   8–3C
"Don't be deceived by the humble surroundings", or the "run down" location – this "friendly" tapas bar, near Euston, serves "delicious food at remarkably good prices". / www.elparadorlondon.com; 11 pm, Fri & Sat 11.30 pm, Sun 9.30 pm; closed Sat L & Sun L.

The Park
Mandarin Oriental SW1 £68 ❷❸❸
66 Knightsbridge   7235 2000   5–1D
This Knightsbridge hotel's 'other' restaurant – the main one is Foliage – is a surprisingly good all-rounder, with "top-notch" food, and views of Hyde Park which make lunch or brunch here a "memorable" experience; but it's to be swept away in the spring of 2010, to make way for the arrival of Heston Blumenthal later in the year. / www.mandarinoriental.com; 10.30 pm.

Pasha SW7 £49 ⑤④❷
1 Gloucester Rd 7589 7969 5–1B
*With its "little coves", rose petals and belly dancing, this "fun" South
Kensington townhouse-Moroccan "is definitely the place to go for
romance"; shame about the food, though – it's sometimes "revolting".
/ www.pasha-restaurant.co.uk; midnight, Thu-Sat 1 am.*

Pasta Brown £44 ④❸⑤
31-32 Bedford St, WC2 7836 7486 4–3C
35-36 Bow St, WC2 7379 5775 4–2D
*Presumably because they seem to be aimed at tourists, these
Theatreland pasta-stops attracted little survey commentary; such as
there was gives a lukewarm endorsement "for a pre-theatre or opera
meal". / www.pastabrown.com; 11 pm, Fri & Sat 11.30 pm, Sun 7 pm; closed
Sun D; no booking Sat before 8 pm.*

Patara £45 ❷❷❸
15 Greek St, W1 7437 1071 4–2A
3-7 Maddox St, W1 7499 6008 3–2C
181 Fulham Rd, SW3 7351 5692 5–2C
9 Beauchamp Pl, SW3 7581 8820 5–1C
*"Lovely refined Thai cooking" and "elegantly performing" staff have
won a big following for this "pleasant" (if slightly "dull") group;
however a slight recent "drop-off in service" seems symptomatic
of slipping standards generally. / www.pataralondon.com; 10.30 pm.*

Paternoster Chop House EC4 £52 ④④④
Warwick Ct, Paternoster Sq 7029 9400 9–2B
*"The view of St Paul's is really the best part" of a visit to this
"fantastically-situated" City eatery (which has some "perfect" outside
tables too); it's "overpriced", but – by the dreary standards of the
D&D group – can serve some "surprisingly good" food.
/ www.danddlondon.com; 10.30 pm; closed Sat & Sun D; set always available
£30 (FP).*

Patio W12 £30 ④❷❶
5 Goldhawk Rd 8743 5194 7–1C
*"For a fun and filling night out" (especially in a group), this "old-
fashioned" Shepherd's Bush venue – where "ebullient" staff serve
up "enormous" portions of "tasty" Polish stodge – is "a hoot".
/ 11.30 pm; closed Sat L & Sun L.*

Pâtisserie Valerie £26 ④⑤❸
Branches throughout London
*The "lovely" pastries ("terrific croissants") and "excellent coffee"
survive – for now – but other aspects of these much-loved cafés are
"going downhill fast", as entrepreneur Luke Johnson 'rolls the concept
out' across the high streets of Britain – the food is too often
"slapdash" nowadays, and service can be plain "rude".
/ www.patisserie-valerie.co.uk; 6 pm-8 pm; Old Compton St 7.30 pm, Wed-Sat
10.30 pm; Hans Cr 11.30 pm; no booking except Old Compton St Sun-Thu.*

Patterson's W1 £65 ❸❸④
4 Mill St 7499 1308 3–2C
*An "off-the-beaten-track", family-run Mayfair establishment, whose
"interesting" cuisine and "consistent good value" (especially
at lunchtime) makes it "a winner every time"; ambience-wise it's
"a bit bland" (but "not bad for business").
/ www.pattersonsrestaurant.co.uk; 11 pm; closed Sat & Sun; set weekday L
£37 (FP).*

Paul £28 ❸④④
115 Marylebone High St, W1   7224 5615   2–1A
29-30 Bedford St, WC2   7836 3304   4–3C
73 Gloucester Rd, SW7   7373 1232   5–2B
43 Hampstead High St, NW3   7794 8657   8–1A
147 Fleet St, EC4   7353 5874   9–2A
France's largest chain of high-street bakers continues to take the capital by storm with its "authentic" bread, "divine" pastries, "delicious" sandwiches and "great" coffee; the service in the adjoining tea rooms, though, is often "atrocious" – "do they do it on purpose?" / www.paul-uk.com; 7 pm-8.30 pm; no booking.

Pearl WC1 £79 ❸❸❸
252 High Holborn   7829 7000   2–1D
Jun Tanaka's "exquisite" cooking has made quite a name for this "discreet" Holborn dining room, in a "vast" and "elegant" (but slightly "soulless") former banking hall; even some fans are "dubious about the prices", though, and ratings generally slipped a little this year. / www.pearl-restaurant.com; 10 pm; closed Sat L & Sun; set weekday L £50 (FP).

Pearl Liang W2 £37 ❷❷❷
8 Sheldon Sq   7289 7000   6–1C
"What an excellent find in bleak Paddington Basin!"; this surprisingly atmospheric, basement all-rounder is really quite a "hidden gem", and it serves up some "superb Chinese food" at very "decent prices" – most notably "fantastic" dim sum "on a par with Royal China's". / www.pearlliang.co.uk; 11 pm.

The Peasant EC1 £42 ❸④❷
240 St John St   7336 7726   8–3D
This 'early-wave' Farringdon gastropub seems to be on the way back to greatness, thanks not least to its "ever-improving" and "good-value" cuisine; it's a "beautiful" place too – if in a very Victorian way – and has a "great terrace". / www.thepeasant.co.uk; 11 pm, Sun 9.30 pm.

Pellicano SW3 £45 ❸❷❸
19-21 Elystan St   7589 3718   5–2C
"Reliable" food and "charming" service win continued support for this "good-value" Chelsea Italian stand-by. / www.pellicanorestaurant.co.uk; 11 pm, Sat 10.30 pm.

E Pellicci E2 £14 ④❶❶
332 Bethnal Green Rd   7739 4873   12–1C
This East End caff is famous for its "fabulous" (listed) Art Deco interior; while service is "adorable", the food is generally "little better than your average greasy spoon", but fans insist that breakfast is the "best in London by a Cockney mile!" / 4.15 pm; L only, closed Sun; no credit cards.

The Pembroke SW5 𝗡𝗘𝗪 £37 ❸❷❷
261 Old Brompton Rd   7373 8337   5–2A
"No longer catering just for a minority!"; Earl's Court legend the Coleherne (RIP) – in its day, the Most Famous Gay Pub in the World – has been "completely reincarnated" as this "engaging" gastropub, and offers a "regularly-changing" menu that's "more interesting than most". / www.realpubs.co.uk; 11 pm, Fri & Sat midnight, Sun 10.30 pm; no Amex.

Peninsular
Holiday Inn Express SE10 £30 ❸④⑤
85 Bugsbys Way 8858 2028 1–3D
An oddly-sited Greenwich oriental that's "nothing to look at"; "top-class dim sum", however, heads up its menu of "solid and authentic fare" which, in particular, attracts "crowds of Chinese customers".
/ www.mychinesefood.co.uk/; 11.30 pm, Sun 11 pm.

The Pepper Tree SW4 £22 ❸❷❷
19 Clapham Common S'side 7622 1758 10–2D
Prepare to queue for the "cheap-as-chips" Thai food on offer at this "really buzzy" canteen, by Clapham Common tube.
/ www.thepeppertree.co.uk; 11 pm, Sun & Mon 10.30 pm; no Amex; no booking at D.

Père Michel W2 £42 ❸❷④
11 Bathurst St 7723 5431 6–2D
A veteran Gallic bistro, in Bayswater, characterised by "old-fashioned charm, faded red velour and white table linen"; it attracts a "regular clientele" with its "reliable, if unexceptional" cuisine; fish is a highlight.
/ 11 pm; closed Sat L & Sun.

Pescatori £50 ❸❷❸
11 Dover Street, W1 7493 2652 3–3C
55-57 Charlotte St, W1 7580 3289 2–1C
Some reporters feel the formula "needs a revamp", but this long-running West End chain is generally seen as a "good, standard fall-back" thanks to its "easy-going" service and its "well-presented" fish dishes. / www.pescatori.co.uk; 11 pm; closed Sat L & Sun.

Petek N4 £25 ❸❸④
94-96 Stroud Green Rd 7619 3933 8–1D
"Just doubled in size, and you can see why" – in under-provided Finsbury Park, this "cosy" spot has quite a name for its "reasonably-priced" Turkish fare, and it comes in "enormous portions" too.
/ www.petekrestaurant.co.uk; 11 pm; Mon-Thu D only, Fri-Sun open L & D.

Petersham Hotel TW10 £56 ❸❸❷
Nightingale Ln 8940 7471 1–4A
"Enchanting" views over the Thames, "high-quality" cooking and "impeccable" service make this rather "old-fashioned" Richmond dining room a "lovely place", especially "for a family celebration"; "book early for the best seats". / www.petershamhotel.co.uk; 9.45 pm, Sun 8.45 pm.

Petersham Nurseries TW10 £56 ❷④❶
Off Petersham Rd 8605 3627 1–4A
Skye Gyngell's "imaginative" cuisine is "really incredible", say fans of this "unique" venue, whose "delightful", "Boho-chic" setting – a glass house within a fully-functioning garden centre – makes a "perfect place for lunch"; the "self-conscious quirkiness" can grate, though, and critics find the operation "smug" and "overpriced".
/ www.petershamnurseries.com; L only, closed Mon.

La Petite Auberge N1 £33 ④④❷
283 Upper St 7359 1046 8–2D
A "rustic-French" Islington bistro that's often "bustling"; rather inauthentically, it does "a very good-value Sunday roast" – at other times it's a "useful" stand-by (if, on some accounts, "not much more"). / www.petiteauberge.co.uk; 11 pm, Fri-Sat 11.30 pm, Sun 10.30 pm.

La Petite Maison W1 £77 ❷❸❷
54 Brooks Mews 7495 4774 3–2B
Nice comes to London in ever-more impressive fashion, at this
"casual" but "chic" Mayfair two-year-old, where the "perfect, light
and delicious" take on provençal cuisine (designed for sharing) only
gets better; "pricey but worth it!". / www.lpmlondon.co.uk; 10.15 pm,
Sun 9 pm.

Pétrus SW1 NEW £90
1 Kinnerton St 5–1D
Opening in late-2009, this Belgravia newcomer from the Gordon
Ramsay group revives the name until recently associated with Marcus
Wareing's venture at the nearby Berkeley; an undoubted success here
might do wonders for the group's somewhat battered reputation;
price is our guesstimate.

Pham Sushi EC1 £27 ❶❷④
159 Whitecross St 7251 6336 12–2A
This "simple" Formica-tables Japanese café, in a "slightly dingy area"
near the Barbican, again inspires raves for its "sublime" and
"very original" sushi (especially the crunchy tuna roll)… and
at "half the price of the big names". / www.phamsushi.co.uk; 10 pm;
closed Sat L & Sun.

Pho £25 ④❸④
3 Great Titchfield St, W1 7436 0111 3–1C
Westfield, Ariel Way, W12 7436 0111 7–1C
86 St John St, EC1 7253 7624 9–1A
"Quick and reasonably-priced Vietnamese soup dishes" have won
a big following for this fast-growing mini-chain; looks as if it's
becoming "a victim of its own success", though, inspiring many gripes
this year about "insipid" food and "inefficient" service.
/ www.phocafe.co.uk; EC1 10 pm, Fri & Sat 10.30 pm; W1 10.30 pm;
W12 9 pm, Sat 7 pm, Sun 6 pm; EC1 closed Sat L & Sun; W1 closed Sun;
no Amex; no booking.

The Phoenix SW1 £34 ❸④④
14 Palace St 7828 8136 2–4B
"A good place to know about near Victoria"; this backstreet
gastroboozer may be a tad "clinical", and have sometimes "slow"
service, but the food rarely disappoints. / www.geronimo-inns.co.uk;
10 pm, Sun 9 pm.

The Phoenix SW3 £43 ④❸❸
23 Smith St 7730 9182 5–2D
"A great Sunday roast" is the top draw to this "always-busy" pub,
just a little removed from the hubbub of the King's Road.
/ www.geronimo-inns.co.uk; 10 pm, Sun 9.30 pm.

Phoenix Bar & Grill SW15 £43 ❸④❸
162-164 Lower Richmond Rd 8780 3131 10–1A
This Putney neighbourhood spot typically wins praise for its "good"
Italian food, "helpful" staff and "pleasant" ambience – this year,
however, saw a few gripes about "slow" service and "undistinguished"
cooking. / www.sonnys.co.uk; 10.30 pm; closed Sun D; set weekday L
£27 (FP).

Phoenix Palace NW1 £35 ❷④④
3-5 Glentworth St 7486 3515 2–1A
*"Always packed with Chinese people", this "Hong Kong-style"
(and "surprisingly large") spot, near Baker Street tube, is "hard to
beat for dim sum", and serves a "very comprehensive" à la carte
menu too; service, though, is "a lottery". / www.phoenixpalace.uk.com;
11.15 pm, Sun 10.30 pm.*

Piccolino £39 ④④④
21 Heddon St, W1 7287 4029 3–2C
27-29 Bellevue Rd, SW17 8767 1713 10–2C
38 High St, SW19 8946 8019 10–2B
11 Exchange Sq, EC2 7375 2568 12–2B
*"Just what we needed – another chain selling lazy stodge!"; these
aspirational Italians once seemed promising, but have become "highly
variable" – fans say they're "fine for a quick pizza or pasta",
but overall they're rated "average at best".
/ www.piccolinorestaurants.co.uk; 11 pm, Sun 10 pm.*

PIED À TERRE W1 £93 ❷❷❸
34 Charlotte St 7636 1178 2–1C
*David Moore's "beacon of excellence", in a Fitzrovia townhouse,
continues to put in an "exemplary" performance, thanks to Shane
Osborn's "truly original" cuisine, the "biblical" wine list and the
"exceptionally professional" service. / www.pied-a-terre.co.uk; 10.45 pm;
closed Sat L & Sun; booking: max 6; set weekday L £52 (FP).*

The Pig's Ear SW3 £39 ❸❸❷
35 Old Church St 7352 2908 5–3C
*"Quirkily decorated" in Art Nouveau style, this "fun" pub, in a
Chelsea side street, is a supremely "cosy", spot with "good and
honest" food – lighter dishes in the ground floor bar, more ambitious
fare in the "smarter" upstairs room. / www.thepigs-ear.com; 10.30 pm;
closed Sun D.*

The Pigalle Club W1 £65 ④④❷
215-217 Piccadilly 988 5470 3–3D
*Scant reports again on this Piccadilly Circus supper club, where the
food is really a "sideline"; standards of its "limited" menu seem
on the up, though, leaving some reporters "pleasantly surprised".
/ www.thepigalleclub.com; 11.30 pm; D only, closed Sun.*

Pinchito EC1 £31 ④❸❷
32 Featherstone St 7490 0121 12–1A
*A "vibrant" year-old bar, near Old Street tube; fans still praise its
"simple" and "excellent" tapas, but critics find this place something
of a "let-down". / www.pintxopeople.co.uk; 11 pm; closed Sat L & Sun.*

ping pong £29 ④④❸
10 Paddington St, W1   7009 9600   2–1A
29a James St, W1   7034 3100   3–1A
45 Gt Marlborough St, W1   7851 6969   3–2C
48 Eastcastle St, W1   7079 0550   3–1C
48 Newman St, W1   7291 3080   3–1C
74-76 Westbourne Grove, W2   7313 9832   6–1B
83-84 Hampstead High St, NW3   7433 0930   8–2A
Southbank Centre, SE1   7960 4160   2–3D
3-6 Steward St, E1   7422 7650   9–2D
St Katharine Docks, E1   7680 7850   9–3D
3 Appold St, EC2   7422 0780   12–2B
Bow Bells Hs, 1 Bread St, EC4   7651 0880   9–2B
For a "dim sum frenzy" – with "delicious" cocktails, and "wonderful
teas" too – many reporters still tip this "sleekly-designed" chain;
it's "not as good as it used to be", though, and sterner critics just say
it's "vile". / www.pingpongdimsum.com; varies; EC2 & EC4 closed Sat & Sun;
booking: min 8.

El Pirata W1 £32 ❸②②
5-6 Down St   7491 3810   3–4B
A "buzzy" ("slightly manic") tapas veteran, that's long been a rare
"very affordable" Mayfair destination. / www.elpirata.co.uk; 11.30 pm;
closed Sat L & Sun; set weekday L £12 (FP).

El Pirata de Tapas W2 NEW £30 ❸❸❸
115 Westbourne Grove   7727 5000   6–1B
"Imaginative" and "beautifully-presented" tapas have won an instant
following for this "unassuming" but "lively" Bayswater newcomer
(where desserts, somewhat inauthentically, are particularly good);
service can be "slow" though, and not everyone is taken with the
overall experience. / www.elpiratadetapas.co.uk; 11 pm.

Pissarro's W4 £40 ④④❶
Corney Reach Way   8994 3111   10–1A
"It's especially lovely on sunny days", in the conservatory of this "well-
hidden" spot, "right on the river", near Chiswick House; perhaps
unsurprisingly, the "reasonable" Gallic fare is somewhat "expensive
for what it is". / www.pissarro.co.uk; 10 pm; closed Sun D.

Pizza Metro SW11 £36 ❷❸④
64 Battersea Rise   7228 3812   10–2C
"It introduced London to pizza-by-the-metre", but this "once-great"
Battersea Neapolitan is "resting on its laurels"; on a good day,
the food is still "fantastic", but "prices are heading up, as standards
come down"; (coming soon – a dance floor in the basement).
/ www.pizzametropizza.co.uk; midnight; closed weekday L.

Pizza on the Park SW1 £35 ❸❸❸
11 Knightsbridge   7235 5273   5–1D
"Though possibly in need of a slight refresh", this "efficient" '70s
stalwart, near Hyde Park Corner, has an agreeably airy ambience and
an affordable pizza-to-burgers menu; the top attraction, however,
is its "brilliant basement jazz club" (entry charge applies).
/ www.pizzaonthepark.co.uk; 10.45 pm, Sun 9.45 pm.

(Ciro's) Pizza Pomodoro SW3 £38 ❸④❷
51 Beauchamp Pl   7589 1278   5–1C
"Rocking" pizza, and "good live music" have made this "boisterous"
cellar a popular Knightsbridge rendezvous for decades (especially
later in the evening); its City offshoot has now closed.
/ www.pomodoro.co.uk; 1 am; D only; no booking.

PizzaExpress £28 ④❸❸

Branches throughout London

More "adventurous" menu additions (such as "pizzas with a salad in the middle") "have added a new dimension" to this ultra-"trusty" multiple – "still by far the best of the chain pizzerias"; kids, famously, "love it". / www.pizzaexpress.co.uk; 11.30 pm-midnight; most City branches closed all or part of weekend; no booking at most branches.

Pizzeria Oregano N1 £31 ❸❷❸

19 St Albans Pl 7288 1123 8–3D

"Just yards from the hell holes of Upper Street", this "friendly", "no-frills" Islington café is a "reliable" sort of place, serving "scrumptious and genuine pizza" and "fine pasta". / 11.30 pm, Sun 10.30 pm; closed Mon, Tue-Fri D only, Sat & Sun open L & D; no Amex.

PJ's SW3 £48 ④❸❸

52 Fulham Rd 7581 0025 5–2C

An "eternal favourite" of Chelsea's younger "beautiful people", this US-style hang-out is "THE place for weekend brunch" hereabouts; it can make a "fun" venue for "burgers and ribs" too. / www.pjsbarandgrill.co.uk; 11.45 pm, Sun 11.15 pm.

The Place Below EC2 £19 ❸④❸

St Mary-le-Bow, Cheapside 7329 0789 9–2C

A "great veggie lunch spot" located in the crypt of an impressive City church, where you choose from the "regularly changing" selection at the counter, and eat at benches or wooden tables; BYO (but possibly coming soon – a licence, and evening opening). / www.theplacebelow.co.uk; L only, closed Sat & Sun; no Amex; need 10+ to book.

Planet Hollywood SW1 £41

57-60 Haymarket 7437 7639 4–4A

Following redevelopment of the original site, the new London outpost of the Tinseltown-themed chain re-opened in mid-2009 at a new West End location; we somehow didn't get there in time to review it for this guide, but early press reviews have been truly terrible. / www.planethollywoodlondon.co.uk; 1 am, Sun 12.30 am.

Plateau E14 £65 ④④❸

Canada Pl 7715 7100 11–1C

"Fabulous views" and "a beautiful summer terrace" help this very "corporate" operation fill a "much-needed niche" – "a serious restaurant in Canary Wharf"; service is "patchy", though, and the place exemplifies what one reporter describes as the D&D group's "cynical and careless attitude to food". / www.plateaurestaurant.co.uk; 10.30 pm; closed Sat L & Sun.

Pod EC2 £7 ❸❸④

162-163 London Wall 7256 5506 9–2C

Local office workers are lucky to have this (non-chain) City snackery to hand; the "very healthy" and "wholesome" fare it offers includes some "masterful" soups. / www.podfood.co.uk; L only, closed Sat & Sun.

Poissonnerie de l'Avenue SW3 £59 ❷❷❸

82 Sloane Ave 7589 2457 5–2C

A "timeless" Brompton Cross parlour that's still "a favourite for seafood", thanks to its "impeccable" cuisine and "discreet" service; "it's not a place for young people", though – "most of the customers are well over 60". / www.poissonneriedelavenue.co.uk; 11.15 pm, Sun 11 pm.

(Ognisko Polskie)
The Polish Club SW7 £42 ④❸❸
55 Prince's Gate, Exhibition Rd   7589 4635   5–1C
A visit to this "wonderful" time warp – an émigrés' club in South
Kensington – can be quite an experience; the "heavy" Polish fare isn't
art, but it is "plentiful" and quite "good of its type"; pleasant terrace
for sunny days. / www.ognisko.com; 11 pm; no trainers; set always available
£22 (FP).

Le Pont de la Tour SE1 £62 ⑤④❷
36d Shad Thames   7403 8403   9–4D
"You simply pay a fortune for the view" at D&D's "fabulously
situated", but "unjustifiably expensive" riverside operation, where
staff can be "completely uninterested" and the ever more "mediocre"
food "desperately needs to improve". / www.lepontdelatour.co.uk; 11 pm,
Sun 10 pm; no trainers; set Sun L £47 (FP).

Popeseye £42 ❷❸④
108 Blythe Rd, W14   7610 4578   7–1C
277 Upper Richmond Rd, SW15   8788 7733   10–2A
With their "superb quality steaks" and "sensibly-priced" clarets, these
"outstanding" little steakhouses "always hit the spot"; "it hardly looks
like they can have spent more than £100 on the décor", however,
and Putney – in contrast to Brook Green – is often "quiet".
/ www.popeseye.com; 10.30 pm; D only, closed Sun; no credit cards.

La Porchetta Pizzeria £28 ❸❸❸
33 Boswell St, WC1   7242 2434   2–1D
141-142 Upper St, N1   7288 2488   8–2D
147 Stroud Green Rd, N4   7281 2892   8–1D
74-77 Chalk Farm Rd, NW1   7267 6822   8–2B
84-86 Rosebery Ave, EC1   7837 6060   9–1A
"Noisy, chaotic, great fun and very child-friendly" – this "jolly" Italian
chain serves "lovely, thin pizza" (and "lots of it"), at "very reasonable
prices"; the Crouch Hill original "is certainly the best". / last orders
varies by branch; WC1 closed Sat L & Sun; N1 closed Mon-Thu L; N4 closed
weekday L; no Amex.

Port of Manila W6 NEW £29
129-131 Brackenbury Rd   8741 2099   7–1C
This Hammersmith backstreet newcomer (on the site of The
Brackenbury, RIP) opens just as this guide goes to press; hopefully the
rarity value of a Philippino menu will make up for a makeover
seemingly done on a shoestring budget. / www.portofmanila.co.uk; 11 pm;
closed Sun D.

Portal EC1 £57 ❸❸❷
88 St John St   7253 6950   9–1B
"Distinctive" Portuguese cuisine, "excellent" wines and a "light" and
"lovely" setting make this "spacious" Clerkenwell venture a "smart"
business choice, in particular; if it were not for continued reports
of "highs and lows", it could truly be a "great all-rounder".
/ www.portalrestaurant.com; 10.15 pm; closed Sat L & Sun.

La Porte des Indes W1 £56 ❸❸❷
32 Bryanston St   7224 0055   2–2A
For an overall "experience", this "Tardis-like" Marble Arch "oasis" –
complete with "palm trees and water features" – can be
"impressive"; service is a bit "random", though, and prices for the
Franco-Indian cuisine are "steep". / www.pilondon.net; 11.30 pm,
Sun 10.30 pm.

Porters English Restaurant WC2 £31 ④④④
17 Henrietta St 7836 6466 4–3C
Little (and, as ever, mediocre) feedback this year on this English-themed eatery in Covent Garden; owner Lord Bradford doesn't like us calling it a 'tourist trap' – how else, though, to explain why reporters so conscientiously seem to avoid it? / www.porters.uk.com; 11.30 pm, Sun 10.30 pm; no Amex.

Il Portico W8 £40 ❸①❷
277 Kensington High St 7602 6262 7–1D
"Behind a dull exterior", by the Kensington Odeon, an old-time family-run Italian that "never fails to delight"; it's the "great" ambience that makes it special, though, rather than the "staple" cuisine. / www.ilportico.co.uk; 11.15 pm; closed Sun.

Portobello Ristorante W11 [NEW] £37 ❸④❸
7 Ladbroke Rd 7221 1373 6–2B
"Convincing Neapolitan pizza by the metre" – plus other "traditional southern Italian food" – helps make this inexpensive Notting Hill Gate newcomer worth knowing about, and it has a "fantastic" terrace too; service is "charming", but it can "struggle" . / www.portobellolondon.co.uk; 11.30 pm, Sun 10.15 pm.

The Portrait
National Portrait Gallery WC2 £46 ④④①
St Martin's Pl 7312 2490 4–4B
"Breathtaking views" ("get a window table to be at eye-level with Nelson's Column") are the star turn at this "attractive" and "bustling" top-floor venue, just off Trafalgar Square; to enjoy them, however, you risk "institutionalised" food and "awful" service. / www.searcys.co.uk; Thu-Fri 8.30 pm; Sat-Wed closed D.

Potemkin EC1 £36 ❸④④
144 Clerkenwell Rd 7278 6661 9–1A
A low-key Clerkenwell hang-out, where the food ("quite good") is best sampled as snacks in the ground-floor vodka bar, rather than in the restaurant below; service is "not bad, just Russian". / www.potemkin.co.uk; 10.30 pm; closed Sat L & Sun.

LA POULE AU POT SW1 £50 ❸❸①
231 Ebury St 7730 7763 5–2D
On a Pimlico corner, a "clichéd but perfect" slice of "rural France", which – with its "secluded and dark" nooks – is, yet again, the survey's top choice for romance; the fare is "heart-warming", and service "authentically brusque". / 11 pm, Sun 10 pm.

Pret A Manger £12 ❸❷④
Branches throughout London
"In a world of mediocre sandwiches", this phenomenally "consistent" chain still "sets the standard", thanks to its "generous" and "always fresh" fare, and its "lovely" coffee; service, as ever, is "achingly enthusiastic". / www.pret.com; 4 pm-6 pm; Trafalgar Sq 8 pm; St. Martin's Ln 9 pm; closed Sun (except some West End branches); City branches closed Sat & Sun; no Amex; no booking.

Preto SW1 £30 ④❸④
72 Wilton Rd 7233 8668 2–4B
"Eat – or rather over-eat – as much as you can" at this new Brazilian buffet near Victoria, which offers a "good salad selection" and "hit or miss skewered meat".

The Prince Arthur E8 £37 ❸❷❸
95 Forest Rd 7249 9996 1–1D
"At last, a truly 'gastro' gastropub!" – London Fields residents are delighted with this "reliable" year-old sibling to The Gun, which has made a marked "improvement to the local scene".
/ www.theprincearthurlondonfields.com; 10 pm; Mon-Thu D only, Fri-Sun open L & D; no Amex.

The Prince Of Wales SW15 £39 ❸❸❸
138 Upper Richmond Rd 8788 1552 10–2B
"A great pub for Putney" – this locally-celebrated yearling continues to attract praise for its "solid" food, "friendly" service and "lovely" setting. / www.princeofwalesputney.co.uk; 10 pm, Sun 9.30 pm; no Amex.

The Princess EC2 £42 ❸④❸
76 Paul St 7729 9270 12–1B
Up a spiral staircase above a bustling Shoreditch pub, there's a dining room where the cooking is generally "very reliable".
/ www.theprincessofshoreditch.com; 10.30 pm; closed Sat L & Sun D.

Princess Garden W1 £52 ❷❷④
8 North Audley St 7493 3223 3–2A
For a "luxurious" Chinese meal, this "little-known" stalwart offers a "very spacious" setting and "reliable" food (notably, "excellent" dim sum); the décor can seem "sterile" however, and the experience undoubtedly comes "at Mayfair prices".
/ www.princessgardenofmayfair.co.uk; 11.15 pm.

Princess Victoria W12 £37 ❸❸❷
217 Uxbridge Rd 8749 5886 7–1B
Marooned in a remote bit of Shepherd's Bush, this "beautifully restored" pub has quickly won a huge fan club, thanks primarily to its "stunning" setting and "tremendous" wine list, but also to the "competent" cuisine. / www.princessvictoria.co.uk; 10.30 pm, Sun 9.30 pm; no Amex.

Princi W1 NEW £18 ❸④❶
135 Wardour St 7478 8888 3–2D
The new Soho outpost of Milanese baker Rocco Princi (the 'Armani del pane'), in conjunction with our own 'local hero', Alan Yau, feels like a "little bit of Milan", offering a "stunning array" of baked goods, and pizza, and "gorgeous" coffee too; "go for a calm breakfast", though – "it's too much of a scrum at other times". / www.princi.co.uk; midnight, Sun 10 pm; no booking.

Priory House W14 £28 ❸❸❷
58 Milson Rd 7371 3999 7–1C
"A very cosy and moody" little hang-out in the back streets of Olympia, serving "tempting" cocktails and tapas that "owe little to Spain, but are sound and tasty". / www.priorybars.com; 10 pm; closed Sat L & Sun.

Prism EC3 £70 ⑤④⑤
147 Leadenhall St 7256 3875 9–2D
Harvey Nics's "cavernous" former banking hall can "set the right tone" for a City lunch; it's easy to "feel lost" in this "soulless" space, however, and its "eye-watering" prices, and "more-show-than-substance" cuisine make it best on "someone else's expenses".
/ www.harveynichols.com; 10 pm; closed Sat & Sun.

Le Provence SW13 NEW £38
7 White Hart Ln 8878 4092 10–1A
John McClements has rebranded this former branch of Ma Cuisine
in Barnes – the most successful of his cosy, bistro chain; we didn't visit
before this guide went to press, but first impressions of its mid-priced
French formula are: 'plus ça change…' / www.leprovence.co.uk;
10.30 pm.

The Providores W1 £61 ❸❷④
109 Marylebone High St 7935 6175 2–1A
The "intimate" ("squeezed in") restaurant above the Tapa Room
offers "brilliantly creative" fusion fare plus a "terrific" Kiwi wine list;
for critics, though, the premium over downstairs is "hard to justify" –
"the food's the same quality, but comes at almost twice the price!"
/ www.theprovidores.co.uk; 10.30 pm; booking: max 12.

(Tapa Room)
The Providores W1 £45 ④④❸
109 Marylebone High St 7935 6175 2–1A
Peter Gordon's "fusion" food is "so interesting", say fans, and the
"incredible brunches" on offer at this "buzzy" Marylebone bar/diner
have a particular reputation; it's "noisy", "crowded" and "extremely
expensive", though, and doubters find it simply "hyped".
/ www.theprovidores.co.uk; 10.30 pm.

The Punch Tavern EC4 £27 ❸④❸
99 Fleet St 7353 6658 9–2A
Near Ludgate Circus, an historic City tavern, where "a good-value
lunchtime buffet" is an unusual feature. / www.punchtavern.com; 11 pm,
Thu & Fri midnight; closed Sat D & Sun.

Pure £18 ❸❷④
39 Beak St, W1 7287 3708 3–2D
47 Goodge St, W1 7436 3601 2–1C
'California' is apparently to be dropped from the name of this small
chain as this guide goes to press; no other change is planned, though,
to its "wide range of wraps, juices and salads" which fans say offer
"the healthiest and tastiest of office lunches". / www.purecalifornia.co.uk;
5 pm-7 pm by branch; Beak Street closed Sun; no booking.

Putney Station SW15 £30 ❸❷❷
94-98 Upper Richmond Rd 8780 0242 10–2B
"John Brinkley's excellent-value wine list" is the prime attraction
at this "cheerful" venture, by East Putney tube, which serves a "well-
realised" menu of burgers, pizza and more; nice sunny-day terrace.
/ www.brinkleys.com; midnight, Mon & Sun 11.30 pm.

Quadrato
Four Seasons Hotel E14 £74 ❸❷⑤
Westferry Circus 7510 1857 11–1B
With its "efficient" service and "competent" cooking, this grand
Canary Wharf hotel dining room has its uses, especially for business
(even if it can "lack ambience)"; "excellent Sunday brunch".
/ www.fourseasons.com; 10.30 pm; booking: max 14; set always available
£47 (FP).

Quaglino's SW1 £50 ⑤⑤⑤
16 Bury St 7930 6767 3–3D
It may "thrill" the odd first-time visitor, but D&D group's "ocean liner-style" St James's brasserie is really just "incredibly naff" nowadays, too often criticised for "poor" food, "rude" service and "ridiculous" prices. / www.quaglinos.co.uk; midnight; closed Sun; no trainers.

The Quality Chop House EC1 £39 ❷❷❸
94 Farringdon Rd 7837 5093 9–1A
"Charming, old-school décor" (with "infamously uncomfy" benches) sets a "enjoyably nostalgic" tone at this former 'working class caterer', in Farringdon – it has long been at the forefront of raising "traditional British basics" to a sometimes "brilliant" level.
/ www.qualitychophouse.co.uk; 11 pm, Sun 10 pm; closed Sat L.

Queen's Head W6 £28 ④④❸
13 Brook Grn 7603 3174 7–1C
Just an "average" (if ancient and rambling) Brook Green boozer... which we list because it has a truly "great garden for the summer".
/ www.thespiritgroup.com; 10 pm, Sun 9 pm; no booking.

Queen's Head & Artichoke NW1 £36 ④❸❸
30-32 Albany St 7916 6206 8–4B
For a "casual" tapas meal, the bar of this "buzzing" gastropub, near Regent's Park, still wins praise (and there's also an "interesting", more "formal" dining room upstairs); recently, however, there have been some "hit-or-miss" reports. / www.theartichoke.net; 10.15 pm.

The Queens Arms SW1 £35 ④❸❸
11 Warwick Way 7834 3313 2–4B
The fact that this "relaxed" gastropub is "one of the buzziest places in Pimlico" is perhaps as much a comment on the area as on the establishment – the food tends to "average".
/ www.thequeensarmspimlico.co.uk; 10 pm.

Le Querce SE23 £32 ❷❷❸
66-68 Brockley Rise 8690 3761 1–4D
The exterior may look "unprepossessing", but this Sardinian "gem", in deepest Brockley, is well worth seeking out for its "terrific" fare; it "helps to know what to order", though – highlights include "excellent pasta" and "amazing ice cream in weird and wonderful flavours". / www.lequercerestaurant.co.uk; 10 pm, Sun 9 pm; closed Mon & Tue L; set Sun L £22 (FP).

Quilon SW1 £55 ❷❶⑤
41 Buckingham Gate 7821 1899 2–4B
"You're painfully aware you're in an hotel dining room", when you visit this posh Indian, near Buckingham Palace; otherwise it really is "a star" – staff are both "efficient" and "friendly", and the cooking is "superb". / www.quilon.co.uk; 11 pm, Sun 10.30 pm; closed Sat L; set weekday L £33 (FP).

Quirinale SW1 £53 ❷❷❸
North Ct, 1 Gt Peter St 7222 7080 2–4C
"Popularity with MPs and civil servants" is a defining feature of this Westminster "gem", which is "hidden-away" in a "light and airy" basement; it offers "mouthwatering" Italian food and "brilliant" wine, and service is notably "competent" too. / www.quirinale.co.uk; 10.30 pm; closed Sat & Sun.

Quo Vadis W1   £52   ❸❸❸
26-29 Dean St   7437 9585   4–2A
Fans give "top marks" to the Hart brothers' reworking of this Soho veteran as a "crisp table-cloth" British grill-restaurant ("a bit like a younger Ivy"), with a "simple" and "solid" menu; doubters – in which camp we place ourselves – find it "over-safe", "overhyped" and "overpriced". / www.quovadissoho.co.uk; 10.30 pm; closed Sun.

Racine SW3   £51   ❷❷❸
239 Brompton Rd   7584 4477   5–2C
"Forever a piece of France", Henry Harris's "high-class" Knightsbridge bistro has a big name for its "immaculate" cooking, and "attentive" service; standards remain high, but there's some feeling that the place is "not the same" since last year's departure of maître d' (and co-founder) Eric Garnier. / 10.30 pm; set Sun L £34 (FP).

Ragam W1   £27   ❶❶⑤
57 Cleveland St   7636 9098   2–1B
"What a dive, but what a great place"!; this "welcoming" and "overcrowded" south Indian veteran, by the Telecom Tower, was seemingly "last decorated in the '70s", but it serves up "stunning, fresh, well-flavoured and really different" food, at "incredible prices"; BYO. / www.ragam.co.uk; 11 pm, Fri & Sat 11.30 pm, Sun 10.30 pm; set weekday L £14 (FP).

Rajasthan   £34   ❸❷④
38-41 Houndsditch, EC3   7626 0033   9–2D
49 Monument St, EC3   7626 1920   9–3C
8 India St, EC3   7488 9777   9–2D
Even if it's "a bit on the safe side", this City Indian chain makes a "good-value" stand-by. / www.rajasthan.co.uk; 11 pm; closed Sat & Sun.

Randa W8   £37   ❸❷④
23 Kensington Church St   7937 5363   5–1A
This "good, honest neighbourhood Lebanese" – an offshoot of the Maroush empire – is a useful "value-for-money" choice in Kensington, albeit one that's "a little lacking in atmosphere". / www.maroush.com; midnight.

Randall & Aubin W1   £45   ❷❷❶
16 Brewer St   7287 4447   3–2D
"People-watching inside, or street-watching outside" – both are attractions to rival the "simple" but "divine" fare at this "ebullient" seafood and champagne bar, "in the heart of Soho"; you may have to queue. / www.randallandaubin.co.uk; 11 pm, Sun 10.30 pm; closed Sun L; no booking.

Rani N3   £26   ❷❷④
7 Long Ln   8349 4386   1–1B
This Finchley old favourite can still produce "excellent" Indian veggie dishes; it draws fans from across London for its "fantastic" buffets and "filling" thalis. / www.raniuk.com; 10 pm.

Ranoush   £34   ❸④④
22 Brompton Rd, SW1   7235 6999   5–1D
338 King's Rd, SW3   7352 0044   5–3C
43 Edgware Rd, W2   7723 5929   6–1D
86 Kensington High St, W8   7938 2234   5–1A
"Awesome shawarmas", "ultra-fresh mezze" and "a large choice of juices" make these Lebanese café/take-aways very popular; service and surroundings, though, are "rather poor". / www.maroush.com; 1 am-3 am.

Ransome's Dock SW11 £44 ④❸❸
35 Parkgate Rd   7223 1611   5–4C
Martin Lam's "passionately-assembled" wine list "beats any
in London for choice and value", so the food at this "laid-back"
Battersea veteran is arguably "beside the point" – like service and
ambience, though, it has "declined in quality" of late.
/ www.ransomesdock.co.uk; 11 pm; closed Sun D.

Raoul's Café £38 ④④❸
105-107 Talbot Rd, W11   7229 2400   6–1B
13 Clifton Rd, W9   7289 7313   8–4A
Queues for brunch at the Maida Vale original of this "buzzy" diner
duo "go round the block" (and its Notting Hill branch also "stands
out from local rivals"); the pay-off is "the best fry-up", using
"incredible eggs imported from Italy" – the downside, "slow and
forgetful" service. / www.raoulsgourmet.com; 10.15 pm; booking after
5 pm only.

Rasa N16 £27 ❶❶❸
55 Stoke Newington Church St   7249 0344   1–1C
"I think about it almost every day!"; this "highly addictive" Stoke
Newington Keralan – "the original and still the best" in the group –
is one of the highest-rated Indians in town, thanks to its "imaginative"
and "absolutely delicious" veggie cooking. / www.rasarestaurants.com;
10.45 pm, Fri & Sat 11.30 pm; closed weekday L.

Rasa £30 ❷❷❸
5 Charlotte St, W1   7637 0222   2–1C
6 Dering St, W1   7629 1346   3–2B
Holiday Inn Hotel, 1 Kings Cross, WC1   7833 9787   8–3D
56 Stoke Newington Church St, N16   7249 1340   1–1C
"Light years ahead of typical curry houses"; these spin-offs from the
N16 original also provide "wonderfully interesting" Keralan dishes and
a "cordial" welcome; though mostly veggie, Dering St and N16
(Travancore) also serve meat, while the "vividly pink" Charlotte Street
(Samudra) branch specialises in seafood. / www.rasarestaurants.com;
10.45 pm; variable hours especially on weekends.

RASOI SW3 £87 ❷❸④
10 Lincoln St   7225 1881   5–2D
The "kaleidoscopic" flavours offered by Vineet Bhatia's "modern
fusion-riff on subcontinental cuisine" make this Chelsea townhouse
one of London's top Indians; "slow service" and a "too-quiet
ambience" can be a let-down, though… not to mention the "second
mortgage you'll need on the way out". / www.rasoirestaurant.co.uk;
11 pm; closed Sat L & Sun; no trainers; set weekday L £48 (FP).

The Real Greek £27 ⑤⑤④
56 Paddington St, W1   7486 0466   2–1A
60/62 Long Acre, WC2   7240 2292   4–2D
Westfield, Ariel Way, W12   8743 9168   7–1C
15 Hoxton Market, N1   7739 8212   12–1B
1-2 Riverside Hs, Southwark Br Rd, SE1   7620 0162   9–3B
31-33 Putney High St, SW15   8788 3270   10–2B
6 Horner Sq, E1   7375 1364   12–2B
140-142 St John St, EC1   7253 7234   9–1A
"What a dump!"; these "random" chain Greeks have "declined
alarmingly" in recent years – many reporters just think they should
be "avoided at all costs". / www.therealgreek.com; 10.45 pm; WC2 11 pm;
EC1 closed Sun; no Amex; WC2 no booking .

Rebato's SW8 £32 ❸①①
169 South Lambeth Rd   7735 6388   10–1D
It's hard not to love this "slice of Spain in the heart of Stockwell" –
an "old-school" tapas bar, plus "cheesy" rear restaurant, where the
"pure '70s décor" only "adds to the charm"; staff are "wonderful",
and the food is "always good and hearty". / www.rebatos.com; 10.45 pm;
closed Sat L & Sun.

Red Fort W1 £58 ❷④④
77 Dean St   7437 2525   4–2A
This veteran Soho Indian is still "first choice" for some reporters,
thanks to its "consistently great" contemporary cuisine; with its
"inattentive" staff and lacklustre ambience, though, even supporters
can find it "outrageously expensive". / www.redfort.co.uk; 11.15 pm,
Sun 10.30 pm; closed Sat L & Sun L.

The Red Pepper W9 £37 ❷④④
8 Formosa St   7266 2708   8–4A
"Excellent pizzas and other Italian dishes are only spoilt by the very
crowded conditions" – almost invariably the theme of reports on this
Maida Vale linchpin, ever since it opened in 1994. / 11 pm, Sat & Sun
10.30 pm; closed weekday L; no Amex.

Refettorio
The Crowne Plaza Hotel EC4 £50 ❸❸④
19 New Bridge St   7438 8052   9–3A
"Cold" ambience notwithstanding, this Italian dining room,
by Blackfriars Bridge, has become a "favourite" City rendezvous;
"sharing platters" are a speciality, accompanied by some "great
bread". / www.refettorio.com; 10.30 pm, Fri & Sat 10 pm; closed Sat L & Sun;
booking: max 8.

The Refinery SE1 NEW £32 ④❸④
110 Southwark St   468 0186   9–4B
A large bar/restaurant, in a new pedestrian street largely populated
with restaurants, behind Tate Modern; it's a jolly enough place,
and handy for culture vultures, but the food is mundane in the
extreme. / Rated on Editors' visit; www.therefinerybar.co.uk; 9.45 pm, Sat &
Sun 7 pm.

Refuel
Soho Hotel W1 £48 ④④④
4 Richmond Mews   7559 3007   3–2D
It inhabits the foyer of an "excellently stylish hotel", but few reporters
go a bundle on this Soho 'scene' – service is "chaotic", the food's
"very expensive for what it is", and the space "co-exists with a noisy
bar". / www.sohohotel.com; midnight, Sun 11 pm.

Le Relais de Venise L'Entrecôte £37 ❸④❸
120 Marylebone Ln, W1   7486 0878   2–1A
5 Throgmorton St, EC2   7638 6325   9–2C NEW
"The formula works!"; these Parisian imports – in Marylebone and,
now, the City – offer "decent steak/frites at decent prices" (plus an
"addictive" secret sauce); be prepared to queue (no bookings),
and then to be "rushed" through by sometimes "grumpy" staff.
/ www.relaisdevenise.com; W1 10.45 pm, Sun 10.30 pm; EC2 10 pm;
EC2 closed Sat & Sun; no booking.

Le Rendezvous du Café EC1 £42 ❸❷❸
22 Charterhouse Sq 7336 8836 9–1B
This "charming" Smithfield bistro – an offshoot from the nearby Café du Marché – is as "authentic" a Gallic destination as you'll find, offering "well cooked" dishes, and a "solid" wine list. / www.cafedumarche.co.uk; 10 pm; closed Sat L & Sun; no Amex.

The Restaurant At St Paul's
St Paul's Cathedral EC4 NEW £33 ❸❷❸
St Paul's Churchyard 7248 2469 9–2B
In the impressive crypt of St Paul's, an airy new British restaurant with a surprisingly get-away-from-it-all feel to it; the food doesn't try too hard, but that's all part of a package which, on an early-days visit, we found surprisingly winning. / Rated on Editors' visit; www.restaurantatstpauls.co.uk; L only.

Retsina NW3 £37 ❸④④
48-50 Belsize Ln 7431 5855 8–2A
"Like being on holiday in Greece, only with better food!" – that's the appeal of this "crowded and busy" taverna in Belsize Park; service is "variable but generally OK". / www.retsina-london.com; 11 pm; no Amex.

Reubens W1 £43 ④⑤⑤
79 Baker St 7486 0035 2–1A
With its "bland" cuisine and "school dinners-style" service, this long-established kosher restaurant (cum deli), in Marylebone, does not impress all reporters; fans, however, insist that it is "traditional and hospitable". / www.reubensrestaurant.co.uk; 10 pm; closed Fri D & Sat; no Amex.

Rhodes 24 EC2 £70 ④❸❷
25 Old Broad St 7877 7703 9–2C
Fortunately, the "spectacular view" distracts from the "corporate" décor of this 24th-floor dining room, which "couldn't be better placed for a City lunch"; its "British classics" cuisine "doesn't embarrass", but complaints about "sky-high" prices rocketed this year. / www.rhodes24.co.uk; 9 pm; closed Sat & Sun; no shorts; booking essential.

Rhodes W1 Brasserie
Cumberland Hotel W1 £52 ④④⑤
Gt Cumberland Pl 7616 5930 2–2A
"Solid, but lacking value for money", or "nice but empty" – about as positive as reports (few) get on Gary Rhodes's vast, and sometimes "awful", brasserie, near Marble Arch. / www.rhodesw1.com; 10.30 pm.

Rhodes W1 Restaurant
Cumberland Hotel W1 £91 ④❸④
Gt Cumberland Pl 7616 5930 2–2A
Gary R's luxurious two-year-old fine dining room, near Marble Arch, inspires amazingly few reports, and they're very mixed – fans applaud it as a "fantastic all-round experience", but detractors find the food "very uninspiring". / www.rhodesw1.com; 10.30 pm; closed Mon, Sat L & Sun; no trainers.

Rib Room
Jumeirah Carlton Tower Hotel SW1   £79   ④❷⑤
2 Cadogan Pl   7858 7250   5–1D
The prices at this "sterile" Knightsbridge grill room are infamously "exorbitant", but fans identify three factors to justify the expense of entertaining clients here – "melting" beef (including "the best steaks in London"), "discreetly spaced" tables, and "five-star" service. / www.jumeirah.com; 10.45 pm, Sun 10.15 pm; booking: max 24; set weekday L £60 (FP).

RIBA Café
Royal Ass'n of Brit' Architects W1   £42   ④④❷
66 Portland Pl   7631 0467   2–1B
"A wonderful, tucked-away, pretty garden" and an "impressive Art Deco interior" are the main draws to the café of this '30s-built Marylebone institution; the food is incidental. / www.riba-venues.com; L only, closed Sat & Sun.

Riccardo's SW3   £40   ❷❸❷
126 Fulham Rd   7370 6656   5–3B
"Always fun, and full of glamorous people", this "affordable" (by Chelsea standards) Italian retains its "stalwart" charms, not least its "simple" fare (served "tapas-style" since long before it was fashionable); good terrace. / www.riccardos.it; 11.30 pm, Sun 10.30 pm.

Richoux   £37   ⑤⑤④
172 Piccadilly, W1   7493 2204   3–3C
41a South Audley St, W1   7629 5228   3–3A
86 Brompton Rd, SW3   7584 8300   5–1C
3 Circus Rd, NW8   7483 4001   8–3A
"For a lazy breakfast" or a "cream tea", or just for "relaxing after shopping", this grand tea-room chain has its charms, with its sometimes "awful" food (and service), though, some reporters find it just "so poor nowadays". / www.richoux.co.uk; 11 pm; SW3 9 pm; W1 Sat 11.30 pm; NW8 10.30 pm, Sat 11 pm.

Rick's Café SW17   £34   ❷❷❷
122 Mitcham Rd   8767 5219   10–2C
"Rick is back, thank goodness", at "Tooting's best restaurant" (of the non-ethnic sort, anyway) – a "simple" place, with "welcoming" service and "very good" food. / 11 pm, Sun 4 pm; closed Mon L; no Amex.

El Rincón Latino SW4   £28   ❸❶❶
148 Clapham Manor St   7622 0599   10–2D
An "excellent", if "noisy", family-run bar in Clapham; it serves "very good tapas", and "reasonably-priced weekend brunch menus" (featuring "full Spanish fry ups") are a highlight. / www.rinconlatino.co.uk; 11.30 pm; closed Mon, Tue-Fri L & Sun D.

Ristorante Semplice W1   £56   ❷❷❸
9-10 Blenheim St   7495 1509   3–2B
"We need more West Enders like this!"; this "slick" Italian two-year-old on the northern fringe of Mayfair has "impeccable" cuisine; staff are "passionate" too, helping create "a good buzz" in the somewhat "cramped" space. / www.ristorantesemplice.com; 10.30 pm; closed Sat L & Sun; booking: max 12; set weekday L £25 (FP).

The Ritz Restaurant
The Ritz W1 £104 ④❸❶
150 Piccadilly 7493 8181 3–4C
This "breathtaking" Louis XVI-style chamber, overlooking Green Park,
is often cited as "the prettiest dining room in London"; the cuisine,
though, has long been "a little average" and "horrendously expensive"
too (but, for a "special occasion", it can still be a "treat"); "top-class
breakfasts". / www.theritzlondon.com; 10 pm; jacket & tie required;
set weekday L £57 (FP), set dinner £66 (FP).

Riva SW13 £53 ❷❶④
169 Church Rd 8748 0434 10–1A
"Honest, seasonal and delicious" Italian cooking has long made
Andreas Riva's "professional" Barnes venture quite a well-known
foodie destination; the uninitiated, though, can find the atmosphere
rather "strange". / 10.30 pm; closed Sat L.

The River Café W6 £69 ❷❷❸
Thames Wharf, Rainville Rd 7386 4200 7–2C
Phoenix-like, this world-famous Hammersmith Italian has re-opened
(after a refurbishment forced by a fire) with "divine" food (better than
it's been for years); its "lighter" interior remains "crowded", though,
and its "eye-popping" prices are still "too high for such simple fare".
/ www.rivercafe.co.uk; 9 pm, Sat 9.15 pm; closed Sun D.

Rivington £45 ❸④❸
178 Greenwich High Rd, SE10 8293 9270 1–3D
28-30 Rivington St, EC2 7729 7053 12–1B
Given its trendy location, the "lively" Shoreditch original of this
bar/brasserie duo – run by Caprice Holdings – is a surprisingly
"dependable" and "straightforward" operation... to the extent that
it can seem a little "ho hum"; its Greenwich spin-off is also a "useful"
haunt, especially for brunch. / www.rivingtongrill.co.uk; 11 pm, Sun 10 pm;
SE10 closed Mon, Tue L & Wed L.

Roast
The Floral Hall SE1 £55 ④④❸
Stoney St 7940 1300 9–4C
"An enormous, light room overlooking Borough Market" provides the
"dynamic" location for this "showcase for British produce"; a shame,
then, that the food's "so distinctly average" – "only breakfast's really
worth eating" – and that service can be "very poor".
/ www.roast-restaurant.com; 10.45 pm; closed Sun D.

Rocca Di Papa SW7 🆕 £28 ⑤❸④
73 Old Brompton Rd 7225 3413 5–2B
"Nice to see a South Kensington space that's long been empty
brought back to life"; although this newcomer is "convenient and
cheap", however, and attracts quite a crowd, its pizzas are
"very average". / www.roccarestaurants.com; 11.30 pm; set weekday L
£18 (FP).

Rock & Sole Plaice WC2 £26 ❸④④
47 Endell St 7836 3785 4–1C
How has this "decent" chippy survived for decades in trendy Covent
Garden? Simply because – though service is "casual" and the interior
"cramped" – the food is "better than at 90% of other outlets locally",
and the place is particularly useful for a group meal on a budget.
/ www.rockandsoleplaice.co.uk; 11 pm; no Amex.

Rock & Rose TW9 £42 ⑤⑤❷
106-108 Kew Rd 8948 8008 1–4A
A "would-be achingly trendy" Richmond yearling, where
"first appearances are great"; it's "all style and no content", though,
with the food being found "very uninspiring", and service "slipshod".
/ www.rockandroserestaurant.co.uk; 10.30 pm; set always available £26 (FP).

Rocket £42 ④❸❷
4-6 Lancashire Ct, W1 7629 2889 3–2B
6 Adams Ct, EC2 7628 0808 9–2C
"Top-end locations" (including in a cute courtyard off Bond Street,
but sadly no longer by the river in Putney) add to the appeal of these
"fun and lively" outfits, which serve "slightly unusual" pizzas and
"unique" salads. / www.rocketrestaurants.co.uk; 10.45 pm; W1 closed Sun;
EC2 closed Sat & Sun; SW15 Mon-Wed D only.

Rodizio Rico £42 ④⑤④
111 Westbourne Grove, W2 7792 4035 6–1B
77-78 Upper St, N1 7354 1076 8–3D
If you like "meat, meat, and more meat", these Brazilian barbecue
buffets can be "fun" (especially "for larger groups"); visits can be a
"hit-and-miss" experience, though, and – on a bad day – the food's
"not great", and service "terrible". / www.rodiziorico.com; W2 11.30 pm;
N1 midnight, Sun 11 pm; SE10 11 pm, Fri & Sat midnight; W2 & N1 closed
weekday L; no Amex.

The Roebuck W4 £38 ❸❷❸
122 Chiswick High Rd 8995 4392 7–2A
A "lovely" rear garden, and "spacious" interior lend an "airy" and
"bustling" atmosphere to this "popular" (and "kid-friendly") Chiswick
gastropub; service is "professional", and the food "spot-on".
/ www.theroebuckchiswick.co.uk; 10.30 pm, Sun 10 pm.

Roka £85 ❷④❷
37 Charlotte St, W1 7580 6464 2–1C
Unit 4, Park Pavilion, 40 Canada Sq, E14 11–1C NEW
This "always buzzing" Zuma-sibling, in Fitzrovia, echoes to the sound
of those enjoying its "vibrant" Japanese fare – both sushi and 'robata'
(grill) dishes; it's becoming "expensive for what you get", though,
and service is increasingly "haphazard"; an offshoot opens in Canary
Wharf in October 2009. / www.rokarestaurant.com; 11.15 pm; booking:
max 8.

Ronnie Scott's W1 £45 ⑤④❶
47 Frith St 7439 0747 4–2A
This famous Soho jazz club, majorly refurbished in recent years,
remains "a great place for a date"; be warned, though – "you don't
go for the food". / www.ronniescotts.co.uk; 3 am, Sun midnight; D only.

Rooburoo N1 £27 ❸❸❸
21 Chapel Mkt 7278 8100 8–3D
A modern Indian in Islington's Chapel Market, which – with its "wide-
ranging, innovative and healthy menu" – often "exceeds
expectations". / www.rooburoo.com; 11 pm; closed Mon, Sat L & Sun L.

Rosa's E1 NEW £30 ❸❸❸
12 Hanbury St 7247 1093 12–2C
"Just off Brick Lane", this Thai newcomer is proving a "good-value"
arrival, serving "genuine" and "very spicy" food, in a "tightly-packed"
space. / www.rosaslondon.com; 10.30 pm.

The Rose & Crown N6 NEW   £39   ④④④
86 Highgate High St   8340 0770   1–1C
"In lovely Highgate", this newly-converted hostelry is now a "quite smart", "pub-type" restaurant with a "high level of cooking" and decent wine list; it can seem "expensive" for what it is, though.
/ www.roseandcrownhighgate.com; 10 pm; closed Mon L & Sun D; no Amex.

Rosemary Lane E1   £44   ❸❸④
61 Royal Mint St   7481 2602   11–1A
In the wasteland east of Tower Hill, this former pub can come as "a real surprise" – "ideal for a discreet business meeting"; the Gallic-influenced fare is sometimes "unexpectedly good".
/ www.rosemarylane.btinternet.co.uk; 10 pm; closed Sat L & Sun; set always available £28 (FP).

The Rosendale SE21   £38   ④❸④
65 Rosendale Rd   8670 0812   1–4D
"High-quality bar food and an excellent, wide-ranging wine list" have made quite a name for this grand and rather "refined" West Dulwich gastropub; this year, however, overall satisfaction was undercut by a few negative reports. / www.therosendale.co.uk; 10.30 pm; no Amex.

Rossopomodoro   £37   ❸④④
50-52 Monmouth St, WC2   7240 9095   4–2B NEW
214 Fulham Rd, SW10   7352 7677   5–3B
184a Kensington Park Rd, W11   7229 9007   6–1A
"You can get a decent pizza" (wood-fired), at this Naples-based chain (which has 70 restaurants worldwide); but whereas fans praise its "fun" style ("really feels like Italy!"), critics complain of "erratic" service and a lack of atmosphere. / midnight; WC2 Sun 11.30 pm.

The Rôtisserie   £40   ④❸④
316 Uxbridge Rd, HA5   8421 2878   1–1A
1288 Whetstone High Rd, N20   8343 8585   1–1B
82 Fortune Green Rd, NW6   7435 9923   1–1B
87 Allitsen Rd, NW8   7722 7444   8–3A
Fans of these "friendly steak joints" say they're "good local staples", even if they do offer "nothing to set the pulse racing".
/ www.therotisserie.co.uk; 10.30 pm, Sun 9.30 pm; NW6, NW8 & NW20 closed Mon L; no Amex (except HA5).

Rôtisserie Jules SW7   £29   ④④④
6-8 Bute St   7584 0600   5–2B
"Roast chicken 'n' chips, and not a lot else" is to be found at this "busy", "little" BYO canteen – a healthy "cheap 'n' cheerful" option, in South Kensington. / www.rotisseriejules.com; 10.30 pm.

Rotunda Bar & Restaurant
Kings Place N1 NEW   £42   ④❸❷
90 York Way   7014 2840   8–3C
"An oasis in the King's Cross desert" – this swish new cultural-centre brasserie has an "attractive" interior and a "lovely setting", right by the canal; the food is "generally good" too, but some concern is expressed that it is "already falling off".
/ www.rotundabarandrestaurant.co.uk; midnight, Sat 10.30 pm; closed Sat L & Sun D.

The Roundhouse SW18 NEW £35 ❸❸❸
2 Wandsworth Common Northside 7326 8580 10–2C
Wandsworth's Freemasons (RIP) has been transformed into this "fun" and "buzzy" gastropub newcomer (of the type that "blurs the line with being a restaurant"); its food is "tasty", if arguably pricey for what it is. / 10 om.

ROUSSILLON SW1 £76 ❶❶❸
16 St Barnabas St 7730 5550 5–2D
Hidden-away "in deepest Pimlico" – but just five minutes' walk from Sloane Square – this "classy" but rather "sedate" outfit remains "under the radar" of many Londoners... despite the quality of Gerard Virolle's "breathtaking" Gallic cooking, and of service that just "couldn't be more friendly"; (this is also the home of London's grandest veggie menu). / www.roussillon.co.uk; 11 pm; closed Sat L & Sun; no trainers; set weekday L £43 (FP).

Rowley's SW1 £57 ④④④
113 Jermyn St 7930 2707 3–3D
"Old-school" style and a handy location help maintain the following of this attractive St James's steakhouse, especially as "a business favourite"; it remains, however, gravely "overpriced". / www.rowleys.co.uk; 11 pm.

Royal Academy W1 £33 ⑤⑤❸
Burlington Hs, Piccadilly 7300 5608 3–3C
Handily-located just off Piccadilly, the Academy's airy, self-service canteen makes a "civilised" (if sometimes "crowded") refuge from the West End; fans say the food's "decent" too, but others – finding it "slapdash" – suggest sticking to tea and a cake. / www.royalacademy.org.uk; 8.15 pm; L only, except Fri open L & D; no booking at L.

Royal China £39 ❷④④
24-26 Baker St, W1 7487 4688 2–1A
805 Fulham Rd, SW6 7731 0081 10–1B
13 Queensway, W2 7221 2535 6–2C
30 Westferry Circus, E14 7719 0888 11–1B
Particularly as "THE place for a weekend dim sum blow-out", these weirdly "glitzy", "'70s-style" orientals are always "rammed" – beware "enormous queues", especially at Bayswater; "patchy" service, however, is a growing concern. / www.rcguk.biz; 10.45 pm, Fri & Sat 11.15 pm, Sun 9.45 pm; no booking Sat & Sun L.

Royal China Club W1 £57 ❷❸④
40-42 Baker St 7486 3898 2–1A
"Sold as a classier option than the standard Royal Chinas", this brand's sole remaining 'premium' outlet, in Marylebone, generates a very similar feedback profile. / www.royalchinagroup.co.uk; 11 pm, Fri & Sat 11.30 pm, Sun 10.30 pm.

Royal China SW15 £36 ❷④④
3 Chelverton Rd 8788 0907 10–2B
This Putney oriental (which long ago parted ways with the chain it spawned) may "looks like a bad '80s disco", but it offers "dependable" cuisine, which includes some "excellent dim sum". / www.royalchinaputney.co.uk; 11 pm, Fri & Sat 11.30 pm; only Amex.

The Royal Exchange Grand Café
The Royal Exchange EC3   £47   ④⑤❷
Cornhill   7618 2480   9–2C
A City seafood bar, whose "only 'Grand' feature" is its setting in a
"spacious and historic" atrium – this is a D&D group operation, after
all, so it's no surprise that food and service are "run-of-the-mill".
/ www.danddlondon.com; 10 pm; closed Sat & Sun; no booking at L & D.

Royal Wok E2 NEW   £12   ❸❸⑤
507 Hackney Rd   7739 6663   12–1D
By Cambridge Heath station (BR) – a BYO Chinese newcomer;
it's certainly nothing to look at, but the food is tasty and sometimes
unusual, and good value too. / Rated on Editors' visit; www.royalwok.co.uk;
11 pm; D only; no credit cards.

RSJ SE1   £42   ❸❷⑤
33 Coin St   7928 4554   9–4A
A "Loire wine list to beat all others" helps maintain the impressive
popularity of this "dependable" Gallic stalwart, handily placed for the
South Bank's cultural attractions; pity its interior has "zero ambience".
/ www.rsj.uk.com; 11 pm; closed Sat L & Sun.

La Rueda   £32   ④④❸
642 King's Rd, SW6   7384 2684   5–4A
66-68 Clapham High St, SW4   7627 2173   10–2D
Fans of the "always-fun" Clapham original of this (now "depleted")
Spanish chain say it's "still a great place", and ratings for its
"authentic" tapas picked up again this year.
/ www.larueda-restaurant.co.uk; 11.30 pm; SW6 1 am.

Rules WC2   £60   ❸❸❶
35 Maiden Ln   7836 5314   4–3D
"The quintessential English dining experience"; London's
oldest restaurant (1798), beautifully housed in a quiet Covent Garden
lane, defies its tourist-trap potential with cooking (especially game)
that's "much better than you might expect". / www.rules.co.uk;
11.30 pm, Sun 10.30 pm; no shorts; booking: max 6.

Running Horse W1   £37   ❸❸❸
50 Davies St   7493 1275   3–2B
"A useful pub", reasonably priced by Mayfair standards – a "helpful"
sort of place, it offers food that's generally "well-prepared".
/ www.therunninghorselondon.co.uk; 9.30 pm; closed Sun.

The Rye SE15   £30   ❸❸❷
31 Peckham Rye   7639 5397   1–4D
A "cosy" gastropub near Peckham Rye station; "it's got great food
and ambience – what more can you say?" / 10 pm, Sun 9 pm; no Amex.

S & M Café   £23   ⑤④④
268 Portobello Rd, W10   8968 8898   6–1A
4-6 Essex Rd, N1   7359 5361   8–3D
02 Centre, Peninsular Sq, SE10   8305 1940   11–2D
48 Brushfield St, E1   7247 2252   12–2B
50 Long Ln, EC1   7606 6591   9–1B
28 Leadenhall Mkt, EC3   7626 6646   9–2B
It's presumably over-expansion which is responsible for the
"plummeting" standards at these retro-styled English cafés; it's such
a shame, as the concept – "great sausage 'n' mash at honest prices"
– is hard to knock. / www.sandmcafe.co.uk; N1 & W10 11 pm;
E1 10.30 pm; SE10 6 pm, Fri & Sat 11 pm, Sun 6.30 pm; EC1 10 pm,
Sat 5 pm; EC3 8 pm, Mon-Tue 5 pm; E1 & EC1 closed Sun; EC3 closed
Sat & Sun; no Amex; W10 no booking L; E1 no booking Sun.

Sabor N1 £37 ④❸❸
108 Essex Rd 7226 5551 8–3D
*"A warm welcome" adds life to this "sweet" Islington Latino;
sometimes it's very good, but realisation is "intermittent".
/ www.sabor.co.uk; 10.45 pm; closed Mon, Tue-Fri D only, Sat & Sun open
L & D; no Amex.*

Le Sacré-Coeur N1 £34 ④❸❸
18 Theberton St 7354 2618 8–3D
*It may be "shabby", but the "good-value rustic fare" at this "cheerful"
and "bustling" ("Montmartre-style") bistro has made it an Islington
perennial. / www.lesacrecoeur.co.uk; 11 pm, Sat 11.30 pm; set weekday
L £18 (FP), set Sun L £20 (FP).*

Saf EC2 £39 ④④❸
152-154 Curtain Rd 7613 0007 12–1B
*"High on concept", this "healthy" vegan yearling, in Shoreditch,
promotes the concepts of "raw food"; some of the "surprising and
refreshing" dishes are "amazing", but the "insufferably right-on"
approach is – inevitably – not for everyone. / www.safrestaurant.co.uk;
10.30 pm.*

Sagar £24 ❷❷④
17a, Percy St, W1 7631 3319 3–2B
31 Catherine St, WC2 7836 6377 4–3D
157 King St, W6 8741 8563 7–2C
27 York St, TW1 8744 3868 1–4A
*"Dosas to die for" feature amongst the "delicious and very cheap"
south Indian dishes on offer at this "cheerful" small chain; some of
this year's visits, however, "lacked the expected wow-factor".
/ www.gosagar.com; Sun-Thu 10.45 pm, Fri & Sat 11.30 pm.*

Saigon Saigon W6 £33 ❸❷❸
313-317 King St 8748 6887 7–2B
*A "civilised" Hammersmith Vietnamese, which wins very consistent
praise for its "charming" staff, "pleasant" interior and "reliable" food.
/ www.saigon-saigon.co.uk; 11 pm, Sun & Mon 10 pm, Fri & Sat 11.30 pm;
no Amex; set weekday L £18 (FP).*

St Alban SW1 £52 ❸❶❷
4-12 Regent St 7499 8558 3–3D
*Thanks not least to a "tasteful revamp" of its "airport-lounge" styling,
Messrs Corbin & King's Theatreland two-year-old now has "a real
media buzz" to it, which is "much appreciated by business lunchers";
the Mediterranean cuisine is of "good quality" too, but is outshone
by the "superlative" service. / www.stalban.net; 11 pm; closed Sun; booking:
max 10.*

St Germain EC1 £40 ④❸④
89-90 Turnmill St 7336 0949 9–1A
*A "buzzy" brasserie, near Farringdon tube, that pleases most punters
with its "bistro-style" cuisine; "you reach it through a raucous bar",
though… and some reporters see that as the better part of the
operation. / www.stgermain.info; 11 pm; closed Sat L & Sun D.*

ST JOHN EC1 £52 ❶❷❸
26 St John St 7251 0848 9–1B
*"The flagship of British cuisine!"; Fergus Henderson's "pioneering"
ex-smokehouse, in Clerkenwell is, for its many fans, "the best
restaurant in the UK", thanks to its "totally unpompous" style and
its "unique" and "punchy" menu (which famously features much
"awesome offal"). / www.stjohnrestaurant.com; 11 pm; closed
Sat L & Sun D.*

St John Bread & Wine E1 £46 ❶❸④
94-96 Commercial St 7251 0848 12–2C
The "younger, noisier and more laid-back" offshoot of the Clerkenwell
icon – a Spitalfields canteen which offers "the best of British food"
("without any poncing about") on its "idiosyncratic and challenging"
tapas-style menu. / www.stjohnbreadandwine.com; 10.30 pm, Sun 9pm.

St Johns N19 £40 ❸❷❶
91 Junction Rd 7272 1587 8–1C
A "drab" exterior gives no hint of the "cavernous" dining room –
a former ballroom "charmingly" decked-out in "shabby-chic" style –
at this popular Archway gastropub; its "friendly and efficient" staff
serve up "straightforward" fare that's generally "well cooked". / 11 pm,
Sun 9.30 pm; Mon-Thu D only, Fri-Sun open L & D; booking: max 12.

Le Saint Julien EC1 £45 ④④④
62-63 Long Ln 7796 4550 9–1B
A "very French" Smithfield brasserie that fans claim as a "hidden
gem"; too often, though, it's "let down" by "lackadaisical" service and
"hit-and-miss" cooking. / 10 pm; closed Sat L & Sun.

St Moritz W1 £47 ❸❸❷
161 Wardour St 7734 3324 3–1D
An "utterly cute Swiss chalet", in the heart of Soho; it's "cramped and
expensive, but cool too", with "great fondues" (plus other "authentic
Swiss dishes") and some "interesting" Helvetic wines.
/ www.stmoritz-restaurant.co.uk; 11.30 pm; closed Sat L & Sun; booking:
max 12.

St Pancras Grand
St Pancras Int'l Station NW1 NEW £48 ④④❷
St Pancras International 7870 9900 8–3C
"Glamorous" and "beautiful", this British brasserie has been "a very
welcome addition" to the eponymous railway station; to become
a true "destination restaurant", however, it would need to sharpen
up its "fine but not memorable" cuisine, and to sort out the
sometimes "neglectful" service. / www.stpancrasgrand.com; 10.45 pm.

Sake No Hana SW1 £70 ④④④
23 St James's St 7925 8988 3–4C
Fans insist this St James's Japanese offers "creative" dishes in a
"hugely glamorous" setting; there's still a huge chorus of complaints,
however, that it's "incredibly pretentious" and "hugely overpriced" –
"I went on a half-price deal, and was still shocked by the bill!"
/ 11 pm, Sat 11.30 pm; closed Sun L.

Saki Bar & Food Emporium EC1 £42 ❷❸⑤
4 West Smithfield 7489 7033 9–2A
"Unexpectedly good" cuisine has long been the only real reason
to seek out this "authentic" Smithfield Japanese (whose "bland"
basement setting is "a let down"); it comes in "small portions",
though, and has sometimes seemed "overpriced" of late.
/ www.saki-food.com; 10.30 pm; closed Sat L & Sun.

Sakonis HA0 £19 ❸④⑤
129 Ealing Rd 8903 9601 1–1A
"Filled with noisy families", this capacious Wembley canteen is worth
a visit for its "mix of Bombay street food and Indochinese dishes";
a bargain buffet is a highlight. / www.sakonis.co.uk; 9.30 pm; no Amex;
set weekday L £11 (FP).

Sakura W1 £27 ❷⑤⑤
9 Hanover St 7629 2961 3–2C
*"Golly the service can be rude", at this "dog-eared" Japanese
basement, off Regent Street; it's "always full", though, and a visit can
even be quite "fun", thanks to its "authentic food" (including
"beautifully fresh" sushi) at "good prices". / 10 pm.*

Salaam Namaste WC1 £28 ❸❷④
68 Millman St 7405 3697 2–1D
*"Not your run-of the mill Indian" – this Bloomsbury curry house offers
some "really unusual dishes"; "shame about the unexciting room",
though, which can get "desperately noisy". / www.salaam-namaste.co.uk;
11.30 pm, Sun 11 pm.*

Sale e Pepe SW1 £46 ❸⓿❷
9-15 Pavilion Rd 7235 0098 5–1D
*"Brilliant staff lend a certain madness to the ambience" of this "fun",
"noisy" and "cramped" trattoria, hidden-away off Sloane Street;
the food is "very good" and "unfussy" too. / www.saleepepe.co.uk;
11.30 pm; closed Sun; no shorts.*

Salisbury SW6 £38 ❸❸❸
21 Sherbrooke Rd 7381 4005 10–1B
*"Excellent since the revamp" in late-2008; this deepest Fulham
boozer is now "more restaurant than pub", and offers "above-
average" service and "much-improved" cooking. / www.thesalisbury.com;
10 pm; closed Sun D.*

Salloos SW1 £46 ❷❸④
62-64 Kinnerton St 7235 4444 5–1D
*"Not flashy, but my subcontinental friends say it's the best!"; this
"old-fashioned" establishment, hidden in a Knightsbridge mews,
may be "somewhat overpriced", but its "really original" Pakistani food
is often "divine". / 11 pm; closed Sun.*

Salt House NW8 £40 ❸❷❷
63 Abbey Rd 7328 6626 8–3A
*"A lovely terrace for the summer" is a high-point at this "reliable"
gastropub "all-rounder" – "a rarity in St John's Wood!"
/ www.thesalthouse.co.uk; 10.15 pm, Sun 10 pm.*

Salt Yard W1 £37 ❷⓿❸
54 Goodge St 7637 0657 2–1B
*"Tremendous" tapas (Spanish "with an Italian twist"), "unusual" wine
and "seamless" service again inspire rave reports on this "always-
hopping" Fitzrovia hang-out; it may be "crowded and noisy"
(especially in the basement), but it's "really enjoyable and relaxed"
too. / www.saltyard.co.uk; 11 pm; closed Sat L & Sun.*

The Salusbury NW6 £40 ❸④❸
50-52 Salusbury Rd 7328 3286 1–2B
*"A staple for the area" – this "friendly" Queen's Park local-favourite
gastropub attracts praise for its "hearty" portions of "solid" Italianate
fare; "the downside, maybe, is the crowds". / 10.15 pm; closed Mon L;
no Amex.*

Sam's Brasserie W4 £43 ④❸❸
11 Barley Mow Pas 8987 0555 7–2A
*For fans, these "buzzy" former industrial premises in Chiswick are
just an "excellent local", with an owner who has "a passion for doing
it right" – even supporters, though, admit the food "doesn't always
hit the mark". / www.samsbrasserie.co.uk; 10.30 pm; booking: max 14;
set weekday L £27 (FP), set Sun L £34 (FP).*

San Daniele del Friuli N5 £35 ❸❸❸
72 Highbury Park 7226 1609 8–1D
A "reliable", "old-school" Highbury Italian that's "reputedly
a favourite of the Arsenal team"; it offers "generous portions, a warm
welcome and lovely grub", and it's "not pricey" either. / 10.30 pm;
closed Mon L, Tue L, Sat L & Sun; no Amex.

San Lorenzo SW3 £68 ④④❸
22 Beauchamp Pl 7584 1074 5–1C
Fans of this '60s Knightsbridge trattoria still find it "fun";
the most eloquent commentary on this "dated" celeb-magnet,
however, is just how few reports it attracts nowadays. / 11.30 pm;
closed Sun.

San Lorenzo Fuoriporta SW19 £53 ④④④
38 Wimbledon Hill Rd 8946 8463 10–2B
Views on this potentially "lovely" Wimbledon Italian have long been
clouded by its ambitious pricing, and its "laid-back, going-on
horizontal" service; however, a recent shake-up of its "formula' –
now including "quick lunches and afternoon teas" – seems to have
bucked the place up quite a lot. / www.sanlorenzo.com; 11 pm; closed
Sun D; set always available £35 (FP).

San Remo SW13 £45 ④❷❸
195 Castelnau 8741 5909 7–2B
A "reliable" and "old-fashioned" Italian, just south of Barnes Bridge,
that's generally "bursting-at-the-seams", even if standards are
"no better than 'not bad'". / www.sanremorestaurant.com; 11 pm;
closed Sun.

Sands End SW6 £37 ❷❷❷
135 Stephendale Rd 7731 7823 10–1B
"Don't let Prince Harry's patronage put you off!"; this "nicely shabby"
pub, at the back end of Fulham, may attract an easily-stereotyped
clientele, but its "rustic" cuisine is part of an overall experience
most reports say is "first-class". / www.thesandsend.co.uk; midnight,
Sun 11 pm; booking: max 24.

Santa Lucia SW10 £38 ⑤④④
2 Hollywood Rd 7352 8484 5–3B
This year saw an unsettled performance at this "noisy", "Eurotrash"
pizzeria, on the fringes of Chelsea; normally it's a "pretty handy
local", but it's served a number of "horrid" meals of late – hopefully
just a blip. / www.madeinitalygroup.co.uk; 11.30 pm; closed weekday L.

Santa Maria del Sur SW8 £38 ❷❷❷
129 Queenstown Rd 7622 2088 10–1C
"Just like being in Buenos Aires", this Argentinean steakhouse,
in Battersea, offers "huge and marvellous slabs of meat" – "a match
for anywhere in London" – and a "great atmosphere" too.
/ www.buenayre.co.uk; 10.30 pm, Mon-Wed 10 pm; closed weekday L.

Santini SW1 £67 ④④④
29 Ebury St 7730 4094 2–4B
A Belgravia Italian stalwart which perennially attracts a glossy crowd
despite being "rather expensive for what it is"; "every year I give
it one last try, and every year it disappoints!"
/ www.santini-restaurant.com; 11 pm; closed Sat L & Sun L.

Santo W10 NEW   £33   ❸④④
299 Portobello Rd   8968 4590   6–1A
Such places may be "ten-a-penny in New York", but this new cantina in North Kensington is certainly, by London standards, a promising Mexican newcomer, offering "forthright" dishes, and "good" drinks too; prices, though, can seem a bit "strong". / www.santovillage.com; 10 pm, Fri & Sat 11.30; closed Mon; booking: max 20.

Sapori WC2   £37   ④❸④
43 Drury Ln   7836 8296   4–2D
A "buzzy" and "useful" Italian, near the Royal Opera House, praised as a "reliable" and "good-value" stand-by; for some tastes, though, it's just too "basic and unexciting". / 11.30 pm; no Amex.

Sarastro WC2   £38   ⑤⑤④
126 Drury Ln   7836 0101   2–2D
"Always entertaining", or "an absolutely hideous experience"? – that's open to dispute, but reporters tend to agreed that the food at this "kitsch" Covent Garden opera-restaurant is "disgusting". / www.sarastro-restaurant.com; 11.30 pm.

Sardo W1   £45   ❷❸❸
45 Grafton Way   7387 2521   2–1B
"Sardinian regional cuisine at its best" – served up by "a small, hard-working team" – makes it well worth discovering this "sparse" but "truly Italian-feeling" venture, "nicely hidden-away in Fitzrovia". / www.sardo-restaurant.com; 11 pm; closed Sat L & Sun.

Sardo Canale NW1   £44   ④⑤❸
42 Gloucester Ave   7722 2800   8–3B
It's not only the lack of a canal-view that can make a visit to this Primrose Hill Italian rather "frustrating"; hit lucky, and the food can be "the best of its type in north London", but the experience is "very hit-and-miss" – "overpricing" and "woeful" service are particular bugbears. / www.sardocanale.com; 10 pm; closed Mon L; set weekday L £25 (FP).

Sargasso Sea N21   £55   ❷❷❷
10 Station Rd   8360 0990   1–1C
A "classy" Winchmore Hill spot, where "genuine" and "well-presented" fish and seafood dishes underpin an "excellent" all-round experience. / www.sargassosea.co.uk; 10.30 pm; D only, closed Mon & Sun; booking: max 9, Sat D.

Sarracino NW6   £37   ❷❸④
186 Broadhurst Gdns   7372 5889   1–1B
A West Hampstead hang-out which offers "authentic" pizza – "with just the right crunch" – by the metre; it's "always busy". / www.sarracinorestaurant.com; 11 pm; closed weekday L; set weekday L £22 (FP).

Sartoria W1   £56   ④④❸
20 Savile Row   7534 7000   3–2C
"Spacious tables" and "elegant" surroundings (curiously decorated with tailors' dummies) help make this large D&D-group Mayfair Italian a decent business rendezvous; it's "expensive for what it is", though, and "takes itself too seriously". / www.danddlondon.co.uk; 11 pm; closed Sun.

Satay House W2 £38 ❷❷④
13 Sale Pl 7723 6763 6–1D
It's not much to look at, but this Bayswater fixture serves "very good
Malaysian food" – "the menu is short, but all the favourites are
here", says one (Malaysian) reporter. / www.satay-house.co.uk; 11 pm.

Satsuma W1 £30 ❸④④
56 Wardour St 7437 8338 3–2D
"Very much in the style of Wagamama", this "nice, cheap and
casual" Asian venture – in the very heart of Soho – can be a "quick
and excellent West End stand-by"; there's a slight feeling, though,
that it has "gone downhill" in recent times. / www.osatsuma.com;
10.30 pm, Tue-Thu 11 pm, Fri & Sat 12 pm; no booking.

Sauterelle
Royal Exchange EC3 £57 ④❸❸
Bank 7618 2483 9–2C
The "divine" location of this "discreet" City dining room, "hidden-away
on the mezzanine of the Royal Exchange", always "impresses the
clients"; by D&D group standards, the food is reasonably good too,
but even so, it's "formulaic". / www.danddlondon.com; 9.30 pm; closed
Sat & Sun; set always available £37 (FP).

Scalini SW3 £58 ❸❸❸
1-3 Walton St 7225 2301 5–2C
A Knightsbridge "classic" – this "always-buzzy" Italian is "extremely
crowded" with well-heeled locals, and "very noisy" as a result; prices
are "sky-high", though, and reporters are increasingly "bemused by its
popularity". / www.scalinionline.com; midnight.

Scarpetta TW11 £35 ❸❷❷
78 High St 8977 8177 1–4A
A "really friendly", family-run Teddington Italian, decorated in "rustic"
style; "amazing" pizzas are a highlight of a menu that generally
"avoids cliché". / www.scarpetta.co.uk; 11 pm; no shorts.

The Scarsdale W8 £38 ④❸❸
23a Edwardes Sq 7937 1811 7–1D
"A good place to hide away in on a chilly day, or to sit outside on a
sunny one" – this prettily-situated Kensington tavern offers traditional
fare that's arguably "rather average", but "solid and honest"
nonetheless. / 10 pm.

Scoffers SW11 £37 ❸❷❷
6 Battersea Rise 7978 5542 10–2C
"A large fig tree lit with fairly lights" adds to the "romantic" appeal
of this "cosy" Battersea fixture – your classic local stand-by, noted
also for its "brilliant brunch". / www.scoffersrestaurant.co.uk; 10.30 pm,
Fri & Sat 11 pm; closed Mon, Tue-Thu L, & Sun D.

SCOTT'S W1 £68 ❷❷❶
20 Mount St 7495 7309 3–3A
The "great aura" of this "happening" Mayfair magnet for the "A-list"
is in part due to the "super-glamorous" style of its "classic" and
"elegant" interior; it's a real "all-rounder", though, also offering
"exemplary" fish and seafood dishes, and "very polished" service.
/ www.scotts-restaurant.com; 10.30 pm, Sun 10 pm; booking: max 6.

The Sea Cow SE22 £25 ❸④⑤
37 Lordship Ln   8693 3111   1–4D
"A really good, no-frills sort of pit stop", in East Dulwich; it offers "very good fish 'n' chips", as well as some fancier fare (tempura, crab cakes, and so on). / www.theseacow.co.uk; 11 pm, Sun 10 pm; closed Mon L; no Amex.

Seafresh SW1 £30 ❸❷⑤
80-81 Wilton Rd   7828 0747   2–4B
"Melt-in-the-mouth" fish 'n' chips – with a "wider menu" than most chippies – makes this Pimlico stalwart (just five minutes' walk from Victoria) a "deservedly popular" destination; "not much in the way of atmosphere", though. / www.seafresh-dining.com; 10.30 pm; closed Sun.

Seaport W1 £43 ④④④
24 Seymour Pl   7724 4307   2–2A
A small fan club still praise this Marylebone fish specialist for its "fresh" and "interesting" cuisine; there's some feeling, however, that its standards generally have "slipped back" of late. / www.seaportrestaurant.co.uk; 11 pm; closed Sat L & Sun L.

Searcy's Brasserie EC2 £52 ④❸❸
Level 2, Barbican Centre   7588 3008   12–2A
The Barbican's "calm" in-house brasserie is arguably "surprisingly good" (or, to put it another way, "convenient, and not bad"); with "such a large captive audience", though (especially if you include the residents), it's perhaps surprising that "they still haven't found a formula really to pack 'em in". / www.searcys.co.uk; 10.30 pm; closed Sat L & Sun.

Seashell NW1 £37 ❷❸⑤
49 Lisson Grove   7224 9000   8–4A
"Drastically needing an updated interior", this famous, "traditional" fish 'n' chip parlour, in Marylebone, is "still among the best in town", but the setting certainly encourages you to take out. / www.seashellrestaurant.co.uk; 10.30 pm; closed Sun D.

Seasons Dining Room W6 🆕 £36 ❸❷⑤
323 King St   8748 2002   7–2B
This simple newcomer near Ravenscourt Park tube doesn't seem to be getting the following it deserves – a shame, as the staff are "lovely", and the food is "consistently good". / www.seasonsdiningroom.com; 11 pm; closed Sun.

Serafino W1 £50 ④❸④
8 Mount St   7629 0544   3–3B
A long-established Italian, by the Connaught, sometimes tipped as a useful Mayfair business or breakfasting venue; the ground-floor dining room has been better-rated of late than the basement pasta bar. / www.finos.co.uk; 10.45 pm; closed Sat L & Sun.

Seven Stars WC2 £31 ❸④❶
53 Carey St   7242 8521   2–2D
Roxy Beaujolais is a "great hostess", and her "very characterful" boozer, behind the Royal Courts of Justice, provides "good home-cooking in generous portions"; just one thing – "don't try to move the cat". / 11 pm, Sun 10.30 pm.

1707

Fortnum & Mason W1 £44 ❸❸❷
181 Piccadilly   7734 8040   2–1B
"An incredible wine list, with a great selection of wine flights, and £10 corkage on any wine from the shop floor" is the stand-out draw to this "posh" but "relaxing" wine bar, next to the main food halls of the Queen's grocer; a light menu (overseen by star chef, Shaun Hill) is served. / www.fortnumandmason.co.uk; 9.15 pm; closed Sun.

Shampers W1 £40 ❸❷❸
4 Kingly St   7437 1692   3–2D
"Fashions come, fashions go", but this "convivial and buzzy" Soho wine bar seems to go on for ever; it may be "crowded and chaotic", but it pleases all with its "fantastically varied wine list", its "always helpful" staff and its "reliable, good-value" food. / www.shampers.net; 11 pm; closed Sun (& Sat in Aug).

Shanghai E8 £28 ❸❸❸
41 Kingsland High St   7254 2878   1–1C
"A beautiful former pie 'n' eel shop" – sit at the front if you can – houses this "decent" Dalston destination, which serves "good-quality dim sum", and other "basic Chinese dishes"; regular Karaoke nights. / www.wengwahgroup.com; 11 pm; no Amex.

Shanghai Blues WC1 £57 ❷❷❸
193-197 High Holborn   7404 1668   4–1D
"Excellent on all fronts… except the prices!" – this "upmarket" Holborn oriental offers "cracking" modern Chinese food ("yummy dim sum", in particular) and "quietly efficient" service, in a "dark" and "decadent" setting. / www.shanghaiblues.co.uk; 11.30 pm.

J SHEEKEY WC2 £63 ❶❷❶
28-32 St Martin's Ct   7240 2565   4–3B
This "stellar" Theatreland "institution" was yet again the survey's most-mentioned establishment (as well as topping nominations as London's best fish restaurant); in its "maze" of "cramped" and "characterful" panelled rooms, a "stylish" menu is served (which includes some "old British favourite dishes"). / www.j-sheekey.co.uk; midnight, Sun 11 pm; booking: max 6.

J Sheekey Oyster Bar WC2 £45 ❶❶❷
St Martin's Ct   7240 2565   4–3B
"Why didn't they think of it before?"; the glamorous but "informal" (indeed, slightly louche) new annex to London's favourite fish veteran really is "the perfect place for a glass of bubbly and some oysters" ("especially if you go for the seemingly-permanent 'special offer'"); ideal for "a light meal, pre/post-theatre". / www.j-sheekey.co.uk; midnight, Sun 11 pm; booking: max 3.

Shepherd's SW1 £56 ❸❷❸
Marsham Ct, Marsham St   7834 9552   2–4C
"The whole is greater than the sum of the parts", say fans of this "club-like" Westminster stalwart, whose "sound", "civilised" and "traditional" British values make it "perfect for business lunches". / www.langansrestaurants.co.uk; 11 pm; closed Sat & Sun.

Shikara £29 ❸❷❸
65 Great Titchfield St, W1   7636 5618   2–1B **NEW**
87 Sloane Ave, SW3   7581 6555   5–2C
A pair of "simple" but "good-value" Indians, most notable as budget destinations in pricey areas (Chelsea especially). / www.shikara1.co.uk; 11.30 pm.

Shilpa W6 £27 ❶❷⑤
206 King St 8741 3127 7–2B
*"Zingy and fresh" south Indian food at "amazing" prices makes
it well worth seeking out this "subdued"-looking outfit,
in Hammersmith; if you're lucky, you may get "Bollywood on the TV"
too.* / www.shilparestaurant.co.uk; 11 pm, Thu, Fri & Sat midnight; no Amex.

The Ship SW18 £39 ❸❸❸
41 Jews Row 8870 9667 10–2B
*This Young's pub remains a key 20/30-something hang out, thanks
in particular to its "good summer BBQ" and "beautiful" Thames-side
setting – sitting in the "heaving" crowd, "you forget Wandsworth
Bridge is just metres away".* / www.theship.co.uk; 10 pm; no booking, Sun L.

Shish £28 ④④❸
2-6 Station Pde, NW2 8208 9290 1–1A
313-319 Old St, EC1 7749 0990 12–1B
*Fans of this "industrial"-looking duo say their wraps and mezze are
"good value" and "more interesting than a burger or pizza joint" –
sceptics that they're "OK, but not worth a trip".* / www.shish.com;
11.30 pm, Sun 10.30 pm; booking: 8 min.

Shogun W1 £64 ❸❷⑤
Adam's Row 7493 1255 3–3A
*It may look rather "tired", but this Mayfair Japanese stalwart still
offers "good, honest traditional food", including some "excellent
sushi".* / 11 pm; D only, closed Mon.

Siam Central W1 £29 ❸❷④
14 Charlotte St 7436 7460 2–1C
*Thanks to its very tasty food at "budget prices", this "cramped"
Fitzrovia Thai is "always bustling".* / 11 pm.

Signor Sassi SW1 £45 ❷❷❷
14 Knightsbridge Grn 7584 2277 5–1D
*This "friendly", traditional-style Knightsbridge trattoria is "always
jumping", thanks not least to its "very good" cooking (and "superb
ingredients"); "must the waiters sing?", though.* / 11.30 pm,
Sun 10.30 pm; closed Sun.

Silk
Courthouse Hotel W1 £53 ④❸❸
19-21 Gt Marlborough St 7297 5555 3–1C
*An "interesting" setting – "an old courthouse with most of its original
fixtures" – isn't enough to make a real success of this Soho-fringe
boutique hotel dining room, which "somehow lacks atmosphere";
it doesn't help that the food is "way too expensive".*
/ www.courthouse-hotel.com; 10.30 pm; D only, closed Mon & Sun.

Simpson's Tavern EC3 £29 ④❷❶
38 1/2 Ball Ct, Cornhill 7626 9985 9–2C
*This "timeless" (Dickensian) back-alley chophouse makes City blokes
(mainly) feel "at one with those who've been making deals round
here for centuries"; its "solid" meaty fare is "never going to win any
prizes", but it is "good value".* / www.simpsonstavern.co.uk; L only, closed
Sat & Sun.

Simpsons-in-the-Strand WC2   £57   ④④④
100 Strand   7836 9112   4–3D
The setting may "ooze olde-world charm", but – with its "bland" cuisine – this grand Covent Garden-fringe "institution" (famous for roast beef from the trolley) too often feels like a "tourist trap"; breakfasts, though, are "classic". / www.simpsonsinthestrand.co.uk; 10.45 pm, Sun 9 pm; no trainers.

Singapore Garden NW6   £38   ❷❷❸
83a Fairfax Rd   7624 8233   8–2A
An "interesting mixture of SE Asian cuisines", "attentive" (sometimes "too attentive") service and a "pleasing" ambience maintain the status of this Swiss Cottage veteran – "a 'local' with a loyal following from far and wide". / www.singaporegarden.co.uk; 11 pm, Fri-Sat 11.30 pm.

Sitaaray WC2   £39   ❷❷❷
167 Drury Ln   7269 6422   4–1C
"Substantial set menus of tandoori dishes and shish kebabs" win praise for this "good-value" Covent Garden spot; a "buzzy" place – with booths and Bollywood-theming – it would equally suit a date or a party. / www.sitaaray.com; 10.45 pm; closed Sun.

606 Club SW10   £47   ④④❷
90 Lots Rd   7352 5953   5–4B
"Surprisingly good all round, and brilliant if you like jazz" – this characterful World's End speak-easy is never going to set the world on fire foodwise, but it makes a fun good-night-out destination nonetheless. / www.606club.co.uk; midnight, Sat & Sun 1.30 pm; D only.

06 St Chad's Place WC1   £36   ❸❸❸
6 St Chad's Pl   7278 3355   8–3D
The "odd" but "interesting" location – an impressively-renovated Victorian warehouse, in an alley by King's Cross station – adds to the appeal of this "pleasant" bar/café, which serves up some "reliable, light and healthy" dishes. / www.6stchadsplace.com; 9.30 pm; closed Sat & Sun; no Amex.

(Lecture Room)
Sketch W1   £95   ⑤⑤④
9 Conduit St   7659 4500   3–2C
"Everything's great... until the bill arrives", at this "beautiful" ("pretentious") Mayfair dining room; true, the "elaborate" cuisine, "with an emphasis on novel flavours", can be "exciting", but... "ouch", with such "silly" prices, "who really wants to go?" / www.sketch.uk.com; 10.30 pm; closed Mon, Sat L & Sun; jacket; booking: max 8.

(Gallery)
Sketch W1   £55   ⑤④④
9 Conduit St   7659 4500   3–2C
"Why, why, why, why, why?" do people still go to this "cold", "look-at-me" Mayfair fashionista hang-out, where you "pay through the nose" for "terrible" food – perhaps it's "to try the egg-loos"? / www.sketch.uk.com; 1 am; D only, closed Sun; booking: max 12.

(Parlour)
Sketch W1   £44   ④④❷
9 Conduit St   7659 4500   3–2C
"Incredible hot chocolate", "gorgeous" cakes and "brilliant" croissants make a snack in the pâtisserie section the lowest-risk way to sample the delights of this OTT Mayfair palazzo. / www.sketch.uk.com; closed Sun; no booking.

Skylon
South Bank Centre SE1 £56 ④④❷
Southbank Centre, Belvedere Rd 7654 7800 2–3D
"Shame about the boring food" – and the "feckless" service too –
at the D&D group operation in this vast "'50s-tastic" South Bank
chamber; despite an "unparalleled" view of the Thames, the overall
experience still too often manages to be "underwhelming".
/ www.skylonrestaurant.co.uk; 11 pm, Sun 10.30 pm; no trainers.

Slurp
£19 ❸④④
104-106 Streatham High Rd, SW16 8677 7786 10–2D
138 Merton Rd, SW19 8543 4141 10–2B
"Definitely better than Wagamama" – these "cheap and cheerful"
canteens in Wimbledon and, now, Putney serve up a "good range
of dishes" at "crunch-busting prices". / www.slurprestaurant.co.uk; 11 pm;
no Amex.

Smithfield Bar & Grill EC1
£46 ❸④❸
2-3 West Smithfield 7246 0900 9–2A
Improved reports this year on this self-explanatory City-fringe spot,
which does indeed specialise in "delicious grilled food" (especially ribs
and burgers). / www.blackhouse.uk.com; 11 pm, Sat 10.30 pm; closed
Sat L & Sun.

(Top Floor)
Smiths of Smithfield EC1 £58 ④④❸
67-77 Charterhouse St 7251 7950 9–1A
"Fantastic views", "great steaks" and a "decent wine list" – all factors
which help make this elevated Smithfield dining room (with terrace)
a top venue for "carnivorous City types"; on too many recent
occasions, however, standards have been "way below par"
("especially given the prices"). / www.smithsofsmithfield.co.uk; 10.45 pm;
closed Sat L; booking: max 10.

(Dining Room)
Smiths of Smithfield EC1 £37 ④④④
67-77 Charterhouse St 7251 7950 9–1A
The second-floor brasserie of this Smithfield complex is "going
downhill"; its "meat-based" menu is "unexceptional" nowadays, staff
are "inattentive" and what was once a "buzzy" scene now too often
just seems "loud" (and sometimes "ear-splittingly" so).
/ www.smithsofsmithfield.co.uk; 10.45 pm; closed Sat L & Sun; booking:
max 12.

(Ground Floor)
Smiths of Smithfield EC1 £23 ④④❷
67-77 Charterhouse St 7251 7950 9–1A
There's "a real NYC feel on weekend mornings", at this "fun" hang-
out, on the ground floor of this Smithfield warehouse-conversion –
a hugely popular, "classic brunch" destination, for which you may
have to queue. / www.smithsofsmithfield.co.uk; L only.

Snazz Sichuan NW1
£33 ❸❸④
37 Chalton St 7388 0808 8–3C
"If you like it hot", this "friendly" spot, near Euston, offers some
"exciting" Sichuan cuisine; the place is "not about to win any style
awards", though, and there's the odd suggestion that the cooking
"went slightly downhill this year". / www.newchinaclub.co.uk; 10.30 pm.

So W1 £45 ❸❸⑤
3-4 Warwick St 7292 0767 3–2D
A small oriental establishment, just off Regent Street, which inspires few reports; fans are wild about its "meticulously elegant" style, "fresh" Japanese/fusion cuisine and "wonderful" selection of teas, but others are unconvinced. / www.sorestaurant.com; 10.30 pm; closed Sun.

Sofra £33 ④④④
I St Christopher's Pl, W1 7224 4080 3–1A
18 Shepherd St, W1 7493 3320 3–4B
36 Tavistock St, WC2 7240 3773 4–3D
II Circus Rd, NW8 7586 9889 8–3A
21 Exmouth Mkt, EC1 7833 1111 9–1A
These "cramped" and "noisy" Turkish cafés are regularly tipped as "OK" and "inexpensive" stand-bys; "they lack style", though, and "can get very boring after a few visits". / www.sofra.co.uk; II pm-midnight.

Soho Japan W1 £33 ❸❷❸
52 Wells St 7323 4661 2–1B
"Tasty and well-priced Japanese classics" win praise for this "quite cosy" spot, tucked-away just north of Oxford Street. / www.sohojapan.co.uk; 10.30 pm; closed Sat L & Sun.

Solly's NW11 £39 ④⑤⑤
146-150 Golders Green Rd 8455 0004 1–1B
Since its post-fire relaunch this Golder's Green Israeli – a "crowded" café/take-away, with upstairs restaurant – has attracted mixed reports; fans say it does "the best shawarma" and "fresh and tasty" salads, too – critics that the food's "badly served and far too expensive for what it is". / 10.30 pm; closed Fri D & Sat L; no credit cards.

Somerstown Coffee House NW1 £36 ❸❸④
60 Chalton St 7691 9136 8–3C
"A lovely French-run pub", in a "dodgy" location not far from the British Library; it's a "friendly" place, and the food – cooked up by two sisters from Normandy – is "tasty" too. / www.somerstowncoffeehouse.com; II pm.

Sông Quê E2 £24 ❷④④
134 Kingsland Rd 7613 3222 12–1B
"Probably still London's best Vietnamese" – this "Spartan" Shoreditch canteen serves "wow" dishes at "extremely low" prices, and remains "very popular"; service, though, can be "abrupt". / II pm; no Amex.

Sonny's SW13 £42 ④❸❸
94 Church Rd 8748 0393 10–1A
Once, it was everyone's "favourite local", but this Barnes brasserie "went off the boil" a few years ago; a recent "updating" of the décor has helped win back some lost ground, but the food is still "not special". / www.sonnys.co.uk; 10.30 pm Fri & Sat II pm; closed Sun D; set weekday L £27 (FP).

Sophie's Steakhouse £40 ④❸❷
29-31 Wellington St, WC2 7836 8836 4–3D **NEW**
311-313 Fulham Rd, SW10 7352 0088 5–3B
"Fun" and "sociable", these no-booking Chelsea and, now, Covent Garden steakhouses are "funky" and "buzzy" sorts of places, where the "reasonably well-prepared" food is secondary to the atmosphere. / www.sophiessteakhouse.com; SW10 11.45 pm, Sun 11.15 pm; WC2 12.45 pm, Sun II pm; no booking.

Soseki EC3 NEW — £50 — ❸❸❷
1F, 20 Bury St   7621 9211   9–2D
"Beautifully designed and thought-out", this Japanese tea house-style newcomer is surprisingly "pretty" for a venue right by the 'Gherkin'; "frequent deals" offer particularly good value. / www.soseki.co.uk; 10 pm; closed Sat & Sun; booking: max 12.

Sotheby's Café W1 — £44 — ❷❷❷
34 New Bond St   7293 5077   3–2C
"Tucked-in to the auction house" – off the foyer, in fact – this small but "very classy" Mayfair café offers a perfect perch for a "people-watching lunch"; the food is "surprisingly good value", too. / www.sothebys.com; L only, closed Sat & Sun; booking: max 6.

Souk Medina WC2 — £34 — ❹❸❶
1A Short Gdns   7240 1796   4–2B
With its "Arabian Nights" atmosphere, this "lovely" Covent Garden 'riad' makes a great setting "for groups and parties", even if the food is rather "variable". / www.soukrestaurant.co.uk; midnight.

Spacca Napoli W1 — £34 — ❷❹❸
101 Dean St   7437 9440   3–1D
"If you like noise and chaos", this "authentic" Soho trattoria ("rammed full of Italians") is "a great place", serving "proper Neapolitan pizza" (by the metre); service, however, "needs work". / www.spaccanapoli.co.uk; 11 pm.

Spago SW7 — £30 — ❸❹❹
6 Glendower Pl   7225 2407   5–2B
It can seem rather "noisy and scruffy", but this budget South Kensington Italian of long standing still has its supporters, especially for its "authentic" thin-crust pizza. / www.spagolondon.co.uk; midnight; no Amex.

Spaniard's Inn NW3 — £20 — ❹❸❷
Spaniards Rd, Hampstead Heath   8731 8406   8–1A
"An atmospheric destination after a walk on Hampstead Heath"; this "welcoming" inn (with large garden) is "steeped in history", and serves tolerable grub at "reasonable prices". / www.thespaniardshampstead.co.uk; 10 pm, Sat & Sun 11 pm.

The Spencer Arms SW15 — £38 — ❸❹❸
237 Lower Richmond Rd   8788 0640   10–1B
By Putney Heath, this modernised "proper pub" recently introduced a more tapas-style menu – early-days reporters disagree as to whether or not this was a good thing! / www.thespencerarms.co.uk; 10 pm, Sun 9 pm.

Spianata & Co — £10 — ❷❷❸
41 Brushfield St, E1   7655 4411   12–2B
20 Holborn Viaduct, EC1   7236 3666   9–2A
12 Moorfields, EC2   7638 6118   12–2A
29-30 Leadenhall Mkt, EC3   7929 1339   9–2D
73 Watling St, EC4   7236 3666   9–2B
"Proper paninis, with fresh and simple fillings", "the best coffee", and "other Italian delights" inspire rave reviews on these "chaotic" but "friendly" pit stops. / www.spianata.com; 3.30 pm; EC3 11 pm; closed Sat & Sun; E1 closed Sat; no credit cards; no booking.

The Spread Eagle SE10　　　　£50　　❸④④
1-2 Stockwell St　8853 2333　1–3D
This "lovely", olde-worlde tavern has been converted into Greenwich's
grandest restaurant; like many of the places we list in the area though
– many of which are owned by the same man! – its appeal can
be spoilt by "amateurish service" and "high prices".
/ www.spreadeaglerestaurant.co.uk; 10 pm, Sat 10.30 pm, Sun 9 pm;
no Amex.

THE SQUARE W1　　　　　　　£96　　❷❷❸
6-10 Bruton St　7495 7100　3–2C
Philip Howard's "consistently superb" cuisine and an utterly
"fabulous" wine list have long put this "understated and confident"
Mayfair dining room in London's first rank; the "polished" service has
sometimes contributed to a rather "serious" ambience, but there are
signs of late that it has 'lightened up'. / www.squarerestaurant.com;
10 pm, Sat 10.30 pm; closed Sat L & Sun L; booking: max 8; set weekday L
£79 (FP).

Square Pie Company　　　　　£15　　❷❷❸
Selfridges, 400 Oxford St, W1　7318 2460　3–1A
Unit 9, The Brunswick Centre, WC1　7837 6207　8–4C
Westfield, Ariel Way, W12　8222 6697　7–1C **NEW**
1 Canada Sq, Jubilee Line Mall, E14　7519 6071　11–1C
16 Horner St, Old Spitalfields Mkt, E1　12–2C
"Quick, simple and good-value" British pit stops, where "top pies" are
indeed the star attraction. / www.squarepie.com; E14 4 pm-8 pm;
E1 4.30 pm, Sun 5.30 pm; W1 6 pm-8 pm; WC1 10.30 pm; E1 L only, closed
Sat; E14 closed Sun; no booking.

Sree Krishna SW17　　　　　£24　　❷❸❸
192-194 Tooting High St　8672 4250　10–2C
This "wonderful" Tooting veteran has forever been a "great-value"
destination; it serves "some of the best south Indian cooking
in London", with "especially interesting" veggie fare.
/ www.sreekrishna.co.uk; 10.45 pm, Fri & Sat midnight; set Sun L £19 (FP).

Star Café W1　　　　　　　£26　　④❸❸
22 Gt Chapel St　7437 8778　3–1D
"Nothing changes", at this "marvellous Soho institution", where
"great fry-ups" are the main event. / www.thestarcafe.co.uk; L only, closed
Sat & Sun; no Amex.

Star of India SW5　　　　　£40　　❷④❸
154 Old Brompton Rd　7373 2901　5–2B
With its "subtle" cooking and "elegant" décor, this Earl's Court
veteran curry house remains "a cut above" most subcontinentals;
service, though, is "brusque". / www.starofindia.eu; 11.45 pm, Sun 11 pm.

Starbucks　　　　　　　　£14　　④❸④
Branches throughout London
Standards are "all a bit average" – "mediocre" snacks in particular –
but this "ubiquitous" chain is still a "guilty pleasure" for many
reporters, who praise its "yummy frappucinos", "great skinny chai
lattes" and "decent" filter coffee. / www.starbucks.com; 6.30 pm-11 pm;
most City branches closed all or part of weekend; no booking.

Stein's TW10　　　　　　　£24　　④④❸
Towpath (Rear of 55 Petersham Rd)　8948 8189　1–4A
A "lovely German beer garden next to the river", at Richmond, which
makes "an extremely pleasant place to spend an afternoon" –
"the requirement to order food" (primarily huge platters of 'wurst')
"keeps out the riff-raff". / www.stein-s.com; 10 pm; no Amex.

Stick & Bowl W8 £22 ❷❷④
31 Kensington High St 7937 2778 5–1A
*Ever "busy", this Kensington "hole in the wall" feels like "a little bit
of Hong Kong"; perch on a "high stool" to enjoy some "tasty" and
"excellent-value" chow. / 11 pm; no credit cards; no booking.*

Sticky Fingers W8 £37 ④④❸
1a Phillimore Gdns 7938 5338 5–1A
*For "unreconstructed" US-style burgers – to eat "with mates or kids"
– some reporters still recommend this "old-favourite" Kensington
diner (which is full of Bill Wyman's rock memorabilia"); others,
though, say it's "old and tired"… "like the Stones!"
/ www.stickyfingers.co.uk; 11.30 pm.*

Stock Pot £18 ④❸④
40 Panton St, SW1 7839 5142 4–4A
273 King's Rd, SW3 7823 3175 5–3C
*"Relive your school dinners!", at these "London institutions" of the
'60s, which offer "basic" but "reliable" comfort food, at "unbeatable"
prices. / 11.30 pm, Wed-Sat midnight, Sun 10.30 pm; no credit cards.*

The Stonhouse SW4 £37 ④④❸
165 Stonhouse St 7819 9312 10–1D
*A back street gastropub, in Clapham Old Town, where
a "good atmosphere" is the high-point – the menu, with some
emphasis on steak, is hit-and-miss. / www.renaissancepubs.co.uk; 11 pm.*

Story Deli
The Old Truman Brewery E1 £29 ❷⑤❷
3 Dray Walk 7247 3137 12–2C
*"Brick Lane's best place to eat" isn't one of its myriad curry houses,
but rather this "very cool", "rustic" haunt, which features "seriously
good" pizza (with "the thinnest bases ever"); service is often off the
case, but at least you get "good people-watching" while you wait.
/ 10.30 pm; no booking.*

Strada £34 ④④❸
Branches throughout London
*Fans tout this "reliable" Italian chain as an "upmarket PizzaExpress",
and claim it has "much better" standards too; its survey grades,
however, trail the market leader's across the board (and by
an appreciable margin too). / www.strada.co.uk; 10.30 pm-11 pm;
some booking restrictions apply.*

Stringray Café £25 ❷④❸
36 Highbury Pk, N5 7354 9309 8–2D
Tufnell Pk, NW5 7482 4855 8–2B
109 Columbia Rd, E2 7613 1141 1–2D
*"After a busy day at Columbia Road flower market", you might like
to try this "chaotic" Italian for some "really tasty, crisp pizza"; it also
has a pair of lesser-known north London siblings – the Highbury
branch is "great before Arsenal matches". / www.stringraycafe.co.uk;
11 pm; NW5 11.30 pm, Sun 11 pm.*

Sufi W12 £22 ❷❶❸
70 Askew Rd 8834 4888 7–1B
*This "family-owned Persian place", in Shepherd's Bush, delivers
up "wonderful" food (including "excellent" meats, "addictive" dips
and "lovely fresh flat-bread"); service "couldn't be nicer".
/ www.sufirestaurant.com; 11 pm.*

Sugar Hut SW6 £47 ❸❸❸
374 North End Rd   7386 8950   5–3A
"You practically get a bed to lie on", in the bar of this "nightclubby"
and "romantic" Fulham Thai – "a cool spot to chill out and drink
great cocktails"; "the food isn't bad either". / www.sugarhutworld.com;
midnight; D only; no trainers.

Sugar Reef W1 £35 ④④④
42-44 Gt Windmill St   7851 0800   3–2D
A large and "busy" Soho nightclub sometimes tipped as a "lively" pre-
theatre destination; critics say its "unmemorable" food
is best "avoided", but it strikes some reporters as "better than
expected". / www.sugarreef.co.uk; 11.30 pm; D only, closed Sun.

Suk Saran SW19 £39 ❸④④
29 Wimbledon Rd   8947 9199   10–2B
"Outclassing its All-Bar-One-style neighbours" – this Thai outfit,
near Wimbledon station, may look a bit "nondescript", but it serves
food that's "a cut above the average". / www.sukhogroup.com; 11 pm;
booking: max 20.

Suka
Sanderson W1 £70 ④④⑤
50 Berners St   7300 1444   3–1D
This once-trashily-trendy boutique hotel dining room, just north
of Oxford Street, inspires little feedback nowadays… mainly to the
effect that it's "very overpriced, and average at best".
/ www.morganshotel.com; 11 pm, Sun 11.30 pm.

Sukho Thai Cuisine SW6 £41 ❶❶❸
855 Fulham Rd   7371 7600   10–1B
"Outstanding" and "delicate" Thai cooking again wins the
highest praise for this "tightly-configured" café, in the distant reaches
of the Fulham Road, as does its "faultless" service; (the occasional
purist, though, says the food's "too sweet"). / www.sukhogroup.co.uk;
11 pm.

Sumosan W1 £65 ❷❸④
26b Albemarle St   7495 5999   3–3C
"It's just as good as Nobu, but minus the attitude and prices",
say fans of this trendy-looking but "calm" Mayfair Japanese;
"they need to inject more life into the atmosphere", though, but at
least the place is "much easier to get in to" than its more famous
peers. / www.sumosan.com; 11.30 pm; closed Sat L & Sun L; set weekday L
£44 (FP).

Le Suquet SW3 £53 ❸❸❸
104 Draycott Ave   7581 1785   5–2C
"Absolutely superb fruits de mer" and other "traditional" fish dishes
have long helped create a "very French" experience at this
"squashed", South Kensington veteran; nowadays, however, it can
sometimes seem a bit "tired". / 11.30 pm; set weekday L £34 (FP).

Sushi Hiroba WC2 £28 ④④④
50-54 Kingsway   7430 1888   2–2D
A "functional" Holborn venue (open 365 days a year), praised
by some – but not all – reporters for offering "good sushi
at reasonable prices". / www.sushihiroba.co.uk; 11 pm; closed Sun L;
booking: max 6.

Sushi-Hiro W5 £39 ❶❸⑤
1 Station Pde   8896 3175   1–3A
"Still London's best place for sushi"; this "tiny" fixture, stuck out near
Ealing Common tube, may look "grim", but appearances are
"more than compensated for" by dishes that are "almost too good
to be true" ("prepared before your eyes by a master of the art").
/ 9 pm; closed Mon; no credit cards.

Sushi-Say NW2 £40 ❶❶④
33b Walm Ln   8459 7512   1–1A
"You could be sitting in Ginza, Tokyo" – not Willesden Green! –
at the Shimizu family's "wonderful" (recently refurbished) café, which
offers "brilliantly-crafted sushi" and "unbeatable service". / 10 pm,
Sat 10.30 pm, Sun 9.30; closed Mon, Tue-Fri D only, Sat & Sun open L & D;
no Amex.

Sushinho SW3 NEW £46 ④④④
312-314 Kings Rd   7349 7496   5–3C
With its ambitious Brazilian-Japanese menu and funky styling,
this new Chelsea bar/restaurant has been a truly "memorable"
discovery for some reporters; critics, though, were "expecting much
more after all the hype", and find it "very expensive for what it is".
/ www.sushinho.com; midnight; closed Sun L.

The Swag & Tails SW7 £44 ❸❷❷
10-11 Fairholt St   7584 6926   5–1C
"Hidden-away in a mews opposite Harrods", this upmarket but
"friendly" gastroboozer can seem something of a "find"; its "fresh,
tasty and consistent" fare includes "delicious" burgers.
/ www.swagandtails.com; 10 pm; closed Sat & Sun.

The Swan W4 £39 ❸❸❷
119 Acton Ln   8994 8262   7–1A
"Tucked-away" in Chiswick, this "pub for all seasons" boasts a "cosy,
wood-panelled" interior and "great garden"; its "good, solid food" also
impresses many reporters, but a few sceptics feel the kitchen has
"lost its way a bit" in recent times. / theswanchiswick.co.uk; 10 pm, Fri &
Sat 10.30 pm, Sun 10 pm; closed weekday L; no booking.

The Swan & Edgar NW1 NEW £29
43 Linhope St   7724 6268   2–1A
A really tiny new Marylebone pub tipped by an early-days reporter for
its "interesting" ambience, "good food" and "value for money"; there
was too little feedback, though, to make a rating appropriate.
/ www.swanandedgar.co.uk; 10 pm, Sun 9 pm; D only, ex Sun open L & D.

The Swan At The Globe SE1 £46 ④❸❷
21 New Globe Walk   7928 9444   9–3B
Despite "gorgeous views of the Thames and St Paul's",
this "charming" South Bank first-floor brasserie is "not quite down
to tourist-trap levels"; that said, the food is still "pretty mediocre".
/ www.swanattheglobe.co.uk; 10 pm; closed Sun D; set Sun L £31 (FP).

Sweetings EC4 £48 ❸❸❷
39 Queen Victoria St   7248 3062   9–3B
An "old-school" City experience – this "bustling" Victorian
"time warp" serves "quality" ("expensive") seafood, "prepared in the
classic British style"; arrive early, though – it's always "exceptionally
busy", and you can't book. / L only, closed Sat & Sun; no booking.

Taberna Etrusca EC4　　　£45　　④④④
9 Bow Churchyard　7248 5552　9–2C
*"For a good business lunch", some City folk find this is a "perfect little
Italian"; it certainly has good al fresco tables, but critics are "unsure
why it's so popular" – "you get better food nearby at better prices".
/ www.etruscarestaurants.com; L only, closed Sat & Sun.*

The Table SE1　　　£33　　❷❷❷
83 Southwark St　7401 2760　9–4B
*In a "cool" building housing a notable architectural practice,
this "trendy", self-service café – serving salads, plus other "light"
dishes – makes a "brisk" weekday lunch venue; it's also "perfect" for
a "chilled" brunch after a trip to nearby Borough Market.
/ www.thetablecafe.com; L only.*

Taiwan Village SW6　　　£28　　❶❶❸
85 Lillie Rd　7381 2900　5–3A
*"Choose the Leave It To Us feast", to enjoy a "seemingly endless"
stream of "sensational dishes", at this "off-the-beaten-track" Fulham
Chinese; it's a "cosy" place too, with "lovely" staff.
/ www.taiwanvillage.com; 11.30 pm; closed weekday L; booking: max 20.*

Tajima Tei EC1　　　£31　　❷❷④
9-11 Leather Ln　7404 9665　9–2A
*"Tucked-away" off Hatton Garden, an "authentic" and "busy"
Japanese, serving "excellent" sushi and other "good-quality" fare.
/ www.tajima-tei.co.uk; 10 pm; closed Sat L & Sun; no booking, L.*

Talad Thai SW15　　　£26　　❸❷⑤
320 Upper Richmond Rd　8789 8084　10–2A
*Fans of this Putney Thai – which is attached to an oriental
supermarket – still acclaim its "authentic", "cheap" and "delicious"
scoff; its survey ratings, though, aren't a patch on a few years ago.
/ www.taladthai.co.uk; 10.30 pm, Sun 9.30 pm; no Amex.*

Taman Gang W1　　　£52　　❸❸④
141 Park Ln　7518 3160　2–2A
*It's easy to assume the main point of this blingy (and somewhat
"overpriced") basement oriental near Marble Arch is to hang out with
its "glitzy" crowd, but reports suggest it's rather the other way round
– "this is a good all-rounder until later on in the evening, when it
becomes a tacky nightclub". / www.tamangang.com; 11.30 pm; D only,
closed Mon & Sun; booking: max 6.*

Tamarai WC2　　　£54　　❸④❸
167 Drury Ln　7831 9399　4–1C
*In a glammed-up Covent Garden basement, a cocktail bar where the
Indian food is "surprisingly good, for a nightspot"; "it tastes even
better if you go on one of their regular 50%-off deals".
/ www.tamarai.co.uk; 11.30 pm; D only, closed Sun.*

Tamarind W1　　　£58　　❷❷❸
20 Queen St　7629 3561　3–3B
*Alfred Prasad's "complex and subtle" cuisine wins continued acclaim
for this "high-class" Mayfair Indian, where a "slightly dark" basement
setting hardly detracts from the "very superior" overall experience.
/ www.tamarindrestaurant.com; 11 pm, Sun 10.15 pm; closed Sat L;
set weekday L £26 (FP).*

tamesa@oxo
Oxo Tower SE1 £43 ⑤⑤④
2nd Fl, Oxo Tower Wharf, Barge House St 7633 0088 9–3A
This South Bank room-with-a-river-view (on the second floor of the landmark Oxo Tower) inspired few and largely "disappointing" reports this year – service is consistently mediocre, and the food's "inconsistent at best". / www.tamesaatoxo.com; 10.30 pm; closed Mon & Sun; set dinner £28 (FP).

Tampopo SW10 £32 ❸❷❸
140 Fulham Rd 7370 5355 5–3B
"This is how Wagamama should have turned out", say fans of this "buzzy" and "slickly-managed" Chelsea pan-Asian (an offshoot of a chain based in NW England); it's "ideal pre/post cinema". / www.tampopo.co.uk; 11 pm, Fri & Sat 11.30 pm, Sun 10 pm.

Tandoori Lane SW6 £26 ❷❷❸
131a Munster Rd 7371 0440 10–1B
A "great neighbourhood Indian", at the far end of Fulham – it looks a bit "odd", but serves food that's "delicious, and cheap too". / 11 pm; D only; no Amex.

Tandoori Nights SE22 £32 ❷❷❷
73 Lordship Ln 1–4D
This "great non-standard curry house" offers "fresh" and "fantastic" food, say fans of this cramped East Dulwich Indian; others, though "fail to see what all the (local) fuss is about". / www.tandoorinightsdulwich.co.uk; 11.30 pm; closed weekday L & Sat L.

Tangawizi TW1 £31 ❷❸❸
406 Richmond Rd 8891 3737 1–4A
A "better-than-average Indian restaurant with a puzzling Swahili name" – this "top-class" Twickenham local wins praise for its "incredibly friendly" service, and its "excellent" cooking. / www.tangawizi.co.uk; 10.30 pm; D only, closed Sun.

Tapas Brindisa SE1 £36 ❷❸❸
18-20 Southwark St 7357 8880 9–4C
"You could be in Madrid", when you visit this Borough Market bar, run by a major firm of food importers, which serves up "exceptionally authentic tapas" in a "bustling" ("slightly manic") setting; "the only catch is that you can't book". / www.tapasbrindisa.com; 10.45 pm; booking: max 8.

Taqueria W11 £31 ❸❸❸
139-143 Westbourne Grove 7229 4734 6–1B
"The best tacos" and other "sparky" street fare – not to mention "hold-on-to-your-hats" margaritas – lead some fans to hail this "casual" Notting Hill cantina as "London's best Mexican"; quality is "variable", however, and "the cost of all those little dishes mounts up". / www.coolchiletaqueria.co.uk; Mon-Thu 11 pm, Fri & Sat 11.30 pm, Sun 10.30 pm; no Amex; no booking.

Taro £23 ❸❸④
10 Old Compton St, W1 7439 2275 4–2B
61 Brewer St, W1 7734 5826 3–2D
136 Brompton Rd, SW3 7581 7777 5–1C
Mr Taro's "fast and furious" Soho canteens offer "reliable nosh on the hop", not least, "big bowls of ramen and good sushi portions". / www.tarorestaurants.co.uk; 10.30 pm, Sun 9.30 pm; no Amex; Brewer St only small bookings.

Tartine SW3 £38 ❸❸❸
114 Draycott Ave   7589 4981   5–2C
A "handy snack place" for "a glass of wine and catch up with the girls" – this "stylish" Brompton Cross café offers "reliable" open sandwiches (using pain Poilâne) and other light bites.
/ www.tartine.co.uk; 11 pm; need 6+ to book at D.

Tas £30 ❹❸❸
22 Bloomsbury St, WC1   7637 4555   2–1C
33 The Cut, SE1   7928 2111   9–4A
72 Borough High St, SE1   7403 7200   9–4C
37 Farringdon Rd, EC1   7430 9721   9–1A
For "fresh" and "decent" food (with mezze a highlight) at "fair" prices, these "noisy" and "crowded" Turkish bistros still have many fans; overall, though, performance is really only "passable" nowadays.
/ www.tasrestaurant.com; 11.30 pm, Sun 10.30 pm.

Tas Pide SE1 £28 ❸❹❸
20-22 New Globe Walk   7928 3300   9–3B
"For decent food at fair prices", this "cramped" Anatolian café, by Shakespeare's Globe, is worth bearing in mind; "it's more homely and traditional than others in the Tas chain", and specialises in pide – Turkish 'pizza'. / www.tasrestaurant.com; 11.30 pm, Sun 10.30 pm.

La Tasca £29 ⑤⑤④
23-24 Maiden Ln, WC2   7240 9062   4–4C
404-406 Chiswick High Rd, W4   8994 4545   7–2A
21 Essex Rd, N1   7226 3272   8–3D
West India Quay, E14   7531 9990   11–1C
15-17 Eldon St, EC2   7256 2381   12–2B
It may be wildly successful, commercially speaking, but the "dreadful" food on offer at this "faux-Spanish" chain is a turn-off to most reporters. / www.latasca.co.uk; 11 pm; E14 10.45 pm; booking: min 8.

A Taste Of McClements TW9 NEW £52 ❷❷④
8 Station Approach   8940 6617   1–3A
"It's good to see John McClements returning to his roots", say fans of his ambitious Twickenham newcomer; "it's trying hard" ("maybe too hard"), and offers an "overwhelming" tasting menu, which at best is "exquisite". / www.tasteofmcclements.com.

(Rex Whistler)
Tate Britain SW1 £47 ❹❸❷
Millbank   7887 8825   2–4C
"Rex Whistler's frescoes make this a very special venue", but the other "hallmark" of this "charming" Westminster gallery dining room is sommelier Hamish Anderson's "fabulous" wine list – known for its "good value", and with "a lot of halves to encourage experimentation"; "stock British dishes" play a supporting role.
/ www.tate.org.uk; L & afternoon tea only.

(Restaurant, Level 7)
Tate Modern SE1 £42 ④④❶
Bankside   7887 8888   9–3B
"Stunning views" are the highlight of this "light and airy" 7th-floor "canteen"; the "seasonal" British food is often "thoughtfully prepared" too, but reports (as on service) are rather up-and-down.
/ www.tate.org.uk; 9.30 pm; Sun-Thu closed D.

(Café, Level 2)
Tate Modern SE1   £36   ④④④
Bankside   7401 5014   9–3B
*An "impressive" interior, "great" views and good kid-friendly attitude
are selling points of this "buzzy" ground floor café in the world's
most popular museum of modern art; its snacks, coffee and cakes
are "a tad dear", but "perfectly acceptable".*
*/ www.tate.org.uk/modern/eatanddrink; Fri 9.30 pm; L & tea only, except Fri
open L & D.*

Tawana W2   £34   ❸②④
3 Westbourne Grove   7229 3785   6–1C
*By the junction with Queensway, an unpretentious Bayswater Thai
establishment of long standing, generally hailed for its "consistent"
cooking. / www.tawana.co.uk; 11 pm, Sun 10 pm.*

Ten Ten Tei W1   £35   ❸❸④
56 Brewer St   7287 1738   3–2D
*A grungy-looking Soho Japanese, mostly praised as a handy "cheap
and cheerful" option "for a quick snack". / 10 pm; closed Sun; no Amex;
no booking, Fri & Sat.*

Tendido Cero SW5   £36   ❷❷❷
174 Old Brompton Rd   7370 3685   5–2B
*"First-class all round", this "cool" and "very buzzy" South Kensington
tapas bar – an offshoot of Cambio de Tercio, opposite – is currently
on a 'high'; service is "prompt" too (but the two-seatings policy can
be "a real pain"). / www.cambiodetercio.co.uk; 11 pm; booking: max 16.*

Tendido Cuatro SW6   £38   ❸❷❸
108-110 New King's Rd   7371 5147   10–1B
*Tapas that are "a cut above" – plus a "great buzzy ambience" –
win praise for Parsons's Green's year-old offshoot of the celebrated
Cambio de Tercio; it seems to be getting "seriously pricey", though.
/ www.cambiodetercio.co.uk; 11 pm; set weekday L £19 (FP).*

Tentazioni SE1   £49   ❷❶❸
2 Mill St   7394 5248   11–2A
*Try to overlook the back street Bermondsey location and the slightly
"odd" interior of this lesser-known Italian – it continues to provide
"superb", "robust" cooking (with suggested wine-matches) and the
"friendliest" service; ("excellent-value set menus – lunch especially").
/ www.tentazioni.co.uk; 10.45 pm; closed Mon L, Sat L & Sun; set weekday L
£17 (FP).*

The Terrace in the Fields WC2   £32   ❸❷❸
Lincoln's Inn Fields   7430 1234   2–2D
*"Watching the squirrels play" sets an away-from-it-all tone at this
"modern, white and wooden" shed, in the middle of Lincoln's Inn
Fields; "the chef's Caribbean background adds a light and spicy edge
to his modern British menu". / www.theterrace.info; 7 pm; L only,
closed Sun.*

Terranostra EC4   £44   ❸❷⑤
27 Old Bailey   3201 0077   9–2A
*A "simple", "friendly" and "dependable" Sardinian, with a location
that's "handy if you're watching a trial at the Old Bailey"; it's a shame
that its "decidedly unpretentious" premises seems to put off
a broader following. / www.terranostrafood.co.uk; 10 pm; closed Sat L & Sun.*

Terroirs WC2 NEW £36 ❷④❷
5 William IV St 7036 0660 4–4C
*"Beautifully-executed" small French plates, served with "real gusto" –
plus an "epic" wine list – have made this "simple bistro",
near Charing Cross, one of the year's hottest openings (to the extent
that service can "struggle" to keep up).* / www.terroirswinebar.com;
11 pm; closed Sun.

Texas Embassy Cantina SW1 £37 ⑤⑤⑤
1 Cockspur St 7925 0077 2–2C
*This "noisy" Tex/Mex, off Trafalgar Square, is often "full of REAL
Americans", and fans say it's "kind of gritty, but fun and not bad
at all"; critics simply find it "hard to express how poor it is".*
/ www.texasembassy.com; 11 pm, Sat 11.30 pm, Sun 10 pm.

Texture W1 £70 ❸❸④
34 Portman St 7224 0028 2–2A
*It's a shame that the "odd" location (a slightly awkward space,
"sharing loos with the adjacent Quality Inn") – combined with
a feeling that the menu is "grossly overpriced" – puts a cap
on appreciation of this ambitious yearling, just north of Oxford Street;
fans say the "very creative" cuisine is "exquisite", and there's
a "strong" wine list too.* / www.texture-restaurant.co.uk; 11 pm; closed
Mon & Sun; set weekday L £40 (FP).

Thai Café SW1 £29 ❸❸④
22 Charlwood St 7592 9584 2–4C
*A self-explanatory establishment, in Pimlico, offering food that's
"authentic" and "good value".* / 10.30 pm; closed Sat L & Sun L;
set weekday L £17 (FP).

Thai Corner Café SE22 £25 ❸❷❸
44 North Cross Rd 8299 4041 1–4D
*A "crammed" East Dulwich "mainstay" which gets "overwhelmingly
busy"; "the menu doesn't hold too many surprises", but the food
tastes "great" and it's "reasonably priced" too; BYO.* / 10.30 pm;
no credit cards.

Thai Garden SW11 £28 ❸❸④
58 Battersea Rise 7738 0380 10–2C
*"Our comfort blanket!" – if you're looking for unchallenging Thai food
in Battersea, this "dependable" stand-by may be just the spot.*
/ www.thaigarden.co.uk; 11 pm; D only.

Thai on the River SW11 £37 ❸❸❸
2 Lombard Rd 7924 6090 5–4B
*"Visit on a balmy summer's evening, and try and get a table outside",
if you seek out this "wonderfully-located" Battersea Thai, which also
benefits from "consistent food and charming service".*
/ www.thaiontheriver.com; 11 pm.

Thai Pot WC2 £32 ④❷④
1 Bedfordbury 7379 4580 4–4C
*Behind the Coliseum, a "reliable stand-by" with "very friendly" staff;
it is much in demand pre-theatre, even if the food is "fairly standard".*
/ www.thaipot.biz; 11.15 pm; closed Sun.

Thai Square £30 ④④❸
21-24 Cockspur St, SW1 7839 4000 2–3C
27-28 St Annes Ct, W1 7287 2000 3–1D
5 Princess St, W1 7499 3333 3–1C
148 The Strand, WC2 7497 0904 2–2D
166-170 Shaftesbury Ave, WC2 7836 7600 4–1B
229-230 Strand, WC2 7353 6980 2–2D
19 Exhibition Rd, SW7 7584 8359 5–2C
347-349 Upper St, N1 7704 2000 8–3D
2-4 Lower Richmond Rd, SW15 8780 1811 10–1A
136-138 Minories, EC3 7680 1111 9–3D
1-7 Great St Thomas Apostle, EC4 7329 0001 9–3B
*These attractive-looking orientals have "gone downhill" over the years;
as things stand, they "aren't the greatest" places ("or the worst"),
and serve food somewhere between "reliable" and "tired";
NB "fantastic river views" from SW15. / www.thaisquare.net;
10 pm-11.30 pm; SW1 Fri & Sat 1 am; WC2, EC3, EC4 & St Annes Ct closed
Sat & Sun.*

Thailand SE14 £29 ④❸④
15 Lewisham Way 8691 4040 1–3D
*This "uninspiring"-looking New Cross Thai has long been "a local
treasure", thanks to its "superb" Laotian specialities and its
"charming" service; feedback has dwindled in recent years, though,
tending to support the suggestion that, "good-value lunches aside,
it's lost its way". / 11.30 pm; set always available £15 (FP).*

The Thatched House W6 £39 ④④④
115 Dalling Rd 8748 6174 7–1B
*"Hearty" pub grub, a big garden and a cosy ambience make this
welcoming local a useful Hammersmith stand-by.
/ www.thatchedhouse.com; 10 pm.*

Theo Randall
InterContinental Hotel W1 £70 ❷❸⑤
1 Hamilton Pl 7318 8747 3–4A
*All the "big" and "rustic" flavours of "River Café cuisine" –
Theo Randall was formerly head chef there – can be had at this
Mayfair two-year-old; service is "a little erratic", though, and it's
a "shame about the room"… perhaps "bunker" would be a better
description. / www.theorandall.com; 11.15 pm; closed Sat L & Sun;
set weekday L & pre-theatre £44 (FP).*

The Thomas Cubitt SW1 £52 ❸❸❷
44 Elizabeth St 7730 6060 2–4A
*This "stylish" and "very congenial" Belgravia gastropub is "always
busy, with a great crowd" – there's a quieter restaurant above;
it's undeniably "expensive", but – for the area – offers decent value.
/ www.thethomascubitt.co.uk; 10 pm; booking only in restaurant.*

The Three Bridges SW8 £42 ❸❶④
153 Battersea Park Rd 7720 0204 10–1C
*"The owner's bonhomie" does a lot for this Italian yearling, which
arguably "deserves a better location" than by Battersea Dogs Home;
the cooking is "authentic", if sometimes "more competent than
inspired". / www.thethreebridges.com; 11 pm; closed Mon L & Sun D.*

The Three Crowns N16 £41 ④④④
175 Stoke Newington High St 7241 5511 1–1D
For fans, this Stoke Newington yearling is still "a great gastropub in a
trendy area"; it's hard, though, to avoid the impression that it's
"not as good as it first was". / www.threecrowns-n16.com; 10 pm,
Sat 10.30 pm, Sun 9.30 pm; no Amex.

tibits W1 NEW £25 ❸④④
12-14 Heddon St 7758 4110 3–2C
"Zingingly fresh" veggie dishes, served "pick 'n' mix" style, have won
praise from most early reporters on this stylish chain outlet, recently
imported from Switzerland; a Westfield version, however, did not last.
/ www.tibits.co.uk.

Tierra Brindisa W1 NEW £40 ❸❸❸
46 Broadwick St 7534 1690 3–2D
The odd sceptic feels it's "not up to its pedigree", but this "bustling"
(slightly "cramped") new Soho offshoot of the renowned Spanish
importers mostly wins high praise for its "airy and modern" looks and
"lovely" tapas. / www.tierrabrindisa.com; 11 pm; closed Sun; booking:
max 14.

Timo W8 £48 ❸❸❸
343 Kensington High St 7603 3888 7–1D
This "very buzzy" – and slightly "cramped" – Kensington local
is hailed by its small fan club as "a modern Italian gem",
with "quality" food and "unobtrusive" service; the odd hiccup,
however, is not unknown. / www.timorestaurant.net; 11 pm; closed Sun.

Toff's N10 £31 ❷❷❸
38 Muswell Hill Broadway 8883 8656 1–1B
It's "nothing fancy", but "vast portions" of "great fresh fish (and good
chips)" have built a formidable reputation for this veteran chippy,
in Muswell Hill; "very friendly" service too. / www.toffsfish.co.uk; 10 pm;
closed Sun.

Toku
Japan Centre W1 £33 ❸④④
212 Piccadilly 7255 8255 3–3D
For a "bargain fix" of "authentic Japanese fast food", this "busy"
culture-centre café, by Piccadilly Circus, is "dependably good"
(if "not the cheapest"). / www.japancentre.com; 11 pm, Sun 10 pm;
no Amex.

Tokyo City EC2 £40 ❸④④
46 Gresham St 7726 0308 9–2B
It may look "uninspiring", but this City Japanese is a notably
"reliable" destination, with "very good sushi and bento boxes";
it's "always full". / 10 pm; closed Sat & Sun.

Tokyo Diner WC2 £19 ④❸④
2 Newport Pl 7287 8777 4–3B
It looks "a bit of a dump" – and its sushi-to-noodles nosh is merely
"adequate" – but this Japanese diner in, er, Chinatown has long been
"a great, central cheap eat" that's "reliable", "fast" and "good-value".
/ www.tokyodiner.com; midnight; no Amex; no booking, Fri & Sat.

Tom Aikens SW3 £96 ❸❸④
43 Elystan St 7584 2003 5–2C
*The cuisine at Tom Aikens's Chelsea flagship can be "outstanding",
but – what with all its "foams and jellies" and all – it can also seem
"too clever by half"; critics find prices "extortionate" too, and the
ambience rather "stiff". / www.tomaikens.co.uk; 11 pm; closed Sat & Sun;
jacket and/or tie; booking: max 8; set weekday L £50 (FP).*

Tom Ilic SW8 £42 ❶❸④
123 Queenstown Rd 7622 0555 10–1C
*Tom Illic is a "genius", say his fans, and "serious meat-eaters",
in particular, will find it "well worth the trip" to his Battersea
restaurant, somewhat "grim" décor notwithstanding. / www.tomilic.com;
10.30 pm; closed Mon, Tue L, Sat L & Sun D.*

Tom's Deli W11 £29 ④④❷
226 Westbourne Grove 7221 8818 6–1B
*For a "fantastic but pricey" brunch or for "coffee and a cake",
Tom Conran's café/deli makes a good "hang-out", and it remains
a linchpin of the Notting Hill scene. / www.tomsdelilondon.co.uk; 5.30 pm;
L only; no Amex; no booking.*

Tom's Kitchen SW3 £50 ❸④④
27 Cale St 7349 0202 5–2C
*For "food without fuss" (especially a "perfect brunch") in a "fun and
buzzy" setting, Tom Aikens's Chelsea bistro can be a "great all-
rounder"; service is sometimes "the worst ever", though,
and "you pay a lot" to be so "squashed". / www.tomskitchen.co.uk;
11 pm; set weekday L & pre-theatre £32 (FP).*

Tootsies £33 ④④④
35 James St, W1 7486 1611 3–1A
120 Holland Park Ave, W11 7229 8567 6–2A
148 Chiswick High Rd, W4 8747 1869 7–2A
196-198 Haverstock Hill, NW3 7431 3812 8–2A
1 Battersea Rise, SW11 7924 4935 10–2C
Putney Wharf, 30 Brewhouse St, SW15 8788 8488 10–2B
48 High St, SW19 8946 4135 10–2B
*"Good burgers and breakfasts" still win fans for this "family-friendly"
chain; it seems very "formulaic", though, nowadays, with "hit-and-
miss" service and "bland" food. / www.tootsiesrestaurants.co.uk; 10.30 pm;
some booking restrictions apply.*

Tosa W6 £33 ❸④④
332 King St 8748 0002 7–2B
*On Hammersmith's main drag, an "excellent local Japanese" which
may be "a little cramped", but which serves "great food
at reasonable prices" – not least "authentic" sushi and "more-ish"
yakitori. / 11 pm, Sun 10.30 pm; no Amex; set weekday L £20 (FP).*

Toto's SW1 £67 ❸❷❷
Lennox Gardens Mews 7589 0075 5–2C
*"Slightly out-dated" but "lovely" – this Italian restaurant, tucked-away
near Harrods, is "just the place for a Eurotrashy date" (possibly
of the more mature sort); staff are "very professional", and the food
– though "pricey" and "unadventurous" – is of "really high quality";
pretty garden too. / 11 pm, Sun 10.30 pm.*

Trader Vics
Hilton Hotel W1   £58   ⑤❸❸
22 Park Ln   7208 4113   3–4A
*Kitschier-than-kitsch "cod-Polynesian" décor makes this Mayfair
basement "a wonderful blast from the past" (if only "for the sheer
madness of it all"); stick to the "superlative cocktails", though –
the food is "disappointing" and "overpriced". / www.tradervics.com;
12.30 am; D only.*

The Trafalgar Tavern SE10   £40   ⑤⑤❸
Park Row   8858 2909   1–3D
*You really couldn't get a finer pub than this grand Georgian tavern,
overlooking the Thames at Greenwich; "pity the tourists", though –
"it seems to get more and more expensive without any improvement
in quality". / www.trafalgartavern.co.uk; 10 pm; closed Sun D; no Amex;
no booking, Sun L.*

Tree House SW13   £38   ④④❸
73 White Hart Ln   8392 1617   10–1A
*A "quirky" Barnes-fringe gastropub, with "decent"-enough cooking,
a "buzzy and cheerful atmosphere", and a "nice garden"; it's a
family-friendly place, with brunch a speciality.
/ www.treehousepeople.com; 11pm, Sat & Sun midnight.*

Trenta W2   £42   ❸④④
30 Connaught St   7262 9623   6–1D
*This "small and intimate" Bayswater Italian still elicits varied
(and limited) feedback from reporters – fans say it's "never a let-
down", but there's also the odd "dismal" report. / 10.30 pm; closed
Mon L, Sat L & Sun.*

Trinity SW4   £51   ❷❷❸
4 The Polygon   7622 1199   10–2D
*"A shining beacon of gastronomy in the SW4 wasteland"; Adam Byatt
has "notably raised his game" at this "laid-back" Clapham spot –
his "idiosyncratic" cuisine is often "brilliant", and service is trying
"very hard" too; "midweek prix-fixe offers exceptional value".
/ www.trinityrestaurant.co.uk; 10.30 pm; closed Mon L & Sun D.*

Trinity Stores SW12   £18   ❷❷❷
5-6 Balham Station Rd   8673 3773   10–2C
*"Continuing to set a standard for deli/cafés" – this "fun" Balham
"beacon" just "seems to get better and better". / www.trinitystores.co.uk;
8pm, Sat 5.30 pm, Sun 4 pm; L only.*

Trishna W1 NEW   £48   ❶❸④
15-17 Blandford St   7935 5624   2–1A
*"Truly wonderful Indian-style seafood" – served in a tapas format –
makes this notable newcomer a worthy namesake to the famous
Mumbai original; service can be rather "amateur", however, and the
styling of the Marylebone premises is rather "cold".
/ www.trishnalondon.com; 10.45 pm, Sun 10 pm.*

Les Trois Garçons E1   £72   ④❸❶
1 Club Row   7613 1924   12–1C
*It's "like walking into a fairy tale", when you enter this "very quirky"
East End fixture, whose "crazy" décor – "from a giraffe's head
to hanging handbags" – makes it "a great choice for a date";
the Gallic cuisine is "adequate". / www.lestroisgarcons.com; 10.15 pm;
D only, closed Sun; set dinner £50 (FP).*

Trojka NW1 £29 ④⑤❸
101 Regent's Park Rd 7483 3765 8–4A
The service is sometimes "@$%!", but this "atmospheric" Russian café, in Primrose Hill, is still pretty popular – "prepare to fight for a weekend table"; "it's the cheapest place around for a quick bite", and the food is at least "hearty". / www.trojka.co.uk; 10.30 pm; no Amex.

LA TROMPETTE W4 £57 ❶❶❷
5-7 Devonshire Rd 8747 1836 7–2A
"Perhaps the best food for the price anywhere in London" – this "charming" and "reasonably-priced" Chiswick sibling to the fabled Chez Bruce is similarly "outstanding" all-round; we had over 250 reports this year, and not a single 'disappointment' – an almost unbelievable level of consistency. / www.latrompette.co.uk; 10.30 pm, Sun 10 pm; booking: max 6.

Troubadour SW5 £33 ⑤④❶
263-267 Old Brompton Rd 7370 1434 5–3A
"A nice time warp for one's inner hippy" – this "chill-out" Earl's Court veteran has a "wonderful café atmosphere" and "good garden" too; the very "average" food is "not what it might be", but "good for breakfast". / www.troubadour.co.uk; 11 pm.

La Trouvaille W1 £52 ❸❸❸
12a Newburgh St 7287 8488 3–2C
A "very authentic French bistro", just off Carnaby Street – "cramped" but "enjoyable", it features an "interesting biodynamic wine list"; service, in particular, has been a bit "patchy" of late, though, and the wine bar (downstairs) is sometimes preferred to the restaurant. / www.latrouvaille.co.uk; 11 pm; closed Sun.

Truc Vert W1 £46 ❸④❷
42 North Audley St 7491 9988 3–2A
"A perfect escape from Selfridges!"; this "French-rustic" deli-café, in Mayfair, is most notable for its "fabulous" breakfasts – at other times, it's more "variable". / www.trucvert.co.uk; 10 pm; closed Sun D.

Tsunami £46 ❸④❸
93 Charlotte St, W1 7637 0050 2–1C **NEW**
5-7 Voltaire Rd, SW4 7978 1610 10–1D
"Top-quality sushi without a Zuma price tag" has long made a big name for this backstreet Clapham oriental, which opened a "trendy" Fitzrovia offshoot this year; "veerrrry slow" service dogs both ventures, though, and the original's sky-high ratings have suffered all-round in recent times. / www.tsunamirestaurant.co.uk; SW4 10.30 pm, Fri & Sat 11 pm, Sun 9.30 pm; W1 11 pm; SW4 Mon - Fri D only; W1 closed Sun; no Amex.

Tuttons WC2 £44 ④④④
11-12 Russell St 0844 3712 550 4–3D
"It's expensive, predictable, and has a great location for tourist-watching", but – surprisingly – this long-established brasserie gets an "acceptable" write-up from reporters; if you're looking for "a light bite" in Covent Garden, it's really "not too bad". / www.tuttons.com; 11.30 pm.

2 Amici SW1 £43 ④④④
48a Rochester Rw 7976 5660 2–4C
An Italian yearling worth knowing about "'if you just want pasta"; even in the desert that is Westminster, however, it only generates rather lukewarm reports. / 11 pm; closed Sat L & Sun.

Two Brothers N3 £31 ❷❷④
297-303 Regent's Park Rd   8346 0469   1–1B
*"Still North London's most popular chippy"; under new management,
this "busy and noisy" Finchley stalwart still wins much praise for its
"fantastic" and "efficiently-served" fish 'n' chips.*
/ www.twobrothers.co.uk; 10.15 pm; closed Mon & Sun; no booking at D.

202
Nicole Farhi W11 £41 ❸❸❸
202 Westbourne Grove   7792 6888   6–1B
*"You wouldn't expect the food to match up to the 'scene', but it
does!" – this diner-plus-clothes-store, in Notting Hill's "beautiful-
people zone", serves up some "surprisingly good" dishes, especially
for brunch.* / www.nicolefarhi.com; 9.30 pm; closed Mon D & Sun D;
no booking.

2 Veneti W1 £52 ❸❷④
10 Wigmore St   7637 0789   3–1B
*"Competent, if a little lacking in zing"; this "reliable" (and "not-
cheap") Italian, near the Wigmore Hall, is sometimes said to be
"under-rated" – it is tipped as "an excellent venue for a business
lunch".* / www.2veneti.com; 10.30 pm; closed Sat L & Sun.

twotwentytwo
The Landmark NW1 NEW £48 ④④⑤
222 Marylebone Rd   7631 8235   8–4A
*The food at this grandly panelled – but wholly uninspired –
Marylebone hotel dining room is "just not special enough for the
enormous prices", says one early-days reporter; on the basis of our
own visit, we'd be much less polite.* / Rated on Editors' visit;
www.landmarklondon.co.uk; 10 pm; closed Sat & Sun.

Uli W11 £33 ❷❶❸
16 All Saints Rd   7727 7511   6–1B
*"Michael is a wonderful host", and the "delicious and varied" pan-
Asian dishes on offer at his "unassuming" Notting Hill "favourite"
make it a real local treasure; a slight slip in ratings this year, however,
supports the long-term fan who feels "standards are down a notch
recently".* / www.uli-oriental.co.uk; 11 pm; D only; no Amex.

Ultimate Burger £23 ④④❸
127 Tottenham Court Rd, W1   7436 5355   2–1B
36-38 Glasshouse St, W1   7287 8429   3–3D NEW
334 New Oxford St, WC1   7436 6641   4–1C
*A small chain of central London (and, oddly, Lincoln) burger parlours,
that's consistently well-rated by practically all who comment on it.*
/ www.ultimateburger.co.uk; 11 pm, Sun 10 pm; W1 11 pm; no bookings for L.

Umu W1 £120 ❷❸❸
14-16 Bruton Pl   7499 8881   3–2C
*"Transcendent sashimi and sushi" are amongst the "exceptional"
Japanese fare on offer at Marlon Abela's "tranquil" Kyoto-style
venture, in a Mayfair mews; it's "outstandingly expensive", though –
"only go if an oligarch is paying!"* / www.umurestaurant.com; 10.30 pm;
closed Sat L & Sun; no trainers; booking: max 14.

The Union Café W1 £45 ❸❸④
96 Marylebone Ln   7486 4860   3–1A
*"One of the best-value wine lists in town" is the main draw to John
Brinkley's "casual" (and "rather noisy") modern café, quietly-located
in Marylebone; "well-prepared" cooking plays an honourable
supporting role.* / www.brinkleys.com; 11 pm; closed Sun D.

Uno SW1 £45 ④⑤④
1 Denbigh St   7834 1001   2–4B
*Some dishes at this attractive, if noisy, Pimlico Italian can
be "delicious" (especially pizza, recently reintroduced), but the
number of "disappointing" reports of late give an unshakeable
impression that it has 'gone off'. / www.uno1.co.uk; 10 pm, Fri & Sun
10.30 pm.*

Upstairs Bar SW2 £40 ❷❶❶
89b Acre Ln (door on Branksome Rd)   7733 8855   10–2D
*Entered "speakeasy-style", this "hidden" Brixton "jewel" seems like
a "great secret"; it inspires a hymn of praise for its "genial" and
"romantic" style and its "lovingly-prepared" Gallic cuisine (albeit from
a "limited" menu); "sexy" little bar too. / www.upstairslondon.com;
10.30 pm; D only, closed Mon & Sun.*

Urban Turban W2 £42 ④④④
98 Westbourne Grove   7243 4200   6–1B
*A year on, Vineet Bhattia's "new wave" Indian tapas "concept",
in Bayswater, remains a work-in-progress – it won more praise this
year for "truly innovative" dishes, but a lot of continuing flak for being
"disappointing and expensive" too. / www.urbanturban.uk.com; 11 pm.*

Le Vacherin W4 £50 ❸❸❸
76-77 South Pde   8742 2121   7–1A
*"Hidden-away" on the Chiswick/Acton borders, Malcolm John's
"understated" bistro is a great "culinary asset" for the area, with a
"very definite" French feel – the "traditional" fare, however, is "not as
memorable" as it once was. / www.levacherin.co.uk; 10.30 pm, Fri & Sat
11 pm, Sun 10 pm; closed Mon L; set Sun L £34 (FP).*

Vama SW10 £42 ❷❷④
438 King's Rd   7351 4118   5–3B
*An "unusual nouvelle Indian", in World's End, where "some dishes are
truly mind-blowing"; the décor, though, "could use some smartening
up", and the place attracts nothing like the attention it once did.
/ www.vama.co.uk; 11 pm, Sun 10.30 pm; D only, ex Sun open L & D.*

Vanilla W1 £55 ❷❷❷
131 Great Titchfield St   3008 7763   2–1B
*"Decorated like a '60s film set", this "fun" Fitzrovia basement
bar/restaurant scores well with a crowd – almost all of whom were
born after that decade – for its "pure theatre"; the cooking "tries
hard" too, and the results are often "simply fantastic".
/ www.vanillalondon.com; 10 pm; closed Mon, Sat L & Sun; no trainers;
booking: max 6; set weekday L £26 (FP).*

Vanilla Black EC4 £45 ❸❷❸
17-18 Tooks Ct   7242 2622   9–2A
*"A rare example of a gourmet vegetarian" – this unlikely import
to legal-land (from York) even leaves carnivores "impressed"; the odd
critic may complain of an "absence of buzz" in the dining room,
but fans say the atmosphere is just "civilised". / www.vanillablack.co.uk;
10 pm; closed Sat & Sun; booking: max 14; set weekday L £25 (FP).*

Vapiano W1 £24 ④④❷
19-21 Great Portland St   7268 0080   3–1C
*There are "no waiting staff" at this "gimmicky and complex" offshoot
of a German cafeteria chain, where you "DIY" (using a swipe card
to keep account) as you go; critics find it a "faceless" and
disappointing experience, but it can be handy enough for a "cheap
and fast" pizza, pasta or salad, near Oxford Circus.
/ www.vapiano.co.uk; 11 pm, Sat 10 pm.*

Il Vaporetto SW1 NEW £55 ④⑤❸
61 Elizabeth St 7730 5406 5–2D
A chic Venetian newcomer, on the Belgravia site that was for many years Mimmo d'Ischia (RIP); it's no surprise that it is, as a first-week reporter notes, "a little pricey", but we were shocked by the complacency of both food and service on our own early-days visit. / Rated on Editors' visit; www.ilvaporetto.co.uk; 11 pm; closed Sun.

Vasco & Piero's Pavilion W1 £50 ❷❸④
15 Poland St 7437 8774 3–1D
An age-old Italian "hide-away" that's "about as un-trendy as you can get in Soho nowadays", and is loved by regulars for its "simple food, simply done very well"; the ambience can seem "tepid", though, and the service has been a touch "variable" of late. / www.vascosfood.com; 10.30 pm; closed Sat L & Sun.

Veeraswamy W1 £54 ❷❷❷
Victory Hs, 99-101 Regent St 7734 1401 3–3D
With its "vibrant" contemporary décor, London's oldest Indian, near Piccadilly Circus, has certainly moved with the times, and it serves up some "very subtle" and "gorgeous" dishes; it has, however, become rather "pricey" of late. / www.realindianfood.com; 10.30 pm, Sun 10.15 pm; booking: max 12.

El Vergel SE1 £19 ❶❷❷
8 Lant St 7357 0057 9–4B
"Incredible South American dishes" come at "laughably cheap prices", at this "cramped and buzzy" refectory in a Borough side street – in fact, "it's hard to think of anywhere in London offering better value"; "amazing" Latin breakfasts too. / www.elvergel.co.uk; breakfast & L only, closed Sat D & Sun; no credit cards.

Vertigo 42
Tower 42 EC2 £64 ④④❷
25 Old Broad St 7877 7842 9–2C
"You only go for the wow of a view", to this 42nd-floor City eyrie – a good (if "overpriced") spot to woo either a client or a date over a glass or two of champagne, together with some fairly "sensible and basic" food. / www.vertigo42.co.uk; 11 pm; closed Sat & Sun; no shorts; booking essential.

Via Condotti W1 £41 ④④④
23 Conduit St 7493 7050 3–2C
"Still a decent bet", this reasonably-priced Italian is certainly worth knowing about, just off Bond Street; it's "not up to its early-days standards", though, with niggles include "amateur" service, and food that's "nice" but nothing more. / www.viacondotti.co.uk; 10.30 pm; closed Sun.

Viajante E2 NEW
Patriot Sq 12–1D
With his daring experimental cuisine, chef Nuno Mendes is one of the capital's most interesting chefs; in 2010, he will move on from the temporary 'pop-up' restaurant ('The Loft') he has been running out of his home, to this new venture in Bethnal Green. / www.viajanterestaurant.co.uk.

Il Vicolo SW1 £45 ❸❷④
3-4 Crown Passage 7839 3960 3–4D
It may look "relatively humble", but this hidden-away St James's Sardinian makes a useful West End "bolt-hole", and offers cooking that's "better than some of its more expensive near-neighbours". / 10 pm; closed Sat & Sun.

The Victoria SW14 £40 ❸❷❷
10 West Temple 8876 4238 10–2A
"Revived by new owners" (including chef Paul Merrett),
this East Sheen gastropub, which is "very handy for Richmond Park",
wins praise for its "simple" food at "reasonable prices"; for sunny
days, it has a "nice conservatory" too. / www.thevictoria.net; 10 pm,
Sat 10.30 pm; closed Sun D; no Amex; set always available £25 (FP).

Viet W1 £19 ❷⑤④
34 Greek St 7494 9888 4–3A
"The pho soups are mouthwatering", at this "packed" and "great-
value" Soho gem (where you can BYO – £2.50 corkage); "so the
tables are bare and the service is rude – what did you expect?"
/ 11 pm, Fri 11.30 pm; closed Sun; no Amex; no booking: Fri & Sat D.

Viet Garden N1 £27 ❸❸④
207 Liverpool Rd 7700 6040 8–2D
This dated-looking spot near Angel is an "absolute joy", thanks to its
"fresh and light" Vietnamese fare that "never disappoints"; "in spite
of the out-of-the-way location, you need to book in advance".
/ www.vietgarden.co.uk; 11 pm; no Amex; set weekday L £15 (FP).

Viet Grill E2 £28 ❸❸❸
58 Kingsland Rd 080624 12–1B
"You can stuff yourself silly" on "really tasty" Vietnamese food, at this
"amazingly cheap" and "cheerful" Shoreditch sibling to Cây Tre;
unusually, it also features a "clever mixing of wines" ("selected
by maestro Malcolm Gluck"). / www.vietnamesekitchen.co.uk; 11 pm, Fri &
Sat 11.30 pm, Sun 10.30 pm.

Viet Hoa E2 £25 ❸④④
70-72 Kingsland Rd 7729 8293 12–1B
You get "no ceremony" – just "no-nonsense" Vietnamese cuisine –
at this "communal café", in Shoreditch, and at "remarkably
affordable" prices too; BYO. / www.viethoarestaurant.co.uk; 11.30 pm.

Vijay NW6 £27 ❷❷④
49 Willesden Ln 7328 1087 1–1B
"Still my favourite!"; this "extremely cheap" and "surprisingly good"
Kilburn veteran looks little-changed since the '60s, but – thanks to its
"gorgeous" south Indian food – it "never fails to hit the spot".
/ www.vijayrestaurant.co.uk; 10.45 pm, Fri & Sat 11.45 pm.

Vijaya Krishna SW17 £21 ❷❷❸
114 Mitcham Rd 8767 7688 10–2C
"Highly recommended" in all reports, this Tooting south Indian offers
"excellent, freshly-spiced food"; by the standards of the area,
the setting is quite "upmarket" too. / 11 pm, Fri & Sat midnight; no Amex.

Villa Bianca NW3 £48 ④④④
1 Perrins Ct 7435 3131 8–2A
A "very quaint" Italian in "such a pretty" Hampstead lane; to fans,
it's an "old favourite", with a "lively" style and "decent enough" food
– to critics, it's just "dull and old-fashioned", and charges "silly"
prices. / www.villabiancanw3.com; 11.30 pm.

Village East SE1 £45 ❸④❸
171-173 Bermondsey St 7357 6082 9–4D
The "relaxed" vibe is the particular feature of this "fun" Bermondsey
hang-out, where the forte is a "high-end, New York-style brunch".
/ www.villageeast.co.uk; 10 pm; closed Sat D & Sun D; set Sun L £34 (FP).

Villandry W1   £47   ④⑤⑤
170 Gt Portland St   7631 3131   2–1B
"Overcrowded, but for no apparent reason" – this Marylebone deli-
café remains "beset by terrible service", and too often serves
up "bland and poorly-presented" fare at "exorbitant" prices; if you
do go, breakfast (or, perhaps, a burger) is best. / www.villandry.com;
10.30 pm; closed Sun D; booking: max 18.

Villandry Kitchen WC1 NEW   £29   ❸②❸
95/97 High Holborn   7242 4580   2–1D
Much better value than its parent establishment, in Marylebone,
this first branch of a proto-chain, near Holborn tube, offers a sensibly
short menu of bistro staples (and pizzas too) at reasonable prices;
it was already remarkably busy on our early-days visit. / Rated
on Editors' visit; www.villandry.com; 11 pm, Sun 10.30 pm.

Villiers Terrace N8 NEW   £34   ❷❷❸
120 Park Rd   8245 6827   1–1C
Early-days reports on this "stylish" and "quirky" new Crouch End
gastropub are all upbeat (and "they even think of vegetarians,
and real food for kids"). / www.villiersterracelondon.com; 10.30 pm;
no Amex; need 8+ to book.

Vincent Rooms
Westminster Kingsway College SW1   £27   ④④④
Vincent Sq   7802 8391   2–4C
This Westminster dining room is a training ground for "the chefs and
waiters of tomorrow", so the odd slip-up "can be forgiven";
the cooking can show "some originality", but it's the very reasonable
prices that make the place of note. / www.thevincentrooms.com; 9 pm;
times vary; only term times; closed Mon D, Wed D, Fri D, Sat & Sun; no Amex.

Vineria NW8 NEW   £49
1 Blenheim Ter   7328 5014   8–3A
The first UK branch of this small Italian chain, on the St John's Wood
site of Osteria Stecca (RIP) – the focus is contemporary Italian cuisine
and a large, mostly Italian, wine list. / www.vineria.it; 10.30 pm,
Sat 11 pm, Sun 10 pm; closed Mon.

Vingt-Quatre SW10   £41   ④④④
325 Fulham Rd   7376 7224   5–3B
A Chelsea 24/7 stand-by, popular "for breakfast or brunch at any
time of day" or more particularly any time of night; more generally,
though, there's a feeling you "don't get much for your money".
/ www.vingtquatre.co.uk; open 24 hours; no booking.

Vinoteca EC1   £37   ❸⓪❷
7 St John St   7253 8786   9–1B
"A truly astounding" wine list at "fair" prices, and "caring staff who
know their stuff" ensure that this "very buzzy" Clerkenwell outfit
is "always packed" – "expect a wait for a table"; the "hearty" food
is "very decent" too. / www.vinoteca.co.uk; 10 pm; closed Sun D; no Amex;
no booking D, max 8 L.

Vital Ingredient   £16   ❸❸④
18a Maddox St, W1   3–2C
36 Berwick St, W1   3–1D
6 Vigo St, W1   no tel   3–3C
1 Garlick Hill, EC4   7248 9822   9–3B
"Big and chunky", salads "freshly made for you", is proving a winning
formula for this small chain (although "they need to do something
about the queues"); "delicious soups" too. / www.vitalingredient.co.uk;
L only, closed Sat & Sun; no credit cards; no booking.

Vivat Bacchus £46 ④❷❸
4 Hay's Ln, SE1 7234 0891 9–4C
47 Farringdon St, EC4 7353 2648 9–2A
"Oooooooh the cheese room!", and the "stunning" (mostly South
African) walk-in wine cellar too – both win fans for this
bar/restaurant, near Holborn Viaduct; the meat-heavy à la carte
offering is only "average", though (and the year-old SE1 spin-off
is "nothing like as appealing as the original"). / www.vivatbacchus.co.uk;
9.30 pm; EC4 closed Sat & Sun; SE1 closed Sat L & Sun.

Vivezza SW1 £43 ④④④
101 Pimlico Rd 7730 0202 5–2D
"Struggling to find its own identity", this Pimlico offshoot of the nearby
Carraffini still doesn't seem to have got its 'offer' quite right;
fans insist it's as good as its more famous Italian stable-mate, but it's
still often seen as just a "fall-back". / www.vivezza.co.uk; 11 pm; closed
Sun D; booking: max 12.

Vrisaki N22 £30 ❸❸❸
73 Myddleton Rd 8889 8760 1–1C
"Great mezze" in "enormous portions" draw a big following to this
"busy and cheerful" – and surprisingly large-scale – Greek operation,
behind a Bounds Green take-away; "not that cheap, but super value".
/ midnight, Sun 9 pm.

Wagamama £29 ④❸④
8 Norris St, SW1 7321 2755 4–4A
Harvey Nichols, Knightsbridge, SW1 7201 8000 5–1D
101a Wigmore St, W1 7409 0111 3–1A
10a Lexington St, W1 7292 0990 3–2D
4a Streatham St, WC1 7323 9223 2–1C
1 Tavistock St, WC2 7836 3330 4–3D
14a Irving St, WC2 7839 2323 4–4B
26a Kensington High St, W8 7376 1717 5–1A
N1 Centre, 37 Parkfield St, N1 7226 2664 8–3D
11 Jamestown Rd, NW1 7428 0800 8–3B
Royal Festival Hall, Southbank Centre, SE1 7021 0877 2–3D
50-54 Putney High St, SW15 8785 3636 10–2B
46-48 Wimbledon Hill Rd, SW19 8879 7280 10–2B
Jubilee Place, 45 Bank St, E14 7516 9009 11–1C
1a Ropemaker St, EC2 7588 2688 12–2A
22 Old Broad St, EC2 7256 9992 9–2C
Tower Pl, EC3 7283 5897 9–3D
109 Fleet St, EC4 7583 7889 9–2A
30 Queen St, EC4 7248 5766 9–3B
It's "perhaps rather predictable", but for a "quick", "simple" and
"healthy" meal – and a "cheap" one too – London's original oriental-
noodle chain is "still a good stand-by"; indeed, after a recent dip,
ratings strengthened again this year. / www.wagamama.com;
10 pm-11 pm; EC4 & EC2 closed Sat & Sun; no booking.

Wahaca £28 ❸❷❷
66 Chandos Pl, WC2 7240 1883 4–4C
Westfield, Ariel Way, W12 8749 4517 7–1C **NEW**
Unit 4, Park Pavilion, 40 Canada Sq, E14 11–1C **NEW**
Thanks to its "zingy" and "good-value" street-food menu, the Covent
Garden original of this "designer-Mexican" duo is often full to the
point of "madness" – be prepared for an "unwieldy" queue; there's
also a (slightly less funky) outpost at Westfield, and a Canary Wharf
branch is to open in late-2009. / www.wahaca.com; WC2 11 pm,
Sun 10.30 pm; W12 11 pm, Sun 10 pm; no booking.

The Wallace
The Wallace Collection W1   £46   ④④❶
Hertford Hs, Manchester Sq   7563 9505   3–1A
The "beautiful" and "cleverly-designed" covered courtyard is the star turn at this Marylebone palazzo's restaurant – a "tranquil" West End rendezvous, "away from the crowds"; the Gallic cuisine is "expensive" for what it is, though, and service can be "painfully slow".
/ www.thewallacerestaurant.com; Fri & Sat 9.30 pm; L only.

The Walmer Castle W11   £35   ❸④❷
58 Ledbury Rd   7229 4620   6–1B
"In the heart of Notting Hill", this trendy pub has long been popular for the "fresh and healthy" Thai fare served, at "cheap" prices, in its "fun" and "cosy" upstairs dining room. / www.walmercastle.co.uk; 10.30 pm; closed weekday L.

Walnut NW6   £35   ❸❸④
280 West End Ln   7794 7772   1–1B
A "friendly" eco-aware West Hampstead local; it isn't massively comfortable, but its "ever-changing" British menu makes it generally "worth a visit". / www.walnutwalnut.com; 11 pm; D only, closed Mon.

Wapping Food E1   £47   ❸④❶
Wapping Power Station, Wapping Wall   7680 2080   11–1A
This "unique" former East End pumping station makes a "most beautiful", if "very eccentric", post-industrial-chic setting – one that rather eclipses the cuisine, "well-prepared" as it is, and even the "very good" all-Ozzie wine list. / www.thewappingproject.com; 10.30 pm; closed Sun D.

The Warrington W9   £44   ⑤⑤⑤
93 Warrington Cr   7592 7960   8–4A
"Gordon Ramsay, hang your head in shame!"; this "dreary" Maida Vale boozer is a "Kitchen Nightmare" of truly astonishing proportions – almost half the reporters who mention the place nominate it as their 'most disappointing meal of the year'! / www.gordonramsay.com; 10.30 pm; Mon-Thu D only, Fri-Sun open L & D; Casual.

Water House N1   £48   ④④❷
10 Orsman Rd   7033 0123   1–2C
"Perched on Regent's Canal", this decidedly "out-of-the-way" Shoreditch yearling "looks great" and its "very eco" credentials are undoubted; the food, though, is "unspectacular".
/ www.waterhouserestaurant.co.uk; 11 pm; closed Mon D & Sun.

Waterloo Brasserie SE1   £43   ⑤⑤④
119 Waterloo Rd   7960 0202   9–4A
Right by the station, this would-be "snazzy" South Bank brasserie is an ongoing "waste of a great location" – the food on its own is "uninspiring" enough, but it's not helped by the perennially "atrocious" service. / www.waterloobrasserie.co.uk; 11 pm; closed Sun; set always available £29 (FP).

The Waterway W9   £43   ④④❸
54 Formosa St   7266 3557   8–4A
"If you can get a table" – "there's a throng at the first hint of sun" – the terrace of this canalside Maida Vale pub has a "perfect location"; at such times, however, the standard of the otherwise "very acceptable" food and service can deteriorate grievously.
/ www.thewaterway.co.uk; 10.30 pm, Sun 10 pm.

The Well EC1 £40 ❸④④
180 St John St 7251 9363 9–1A
This "long-standing Clerkenwell gastropub" still delivers "above-par" cuisine; "harried" and "off-hand" service, however, contributes to an impression in some quarters that "former standards are not quite being maintained". / www.downthewell.com; 10.30 pm, Sun 10 pm.

The Wells NW3 £40 ❸❸❷
30 Well Walk 7794 3785 8–1A
"Well-located by Hampstead Heath", this elegantly-refurbished boozer (with a grand upstairs dining room) is "especially atmospheric in summer", when you can sit outside; it serves food that's "very consistent" and "enjoyable". / www.thewellshampstead.co.uk; 10 pm, Sun 9.30 pm; no Amex.

Weng Wah House NW3 £32 ④④④
240 Haverstock Hill 7794 5123 8–2A
For some Belsize Park regulars, this Chinese stalwart remains a "consistently reliable local", but increasingly variable feedback suggests it's "not as good as it was". / www.wengwahgroup.com; 11.30 pm, Sat midnight, Sun 11.15 pm.

The Westbourne W2 £36 ❸④❷
101 Westbourne Park Villas 7221 1332 6–1B
"For generally hanging out with friends" – especially on sunny days when the large terrace comes into its own – this boho Bayswater boozer is a key rendezvous; the food is pretty reliable, but "come early" – "service deteriorates as the place fills up". / www.thewestbourne.com; 10 pm, Sun 9.30 pm; closed Mon L; need 4+ to book.

The Wet Fish Cafe NW6 £40 ❸❸❷
242 West End Ln 7443 9222 1–1B
A former fishmongers provides a "pleasantly trendy environment" for this "relaxed" West Hampstead local, which serves a "small" but "inventive" menu… that's not just fishy. / www.thewetfishcafe.co.uk; 11 pm; closed Mon; no Amex.

The Wharf TW11 £45 ④④❷
22 Manor Rd 8977 6333 1–4A
This large, converted boathouse near Teddington Lock – nowadays a bar/brasserie – makes a "stunning" and "romantic" location, especially outside on a sunny day; on the food and service fronts, however, reports are mixed. / www.thewharfteddington.com; 10 pm; closed Mon; set always available £25 (FP), set Sun L £32 (FP).

White Horse SW6 £37 ❸④❷
1-3 Parsons Grn 7736 2115 10–1B
Parson's Green's large and "buzzy" landmark, long nicknamed the 'Sloaney Pony', "could try harder" on the food front, but it has other attractions – these include "a good summer barbecue", "the best beer selection" and a "great" wine list. / www.whitehorsesw6.com; 10.30 pm.

The White Swan EC4 £46 ❸❸❸
108 Fetter Ln 7242 9122 9–2A
"Press on through the average boozer downstairs", to find this "surprisingly smart" upstairs City dining room, where the cuisine is very "reliable" – it's particularly "good for a business lunch". / www.thewhiteswanlondon.com; 10 pm; closed Sat & Sun.

Whitechapel Gallery Dining Room
Whitechapel Gallery E1 NEW £41 ❶❷❸
77-82 Whitechapel High St 7522 7896 12–2C
The "bright and intimate" dining room of this revamped East End gallery has proved an "unexpectedly good new opening", thanks largely to the "precise modern cooking" from Maria Elia (formerly of Delfina Studios). / www.whitechapelgallery.org; 9.30 pm; closed Mon & Sun D.

Whits W8 £44 ❷❶❸
21 Abingdon Rd 7938 1122 5–1A
"A lady who never forgets a face" oversees this small Kensington bistro with "charm and energy"; for a place that serves "traditional" Gallic food "done very well", it's perhaps rather under-appreciated. / www.whits.co.uk; 10.30 pm; closed Mon, Tue L, Sat L & Sun.

Wild Honey W1 £50 ❷❷❸
12 St George St 7758 9160 3–2C
Like its sibling Arbutus, this "gourmet" favourite wins rave reviews for its "sensitively-prepared" Gallic classics, its "superb wines by the carafe" and its "decent prices" (especially the set lunch); "get a booth", though – these panelled Mayfair premises can otherwise seem a bit "dull". / www.wildhoneyrestaurant.co.uk; 11 pm, Sun 10 pm; set weekday L £30 (FP), set pre-theatre £32 (FP).

William IV NW10 £31 ❸❷❷
786 Harrow Rd 8969 5944 1–2B
Out on a limb, in Kensal Green, this large pub hasn't quite maintained its one-time 'destination' status; with its "tasty tapas" and its beautiful garden, however, fans still say it's "a gem". / www.williamivlondon.com; 10.30 pm, Fri & Sat 11 pm, Sun 9.30 pm.

Wiltons SW1 £92 ❸❷❷
55 Jermyn St 7629 9955 3–3C
A "rather stuffy" clubland institution, where the "finest" British oysters, fish and game are treated "with respect", and presented in "brilliantly old-fashioned" style; critics, however, condemn the place as a "home for the elderly", and the "undemanding rich". / www.wiltons.co.uk; 10.30 pm; closed Sat & Sun; jacket required; set weekday L £74 (FP).

The Windmill W1 £35 ❸❸④
6-8 Mill St 7491 8050 3–2C
"The pies are fantastic, and the beer is good too!", at this very traditional Mayfair boozer; "for best value, sit downstairs". / www.windmillmayfair.co.uk; 9.30 pm; closed Sat D & Sun.

The Windsor Castle W8 £29 ❸❸❶
114 Campden Hill Rd 7243 8797 6–2B
Just off Notting Hill Gate, an ancient coaching inn known for its quirky interior and charming walled garden; reports (relatively few this year) say its simple "traditional British" fare is usually "great". / www.thewindsorcastlekensington.co.uk; 10 pm, Sun 9pm; no booking.

Wine Factory W11 £36 ❸❸④
294 Westbourne Grove 7229 1877 6–1B
"An emphasis on good, cheap wine" has long fuelled the local popularity of John Brinkley's Notting Hill hang-out; "excellent pizza" stars on a menu of "well-priced" staples. / www.brinkleys.com; 11 pm; closed Sun D.

Wine Gallery SW10 £36 ④❸❷
49 Hollywood Rd 7352 7572 5–3B
*John Brinkley's bustling Chelsea bistro is an "institution" –
the realisation of the "classic comfort dishes" may be "average",
but it offers "great" wines at "very affordable" prices.*
/ www.brinkleys.com; 11.30 pm; closed Sun D; booking: max 12.

The Wine Library EC3 £24 ④❷⓪
43 Trinity Sq 7481 0415 9–3D
*A selection of "over 200 wines" (all at shop price plus corkage) make
this City cellar "hide-away" a "super venue for serious wine
browsers"; don't expect much of the food, however – it's just a simple
buffet of pâté and cheese.* / www.winelibrary.co.uk; 8 pm, Mon 6 pm;
L & early evening only, closed Sat & Sun.

The Wine Theatre SE1 NEW £34 ④❸⑤
202-206 Union St 7261 0209 9–4B
*A grandiosely-named newcomer that has its uses if you're looking for
a quick meal somewhere round the South Bank end of Blackfriars
Bridge; otherwise, it's difficult to see that a journey would
be worthwhile.* / Rated on Editors' visit; www.thewinetheatre.co.uk; 11.30 pm.

Wódka W8 £41 ❸❷❸
12 St Alban's Grove 7937 6513 5–1B
*Hidden-away in a Kensington backwater, a "cosy" spot, where
"huge portions" of "hearty" Polish fare ("better than we expected!")
– not to mention copious quantities of vodka – fuel many a "happy"
evening.* / www.wodka.co.uk; 11.15 pm; closed Mon L & Sat L.

Wolfe's WC2 £40 ❸④④
30 Gt Queen St 7831 4442 4–1D
*"Burgers like you'd get in NYC" still carve out a loyal fan club for this
'70s-style eatery, in Covent Garden; critics, though, find it too "old-
fashioned".* / www.wolfes-grill.net; 11 pm, Fri & Sat midnight, Sun 9 pm.

THE WOLSELEY W1 £55 ❸❷⓪
160 Piccadilly 7499 6996 3–3C
*"A buzzing hub of London life!"; Corbin & King's "electric" grand
café, by the Ritz, suits most occasions, not least a "peerless
breakfast", "impressing a client" or "discreet celeb-spotting" (or all
three at once!); the "steadfast" food is rather beside the point.*
/ www.thewolseley.com; midnight, Sun 11 pm.

Wong Kei W1 £22 ❸⑤❷
41-43 Wardour St 7437 8408 4–3A
*It's famous for "frankly rude" service – to the extent it's "a giggle" –
but this "unchanging" Chinatown landmark is also a top 'cheap eat',
serving up "tasty", "fast" and "hot" chow, at "terrific" prices.*
/ 11.30 pm, Fri & Sat 11.45 pm, Sun 10.30 pm; no credit cards; no booking.

Woodlands £30 ❸❸④
37 Panton St, SW1 7839 7258 4–4A
77 Marylebone Ln, W1 7486 3862 2–1A
102 Heath St, NW3 7794 3080 8–1A
*It's a pity about the "stale" décor of this stalwart chain (part of
an international group) – "fresh" south Indian vegetarian fare
at "reasonable prices" makes it a "great stand-by".*
/ www.woodlandsrestaurant.co.uk; 10 pm; W4 Mon-Thu D only.

Wright Brothers SE1 £42 ❶❷❷
11 Stoney St 7403 9554 9–4C
"Three cheers for the best oysters in London!" – they're
"incomparable", at this "cramped" but "fun" seafood bar in Borough
Market; "be warned, it gets VERY busy". / www.wrightbros.eu.com;
10.30 pm; closed Sun; booking: max 8.

XO NW3 £41 ❸❸❸
29 Belsize Ln 7433 0888 8–2A
"Not as good as E&O, but still a favourite local"; Will Ricker's Belsize
Park venture is "a real asset" to the area, even if it's "trendy" style
and "tasty" pan-Asian fusion cuisine don't yet match up to its
siblings'. / www.rickerrestaurants.com; 11 pm, Sun 10.30 pm.

Yalla Yalla W1 NEW £22 ❷❷❸
1 Greens Ct 7287 7663 3–2D
This "sweet" new heart-of-Soho café has been an instant hit with its
"authentic Beirut-style cooking and baking"; it is already invariably
full. / www.yalla-yalla.co.uk; 11 pm, Sun 10 pm; no Amex.

YAUATCHA W1 £55 ❶❸❷
Broadwick Hs, 15-17 Broadwick St 7494 8888 3–2D
"The most ravishing dim sum in London" inspire rave reports on Alan
Yau's "über-trendy" Soho oriental – it doesn't seem to matter than
the experience is "rushed", or that service sometimes "sucks";
NB above the "dark and funky" basement, there's a "lovely" room
additionally offering "exquisite" teas and "jewel-like" pâtisserie.
/ www.yauatcha.com; 11.30 pm.

The Yellow House SE16 £33 ❷❷❸
126 Lower Rd 7231 8777 11–2A
Recently moved to larger premises, this "excellent local restaurant"
is all the more worth knowing about in the Surrey Quays "sea of
mediocrity" – Jamie is a "passionate" chef/patron, and it shows.
/ www.theyellowhouse.eu; 10.30 pm, Sun 9.30 pm; closed Mon, Tue-Fri D only,
Sat & Sun open L & D.

Yelo £24 ❸❸④
136a Lancaster Rd, W11 7243 2220 6–1A
8-9 Hoxton Sq, N1 7729 4626 12–1B
A small noodle chain with "prompt" service and "reliable"
(if "not especially interesting") cuisine. / www.yelothai.com; 10.30 pm,
Fri & Sat 11 pm; no Amex; booking: min 6.

Yi-Ban £31 ❷❷❷
Imperial Wharf, Imperial Rd, SW6 7731 6606 5–4B
Regatta Centre, Dockside Rd, E16 7473 6699 11–1D
With its "lovely views of City airport", this "lively" dockside oriental
is certainly "in the middle of nowhere", and its Fulham sibling, lost in
a soulless riverside development, is even more obscure;
both establishments, however, are worth seeking out for their "fresh
and tasty" Chinese fare (including top dim sum). / www.yi-ban.co.uk;
10.45 pm; SW6 closed Sun.

Yming W1 £33 ❷❶❸
35-36 Greek St 7734 2721 4–2A
"How they remember so many customers is amazing" – Christine
Lau's "charming" Soho restaurant is an unusually "personal" venture,
and always has some "interesting" dishes on its "North Chinese-
focussed" menu; let's hope a few recent 'off' reports are
just a wobble. / www.yminglondon.com; 11.45 pm; closed Sun; set pre theatre
£20 (FP).

Yo! Sushi   £24   ⑤⑤④
Branches throughout London
"Novelty value alone" wins some positive reports on this conveyor-sushi chain, but for too many reporters they're "a joke", and what they serve is just "an excuse for sushi". / www.yosushi.co.uk; 10.30 pm; no booking.

York & Albany NW1   £62   ❸④❸
127-129 Parkway   7388 3344   8–3B
Overseen by Angela Hartnett, this "swish" and "attractive" Ramsay-group yearling – a reworking of an impressive tavern between Camden Town and Regent's Park – offers some "enjoyable" cooking; "after all the hype", though, standards turn out to be resolutely "average" overall. / www.gordonramsay.com; 10.30 pm; set weekday L £35 (FP), set Sun L £43 (FP).

Yoshino W1   £38   ❷❷④
3 Piccadilly Pl   7287 6622   3–3D
"Hidden-away" off Piccadilly, a "super, secret Japanese" that's "always packed with an oriental crowd"; there was the odd misfire this year, but most feedback is still a hymn of praise to its "smiling" staff and "mouth-wateringly good" sushi and sashimi; the interior, though, is slightly "cold". / www.yoshino.net; 9 pm; closed Sun.

Yum Yum N16   £30   ❸❸❷
187 Stoke Newington High St   7254 6751   1–1D
This "fabulous"-looking large-scale Thai has long been a linchpin of Stoke Newington (though not always on this site), thanks largely to its "very reasonably-priced" cuisine. / www.yumyum.co.uk; 11 pm, Fri & Sat midnight.

Yumenoki SW10   £30   ④❷❸
204 Fulham Rd   7351 2777   5–3B
Fans insist this little Fulham Japanese two-year-old offers "lovely food" (including "the best sushi"); it attracts very few reports, however, and the odd critic says "it's still heading downhill". / www.yumenoki.co.uk; 10.30 pm.

Yuzu NW6   £34   ❷⑤⑤
102 Fortune Green Rd   7431 6602   1–1B
"Despite the shocking service, the food (in particular sushi) is awesome", at this tiny West Hampstead Japanese, and "reasonably-priced" too. / www.yuzu-restaurants.com; 10.30 pm, Sun 10 pm; D only, closed Mon.

Zafferano SW1   £63   ❸❸❸
15 Lowndes St   7235 5800   5–1D
Many fans still extol this veteran Belgravia "all-rounder" as "one of London's best Italians"; overall, however, reports suggest it's now "trading on its name" – "it used to be a destination, now it's just a neighbourhood place". / www.zafferanorestaurant.com; 11 pm, Sun 10.30 pm; booking: max 8, 4 Sat & Sun; set weekday L £39 (FP).

Zaffrani N1   £35   ❸❷❸
47 Cross St   7226 5522   8–3D
An "out-of-the-ordinary" Islington Indian combining "stylish" décor, "attentive" service, and "posh food without posh prices"; "some lapses" were, however, again reported this year. / www.zaffrani-islington.co.uk; 11 pm.

Zaika W8 £52 ❶❷❸
1 Kensington High St   7795 6533   5–1A
Sanjay Dwivedi's "subtle but confident" cooking at this "innovative" Kensington spot is nigh on "the very definition of gourmet Indian cuisine"; the former banking-hall premises, however, can seem "cavernous". / www.zaika-restaurant.co.uk; 10.45 pm, Sun 9.45 pm.

Zeen NW1 NEW £28 ❹❹❹
130 Drummond St   7387 0606   8–3C
A Little India basement newcomer, backed by the Noon supermarket-curry fortune; it has totally divided early reporters – fans say it shows the "self-confident but distinctive face of contemporary India"… but we're with those who think the food is plain "ghastly". / www.zeenrestaurant.co.uk; 11.30 pm; closed Sun; no Amex.

Zero Degrees SE3 £31 ❸❹❸
29-31 Montpelier Vale   8852 5619   1–4D
An "extensive range of very well-priced beers" helps fuel the "lively" (sometimes "rowdy") ambience at this "cavernous" Blackheath microbrewery, which is also known for "fresh and tasty pizza" and "good mussels and chips". / www.zerodegrees.co.uk; 11.30 pm, Sun 10.30 pm; set weekday L £19 (FP).

The Zetter EC1 £47 ❸❹❸
St John's Sq, 86-88 Clerkenwell Rd   7324 4455   9–1A
This "funky" corner dining room of a Shoreditch hotel is a "stylish" and "pleasant" – if arguably rather "pricey" – venue, where the food has improved of late; for an "elegant hang-over brunch", it's "fantastic". / www.thezetter.com; 11 pm, Sun-Wed 10.30 pm; set weekday L £28 (FP).

Ziani SW3 £46 ❸❷❸
45 Radnor Walk   7352 2698   5–3C
"Don't expect a 'private' dinner", at this "noisy" and "far-too-crowded" Italian stalwart, in a Chelsea side street; the locals adore it, though, for its "cheeky" waiters and its "fun" style. / www.ziani.uk.com; 11.30 pm, Sun 10.30 pm; set Sun L £29 (FP).

Zilli Fish W1 £55 ❸❹❹
36-40 Brewer St   7734 8649   3–2D
Aldo Zilli's "buzzing" Soho corner-site is well-known for its "superb" fish; it's "pricey", though, for somewhere that feels "more of a café than a restaurant", and was sometimes accused this year of "living on former glories". / www.zillialdo.com; 11.30 pm; closed Sun.

Zizzi £30 ❹❹❹
Branches throughout London
Many reporters nominate this "bright" chain as a "safe bet for a pizza and a glass of wine"; "it needs some new ideas", however – service can be "slow" and the whole operation seems ever more "tired". / www.zizzi.co.uk; 11 pm; some booking restrictions apply.

ZUMA SW7 £69 ❶❸❶
5 Raphael St   7584 1010   5–1C
"Move over Nobu!"; this "happening" Knightsbridge hang-out – with its "stunning" Japanese fusion fare and a "super-chic" vibe – is "so much better"; if you want to eat, though, be prepared to "fight your way through the flash younger crowd at the bar". / www.zumarestaurant.com; 10.45 pm, Sun 9.45 pm; booking: max 8.

INDEXES

BREAKFAST
(with opening times)

Central

Abokado *(7.30)*
Adam Street *(9)*
The Albemarle *(7.30)*
Alloro *(Mon-Fri 7.30)*
Apsleys *(7)*
Asia de Cuba *(6, Sun 7.30)*
Atrium *(8.30)*
Aubaine: W1 *(8, Sat 10)*
Automat *(7, Sat 10)*
Baker & Spice: SW1 *(7)*
Balans: *all branches (8)*
Bar Italia *(7)*
Benugo: *all central branches (7.30)*
Bistro 1: *Beak St W1 (Sun 11)*
Bob Bob Ricard *(7)*
Bord'Eaux *(7)*
The Botanist *(8, Sat & Sun 9)*
La Bottega: *Eccleston St SW1 (8, Sat 9);*
    Lower Sloane St SW1 (8, Sat 9, Sun 10)
Brasserie Roux *(6.30, Sat & Sun 7)*
Brasserie St Jacques *(8, Sat & Sun 10)*
Browns: WC2 *(9, 10 Sat & Sun)*
Café Bohème *(8)*
Café in the Crypt *(Mon-Sat 8)*
Caffè Caldesi *(10 am)*
Caffè Vergnano: WC2 *(8, Sun 11)*
Canela: W1 *(10.30); WC2 (9.30, Sat & Sun 10.30)*
Canteen: *all branches (8, Sat & Sun 9)*
Cafe Caramel *(Sun 9)*
Cecconi's *(7)*
Cha Cha Moon: W1 *(8, Sat & Sun 9)*
The Chelsea Brasserie *(7)*
Chez Gérard: *Chancery Ln WC2 (8)*
Christopher's *(Sat & Sun 11.30)*
The Cinnamon Club *(Mon-Fri 7.30)*
City Café *(6.30, Sat & Sun 7)*
Comptoir Libanais: W1 *(8.30)*
Côte: W1 *(8, Sat & Sun 10)*
Crussh: W1 *(7)*
Daylesford Organic: *B Pimlico*
    Rd SW1 (8, Sun 11); Sloane Sq SW1 (9, Sat
    10, Sun noon)
Diner: W1 *(10, Sat & Sun 9)*
Dorchester Grill *(7, Sat & Sun 8)*
Eagle Bar Diner *(Sat 10, Sun 11)*
Eat & Two Veg *(9, Sun 10, Mon 11)*
The Ebury *(Sat & Sun 11)*
Fernandez & Wells: *Lexington*
    St W1 (7 am)
The Fifth Floor Café *(Mon-Sat*
    9, Sun 11)
5 Cavendish Square *(8)*
Flat White *(8, Sat & Sun 9)*
Fortnum's, The Fountain *(7.30)*
Franco's *(7.30, Sat 8)*
La Fromagerie Café *(8, Sat 9, Sun 10)*
Fuzzy's Grub: SW1 *(7)*
Galvin at Windows *(7)*
Giraffe: W1 *(7.45, Sat & Sun 9)*
The Goring Hotel *(7, Sun 7.30)*
Homage *(7)*
Indigo *(6.30)*
Inn the Park *(8)*
Joe Allen *(8)*
Just St James *(7.30)*
Kastner & Ovens *(8)*
Konditor & Cook: WC1 *(9.30); W1 (9.30,*
    Sun 10.30)
Ladurée: W1 *(9); SW1 (Mon - Sat*
    9, Sun noon - 1.30)

The Landau *(7)*
Leon: WC2 *(7.30, Sat 9, Sun 10);*
    Gt Marlborough St W1 (9.30, Sat & Sun
    10.30)
Maison Bertaux *(8.30, Sun 9)*
Maxwell's *(Sat & Sun 9.30)*
Monmouth Coffee Company: WC2 *(8)*
Mrs Marengos *(8, Sat noon)*
Napket: *Piccadilly W1 (7); Vigo St W1, Brook*
    St W1 (7.30)
The National Dining Rooms *(10)*
National Gallery Café *(8, Sat & Sun10)*
Nicole's *(8.30)*
No.20 *(6.30, Sun 7)*
Nordic Bakery *(Mon-Fri 8)*
Noura: William St SW1 *(8)*
Number Twelve *(7, Sat & Sun 7.30)*
The Only Running Footman *(7.30,*
    Sat & Sun 9.30)
Oriel *(8.30, Sun 9)*
Oscar *(7)*
Ottolenghi: SW1 *(8, Sun 9)*
The Pantechnicon *(Sat & Sun 8.30)*
The Park *(6.30)*
Paul: WC2 *(7.30); W1 (7.30, Sat & Sun 8)*
Pearl *(6.30, Sat & Sun 7)*
The Portrait *(10)*
The Providores *(9, Sat & Sun 10)*
Providores (Tapa Room) *(9, Sat*
    & Sun 10)
Pure: WC1 *(7, Sat 8); Goodge St W1 (8); Beak*
    St W1 (8, Sat 10)
Ranoush: SW1 *(9)*
Refuel *(7, Sun 8)*
Rhodes W1 Brasserie *(6.30, Sat &*
    Sun 7)
Rib Room *(7, Sun 8)*
RIBA Café *(8)*
Richoux: *all branches (8)*
The Ritz Restaurant *(7, Sun 8)*
Royal Academy *(10)*
Serafino *(7)*
Simpsons-in-the-Strand *(Mon-Fri 7.30)*
06 St Chad's Place *(8)*
Sketch (Parlour) *(Mon-Fri 8, Sat 10)*
Sophie's Steakhouse: *all branches (Sat &*
    Sun 11)
Sotheby's Café *(9.30)*
Square Pie Company: W1 *(10, Sat 9.30,*
    Sun midday)
Star Café *(7.30)*
Stock Pot: SW1 *(7)*
Suka *(6.30, Sat & Sun 7)*
Tate Britain (Rex Whistler) *(10)*
The Terrace in the Fields *(Mon-Fri 9)*
tibits *(9, Sun 10)*
Tootsies: W1 *(Sat & Sun 11)*
Truc Vert *(7.30, Sat & Sun 9)*
Tuttons *(9.30)*
The Union Café *(Sat & Sun 11)*
Villandry Kitchen *(8, Sat & Sun 11)*
Vital Ingredient: *all branches (9.30)*
The Wallace *(10)*
The Wolseley *(7, Sat & Sun 8)*
Yalla Yalla *(8, Sat & Sun 10)*

West

Adams Café *(7.30, Sat 8.30)*
Annie's: W4 *(Tue - Thu 10, Fri & Sat 10.30,*
    Sun 10)
Aubaine: SW3 *(8, Sun 9)*
Baker & Spice: SW3 *(7, Sun 8)*
Balans West: *all branches (8)*
Bedlington Café *(8.30)*
Beirut Express: W2 *(7)*

Bistro 190 *(Mon-Fri 7)*
Blakes *(7.30)*
Bluebird Café *(8, Sun 10)*
La Bottega: *SW7 (8, Sun 9, Sun 10)*
La Brasserie *(8, Sat & Sun 9)*
Brompton Quarter Café *(7.30)*
Brunello *(7)*
Bumpkin: *SW7 (Sat 9);W11 (Sat noon)*
Le Café Anglais *(Sat 9.30)*
Café Laville *(10, Sat & Sun 9)*
Canta Napoli *(9)*
Chelsea Bun Diner *(7, Sun 9)*
The Chelsea Kitchen *(7.30, Sun 8)*
Comptoir Libanais: *W12 (9.30)*
Crussh: *W8 (7.30);W12 (8)*
Daylesford Organic: *W11 (8, Sun 11)*
Del'Aziz: *SW6 (7, Sun 9);W12 (8)*
Duke on the Green *(11, Sat & Sun 10.30)*
Electric Brasserie *(8)*
Fresco *(8)*
Gail's Bread: *W11 (7, Sat & Sun 8)*
Gallery Mess *(9)*
Giraffe: *all west branches (7.45, Sat & Sun 9)*
Hammersmith Café *(9)*
Harlem *(Sat & Sun 10)*
Henry J Beans *(11)*
High Road Brasserie *(7, Sat & Sun 8)*
Joe's Brasserie *(Sat & Sun 11)*
Julie's *(9)*
Kensington Square Kitchen *(8.30, Sun 9.30)*
Knaypa *(7)*
Langan's Coq d'Or Bar & Grill *(Sat & Sun 10.30)*
Lisboa Pâtisserie *(7)*
Lola & Simón *(8.30, Sat & Sun 9.30)*
Lucky Seven *(Mon noon,Tue-Thu 10, Fri-Sun 9)*
Le Metro *(7.30)*
Mona Lisa *(7)*
Mulberry Street *(Sat & Sun 9)*
Napket: *SW3 (8)*
Ottolenghi: *W11 (8, Sun 8.30)*
Pappa Ciccia: *Fulham High St SW6 (7.30)*
Paradise by Way of Kensal Green *(Sat noon)*
Paul: *SW7 (7)*
Pissarro's *(Sat & Sun 9)*
PJ's *(Sat & Sun 10)*
Ranoush: *W2 (9); SW3,W8 (noon)*
Raoul's Café & Deli: *W11 (8.30); W9 (8.30 am)*
Richoux: *all branches (8)*
S & M Café: *W10 (10, Fri & Sat 8, Sun 9)*
Sam's Brasserie *(9)*
Sophie's Steakhouse: *all branches (Sat & Sun 11)*
Square Pie Company: *W12 (7, Sat 9, Sun midday)*
Stock Pot: *SW3 (8)*
Tartine *(11)*
Tom's Deli *(8, Sun 9)*
Tom's Kitchen *(7, Sat 10, Sun 11)*
Tootsies: *W4 (Sat & Sun 10);W11 (Sat & Sun 9)*
Troubadour *(9)*
202 *(Mon & Sun 10,Tue-Sat 8.30)*
Vingt-Quatre *(24 hrs)*
White Horse *(9.30)*
Wine Factory *(Sat 11)*

North
The Albion *(Sat & Sun 10)*

The Almeida *( )*
The Arches *(11.30)*
Baker & Spice: *all north branches (7, Sun 8)*
Banners *(9, Sat & Sun 10)*
Camino *(8, Sun 11)*
Chamomile *(7, Sun 8)*
Del'Aziz: *NW3 (8)*
The Elk in the Woods *(10.30)*
The Engineer *(9)*
Fifteen Trattoria *(7.30, Sun 8)*
Fine Burger Company: *all branches (midday, Sat & Sun 11 am)*
Gail's Bread: *NW3 (7, Sat & Sun 8)*
Gallipoli: *Upper St N1, Upper St N1 (10.30)*
Giraffe: *all north branches (7.45, Sat & Sun 9)*
Harry Morgan's *(9)*
The House *(Sat & Sun 11)*
Kenwood (Brew House) *(9)*
Landmark (Winter Gdn) *(7)*
Osteria Emilia *(8.30)*
Ottolenghi: *N1 (8, Sun 9)*
Paul: *NW3 (7, Sat & Sun 7.30)*
Richoux: *all branches (8)*
The Rose & Crown *(Sat & Sun 10.30)*
S & M Café: *N1 (7.30)*
Sabor *(11)*
Stringray Café: *N5 (11);NW5 (Fri-Sun 11)*
Tootsies: *NW3 (Sat & Sun 10)*
Trojka *(Mon-Fri 8)*
Water House *(9, Sat 10)*
The Wet Fish Cafe *(10)*

South
Amano: *Victor Wharf, Clink St SE1 (7, Sat & Sun 9)*
Annie's: *SW13 (Tue-Sun 10)*
Arch One *(8)*
Bar Estrela *(8)*
Bermondsey Kitchen *(Sat & Sun 9.30)*
Boiled Egg & Soldiers *(9)*
The Bolingbroke *(Sat & Sun 10)*
Le Bouchon Bordelais *(Sat & Sun 10)*
Brasserie James *(Sat & Sun 10 am)*
Browns: *SE1 (11 am)*
Butcher & Grill: *SW11 (8.30); SW19 (Sat & Sun 8.30)*
Caffè Vergnano: *SE1 (8, Sat & Sun 11)*
Canteen: *all branches (8, Sat & Sun 9)*
Chapters *(8)*
Le Chardon: *SW4 (9); SE22 (Sat & Sun 9.30)*
Del'Aziz: *all south branches (8)*
The Depot *(Sat 9.30)*
Dexters: *SW4 (Sat & Sun 10)*
The Duke's Head *(11, Sun noon)*
Esca *(8, Sat & Sun 9)*
The Establishment: *SW11 (Sat & Sun midday)*
Fat Boy's: *TW8 (Mon-Fri 11.30)*
Franklins *(Sat 10)*
Garrison *(8, Sat & Sun 9)*
Gastro *(8)*
Gazette: *SW12 (7); SW11 (8)*
Giraffe: *all south branches (7.45, Sat & Sun 9)*
Green & Blue *(9, Sun 11)*
Harrison's *(Sat & Sun 9)*
Hudson's *(9.30, Sat & Sun 9)*
The Inn at Kew Gardens *(7, Sat & Sun 8)*
Joanna's *(10)*
Loch Fyne: *TW2 (9, Sun 10)*
Lola Rojo: *SW11 (Sat & Sun 11)*

BRUNCH MENUS

BUSINESS

The Royal Exchange Grand Café (p)
Royal Wok (h)
S & M Café: all branches (hm)
Saf (hp)
St Germain (hp)
St John (h)
St John Bread & Wine (hp)
Saki Bar & Food Emporium (h)
Sauterelle (p)
Searcy's Brasserie (p)
Shish: all branches (ehm)
Smithfield Bar & Grill (hm)
Smiths (Top Floor) (hp)
Smiths (Dining Rm) (hp)
Smiths (Ground Floor) (hp)
Sofra: EC1 (hp)
Sông Quê (h)
Square Pie Company: all
    east branches (m)
Story Deli (o)
Stringray Globe Café: all branches (hm)
Tas: EC1 (h)
La Tasca: E14 (hm)
Terranostra (p)
Viet Grill (hop)
Viet Hoa (h)
Vinoteca (p)
Wagamama: all east branches (hm)
Wapping Food (h)
The Well (hm)
Whitechapel Gallery (hp)
Yi-Ban: E16 (h)
The Zetter (h)

ENTERTAINMENT
(Check times before you go)

Central
All Star Lanes: WC1
    (bowling, DJ Fri & Sat)
Apsleys
    (jazz brunch, Sun)
Atrium
    (live piano every last Fri)
Bank Westminster
    (DJ, Fri & Sat)
Bentley's
    (live piano, Wed-Sat)
Bincho Yakitori
    (DJ, Mon, occasional live music, Wed)
Boisdale
    (jazz, Mon-Sat)
The Bountiful Cow
    (jazz, Sat)
Browns: WC2
    (live piano)
Buddha Bar
    (DJ, nightly from 10 pm)
Café des Amis
    (pianist, Tue D)
Café in the Crypt
    (jazz, Wed night)
Le Caprice
    (pianist, nightly)
Chez Gérard: SW1
    (jazz, Sun L)
Ciao Bella
    (pianist, nightly)
Dover Street Restaurant & Bar
    (live bands and DJ, nightly)
Eagle Bar Diner
    (DJ, Thu-Sat)
The Easton
    (DJ, Fri)
Efes II: Gt Portland St W1

(belly dancer, nightly)
Fakhreldine
    (bellydancer, Thu-Sat)
Floridita
    (live Cuban music, nightly)
Hakkasan
    (DJ, nightly)
Hard Rock Café
    (regular live music)
Imperial China
    (pianist; private rooms with karaoke)
Joe Allen
    (pianist, Mon-Sat)
Just St James
    (live jazz, Sat)
Kai Mayfair
    (harpist & cellist, Tue & Thu)
Kettners
    (pianist)
Langan's Brasserie
    (jazz, Fri & Sat)
Levant
    (belly dancer, nightly)
Little Italy
    (DJ, Mon-Sat)
Luciano
    (magician, Fri)
Maroush: V) 3-4 Vere St W1
    (music & dancing, nightly)
Mint Leaf: SW1
    (weekend DJ/jazz, Fri D)
Momo
    (live world music, Tue)
Noura: W1
    (belly dancer, Fri&Sat)
L'Oranger
    (pianist, Fri & Sat)
Oscar
    (film club, Sun)
Pearl
    (pianist, Wed-Sat)
The Pigalle Club
    (live music, nightly)
Pizza on the Park
    *(cabaret Mon-Sun (matinee Sun, double
    shows Fri & Sat))*
Planet Hollywood
    (DJ, nightly)
La Porte des Indes
    (jazz, every other Sun)
Quaglino's
    (jazz, Fri & Sat)
Red Fort
    (DJ, Fri & Sat)
Refuel
    (film club, Sun)
The Ritz Restaurant
    (live music, Fri & Sat)
Roka: W1
    (DJ, Thu-Sat)
Ronnie Scott's
    (jazz, nightly)
Royal Academy
    (jazz, Fri)
Sarastro
    (opera, Sun & Mon D)
Shanghai Blues
    (live jazz, Fri & Sat)
Simpsons-in-the-Strand
    (pianist, nightly)
06 St Chad's Place
    (DJ, Fri)
Sketch (Gallery)
    (DJ, Thu-Sat)
Souk Medina

(belly dancer, Thu-Sat)
Sugar Reef
(live music, Thu & Fri)
Taman Gang
(DJ, Thu-Sat)
Tamarai
(club nights, Fri & Sat)
Texas Embassy Cantina
(live band, Fri & Sat)
Thai Square: *SW1*
(DJ, Fri & Sat)
Trader Vics
(guitarist, Thu-Sat)
The Windmill
(quiz night, Tue)

West

All Star Lanes: *W2*
(bowling, DJ Thu-Sat)
Babylon
(live music, Thu D, magician Sun)
Beach Blanket Babylon: *all branches*
(DJ, Fri & Sat)
Belvedere
(pianist, nightly Sat & Sun all day)
Benugo: *SW7*
(jazz, Wed)
Big Easy
(live music, nightly)
Brompton Bar & Grill
(jazz, Thu & occasional Fri)
Le Café Anglais
(magician Sun lunch)
Cheyne Walk Brasserie
(jazz every first Mon)
Chutney Mary
(jazz, Sun L)
The Collection
(DJ, nightly)
Da Mario
(magician, Wed)
Del'Aziz: *W12*
(belly dancer, Fri-Sat); SW6
(belly dancer, Thu-Sat, live jazz, Tue in deli)
The Establishment: *SW6*
(live music, Fri)
Frankie's Italian Bar & Grill: *W4*
(jazz, Fri & Sat); SW3
(magician, Sun)
Harlem
(DJ, Wed-Sat)
Harwood Arms
(quiz night, Tue)
Kensington Square Kitchen
(DJ, occasional weekends)
Maroush: *I) 21 Edgware Rd W2*
(music & dancing, nightly)
Mr Wing
(jazz, Thu-Sat)
Notting Hill Brasserie
(jazz, nightly)
Nozomi
(DJ, Tue-Sat)
Old Parr's Head
(quiz night, Mon; poker, Tue)
Il Pagliaccio
(Elvis impersonator, monthly; talent show, Mon)
Paradise by Way of Kensal Green
(live music and burlesque, Tue & Thu; comedy nights, Wed; DJ, Fri-Sun; jazz, Sun)
Pasha
(belly dancer, nightly; tarot card reader, Wed)
(Ciro's) Pizza Pomodoro

(live music, nightly)
La Rueda: *SW6*
(live music Fri & Sat)
606 Club
(live music, nightly)
Sticky Fingers
(face painter, Sat & Sun L)
Sugar Hut
(DJ, Thu-Sat; live band, Sun)
Sushinho
(live music, Wed)
Tendido Cuatro
(Spanish guitar, Wed D)
Troubadour
(live music, most nights)
The Waterway
(live music, Thu)
William IV
(DJ, Fri & Sat)

North

Bald Faced Stag
(live jazz, occasional)
Bull & Last
(pub quiz, Sun; live band, occasional)
Camino
(DJ, Thu-Sat)
Caponata
(live music, Tue-Sun)
Cottons: *NW1*
(live music, Sun; DJ, Fri & Sat)
Del'Aziz: *NW3*
(childrens entertainer, Wed)
Don Pepe
(singer, Fri & Sat)
The Fellow
(DJ, Thu-Sat)
Gilgamesh
(DJ, Fri & Sat)
The Haven
(jazz, Tue-Thu)
The House
(live music, monthly)
Hoxton Apprentice
(jazz, Tue)
Isarn
(live music)
Landmark (Winter Gdn)
(pianist & musicians, daily)
The Lord Palmerston
(quiz night, Wed)
Mestizo
(DJ, Thu)
The North London Tavern
(jazz, Mon; film night, first Sun of the month)
Rotunda Bar & Restaurant
(jazz, Fri)
St Pancras Grand
(live jazz, Sun)
Shish: *NW2*
(live music Fri, DJ Sat)
Snazz Sichuan
(karaoke)
Spaniard's Inn
(poetry readings, Tue)
Thai Square: *N1*
(DJ, Thu-Sat)
The Three Crowns
(DJ, Fri & Sat)
Trojka
(Russian music, Fri & Sat)
Villa Bianca
(guitarist, Mon-Thu; pianist, Sat & Sun)
Villiers Terrace

(DJ, Fri & Sat)
The Wells
(live music, Mon D)
Weng Wah House
(karaoke, nightly)
Yum Yum
(DJ, Fri & Sat)

South

Al Forno: SW15
(live music, Sat)
Arch One
(live lounge music, Mon; jazz & lounge music, Wed; DJ, Thu-Sat)
Archduke Wine Bar
(jazz, Mon-Sat)
The Avalon
(DJ, Fri & Sat)
Barcelona Tapas: SE22
(live music Wed every fortnight)
Bayee Village
(Mon-Wed, pianist)
Bengal Clipper
(pianist, nightly)
Cantina Vinopolis
(singer, Mon & Wed)
Del'Aziz: Bermondsey Sq SE1
(belly dancer, Fri-Sat); Canvey St SE1
(live music, Sat)
The Establishment: SW11
(live music, Thu D)
The Fentiman Arms
(quiz night, Tue)
The Gowlett
(DJ, Sun; Lucky 7s, Thu)
Harrison's
(acoustic music, Sun)
La Lanterna
(live music)
The Little Bay: SW11
(opera, Thu-Sat; piano, Wed & Sun)
The Mason's Arms
(live bands, Sun)
Meson don Felipe
(guitarist, nightly)
China Boulevard
(live music)
Oxo Tower (Brass')
(live jazz, Sat & Sun L, Sun-Mon D)
Le Pont de la Tour
(pianist, every evening; live jazz trio, Sun L)
The Prince Of Wales
(pianist, Sun)
Putney Station
(live music, every last Thu of the month)
The Refinery
(DJ, Fri)
Roast
(jazz, Sun)
The Roundhouse
(quiz night, Mon)
La Rueda: SW4
(Spanish music & dancing, Fri & Sat; Sun L live music)
The Rye
(quiz night, every other Wed)
Santa Maria del Sur
(live music, Mon)
The Ship
(live music, Sun; quiz, Wed)
The Spencer Arms
(occasional jazz band, pianist)
Tas: all south branches
(guitarist, nightly)
Tentazioni

(various, monthly)
Thai Square: SW15
(DJ, Fri & Sat)
Thailand
(karaoke, Thu-Sat)
Tree House
(occasional live music)
The Victoria
(Singer, one Wed a month)
The Wharf
(Salsa night first Wed of month)

East

All Star Lanes: E1
(bowling)
Barcelona Tapas: EC4
(disco, Thu & Fri); both EC3
(live music Wed every fortnight)
The Bathhouse
(live music, most nights)
Beach Blanket Babylon: all branches
(DJ, Fri & Sat)
Bel Canto
(opera singers & pianists)
Bistrotheque
(transvestite show, varies; cabaret varies, piano brunch)
Browns: E14
(live piano)
Café du Marché
(pianist & bass, Mon-Thu, pianist, Fri & Sat)
Cinnamon Kitchen
(DJ, occasionally)
Coq d'Argent
(jazz Sun L)
Cottons: EC1
(live music or DJs, Tue-Sun)
D Sum 2
(some scheduled live music)
$
(DJ, Fri & Sat)
The Drunken Monkey
(DJ, Wed-Sun)
Eastside Inn
(jazz, Thu & Fri)
Elephant Royale
(live music, Thu-Sat)
Great Eastern Dining Room
(DJs, Fri & Sat)
Green & Red Bar & Cantina
(DJ in bar, Thu-Sat)
The Hoxton Grille
(DJ, Thu-Sat)
Kazan: EC3
(Turkish night, occasional)
Kenza
(belly dancers, Mon-Sat; tarot reader, Fri)
Lena
(live jazz, Wed-Sat)
LMNT
(opera, Sun)
1901
(DJ, Thu-Sat)
Noto Kikuya
(karaoke)
Pacific Oriental
(DJ, Fri)
Potemkin
(occasional live Russian music)
Prism
(circus acts and DJ, Fri)
The Punch Tavern
(poker nights, Mon; wine tasting, quiz & comedy nights, monthly)
Le Rendezvous du Café

LATE
(open till midnight or later as shown; may be earlier Sunday)

Sushinho
Vingt-Quatre *(24 hours)*

North
Ali Baba
L'Artista
Banners *(Fri midnight)*
Emni *(Fri midnight)*
Gaucho: *NW3*
Gem *(Fri & Sat midnight)*
Gilgamesh
Izgara
Landmark (Winter Gdn) *(1 am)*
Le Mercury *(1 am, not Sun)*
La Porchetta Pizzeria: *all north branches*
Rodizio Rico: *N1*
Rotunda Bar & Restaurant *(not Sat)*
Sofra: *all branches*
Vrisaki
Weng Wah House *(Sat midnight)*
Yum Yum *(Fri & Sat midnight)*

South
Bar Estrela
Buona Sera: *all branches*
The Clarence *(midnight, Fri & Sat 1 am)*
The Duke's Head *(Fri & Sat midnight)*
Everest Inn *(Fri & Sat midnight)*
Firezza: *SW11*
Fish in a Tie
Fujiyama *(Fri & Sat midnight)*
Gastro
Green & Blue *(Fri & Sat midnight)*
Kennington Tandoori
Mirch Masala: *all south branches*
Nazmins
Paradiso Olivelli: *all branches*
Pizza Metro
Putney Station *(not Sun & Mon)*
La Rueda: *all branches (Sat & Sun midnight)*
Sands End
Sree Krishna *(Fri & Sat midnight)*
Tree House *(Sat & Sun)*
Vijaya Krishna *(Fri & Sat midnight)*

East
Albion
Barcelona Tapas: *EC4 (2.30 am)*
Brick Lane Beigel Bake *(24 hours)*
Cellar Gascon
Clifton *(midnight, Sat & Sun 1am)*
Devonshire Terrace
The Diner: *EC2 (not Sun & Mon)*
The Drunken Monkey
Elephant Royale *(Fri & Sat)*
The Gaylord
Itsu: *Level 2, Cabot Place East E14 (Fri & Sat midnight)*
Lahore Kebab House
Lutyens
Mangal Ocakbasi
La Porchetta Pizzeria: *EC1*
The Punch Tavern *(Thu & Fri midnight)*
Sofra: *all branches*

OUTSIDE TABLES
(* particularly recommended)

Central
Al Hamra*
Al Sultan
Andrew Edmunds
Aqua Kyoto
Archipelago
L'Artiste Musclé
Atari-Ya: *W1*
Aubaine: *all branches*
Aurora
L'Autre Pied
Back to Basics
Baker & Spice: *SW1*
Balans: *Old Compton St W1*
Balfour
Bam-Bou
Bank Westminster
Bar Italia
Bar Trattoria Semplice
Barrafina
The Beehive
Beiteddine
Bentley's
Benugo: *all central branches*
Bertorelli: *both W1*
Bincho Yakitori
Bistro 1: *Frith St W1, WC2*
Bord'Eaux
The Botanist
La Bottega: *all branches*
Boudin Blanc
Busaba Eathai: *WC1*
Café Bohème
Café des Amis
Café du Jardin
Canela: *all branches*
Caraffini
Cafe Caramel
Cecconi's
Cha Cha Moon: *W1*
Chez Gérard: *SW1, Dover St W1, Charlotte St W1, both WC2*
Chimes
Chisou
Ciao Bella
Cigala
City Café
Comptoir Libanais: *W1*
Côte: *WC2*
Daylesford Organic: *B Pimlico Rd SW1*
Dehesa
Delfino
dim T: *W1*
Diner: *W1*
The Duke of Wellington
The Easton
Ed's Easy Diner: *Moor St W1*
Efes Restaurant: *Gt Titchfield St W1*
Fairuz
The Fifth Floor Café
Franco's
Getti: *all branches*
Giraffe: *W1*
Golden Hind
Goodman
Gordon's Wine Bar*
Gourmet Burger Kitchen: *W1*
Goya
Great Queen Street
Greig's
Grumbles
Hard Rock Café

PRIVATE ROOMS

(for the most comprehensive listing of venues for functions – from palaces to pubs – visit www.hardens.com/party, or buy *Harden's London Party, Event & Conference Guide,* **available in all good bookshops)**

Bleeding Heart *(20,35,45)*
Bonds *(8,8,16)*
Café du Marché *(30,60)*
Café Spice Namaste *(40)*
Cellar Gascon *(20)*
Chamberlain's *(65)*
The Chancery *(25,30)*
Chez Gérard: *EC2 (12)*; *EC3 (45)*
Cicada *(36)*
Cinnamon Kitchen *(12)*
City Miyama *(4,4,8,10)*
The Clerkenwell Dining Room *(40)*
Clifton *(90)*
Cottons: *EC1 (70)*
Dans le Noir *(30)*
Devonshire Terrace *(10,60)*
Dockmaster's House *(40,25)*
$ *(120)*
The Don *(24,12)*
The Drunken Monkey *(10,30)*
The East Room *(16, 50)*
Eastside Inn *(14)*
Fabrizio *(18)*
El Faro *(70)*
Faulkner's *(18)*
Fish Central *(60)*
The Fox *(12)*
George & Vulture *(24)*
Great Eastern Dining Room *(75)*
The Gun *(14,22)*
The Hat & Feathers *(40,30)*
Hawksmoor *(14)*
High Timber *(18)*
The Hoxton Grille *(20,20)*
Imperial City *(12)*
Kenza *(50,15)*
The Larder *(18)*
Lena *(18)*
Luc's Brasserie *(60)*
Lutyens *(20,8,8,12)*
Malmaison Brasserie *(14,8)*
Manicomio: *all branches (30)*
MPW Steakhouse & Grill *(32)*
Medcalf *(18)*
The Mercer *(12,40)*
Missouri Angel *(10,14)*
The Modern Pantry *(40)*
Moro *(14)*
Mugen *(8)*
The Narrow *(14)*
New Tayyabs *(40)*
Northbank *(30)*
Noto Kikuya *(10)*
Ye Olde Cheshire Cheese *(15,50)*
1 Blossom Street *(8,12,26)*
1 Lombard Street *(20)*
Osteria Appennino *(20)*
Pacific Oriental *(20,20)*
Paternoster Chop House *(14)*
The Peasant *(18)*
Piccolino: *EC2 (24)*
Plateau *(24)*
Portal *(14)*
The Princess *(45)*
Prism *(30,55)*
The Punch Tavern *(150)*
Rajasthan II: *India St EC3 (35)*; *Monument St EC3, Houndsditch EC3 (60)*
The Real Greek: *EC1 (35)*
Refettorio *(30)*
Le Rendezvous du Café *(30,60)*
Rivington: *EC2 (25)*
Rocket : *EC2 (25)*
Rosa's *(40)*
Royal China: *E14 (12,12,12)*

The Royal Exchange Grand Café *(26)*
S & M Café: *EC3 (123)*; *E1 (40)*
Saf *(25)*
St John *(18)*
Saki Bar & Food Emporium *(10)*
Sauterelle *(26)*
Searcy's Brasserie *(14)*
Shanghai *(45,50)*
Smithfield Bar & Grill *(10)*
Smiths (Ground Floor) *(24,12,10)*
Soseki *(12,6,6)*
Tajima Tei *(16,6,4)*
Tas: *EC1 (50)*
La Tasca: *E14 (120)*
Les Trois Garçons *(10)*
Viet Grill *(100)*
Vinoteca *(30)*
Vivat Bacchus: *EC4 (45)*
The Well *(70)*
The White Swan *(52)*
Whitechapel Gallery *(12)*
Yi-Ban: *E16 (30)*
The Zetter *(10,50)*

ROMANTIC

Central
Andrew Edmunds
Archipelago
Aurora
Bam-Bou
Boudin Blanc
Buddha Bar
Café Bohème
Le Caprice
Cecconi's
Le Cercle
Chor Bizarre
Clos Maggiore
Corrigan's Mayfair
Crazy Bear
Elena's L'Etoile
L'Escargot
French House
Galvin at Windows
Le Gavroche
Gay Hussar
Gordon Ramsay at Claridge's
Gordon's Wine Bar
Hakkasan
Hush
The Ivy
Kettners
Langan's Bistro
Langan's Brasserie
Levant
Locanda Locatelli
Marcus Wareing
Momo
Mon Plaisir
Odin's
L'Oranger
Orrery
Pied à Terre
The Pigalle Club
La Porte des Indes
La Poule au Pot
The Ritz Restaurant
Roussillon
Rules
St Moritz
Sarastro
J Sheekey
Souk Medina

ROOMS WITH A VIEW

Rhodes 24
Searcy's Brasserie
Smiths (Top Floor)
Vertigo 42
Yi-Ban: *E16*

NOTABLE WINE LISTS

Central
Adam Street
Andrew Edmunds
Arbutus
Bedford & Strand
Boisdale
Café des Amis
Le Cercle
Cigala
Clos Maggiore
Cork & Bottle
Dehesa
The Ebury
L'Escargot
The Fifth Floor Restaurant
Fino
Foliage
Fortnum's, The Fountain
La Fromagerie Café
Galvin Bistrot de Luxe
Le Gavroche
Gordon Ramsay at Claridge's
Gordon's Wine Bar
The Greenhouse
Hardy's Brasserie
Hibiscus
The Ivy
Kai Mayfair
Locanda Locatelli
Marcus Wareing
Olivo
Orrery
Pétrus
Pied à Terre
The Providores
Quo Vadis
Roussillon
St Alban
St Moritz
Salt Yard
Sardo
1707
Shampers
Sotheby's Café
The Square
Tate Britain (Rex Whistler)
Terroirs
Texture
La Trouvaille
The Union Café
Wild Honey
Zafferano

West
Angelus
Bibendum
Brinkley's
Brompton Bar & Grill
Brunello
Cambio de Tercio
Clarke's
Le Colombier
L'Etranger
The Frontline Club
Gordon Ramsay
Joe's Brasserie
The Kensington Wine Rooms

The Ledbury
Marco
Le Metro
Osteria dell'Arancio
Papillon
Princess Victoria
Racine
The River Café
Tom Aikens
La Trompette
White Horse
Wine Factory
Wine Gallery

North
The Arches
La Collina
Metrogusto
The Rose & Crown
Vineria

South
Brinkley's Kitchen
Cantina Vinopolis
Chez Bruce
Emile's
Enoteca Turi
The Glasshouse
Green & Blue
Magdalen
Le Pont de la Tour
Putney Station
Ransome's Dock
Riva
The Rosendale
RSJ
Tentazioni
Vivat Bacchus: *all branches*

East
Alba
Ambassador
Bleeding Heart
Cellar Gascon
Club Gascon
Coq d'Argent
The Don
The East Room
High Timber
Moro
Portal
St John Bread & Wine
Smiths (Top Floor)
Vinoteca
Vivat Bacchus: *all branches*
Wapping Food
The Wine Library

CUISINES

An asterisk (*) after an entry indicates exceptional or very good cooking

AMERICAN
Central
All Star Lanes *(WC1)*
Automat *(W1)*
Bodean's *(W1)*
Chicago Rib Shack *(SW1)*
Christopher's *(WC2)*
Hard Rock Café *(W1)*
Joe Allen *(WC2)*
Maxwell's *(WC2)*
Planet Hollywood *(SW1)*

West
All Star Lanes *(W2)*
Big Easy *(SW3)*
Bodean's *(SW6, W2)*
Harlem *(W2)*
Lucky Seven *(W2)**
PJ's *(SW3)*
Sticky Fingers *(W8)*

South
Bodean's *(SW4)*

East
All Star Lanes *(E1)*
Bodean's *(EC3)*
The Hoxton Grille *(EC2)*
Missouri Angel *(EC3)*

BELGIAN
Central
Belgo *(WC2)*

North
Belgo Noord *(NW1)*

South
Belgo *(SW4)*
Brouge *(TW2, TW9)*

BRITISH, MODERN
Central
About Thyme *(SW1)**
Acorn House *(WC1)*
Adam Street *(WC2)*
Alastair Little *(W1)*
Andrew Edmunds *(W1)*
Arbutus *(W1)**
Artisan *(W1)*
Atrium *(SW1)*
Aurora *(W1)*
The Avenue *(SW1)*
Axis *(WC2)*
Balfour *(WC1)*
Bank Westminster *(SW1)*
Bellamy's *(W1)*
Bob Bob Ricard *(W1)*
The Botanist *(SW1)*
Café du Jardin *(WC2)*
Café Emm *(W1)*
Le Caprice *(SW1)**
Criterion *(W1)*
Daylesford Organic *(SW1)*
Dean Street Townhouse & Dining Room *(W1)*
Le Deuxième *(WC2)*
Dorchester Grill *(W1)*
The Duke of Wellington *(W1)**
The Easton *(WC1)*

Ebury Wine Bar *(SW1)*
The Fifth Floor Restaurant *(SW1)*
French House *(W1)*
The Goring Hotel *(SW1)*
Great Queen Street *(WC2)**
Hardy's Brasserie *(W1)*
Homage *(WC2)*
Hush *(W1)*
Indigo *(WC2)*
Inn in the Park *(SW1)*
The Ivy *(WC2)*
Just St James *(SW1)*
Konstam *(WC1)**
The Landau *(W1)**
Langan's Brasserie *(W1)*
The Little Square *(W1)*
Mews of Mayfair *(W1)*
Nicole's *(W1)*
No.20 *(W1)*
The Norfolk Arms *(WC1)*
The Only Running Footman *(W1)*
Oscar *(W1)*
Ozer *(W1)*
The Pantechnicon *(SW1)*
Patterson's *(W1)*
The Phoenix *(SW1)*
The Pigalle Club *(W1)*
The Portrait *(WC2)*
Quaglino's *(SW1)*
The Queens Arms *(SW1)*
Quo Vadis *(W1)*
Refuel *(W1)*
Rhodes W1 Brasserie *(W1)*
Rhodes W1 Restaurant *(W1)*
RIBA Café *(W1)*
Rowley's *(SW1)*
Running Horse *(W1)*
1707 *(W1)*
Shampers *(W1)*
Sotheby's Café *(W1)**
Tate Britain (Rex Whistler) *(SW1)*
The Terrace in the Fields *(WC2)*
The Thomas Cubitt *(SW1)*
Tuttons *(WC2)*
The Union Café *(W1)*
Vanilla *(W1)**
Villandry *(W1)*
Vincent Rooms *(SW1)*
Wild Honey *(W1)**
The Wolseley *(W1)*

West
The Abingdon *(W8)*
Admiral Codrington *(SW3)*
The Anglesea Arms *(W6)**
The Anglesea Arms *(SW7)*
Babylon *(W8)*
Beach Blanket Babylon *(W11)*
Belvedere *(W8)*
Bistro 190 *(SW7)*
Bluebird *(SW3)*
Brinkley's *(SW10)*
Brompton Bar & Grill *(SW3)*
The Builders Arms *(SW3)*
Butcher's Hook *(SW6)*
The Carpenter's Arms *(W6)*
Clarke's *(W8)**
Commander *(W2)*
The Cow *(W2)**
Daylesford Organic *(W11)*
Devonshire House *(W4)*
Duke Of Sussex *(W4)*
Duke on the Green *(SW6)*
Ealing Park Tavern *(W5)*
The Establishment *(SW6)*

The Farm (SW6)
First Floor (W11)
Fish Hook (W4)*
The Frontline Club (W2)
Gilmour's (SW10)
Harwood Arms (SW6)*
The Havelock Tavern (W14)*
High Road Brasserie (W4)
Hole in the Wall (W4)
Joe's Brasserie (SW6)
Julie's (W11)
Kensington Place (W8)
Kensington Square Kitchen (W8)
The Ladbroke Arms (W11)*
Launceston Place (W8)*
The Ledbury (W11)*
Lots Road (SW10)
Marco (SW6)
Le Metro (SW3)
Notting Hill Brasserie (W11)
Paradise by Way of Kensal
  Green (W10)*
The Phoenix (SW3)
Pissarro's (W4)
PJ's (SW3)
Princess Victoria (W12)
Queen's Head (W6)
The Roebuck (W4)
Salisbury (SW6)
Sam's Brasserie (W4)
Seasons Dining Room (W6)
Tom Aikens (SW3)
Tom's Deli (W11)
Tom's Kitchen (SW3)
Vingt-Quatre (SW10)
The Warrington (W9)
The Waterway (W9)
The Westbourne (W2)
White Horse (SW6)
Whits (W8)*

North

The Albion (N1)
Bald Faced Stag (N2)
The Barnsbury (N1)
Bradley's (NW3)
The Bull (N6)
Café Med (NW8)
Charles Lamb (N1)
The Clissold Arms (N2)
Coast (NW1)
Cruse 9 (N1)
The Duke of Cambridge (N1)
The Elk in the Woods (N1)
The Engineer (NW1)
The Fellow (N1)
Frederick's (N1)
Freemasons Arms (NW3)
The Haven (N20)
The Horseshoe (NW3)
The House (N1)
Hoxton Apprentice (N1)
The Junction Tavern (NW5)
Landmark (Winter Gdn) (NW1)
The Lansdowne (NW1)
The Lock Dining Bar (N17)*
The Lord Palmerston (NW5)
Mango Room (NW1)
Market (NW1)*
Mosaica (N22)*
The North London Tavern (NW6)
Odette's (NW1)
The Old Bull & Bush (NW3)
The Rose & Crown (N6)
Rotunda Bar & Restaurant (N1)

St Pancras Grand (NW1)
The Three Crowns (N16)
Villiers Terrace (N8)*
Walnut (NW6)
Water House (N1)
The Wells (NW3)
The Wet Fish Cafe (NW6)

South

The Abbeville (SW4)
Alma (SW18)
Arch One (SE1)
The Avalon (SW12)
Blueprint Café (SE1)
The Bolingbroke (SW11)
The Bridge (SW13)
The Brown Dog (SW13)
Buchan's (SW11)
The Cadogan Arms (SW3)
Cantina Vinopolis (SE1)
Chapters (SE3)
Chez Bruce (SW17)*
The Clarence (SW11)
The Dartmouth Arms (SE23)
The Depot (SW14)
The Duke's Head (SW15)
Earl Spencer (SW18)
The East Hill (SW18)
Emile's (SW15)*
The Establishment (SW11)
The Fentiman Arms (SW8)
The Fire Stables (SW19)
Four O Nine (SW9)*
Franklins (SE22)
Garrison (SE1)
The Glasshouse (TW9)*
Harrison's (SW12)
The Inn at Kew Gardens (TW9)
Inside (SE10)*
Lamberts (SW12)*
The Lighthouse (SW11)*
Magdalen (SE1)*
The Mason's Arms (SW8)
Menier Chocolate Factory (SE1)
Mezzanine (SE1)
The Orange (SW1)
Oxo Tower (Rest') (SE1)
The Palmerston (SE22)*
Petersham Hotel (TW10)
Petersham Nurseries (TW10)*
Phoenix Bar & Grill (SW15)
Le Pont de la Tour (SE1)
The Prince Of Wales (SW15)
Ransome's Dock (SW11)
The Refinery (SE1)
Rick's Café (SW17)*
Rivington (SE10)
Rock & Rose (TW9)
The Rosendale (SE21)
The Roundhouse (SW18)
RSJ (SE1)
Sands End (SW6)*
Scoffers (SW11)
Skylon (SE1)
Sonny's (SW13)
The Spencer Arms (SW15)
The Swan At The Globe (SE1)
The Table (SE1)*
tamesa@oxo (SE1)
Tom Ilic (SW8)*
The Trafalgar Tavern (SE10)
Tree House (SW13)
Trinity (SW4)*
Trinity Stores (SW12)*
The Victoria (SW14)

The Wharf (TW11)

East
Ambassador (EC1)
Beach Blanket Babylon (E1)
Bevis Marks (EC3)
Bistrotheque (E2)
The Boundary (E2)
The Brickhouse (E1)
The Chancery (EC4)*
Coach & Horses (EC1)
Devonshire Terrace (EC2)
The Don (EC4)*
The Empress of India (E9)
The Fox (EC2)
Gow's (EC2)
The Gun (E14)
The Hat & Feathers (EC1)
High Timber (EC4)
Hilliard (EC4)*
Hix Oyster & Chop House (EC1)
The Larder (EC1)
Malmaison Brasserie (EC1)
Medcalf (EC1)
The Mercer (EC2)
The Modern Pantry (EC1)
The Morgan Arms (E3)
The Narrow (E14)
Northbank (EC4)
1 Lombard Street (EC3)
The Peasant (EC1)
The Prince Arthur (E8)
The Princess (EC2)
Prism (EC3)
The Restaurant At St Paul's (EC4)
Rhodes 24 (EC2)
Rivington (EC2)
Searcy's Brasserie (EC2)
Smithfield Bar & Grill (EC1)
Smiths (Ground Floor) (EC1)
Vertigo 42 (EC2)
Vinoteca (EC1)
Wapping Food (E1)
The Well (EC1)
The White Swan (EC4)
Whitechapel Gallery (E1)*

BRITISH, TRADITIONAL
Central
The Albemarle (W1)
Boisdale (SW1)
Canteen (W1)
Chimes (SW1)
Corrigan's Mayfair (W1)
Fortnum's, The Fountain (W1)
Fuzzy's Grub (SW1)*
Great Queen Street (WC2)*
Green's (SW1)
Greig's (W1)
Grenadier (SW1)
The Guinea Grill (W1)*
Hardy's Brasserie (W1)
The National Dining Rooms (WC2)
Odin's (W1)
Porters English Restaurant (WC2)
Rib Room (SW1)
Rules (WC2)
Scott's (W1)*
Shepherd's (SW1)
Simpsons-in-the-Strand (WC2)
Square Pie Company (W1,WC1)*
Wiltons (SW1)
The Windmill (W1)

West
Bumpkin (SW7,W11)
The Fat Badger (W10)
Ffiona's (W8)
Hereford Road (W2)*
Maggie Jones's (W8)
S & M Café (W10)
Square Pie Company (W12)*
The Windsor Castle (W8)

North
Bull & Last (NW5)*
The Drapers Arms (N1)
The Flask (N6)
Holly Bush (NW3)
Kenwood (Brew House) (NW3)
The Marquess Tavern (N1)
S & M Café (N1)
St Johns (N19)
The Swan & Edgar (NW1)

South
The Anchor & Hope (SE1)*
Butlers Wharf Chop House (SE1)
Canteen (SE1)
Roast (SE1)
S & M Café (SE10)
Sands End (SW6)*
The Trafalgar Tavern (SE10)

East
Albion (E2)
Boisdale of Bishopsgate (EC2)
Canteen (E1)
Cock Tavern (EC1)
54 Farringdon Road (EC1)*
The Fox and Anchor (EC1)
Fuzzy's Grub (EC2, EC3, EC4)*
George & Vulture (EC3)
Green's (EC3)
Hix Oyster & Chop House (EC1)
Ye Olde Cheshire Cheese (EC4)
Paternoster Chop House (EC4)
E Pellicci (E2)
The Quality Chop House (EC1)*
The Restaurant At St Paul's (EC4)
S & M Café (E1, EC1, EC3)
St John (EC1)*
St John Bread & Wine (E1)*
Simpson's Tavern (EC3)
Square Pie Company (E1, E14)*
Sweetings (EC4)
The Wine Library (EC3)

CZECH
North
The Czechoslovak Restaurant (NW6)

EAST & CENT. EUROPEAN
Central
Gay Hussar (W1)
1707 (W1)
The Wolseley (W1)

North
Trojka (NW1)

East
Kipferl (EC1)

FISH & SEAFOOD
Central
Back to Basics (W1)*
Belgo Centraal (WC2)

Bentley's *(W1)**
Cape Town Fish Market *(W1)*
Fishworks *(W1)*
Fung Shing *(WC2)**
Green's *(SW1)*
Keelung *(WC2)*
Livebait *(WC2)*
Loch Fyne *(WC2)*
Olivomare *(SW1)**
One-O-One *(SW1)*
The Pantechnicon *(SW1)*
Pescatori *(W1)*
Quaglino's *(SW1)*
Randall & Aubin *(W1)**
Rasa Samudra *(W1)**
Rib Room *(SW1)*
Royal China Club *(W1)**
Scott's *(W1)**
Seaport *(W1)*
J Sheekey *(WC2)**
J Sheekey Oyster Bar *(WC2)**
Trishna *(W1)**
Wiltons *(SW1)*
Zilli Fish *(W1)*

West
Bibendum Oyster Bar *(SW3)*
Big Easy *(SW3)*
Chez Patrick *(W8)**
The Cow *(W2)**
Fish Hook *(W4)**
Geale's *(W8)*
Mandarin Kitchen *(W2)**
Poissonnerie de l'Avenue *(SW3)**
Le Suquet *(SW3)*

North
Belgo Noord *(NW1)*
Bradley's *(NW3)*
Chez Liline *(N4)**
Coast *(NW1)*
Olympus Fish *(N3)*
Sargasso Sea *(N21)**
Toff's *(N10)**

South
Applebee's Cafe *(SE1)**
Chez Lindsay *(TW10)*
Fish Club *(SW11)**
fish! *(SE1)*
Gastro *(SW4)*
Livebait *(SE1)*
Lobster Pot *(SE11)**
Loch Fyne *(TW2)*
Wright Brothers *(SE1)**

East
Applebee's *(E11)**
Catch *(EC2)*
Chamberlain's *(EC3)*
Curve *(E14)*
Fish Central *(EC1)*
Fish Shop *(EC1)*
Forman's *(E3)*
Gow's *(EC2)*
The Grapes *(E14)*
The Royal Exchange Grand
   Café *(EC3)*
Sweetings *(EC4)*

FRENCH
Central
The Admiralty *(WC2)*
Alain Ducasse *(W1)*
L'Artiste Musclé *(W1)*

L'Atelier de Joel Robuchon *(WC2)**
L'Autre Pied *(W1)**
The Avenue *(SW1)*
Bellamy's *(W1)*
Beotys *(WC2)*
Bord'Eaux *(W1)*
Boudin Blanc *(W1)**
Boulevard *(WC2)*
Brasserie Roux *(SW1)*
Brasserie St Jacques *(SW1)*
Café Bohème *(W1)*
Café des Amis *(WC2)*
Le Cercle *(SW1)**
The Chelsea Brasserie *(SW1)*
Chez Gérard *(SW1,W1,WC2)*
Clos Maggiore *(WC2)**
Côte *(W1,WC2)*
The Ebury *(SW1)*
Elena's L'Étoile *(W1)*
L'Escargot *(W1)*
Foliage *(SW1)*
Galvin at Windows *(W1)*
Galvin Bistrot de Luxe *(W1)**
Le Gavroche *(W1)**
The Giaconda Dining Room *(WC2)**
Gordon Ramsay at Claridge's *(W1)*
The Greenhouse *(W1)*
Hélène Darroze *(W1)*
Hibiscus *(W1)*
Incognico *(WC2)*
Langan's Bistro *(W1)*
Marcus Wareing *(SW1)**
maze *(W1)**
maze Grill *(W1)*
Mon Plaisir *(WC2)*
Odin's *(W1)*
L'Oranger *(SW1)*
Orrery *(W1)**
Pearl *(WC1)*
La Petite Maison *(W1)**
Pétrus *(SW1)*
Pied à Terre *(W1)**
La Poule au Pot *(SW1)*
Randall & Aubin *(W1)**
Le Relais de Venise L'Entrecôte *(W1)*
The Ritz Restaurant *(W1)*
Roussillon *(SW1)**
Sketch (Lecture Rm) *(W1)*
Sketch (Gallery) *(W1)*
The Square *(W1)**
Terroirs *(WC2)**
La Trouvaille *(W1)*
Villandry *(W1)*
Villandry Kitchen *(WC1)*
The Wallace *(W1)*

West
Ambassade de l'Ile *(SW7)*
Angelus *(W2)**
Aubergine *(SW10)*
Belvedere *(W8)*
Bibendum *(SW3)*
La Bouchée *(SW7)*
La Brasserie *(SW3)*
Le Café Anglais *(W2)*
The Capital Restaurant *(SW3)**
Charlotte's Place *(W5)*
Cheyne Walk Brasserie *(SW3)*
Chez Kristof *(W6)*
Chez Patrick *(W8)**
Le Colombier *(SW3)*
Côte *(W8)*
L'Etranger *(SW7)*
Gordon Ramsay *(SW3)*
Langan's Coq d'Or Bar & Grill *(SW5)*

249

Notting Hill Brasserie *(W11)*
Papillon *(SW3)*
Père Michel *(W2)*
The Pig's Ear *(SW3)*
Poissonnerie de l'Avenue *(SW3)**
Racine *(SW3)**
Rôtisserie Jules *(SW7)*
Le Suquet *(SW3)*
Tartine *(SW3)*
La Trompette *(W4)**
Le Vacherin *(W4)*
Whits *(W8)**

North
L'Absinthe *(NW1)*
The Almeida *(N1)*
Les Associés *(N8)*
L'Aventure *(NW8)**
Bistro Aix *(N8)*
Bradley's *(NW3)*
La Cage Imaginaire *(NW3)*
Charles Lamb *(N1)*
Fig *(N1)**
Le Mercury *(N1)*
Morgan M *(N7)**
Oslo Court *(NW8)**
La Petite Auberge *(N1)*
Le Sacré-Coeur *(N1)*
St Johns *(N19)*
Somerstown Coffee House *(NW1)*
The Wells *(NW3)*

South
Bellevue Rendez-Vous *(SW17)*
Le Bouchon Bordelais *(SW11)*
Brasserie James *(SW12)*
Brula *(TW1)**
La Buvette *(TW9)*
Le Cassoulet *(CR2)*
Le Chardon *(SE22, SW4)*
Chez Gérard *(SE1)*
Chez Lindsay *(TW10)*
Côte *(SW19, TW9)*
Gastro *(SW4)*
Gazette *(SW11, SW12)*
Lobster Pot *(SE11)**
Ma Cuisine *(TW1, TW9)*
Le Provence *(SW13)*
The Spread Eagle *(SE10)*
A Taste Of McClements *(TW9)**
Upstairs Bar *(SW2)**
Waterloo Brasserie *(SE1)*

East
Bel Canto *(EC3)*
Bleeding Heart *(EC1)**
Le Bouchon Breton *(E1)*
Café du Marché *(EC1)**
Cellar Gascon *(EC1)*
Chez Gérard *(EC2, EC3, EC4)*
Club Gascon *(EC1)**
Comptoir Gascon *(EC1)**
Coq d'Argent *(EC2)*
The Don *(EC4)**
Eastside Inn *(EC1)*
Flâneur *(EC1)*
Galvin La Chapelle *(E1)*
Luc's Brasserie *(EC3)*
Lutyens *(EC4)*
1901 *(EC2)*
Plateau *(E14)*
Relais de Venise L'Entrecôte *(EC2)*
Le Rendezvous du Café *(EC1)*
Rosemary Lane *(E1)*
The Royal Exchange Grand

Café *(EC3)*
St Germain *(EC1)*
Le Saint Julien *(EC1)*
Sauterelle *(EC3)*
Les Trois Garçons *(E1)*

FUSION
Central
Archipelago *(W1)*
Asia de Cuba *(WC2)*
Nobu *(W1)**
Nobu Berkeley *(W1)*
The Providores *(W1)*
Providores (Tapa Room) *(W1)*

West
E&O *(W11)**
Eight Over Eight *(SW3)**
L'Étranger *(SW7)*
Port of Manila *(W6)*
Sushinho *(SW3)*

North
XO *(NW3)*

South
Beauberry House *(SE21)*
Champor-Champor *(SE1)**
Tsunami *(SW4)*
Village East *(SE1)*

East
Viajante *(E2)*

GAME
Central
Boisdale *(SW1)*
Rules *(WC2)*
Wiltons *(SW1)*

West
Harwood Arms *(SW6)**

North
San Daniele del Friuli *(N5)*

East
Boisdale of Bishopsgate *(EC2)*

GERMAN
South
Stein's *(TW10)*

GREEK
Central
Beotys *(WC2)*
Hellenik *(W1)**
Real Greek *(W1, WC2)*

West
Costa's Grill *(W8)*
Halepi *(W2)*
The Real Greek *(W12)*

North
Daphne *(NW1)*
Lemonia *(NW1)*
The Real Greek *(N1)*
Retsina *(NW3)*
Vrisaki *(N22)*

South
Real Greek *(SE1, SW15)*

East
Kolossi Grill *(EC1)*
Real Greek *(E1, EC1)*

HUNGARIAN
Central
Gay Hussar *(W1)*

INTERNATIONAL
Central
The Avenue *(SW1)*
Balans *(W1)*
Bedford & Strand *(WC2)*
Boulevard *(WC2)*
Boxwood Café *(SW1)*
Browns *(W1, WC2)*
Café in the Crypt *(WC2)*
Cafe Caramel *(SW1)*
City Café *(SW1)*
Cork & Bottle *(WC2)*
Dover Street Restaurant & Bar *(W1)*
Eat & Two Veg *(W1)*
Footstool *(SW1)*
The Forge *(WC2)*
Giraffe *(W1, WC1)*
Gordon's Wine Bar *(WC2)*
Grumbles *(SW1)*
Michael Moore *(W1)*
Motcombs *(SW1)*
National Gallery Café *(WC2)*
Ooze *(W1)*
Oriel *(SW1)*
The Park *(SW1)**
Ronnie Scott's *(W1)*
Sarastro *(WC2)*
Seven Stars *(WC2)*
Star Café *(W1)*
Stock Pot *(SW1)*
Sugar Reef *(W1)*
Terroirs *(WC2)**

West
The Academy *(W11)**
Annie's *(W4)*
Balans West *(SW5, W4, W8)*
Blakes *(SW7)*
Brompton Quarter Café *(SW3)*
The Cabin *(SW6)**
Café Laville *(W2)*
Chelsea Bun Diner *(SW10)*
The Chelsea Kitchen *(SW10)*
Electric Brasserie *(W11)*
The Enterprise *(SW3)*
Foxtrot Oscar *(SW3)*
Gallery Mess *(SW3)*
The Gate *(W6)**
Giraffe *(W4, W8)*
Glaisters *(SW10)*
The Kensington Wine Rooms *(W8)*
Lola & Simón *(W6)*
Mona Lisa *(SW10)*
Ooze *(W12)*
The Pembroke *(SW5)*
The Scarsdale *(W8)*
606 Club *(SW10)*
Stock Pot *(SW3)*
The Swag & Tails *(SW7)*
The Thatched House *(W6)*
202 *(W11)*
The Windsor Castle *(W8)*
Wine Factory *(W11)*
Wine Gallery *(SW10)*

North
The Arches *(NW6)*

Banners *(N8)*
Browns *(N1)*
The Fox Reformed *(N16)*
Giraffe *(N1, NW3)*
The Haven *(N20)*
The Old Bull & Bush *(NW3)*
Orange Tree *(N20)*
Petek *(N4)*
Spaniard's Inn *(NW3)*
twotwentytwo *(NW1)*

South
Annie's *(SW13)*
Applebee's Cafe *(SE1)**
Bingham *(TW10)*
Brinkley's Kitchen *(SW17)*
Browns *(SE1)*
Tate Modern (Level 2) *(SE1)*
Giraffe *(SE1, SW11)*
Green & Blue *(SE22)*
Hudson's *(SW15)*
Joanna's *(SE19)*
The Light House *(SW19)*
More *(SE1)*
Tate Modern (Level 7) *(SE1)*
The Rye *(SE15)*
The Ship *(SW18)*
The Stonhouse *(SW4)*
Vivat Bacchus *(SE1)*
The Wharf *(TW11)*
The Yellow House *(SE16)**

East
Applebee's *(E11)**
The Bathhouse *(EC2)*
Browns *(E14, EC2)*
Dans le Noir *(EC1)*
$ *(EC1)*
The East Room *(EC2)*
Giraffe *(E1)*
LMNT *(E8)*
The Luxe *(E1)*
The Punch Tavern *(EC4)*
Les Trois Garçons *(E1)*
Vivat Bacchus *(EC4)*

IRISH
East
Lutyens *(EC4)*

ITALIAN
Central
Al Duca *(SW1)*
Alloro *(W1)*
Apsleys *(SW1)*
Bar Trattoria Semplice *(W1)*
Il Baretto *(W1)*
The Beehive *(W1)*
Bertorelli *(W1, WC2)*
Bocca Di Lupo *(W1)**
La Bottega *(SW1)*
Caffè Caldesi *(W1)*
Caffè Vergnano *(WC2)*
Caraffini *(SW1)*
Cecconi's *(W1)*
Ciao Bella *(WC1)*
Cipriani *(W1)*
Como Lario *(SW1)*
Il Convivio *(SW1)**
Dehesa *(W1)**
Delfino *(W1)**
Dolada *(W1)*
5 Cavendish Square *(W1)*
Franco's *(SW1)*
Getti *(SW1, W1)*

Gran Paradiso *(SW1)*
Incognico *(WC2)*
L'Incontro *(SW1)*
Latium *(W1)**
Little Italy *(W1)*
Locanda Locatelli *(W1)*
Luciano *(SW1)*
Murano *(W1)**
Number Twelve *(WC1)*
Oliveto *(SW1)**
Olivo *(SW1)**
Olivomare *(SW1)**
Orso *(WC2)*
Osteria Dell'Angolo *(SW1)*
Ottolenghi *(SW1)**
Paolina Café *(WC1)*
Paradiso Olivelli *(W1)*
Pasta Brown *(WC2)*
Pescatori *(W1)*
Piccolino *(W1)*
Pizza on the Park *(SW1)*
La Porchetta Pizzeria *(WC1)*
Princi *(W1)*
Quirinale *(SW1)**
Ristorante Semplice *(W1)**
Rossopomodoro *(WC2)*
Sale e Pepe *(SW1)*
Salt Yard *(W1)**
Santini *(SW1)*
Sapori *(WC2)*
Sardo *(W1)**
Sartoria *(W1)*
Serafino *(W1)*
Signor Sassi *(SW1)**
Spacca Napoli *(W1)**
Theo Randall *(W1)**
Toto's *(SW1)*
2 Amici *(SW1)*
2 Veneti *(W1)*
Uno *(SW1)*
Vapiano *(W1)*
Il Vaporetto *(SW1)*
Vasco & Piero's Pavilion *(W1)**
Via Condotti *(W1)*
Il Vicolo *(SW1)*
Villandry Kitchen *(WC1)*
Vivezza *(SW1)*
Zafferano *(SW1)*
Zilli Fish *(W1)*

West

L'Accento Italiano *(W2)*
Aglio e Olio *(SW10)**
The Ark *(W8)*
Arturo *(W2)*
Assaggi *(W2)**
Bianco Nero *(W6)**
La Bottega *(SW7)*
Brunello *(SW7)*
Buona Sera *(SW3)*
Canta Napoli *(W4)*
Carpaccio's *(SW3)*
Cibo *(W14)*
Da Mario *(SW7)*
Daphne's *(SW3)*
De Cecco *(SW6)*
La Delizia Limbara *(SW3)*
Edera *(W11)*
Elistano *(SW3)*
Essenza *(W11)**
Il Falconiere *(SW7)*
La Famiglia *(SW10)*
Frankie's Italian Bar & Grill *(SW3,W4)*
Frantoio *(SW10)*
Friends *(SW10)*

Il Giardino *(SW3)*
The Green Olive *(W9)*
Locanda Ottomezzo *(W8)*
Lucio *(SW3)*
Luna Rossa *(W11)*
Made in Italy *(SW3)**
Manicomio *(SW3)*
Mediterraneo *(W11)*
Montpeliano *(SW7)*
Mulberry Street *(W2)*
Napulé *(SW6)*
Nuovi Sapori *(SW6)*
The Oak *(W2)**
Osteria Basilico *(W11)*
Osteria dell'Arancio *(SW10)*
Ottolenghi *(W11,W8)**
Il Pagliaccio *(SW6)*
Pappa Ciccia *(SW6)**
Pellicano *(SW3)*
Il Portico *(W8)*
Portobello Ristorante *(W11)*
The Red Pepper *(W9)**
Riccardo's *(SW3)**
The River Café *(W6)**
Rocca Di Papa *(SW7)*
Rossopomodoro *(SW10,W11)*
San Lorenzo *(SW3)*
Santa Lucia *(SW10)*
Scalini *(SW3)*
Spago *(SW7)*
Timo *(W8)*
Trenta *(W2)*
Ziani *(SW3)*

North

Artigiano *(NW3)*
L'Artista *(NW11)*
Il Bacio *(N16, N5)*
La Brocca *(NW6)*
Cantina Italia *(N1)*
Caponata *(NW1)*
La Collina *(NW1)*
Fifteen Dining Room *(N1)*
Fifteen Trattoria *(N1)*
500 *(N19)**
Fratelli la Bufala *(NW3)*
Marine Ices *(NW3)*
Metrogusto *(N1)*
Osteria Emilia *(NW3)*
Ottolenghi *(N1)**
Pizzeria Oregano *(N1)*
La Porchetta Pizzeria *(N1, N4, NW1)*
Salt House *(NW8)*
The Salusbury *(NW6)*
San Daniele del Friuli *(N5)*
Sardo Canale *(NW1)*
Sarracino *(NW6)**
Villa Bianca *(NW3)*
Vineria *(NW8)*
York & Albany *(NW1)*

South

A Cena *(TW1)**
Al Forno *(SW15, SW19)*
Antipasto & Pasta *(SW11)*
Buona Sera *(SW11)*
Cantina del Ponte *(SE1)*
Castello *(SE16)*
Donna Margherita *(SW11)**
Enoteca Turi *(SW15)**
Esca *(SW4)*
Frankie's Italian Bar & Grill *(SW15)*
Isola del Sole *(SW15)*
La Lanterna *(SE1)*
Numero Uno *(SW11)**

Pappa Ciccia *(SW15)**
Piccolino *(SW17, SW19)*
Pizza Metro *(SW11)**
Le Querce *(SE23)**
Riva *(SW13)**
San Lorenzo Fuoriporta *(SW19)*
San Remo *(SW13)*
Scarpetta *(TW11)*
Tentazioni *(SE1)**
The Three Bridges *(SW8)*
The Wine Theatre *(SE1)*

East
Alba *(EC1)*
Amerigo Vespucci *(E14)*
L'Anima *(EC2)**
Bertorelli *(EC3, EC4)*
Il Bordello *(E1)**
Caravaggio *(EC3)*
Fabrizio *(EC1)**
La Figa *(E14)**
Flâneur *(EC1)*
Jamie's Italian *(E14)*
Lena *(EC2)*
Manicomio *(EC2)*
1 Blossom Street *(E1)*
Osteria Appennino *(EC2)**
E Pellicci *(E2)*
Piccolino *(EC2)*
La Porchetta Pizzeria *(EC1)*
Quadrato *(E14)*
Refettorio *(EC4)*
Taberna Etrusca *(EC4)*
Terranostra *(EC4)*

MEDITERRANEAN
Central
About Thyme *(SW1)**
Bistro 1 *(W1,WC2)*
The Fifth Floor Café *(SW1)*
Hummus Bros *(W1,WC1)*
The Norfolk Arms *(WC1)*
Rocket *(W1)*
St Alban *(SW1)*
06 St Chad's Place *(WC1)*
Truc Vert *(W1)*
Tuttons *(WC2)*

West
The Atlas *(SW6)**
Cochonnet *(W9)*
Cumberland Arms *(W14)*
Del'Aziz *(SW6)*
Elistano *(SW3)*
Locanda Ottomezzo *(W8)*
Made in Italy *(SW3)**
Mediterraneo *(W11)*
Priory House *(W14)*
Raoul's Café *(W9)*
Raoul's Café & Deli *(W11)*
The Swan *(W4)*
Tom's Deli *(W11)*
Troubadour *(SW5)*
William IV *(NW10)*

West
Del'Aziz *(W12)*

North
Café Med *(NW8)*
Camden Brasserie *(NW1)*
Del'Aziz *(NW3)*
The Little Bay *(NW6)*
Mem & Laz *(N1)*
Petek *(N4)*

Queen's Head & Artichoke *(NW1)*
Stringray Café *(N5, NW5)**

South
Bermondsey Kitchen *(SE1)*
Cantina del Ponte *(SE1)*
Cantina Vinopolis *(SE1)*
Del'Aziz *(SE1)*
Fish in a Tie *(SW11)*
The Fox & Hounds *(SW11)**
The Little Bay *(SW11)*
Oxo Tower (Brass') *(SE1)*
Putney Station *(SW15)*
The Wharf *(TW11)*

East
Ambassador *(EC1)*
Bonds *(EC2)*
The Clerkenwell Dining Room *(EC1)*
The Eagle *(EC1)*
Eyre Brothers *(EC2)*
Flâneur *(EC1)*
The Little Bay *(EC1)*
Portal *(EC1)*
Rocket *(EC2)*
Stringray Globe Café *(E2)**
Vinoteca *(EC1)*
The Zetter *(EC1)*

ORGANIC
Central
Acorn House *(WC1)*
Daylesford Organic *(SW1)*

West
Daylesford Organic *(W11)*

North
The Duke of Cambridge *(N1)*
Holly Bush *(NW3)*
Walnut *(NW6)*
Water House *(N1)*

East
Saf *(EC2)*
Smiths (Dining Rm) *(EC1)*
Story Deli *(E1)**

POLISH
West
Daquise *(SW7)*
Knaypa *(W6)*
Ognisko Polskie *(SW7)*
Patio *(W12)*
Wódka *(W8)*

South
Baltic *(SE1)*

PORTUGUESE
Central
Canela *(W1,WC2)*

West
Lisboa Pâtisserie *(W10)**

South
Bar Estrela *(SW8)*

East
The Gun *(E14)*
Portal *(EC1)*

RUSSIAN
North
Trojka (NW1)

East
Potemkin (EC1)

SCANDINAVIAN
Central
Garbo's (W1)
Nordic Bakery (W1)
Texture (W1)

West
Madsen (SW7)

SCOTTISH
Central
Albannach (WC2)
Boisdale (SW1)

South
Buchan's (SW11)

East
Boisdale of Bishopsgate (EC2)

SPANISH
Central
Aqua Nueva (W1)
Barrafina (W1)*
Café España (W1)
Cigala (WC1)
Dehesa (W1)*
Fino (W1)*
Goya (SW1)
Ibérica (W1)*
Navarro's (W1)
El Pirata (W1)
Salt Yard (W1)*
La Tasca (WC2)
Tierra Brindisa (W1)*

West
Cambio de Tercio (SW5)*
Casa Brindisa (SW7)
Duke Of Sussex (W4)
Galicia (W10)
L-Restaurant & Bar (W8)
Lola Rojo (SW6)*
El Pirata de Tapas (W2)
La Rueda (SW6)
La Tasca (W4)
Tendido Cero (SW5)*
Tendido Cuatro (SW6)

North
La Bota (N8)
Camino (N1)
Don Pepe (NW8)
The Islington Tapas Bar (N1)
El Parador (NW1)*

South
Barcelona Tapas (SE22)
don Fernando's (TW9)
Lola Rojo (SW11)*
La Mancha (SW15)
Meson don Felipe (SE1)
Rebato's (SW8)
El Rincón Latino (SW4)
La Rueda (SW4)
Tapas Brindisa (SE1)*

East
Barcelona Tapas (EC3, EC4)
Eyre Brothers (EC2)
El Faro (E14)*
Moro (EC1)*
Pinchito (EC1)
La Tasca (E14, EC2)

STEAKS & GRILLS
Central
Black & Blue (W1)
Bodean's (W1)
The Bountiful Cow (WC1)
Chez Gérard (SW1,W1,WC2)
Christopher's (WC2)
Gaucho (W1,WC2)
Goodman (W1)*
Greig's (W1)
The Guinea Grill (W1)*
The Palm (SW1)
Rowley's (SW1)
Sophie's Steakhouse (WC2)
Wolfe's (WC2)

West
Black & Blue (SW7,W8)
Bodean's (SW6)
Bowler Bar & Grill (SW3)
El Gaucho (SW3, SW7)
Gaucho (SW3)
Haché (SW10)*
Kings Road Steakhouse (SW3)
The Meat & Wine Co (W12)
Popeseye (W14)*
Sophie's Steakhouse (SW10)

North
Black & Blue (NW3)
Camden Brasserie (NW1)
Garufa (N5)
Gaucho (NW3)
Haché (NW1)*
Rôtisserie (HA5, N20, NW6, NW8)

South
Archduke Wine Bar (SE1)
Bermondsey Kitchen (SE1)
Black & Blue (SE1)
Bodean's (SW4)
Buenos Aires (SE3)
Butcher & Grill (SW11, SW19)
Chez Gérard (SE1)
Gaucho (SE1, SE10,TW10)
Kew Grill (TW9)
La Pampa Grill (SW11)
Popeseye (SW15)*

East
Buen Ayre (E8)*
Chez Gérard (EC2, EC3, EC4)
Gaucho (E14, EC1, EC2, EC3)
Hawksmoor (E1)
Lower East (E14)
MPW Steakhouse & Grill (E1)
Simpson's Tavern (EC3)
Smithfield Bar & Grill (EC1)
Smiths (Top Floor) (EC1)
Smiths (Dining Rm) (EC1)
Smiths (Ground Floor) (EC1)

SWISS
Central
St Moritz (W1)

VEGETARIAN
Central
Chop'd *(W1,WC1)**
Eat & Two Veg *(W1)*
Food for Thought *(WC2)**
Hummus Bros *(W1,WC1)*
Just Falafs *(W1,WC2)*
Malabar Junction *(WC1)*
Masala Zone *(W1)*
Mildred's *(W1)**
Ragam *(W1)**
Rasa *(W1)**
Rasa Maricham *(WC1)**
Roussillon *(SW1)**
Sagar *(W1)**
Seaport *(W1)*
tibits *(W1)*
Vital Ingredient *(W1)*
Woodlands *(SW1,W1)*

West
Blah! Blah! Blah! *(W12)*
Blue Elephant *(SW6)*
The Gate *(W6)**
Masala Zone *(SW5, SW6,W2)*
Sagar *(W6)**

North
Chop'd *(NW1)**
Chutneys *(NW1)*
Diwana Bhel-Poori House *(NW1)*
Geeta *(NW6)**
Kovalam *(NW6)*
Manna *(NW3)*
Masala Zone *(N1)*
Rani *(N3)**
Rasa *(N16)**
Rasa Travancore *(N16)**
Sakonis *(HA0)*
Vijay *(NW6)**
Woodlands *(NW3)*

South
Ganapati *(SE15)**
Kastoori *(SW17)**
Le Pont de la Tour *(SE1)*
Sagar *(TW1)**
Sree Krishna *(SW17)**

East
Carnevale *(EC1)*
Chop'd *(E1, E14, EC3)**
The Place Below *(EC2)*
Saf *(EC2)*
Vanilla Black *(EC4)*
Vital Ingredient *(EC4)*

AFTERNOON TEA
Central
Brasserie Roux *(SW1)*
The Fifth Floor Café *(SW1)*
Fortnum's, The Fountain *(W1)*
Ladurée *(SW1,W1)*
Napket *(W1)*
Oscar *(W1)*
The Park *(SW1)**
Richoux *(W1)*
The Ritz Restaurant *(W1)*
Royal Academy *(W1)*
Sketch (Parlour) *(W1)*
Villandry *(W1)*
The Wolseley *(W1)*
Yauatcha *(W1)**

West
Daquise *(SW7)*
Napket *(SW3)*
Richoux *(SW3)*

North
Richoux *(NW8)*

South
San Lorenzo Fuoriporta *(SW19)*

East
Napket *(EC3)*

BURGERS, ETC
Central
Automat *(W1)*
Black & Blue *(W1)*
Diner *(W1)*
Eagle Bar Diner *(W1)*
Ed's Easy Diner *(W1)*
Gourmet Burger Kitchen *(W1,WC2)*
Hamburger Union *(W1,WC2)*
Hard Rock Café *(W1)*
Joe Allen *(WC2)*
Kettners *(W1)*
Maxwell's *(WC2)*
Planet Hollywood *(SW1)*
Tootsies *(W1)*
Ultimate Burger *(W1,WC1)*
Wolfe's *(WC2)*

West
Big Easy *(SW3)*
Black & Blue *(SW7,W8)*
Byron *(W12,W8)*
Electric Brasserie *(W11)*
Gourmet Burger Kitchen *(SW5, SW6, SW7,W11,W2,W4)*
Ground *(W4)**
Haché *(SW10)**
Henry J Beans *(SW3)*
Lucky Seven *(W2)**
PJ's *(SW3)*
Sticky Fingers *(W8)*
Tootsies *(W11,W4)*

North
Black & Blue *(NW3)*
The Diner *(NW1, NW10)*
Fine Burger Company *(N1, NW3)*
Gourmet Burger Kitchen *(NW3)*
Haché *(NW1)**
Hamburger Union *(N1)*
Harry Morgan's *(NW8)*
Tootsies *(NW3)*

South
Black & Blue *(SE1)*
Dexter's Grill *(SW17)*
Dexters *(SW4)*
Gourmet Burger Kitchen *(SW11, SW15, SW4)*
Tootsies *(SW11, SW15, SW19)*

East
The Diner *(EC2)*
$ *(EC1)*
Gourmet Burger Kitchen *(EC4)*
Smithfield Bar & Grill *(EC1)*
Smiths (Dining Rm) *(EC1)*

CRÊPES
South
Chez Lindsay *(TW10)*

FISH & CHIPS
Central
The Chippy *(W1)*
Fryer's Delight *(WC1)*
Golden Hind *(W1)**
North Sea Fish *(WC1)**
Rock & Sole Plaice *(WC2)*
Seafresh *(SW1)*

West
Costa's Fish Restaurant *(W8)*
Geale's *(W8)*

North
Nautilus *(NW6)**
Seashell *(NW1)**
Toff's *(N10)**
Two Brothers *(N3)**

South
Brady's *(SW18)*
Fish Club *(SW11, SW4)**
Masters Super Fish *(SE1)**
Olley's *(SE24)**
The Sea Cow *(SE22)*

East
Ark Fish *(E18)**
Faulkner's *(E8)**

ICE CREAM
North
Marine Ices *(NW3)*

PIZZA
Central
Il Baretto *(W1)*
Delfino *(W1)**
Fire & Stone *(WC2)*
Kettners *(W1)*
Oliveto *(SW1)**
Paradiso Olivelli *(W1, WC1)*
Piccolino *(W1)*
Pizza on the Park *(SW1)*
La Porchetta Pizzeria *(WC1)*
Rocket *(W1)*
Sapori *(WC2)*

West
Basilico *(SW6)*
Buona Sera *(SW3)*
Cochonnet *(W9)*
Da Mario *(SW7)*
La Delizia Limbara *(SW3)*
Fire & Stone *(W12)*
Firezza *(W11, W4)**
Frankie's Italian Bar & Grill *(SW3, W4)*
Friends *(SW10)*
Made in Italy *(SW3)**
Mulberry Street *(W2)*
The Oak *(W2)**
Osteria Basilico *(W11)*
(Ciro's) Pizza Pomodoro *(SW3)*
Spago *(SW7)*

North
Il Bacio *(N16, N5)*
Basilico *(N1, NW3)*
La Brocca *(NW6)*
Cantina Italia *(N1)*

Firezza *(N1)**
Furnace *(N1)*
Marine Ices *(NW3)*
Pizzeria Oregano *(N1)*
La Porchetta Pizzeria *(N1, N4, NW1)*

South
Al Forno *(SW15, SW19)*
Basilico *(SW11, SW14)*
Buona Sera *(SW11)*
Castello *(SE16)*
Eco *(SW4)*
Firezza *(SW11, SW18)**
Franco Manca *(SW9)**
Frankie's Italian Bar & Grill *(SW15)*
Gourmet Pizza Company *(SE1)*
The Gowlett *(SE15)**
La Lanterna *(SE1)*
Paradiso Olivelli *(SE1)*
Piccolino *(SW17, SW19)*
Pizza Metro *(SW11)**
Zero Degrees *(SE3)*

East
Il Bordello *(E1)**
Gourmet Pizza Company *(E14)*
Piccolino *(EC2)*
La Porchetta Pizzeria *(EC1)*
Rocket *(EC2)*
Story Deli *(E1)**

SANDWICHES, CAKES, ETC
Central
Aubaine *(W1)*
Baker & Spice *(SW1)*
Bar Italia *(W1)*
Benugo *(W1)*
Crussh *(W1)*
Daylesford Organic Café *(SW1)*
Fernandez & Wells *(W1)**
Flat White *(W1)**
La Fromagerie Café *(W1)**
Fuzzy's Grub *(SW1)**
Kastner & Ovens *(WC2)**
Konditor & Cook *(W1, WC1)**
Ladurée *(SW1, W1)*
Leon *(W1, WC2)*
Maison Bertaux *(W1)**
Monmouth Coffee Company *(WC2)**
Mrs Marengos *(W1)**
Napket *(W1)*
Paul *(W1, WC2)*
Pure *(W1, WC1)*
Richoux *(W1)*
Royal Academy *(W1)*
Sketch (Parlour) *(W1)*

West
Aubaine *(SW3)*
Baker & Spice *(SW3)*
Benugo *(SW7, W12)*
Bluebird Café *(SW3)*
Crussh *(W12, W8)*
Gail's Bread *(W11)**
Lisboa Pâtisserie *(W10)**
Napket *(SW3)*
Paul *(SW7)*
Richoux *(SW3)*
Tom's Deli *(W11)*
Troubadour *(SW5)*

North
Baker & Spice *(NW6, W9)*
Benugo *(NW1)*
Chamomile *(NW3)*

Gail's Bread *(NW3, NW8)**
Kenwood (Brew House) *(NW3)*
Paul *(NW3)*
Richoux *(NW8)*

South
Amano *(SE1)*
Benugo *(SE1)*
Boiled Egg & Soldiers *(SW11)*
Caffé Vergnano *(SE1)*
Fuzzy's Grub *(SE1)**
Leon *(SE1)*
Monmouth Coffee Company *(SE1)**

East
Benugo *(EC1)*
Brick Lane Beigel Bake *(E1)**
Crussh *(E14, EC3, EC4)*
Fuzzy's Grub *(EC2, EC3, EC4)**
Konditor & Cook *(EC3)**
Leon *(E1, E14, EC4)*
Nusa Kitchen *(EC1, EC2)**
Paul *(EC4)*
Pod *(EC2)*
Pure *(EC4)*
Spianata & Co *(E1, EC1, EC2, EC3, EC4)**

SALADS
Central
Chop'd *(W1,WC1)**
Just Falafs *(W1,WC2)*
Pure *(W1,WC1)*
Vital Ingredient *(W1)*

West
Beirut Express *(SW7,W2)**

North
Chop'd *(NW1)**

East
Chop'd *(E1, E14, EC3)**
Vital Ingredient *(EC4)*

ARGENTINIAN
Central
Gaucho *(W1,WC2)*

West
El Gaucho *(SW3, SW7)*
Gaucho *(SW3)*
Lola & Simón *(W6)*

North
Garufa *(N5)*
Gaucho *(NW3)*

South
Buenos Aires *(SE3)*
Gaucho *(SE1,TW10)*
La Pampa Grill *(SW11)*
Santa Maria del Sur *(SW8)**

East
Buen Ayre *(E8)**
Gaucho *(E14, EC2, EC3)*

BRAZILIAN
Central
Canela *(W1,WC2)*
Preto *(SW1)*

West
Rodizio Rico *(W2)*

Sushinho *(SW3)*

North
Rodizio Rico *(N1)*

CUBAN
Central
Floridita *(W1)*

MEXICAN/TEXMEX
Central
Café Pacifico *(WC2)*
Texas Embassy Cantina *(SW1)*
Wahaca *(WC2)*

West
Crazy Homies *(W2)**
Santo *(W10)*
Taqueria *(W11)*
Wahaca *(W12)*

North
Chilango *(N1)*
Mestizo *(NW1)*

East
Chilango *(EC4)*
Green & Red Bar & Cantina *(E1)*
Wahaca *(E14)*

SOUTH AMERICAN
North
Sabor *(N1)*

South
El Vergel *(SE1)**

AFRO-CARIBBEAN
Central
The Terrace in the Fields *(WC2)*

North
Cottons *(NW1)*
Mango Room *(NW1)*

East
Cottons *(EC1)*

MOROCCAN
Central
Original Tajines *(W1)*
Souk Medina *(WC2)*

West
Adams Café *(W12)*
Pasha *(SW7)*

NORTH AFRICAN
Central
Momo *(W1)*
Souk Medina *(WC2)*

West
Del'Aziz *(SW6)*

East
Kenza *(EC2)*

SOUTH AFRICAN
West
Chakalaka *(W4)*

South
Chakalaka *(SW15)*

TUNISIAN
West
Adams Café *(W12)*

EGYPTIAN
North
Ali Baba *(NW1)*

ISRAELI
Central
Gaby's *(WC2)*

North
Solly's *(NW11)*

KOSHER
Central
Reubens *(W1)*

North
Kaifeng *(NW4)*
Met Su Yan *(NW11)*
Solly's *(NW11)*

East
Bevis Marks *(EC3)*

LEBANESE
Central
Al Hamra *(W1)*
Al Sultan *(W1)*
Beiteddine *(SW1)*
Comptoir Libanais *(W1)*
Fairuz *(W1)*
Fakhreldine *(W1)*
Ishbilia *(SW1)*
Levant *(W1)*
Maroush *(W1)*
Noura *(SW1,W1)*
1001 Nights *(W1)*
Ranoush *(SW1)*
Yalla Yalla *(W1)*

West
Al-Waha *(W2)*
Beirut Express *(SW7,W2)*
Chez Marcelle *(W14)*
Comptoir Libanais *(W12,W2)*
Fresco *(W2)*
Maroush *(W2)*
Maroush *(SW3)*
Pasha *(W7)*
Randa *(W8)*
Ranoush *(SW3,W2,W8)*

East
Kenza *(EC2)*

MIDDLE EASTERN
North
Solly's *(NW11)*

South
Esca *(SW4)*

PERSIAN
West
Alounak *(W14,W2)*
Mohsen *(W14)*
Sufi *(W12)*

South
Dish Dash *(SW12)*

SYRIAN
West
Abu Zaad *(W12)*

TURKISH
Central
Cyprus Mangal *(SW1)*
Efes II *(W1)*
Kazan *(SW1)*
Sofra *(W1,WC2)*
Tas *(WC1)*

West
Best Mangal *(W14)*

North
Beyoglu *(NW3)*
Gallipoli *(N1)*
Gem *(N1)*
Izgara *(N3)*
Petek *(N4)*
Shish *(NW2)*
Sofra *(NW8)*

South
Ev Restaurant, Bar & Deli *(SE1)*
Tas *(SE1)*
Tas Pide *(SE1)*

East
Haz *(E1, EC3)*
Kazan *(EC3)*
Mangal Ocakbasi *(E8)*
Shish *(EC1)*
Sofra *(EC1)*
Tas *(EC1)*

AFGHANI
North
Afghan Kitchen *(N1)*

BURMESE
West
Mandalay *(W2)*

CHINESE
Central
Ba Shan *(W1)*
Baozi Inn *(WC2)*
Bar Shu *(W1)*
Cha Cha Moon *(W1)*
China Tang *(W1)*
The Chinese Experience *(W1)*
Chuen Cheng Ku *(W1)*
Fung Shing *(WC2)*
Golden Dragon *(W1)*
Hakkasan *(W1)*
Haozhan *(W1)*
Harbour City *(W1)*
Hunan *(SW1)*
Imperial China *(WC2)*
Jade Garden *(W1)*
Jenny Lo's Tea House *(SW1)*
Joy King Lau *(WC2)*
Kai Mayfair *(W1)*
Keelung *(WC2)*
Ken Lo's Memories *(SW1)*
Mekong *(SW1)*
Mr Chow *(SW1)*
Mr Kong *(WC2)*
New Mayflower *(W1)*

New World *(W1)*
Princess Garden *(W1)**
Royal China *(W1)**
Royal China Club *(W1)**
Shanghai Blues *(WC1)**
Taman Gang *(W1)*
Wong Kei *(W1)*
Yauatcha *(W1)**
Yming *(W1)**

West
Choys *(SW3)*
The Four Seasons *(W2)**
Good Earth *(SW3)*
Ken Lo's Memories of China *(W8)**
Magic Wok *(W2)**
Mandarin Kitchen *(W2)**
Min Jiang *(W8)**
Mr Wing *(SW5)*
New Culture Revolution *(SW3,W11)*
North China *(W3)**
Pearl Liang *(W2)**
Royal China *(SW6,W2)**
Stick & Bowl *(W8)**
Taiwan Village *(SW6)**
Yi-Ban *(SW6)**

North
Alisan *(HA9)**
Goldfish *(NW3)**
Good Earth *(NW7)*
Gung-Ho *(NW6)*
Kaifeng *(NW4)*
Met Su Yan *(NW11)*
New Culture Revolution *(N1)*
Phoenix Palace *(NW1)**
Sakonis *(HA0)*
Singapore Garden *(NW6)**
Snazz Sichuan *(NW1)*
Weng Wah House *(NW3)*

South
Bayee Village *(SW19)*
Dalchini *(SW19)*
Dragon Castle *(SE17)**
Four Regions *(TW9)*
China Boulevard *(SW18)*
O'Zon *(TW1)*
Peninsular *(SE10)*
Royal China *(SW15)**

East
The Drunken Monkey *(E1)**
Gourmet San *(E2)**
Imperial City *(EC3)*
Lotus Chinese Floating
   Restaurant *(E14)*
Royal China *(E14)**
Royal Wok *(E2)*
Shanghai *(E8)*
Yi-Ban *(E16)**

CHINESE, DIM SUM
Central
The Chinese Experience *(W1)*
Chuen Cheng Ku *(W1)*
dim T *(W1)*
Golden Dragon *(W1)*
Hakkasan *(W1)**
Harbour City *(W1)**
Imperial China *(WC2)*
Jade Garden *(W1)*
Joy King Lau *(WC2)**
Leong's Legends *(W1)*
New World *(W1)*

ping pong *(W1)*
Princess Garden *(W1)**
Royal China *(W1)**
Royal China Club *(W1)**
Shanghai Blues *(WC1)**
Yauatcha *(W1)**

West
Cha Cha Moon *(W2)*
Min Jiang *(W8)**
Pearl Liang *(W2)**
ping pong *(W2)*
Royal China *(SW6,W2)**
Yi-Ban *(SW6)**

North
Alisan *(HA9)**
dim T *(N6, NW3)*
Phoenix Palace *(NW1)**
ping pong *(NW3)*
Weng Wah House *(NW3)*

South
dim T *(SE1)*
Dragon Castle *(SE17)**
China Boulevard *(SW18)*
Peninsular *(SE10)*
ping pong *(SE1)*
Royal China *(SW15)**

East
D Sum 2 *(EC4)*
The Drunken Monkey *(E1)**
Lotus Chinese Floating
   Restaurant *(E14)*
ping pong *(E1, EC2, EC4)*
Royal China *(E14)**
Shanghai *(E8)*
Yi-Ban *(E16)**

INDIAN
Central
Amaya *(SW1)**
Benares *(W1)**
Chor Bizarre *(W1)**
Chowki *(W1)*
The Cinnamon Club *(SW1)**
Gaylord *(W1)*
Gopal's of Soho *(W1)*
Imli *(W1)*
Indali Lounge *(W1)*
India Club *(WC2)*
Malabar Junction *(WC1)*
Masala Zone *(W1,WC2)*
Mela *(WC2)*
Mint Leaf *(SW1)*
Moti Mahal *(WC2)**
La Porte des Indes *(W1)*
Ragam *(W1)**
Red Fort *(W1)**
Sagar *(W1,WC2)**
Salaam Namaste *(WC1)*
Shikara *(W1)*
Silk *(W1)*
Sitaaray *(WC2)**
Tamarind *(W1)**
Veeraswamy *(W1)**
Woodlands *(SW1,W1)*

West
Anarkali *(W6)**
Bombay Bicycle Club *(W11)*
Bombay Brasserie *(SW7)*
Bombay Palace *(W2)**
Brilliant *(UB2)**

Chutney Mary *(SW10)**
Five Hot Chillies *(HA0)**
Green Chilli *(W6)*
Haandi *(SW3)*
Indian Zing *(W6)**
kare kare *(SW5)*
Karma *(W14)*
Khan's *(W2)**
Khan's of Kensington *(SW7)*
Madhu's *(UB1)**
Malabar *(W8)*
Masala Zone *(SW5, SW6, W2)*
Memories of India *(SW7)*
Mirch Masala *(UB1, W14)**
Monty's *(SW6, W13, W5)*
Noor Jahan *(SW5, W2)**
The Painted Heron *(SW10)**
Rasoi *(SW3)**
Sagar *(W6)**
Shikara *(SW3)*
Star of India *(SW5)**
Tandoori Lane *(SW6)**
Urban Turban *(W2)*
Vama *(SW10)**
Zaika *(W8)**

North
Anglo Asian Tandoori *(N16)*
Atma *(NW3)**
Bombay Bicycle Club *(NW3)*
Chutneys *(NW1)*
Diwana Bhel-Poori House *(NW1)*
Emni *(N1)*
Eriki *(NW3)**
Geeta *(NW6)**
Great Nepalese *(NW1)*
Indian Rasoi *(N2)**
Kovalam *(NW6)*
Masala Zone *(N1, NW1)*
Rani *(N3)**
Rooburoo *(N1)*
Sakonis *(HA0)*
Vijay *(NW6)**
Woodlands *(NW3)*
Zaffrani *(N1)*
Zeen *(NW1)*

South
Babur *(SE23)**
Bangalore Express *(SE1)*
Bengal Clipper *(SE1)**
Bombay Bicycle Club *(SW12)*
Chutney *(SW18)**
Dalchini *(SW19)*
Everest Inn *(SE3)*
Ganapati *(SE15)**
Holy Cow *(SW11)**
Hot Stuff *(SW8)**
Indian Ocean *(SW17)**
Kastoori *(SW17)**
Kennington Tandoori *(SE11)*
Ma Goa *(SW15)**
Mango & Silk *(SW14)*
Mango Tree *(SE1)**
Mela *(SE24)*
Mirch Masala *(SW16, SW17)**
Mogul *(SE10)*
Nazmins *(SW18)**
Origin Asia *(TW9)**
Sagar *(TW1)**
Sree Krishna *(SW17)**
Tandoori Nights *(SE22)**
Tangawizi *(TW1)**

East
Café Spice Namaste *(E1)**
Cinnamon Kitchen *(EC2)**
Clifton *(E1)**
Dockmaster's House *(E14)*
The Gaylord *(E14)*
Memsaheb on Thames *(E14)*
Mint Leaf *(EC2)*
Mirch Masala *(E1)**
New Tayyabs *(E1)**
Rajasthan *(EC3)*

INDIAN, SOUTHERN
Central
India Club *(WC2)*
Malabar Junction *(WC1)*
Quilon *(SW1)**
Ragam *(W1)**
Rasa *(W1)**
Rasa Maricham *(WC1)**
Sagar *(W1)**
Woodlands *(SW1, W1)*

West
Sagar *(W6)**
Shilpa *(W6)**

North
Chutneys *(NW1)*
Geeta *(NW6)**
Kovalam *(NW6)*
Rani *(N3)**
Rasa *(N16)**
Rasa Travancore *(N16)**
Vijay *(NW6)**
Woodlands *(NW3)*

South
Ganapati *(SE15)**
Sagar *(TW1)**
Sree Krishna *(SW17)**
Vijaya Krishna *(SW17)**

INDONESIAN
Central
Melati *(W1)*
Trader Vics *(W1)*

West
Kiasu *(W2)*

South
Nancy Lam's Enak Enak *(SW11)*

JAPANESE
Central
Abeno *(WC1, WC2)*
Abokado *(WC2)**
Aqua Kyoto *(W1)*
Atami *(SW1)*
Atari-Ya *(W1)**
Benihana *(W1)*
Bincho Yakitori *(W1)*
Centrepoint Sushi *(WC2)**
Chisou *(W1)**
Defune *(W1)**
Dinings *(W1)**
Donzoko *(W1)**
Edokko *(WC1)**
Feng Sushi *(SW1)*
Hazuki *(WC2)*
Ikeda *(W1)**
Inamo *(W1)*
Itsu *(W1)*

Kiku *(W1)**
Kulu Kulu *(W1, WC2)*
Matsuri *(SW1, WC1)*
Misato *(W1)*
Mitsukoshi *(SW1)**
Miyama *(W1)*
Nobu *(W1)**
Nobu Berkeley *(W1)*
Okawari *(WC2)*
Roka *(W1)**
Sake No Hana *(SW1)*
Sakura *(W1)**
Satsuma *(W1)*
Shogun *(W1)*
So *(W1)*
Soho Japan *(W1)*
Sumosan *(W1)**
Sushi Hiroba *(WC2)*
Taman Gang *(W1)*
Taro *(W1)*
Ten Ten Tei *(W1)*
Toku *(W1)*
Tokyo Diner *(WC2)*
Tsunami *(W1)*
Umu *(W1)**
Wagamama *(SW1, W1, WC1, WC2)*
Yoshino *(W1)**

West
Benihana *(SW3)*
Feng Sushi *(SW10, W11, W8)*
Inaho *(W2)**
Itsu *(SW3)*
Kulu Kulu *(SW7)*
Nozomi *(SW3)*
Okawari *(W5)*
Sushi-Hiro *(W5)**
Sushinho *(SW3)*
Taro *(SW3)*
Tosa *(W6)*
Wagamama *(W8)*
Yumenoki *(SW10)*
Zuma *(SW7)**

North
Abeno *(NW3)*
Asakusa *(NW1)**
Atari-Ya *(NW4)**
Benihana *(NW3)*
Bento Cafe *(NW1)**
Café Japan *(NW11)**
Feng Sushi *(NW3)*
Jin Kichi *(NW3)**
Met Su Yan *(NW11)*
Sushi-Say *(NW2)**
Wagamama *(N1, NW1)*
Yuzu *(NW6)**

South
Cho-San *(SW15)**
Feng Sushi *(SE1)*
Fujiyama *(SW9)*
Inshoku *(SE1)*
Matsuba *(TW9)*
Slurp *(SW16, SW19)*
Tsunami *(SW4)*
Wagamama *(SE1, SW15, SW19)*

East
City Miyama *(EC4)**
Itsu *(E14)*
K10 *(EC2)*
Kurumaya *(EC4)**
Mugen *(EC4)*
Noto Kikuya *(EC3)*

Pham Sushi *(EC1)**
Roka *(E14)**
Saki Bar & Food Emporium *(EC1)**
Soseki *(EC3)*
Tajima Tei *(EC1)**
Tokyo City *(EC2)*
Wagamama *(E14, EC2, EC3, EC4)*

JAPANESE, TEPPAN-YAKI
East
Noto Kikuya *(EC3)*

KOREAN
Central
Asadal *(WC1)*
Koba *(W1)*

North
Dotori *(N4)*

MALAYSIAN
Central
C&R Cafe *(W1)**
Jom Makan *(SW1)*
Melati *(W1)*
Suka *(W1)*

West
Awana *(SW3)*
Kiasu *(W2)*
Satay House *(W2)**

North
Singapore Garden *(NW6)**

South
Champor-Champor *(SE1)**
Ekachai *(SW18)*

East
Ekachai *(EC2)*
54 Farringdon Road *(EC1)**

PAKISTANI
Central
Salloos *(SW1)**

West
Mirch Masala *(UB1)**

South
Mirch Masala *(SW16, SW17)**

East
Lahore Kebab House *(E1)**
Mirch Masala *(E1)**
New Tayyabs *(E1)**

PAN-ASIAN
Central
Buddha Bar *(WC2)*
Cocoon *(W1)*
dim T *(SW1, W1)*
Haozhan *(W1)**
Hare & Tortoise *(WC1)*
Noodle Noodle *(SW1)*
Silk *(W1)*
Tamarai *(WC2)*

West
The Collection *(SW3)*
dim T *(SW7)*
E&O *(W11)**

Eight Over Eight *(SW3)**
Hare & Tortoise *(W14,W5)*
Mao Tai *(SW6)**
Tampopo *(SW10)*
Uli *(W11)**

North
The Banana Tree Canteen *(NW6)*
dim T *(N6, NW3)*
Gilgamesh *(NW1)*
XO *(NW3)*

South
The Banana Leaf Canteen *(SW11)*
dim T *(SE1)*
Hare & Tortoise *(SW15)*
Nancy Lam's Enak Enak *(SW11)*
O'Zon *(TW1)*

East
Banana Tree Canteen *(EC1)*
Chi Noodle & Wine Bar *(EC4)**
Cicada *(EC1)*
D Sum 2 *(EC4)*
Great Eastern Dining Room *(EC2)*
Pacific Oriental *(EC2)*

THAI
Central
Benja *(W1)**
Blue Jade *(SW1)*
Busaba Eathai *(W1,WC1)**
C&R Cafe *(W1)**
Crazy Bear *(W1)*
Ekachai *(W1)*
Mango Tree *(SW1)*
Mekong *(SW1)*
Monkey & Me *(W1)**
Nahm *(SW1)*
Patara *(W1)**
Siam Central *(W1)*
Silk *(W1)*
Thai Café *(SW1)*
Thai Pot *(WC2)*
Thai Square *(SW1,W1,WC2)*

West
Addie's Thai Café *(SW5)**
Bangkok *(SW7)*
Bedlington Café *(W4)*
Blue Elephant *(SW6)*
C&R Cafe *(W2)**
Café 209 *(SW6)*
Churchill Arms *(W8)**
Esarn Kheaw *(W12)**
Fat Boy's *(W5)*
Hammersmith Café *(W6)*
Latymers *(W6)**
Number One Café *(W10)**
Old Parr's Head *(W14)*
Patara *(SW3)**
Sugar Hut *(SW6)*
Sukho Thai Cuisine *(SW6)**
Tawana *(W2)*
Thai Square *(SW7)*
The Walmer Castle *(W11)*
Yelo Thai Canteen *(W11)*

North
Isarn *(N1)**
Thai Square *(N1)*
Yelo *(N1)*
Yum Yum *(N16)*

South
Amaranth *(SW18)*
Ekachai *(SW18)*
Fat Boy's *(SW14,TW1,TW8,W4)*
The Paddyfield *(SW12)*
The Pepper Tree *(SW4)*
The Rye *(SE15)*
Suk Saran *(SW19)*
Talad Thai *(SW15)*
Thai Corner Café *(SE22)*
Thai Garden *(SW11)*
Thai on the River *(SW11)*
Thai Square *(SW15)*
Thailand *(SE14)*

East
Ekachai *(EC2)*
Elephant Royale *(E14)*
Hokkien Chan *(EC2)*
Rosa's *(E1)*
Thai Square *(EC4)*
Thai Square City *(EC3)*

VIETNAMESE
Central
Bam-Bou *(W1)**
Mekong *(SW1)*
Pho *(W1)*
Viet *(W1)**

West
Kiasu *(W2)*
Pho *(W12)*
Saigon Saigon *(W6)*

North
Huong-Viet *(N1)**
Khoai *(N8)*
Khoai Cafe *(N12)*
Viet Garden *(N1)*

South
The Paddyfield *(SW12)*

East
Cây Tre *(EC1)*
Namo *(E9)*
Pho *(EC1)*
Sông Quê *(E2)**
Viet Grill *(E2)*
Viet Hoa *(E2)*

AREA OVERVIEWS

CENTRAL

Soho, Covent Garden & Bloomsbury
(Parts of W1, all WC2 and WC1)

Price	Name	Cuisine			
£80+	L'Atelier de Joel Robuchon	French	2	3	2
	Asia de Cuba	Fusion	4	5	3
£70+	Pearl	French	3	3	3
£60+	Homage	British, Modern	4	4	4
	The Ivy	"	4	2	2
	Rules	British, Traditional	3	3	1
	J Sheekey	Fish & seafood	1	2	1
	Matsuri	Japanese	3	3	5
£50+	Christopher's	American	4	4	3
	Adam Street	British, Modern	3	2	2
	Alastair Little	"	–	–	–
	Axis	"	3	2	4
	Bob Bob Ricard	"	5	4	3
	Indigo	"	3	2	3
	Quo Vadis	"	3	3	3
	The National Dining Rooms	British, Traditional	5	5	4
	Simpsons-in-the-Strand	"	4	4	4
	Zilli Fish	Fish & seafood	3	4	4
	The Admiralty	French	4	4	4
	L'Escargot	"	3	2	2
	Incognico	"	4	3	4
	Mon Plaisir	"	4	4	3
	La Trouvaille	"	3	3	3
	Little Italy	Italian	4	3	3
	Orso	"	4	3	4
	Vasco & Piero's Pavilion	"	2	3	4
	Albannach	Scottish	5	5	5
	Gaucho	Steaks & grills	3	3	3
	Floridita	Cuban	5	5	2
	Shanghai Blues	Chinese	2	2	3
	Yauatcha	"	1	3	2
	Red Fort	Indian	2	4	4
	Buddha Bar	Pan-Asian	5	5	3
	Silk	"	4	3	3
	Tamarai	"	3	4	3
£40+	Joe Allen	American	4	3	1
	Acorn House	British, Modern	3	3	5
	Arbutus	"	2	2	3
	Café du Jardin	"	4	3	3
	Le Deuxième	"	4	4	4
	French House	"	3	3	2
	Konstam	"	2	3	3
	No.20	"	4	4	5
	The Portrait	"	4	4	1
	Refuel	"	4	4	4
	Shampers	"	3	2	3
	Tuttons	"	4	4	4
	Cape Town Fish Market	Fish & seafood	4	4	4
	Livebait	"	4	5	5

J Sheekey Oyster Bar	"	❶❶❷
Beotys	French	⑤④④
Café Bohème	"	④④❷
Café des Amis	"	④④④
Chez Gérard	"	⑤⑤④
Clos Maggiore	"	❷❶❶
Randall & Aubin	"	❷❷❶
So	Fusion	❸❸⑤
Bedford & Strand	International	④❸❷
The Forge	"	④❸❸
National Gallery Café	"	⑤⑤④
Ronnie Scott's	"	⑤④❶
Bertorelli	Italian	⑤⑤⑤
Dehesa	"	❷❷❶
Number Twelve	"	❸❷⑤
Pasta Brown	"	④❸⑤
Barrafina	Spanish	❶❶❷
Cigala	"	❸❷④
Tierra Brindisa	"	❷❸❸
The Bountiful Cow	Steaks & grills	❸④④
Sophie's Steakhouse	"	④❸❷
St Moritz	Swiss	❸❸❷
Wolfe's	Burgers, etc	❸④④
Kettners	Pizza	④④⑤
Moti Mahal	Indian	❷❷❸
Edokko	Japanese	❷❷❸
Benja	Thai	❷❷❸
Patara	"	❷❷❸
£35+		
All Star Lanes	American	④⑤❸
Bodean's	"	④④④
Maxwell's	"	④④❸
Belgo	Belgian	④④④
Andrew Edmunds	British, Modern	❸❷❶
Aurora	"	❸❸❷
The Norfolk Arms	"	④④❸
Great Queen Street	British, Traditional	❷❸❸
Loch Fyne	Fish & seafood	④④④
Côte	French	④❸④
The Giaconda	"	❷❶④
Terroirs	"	❷④❷
Gay Hussar	Hungarian	④❸❷
Balans	International	⑤❸④
Boulevard	"	⑤⑤⑤
Browns	"	④④④
Sarastro	"	⑤⑤④
Sugar Reef	"	④④④
Bocca Di Lupo	Italian	❷❷❷
Rossopomodoro	"	❸④④
Sapori	"	④❸④
06 St Chad's Place	Mediterranean	❸❸❸
Bar Shu	Chinese	❷④❸
Fung Shing	"	❷❸⑤
Imperial China	"	❸❸❸
Malabar Junction	Indian	❸❸❸
Sitaaray	"	❷❷❷
Donzoko	Japanese	❷④④
Ten Ten Tei	"	❸❸④

	Asadal	*Korean*	③	④	④
	Haozhan	*Pan-Asian*	❶	❷	④
£30+	Balfour	*British, Modern*	④	❷	❷
	The Easton	"	❸	❸	❸
	Giraffe	"	④	❸	❸
	The Terrace	"	❸	❷	❸
	Porters	*British, Traditional*	④	④	④
	Cork & Bottle	*International*	⑤	④	❷
	Seven Stars	"	❸	④	❶
	Ciao Bella	*Italian*	④	❷	❶
	Spacca Napoli	"	❷	④	❸
	Mildred's	*Vegetarian*	❷	❸	❷
	Fire & Stone	*Pizza*	❸	④	❷
	Paradiso Olivelli	"	④	④	④
	Café Pacifico	*Mexican/TexMex*	④	❸	❷
	Souk Medina	*Moroccan*	④	❸	❶
	Sofra	*Turkish*	④	④	④
	Tas	"	④	❸	❸
	Chuen Cheng Ku	*Chinese*	❸	❸	❸
	Mr Kong	"	❸	❷	❸
	New Mayflower	"	❷	⑤	⑤
	New World	"	④	④	④
	Yming	"	❷	❶	❸
	Mela	*Indian*	❸	❸	❸
	Rasa Maricham	*Indian, Southern*	❷	❷	❸
	Abeno	*Japanese*	❸	❷	❸
	Bincho Yakitori	"	④	❷	❸
	Hazuki	"	❸	❷	④
	Inamo	"	④	❷	❶
	Satsuma	"	❸	④	④
	Melati, Gt Windmill St	*Malaysian*	④	❷	④
	Thai Pot	*Thai*	④	❷	④
	Thai Square	"	④	④	❸
£25+	Café Emm	*British, Modern*	④	④	❸
	Villandry Kitchen	*French*	❸	❷	❸
	Real Greek	*Greek*	⑤	⑤	④
	Star Café	*International*	④	❸	❸
	La Porchetta Pizzeria	*Italian*	❸	❸	❸
	Canela	*Portuguese*	❸	❷	❷
	La Tasca	*Spanish*	⑤	⑤	④
	North Sea Fish	*Fish & chips*	❷	❷	④
	Rock & Sole Plaice	"	❸	④	④
	Fernandez & Wells	*Sandwiches, cakes, etc*	❶	❷	❷
	Paul	"	❸	④	④
	Wahaca	*Mexican/TexMex*	❸	❷	❷
	Gaby's	*Israeli*	❸	❸	④
	Ba Shan	*Chinese*	④	❸	❸
	The Chinese Experience	"	❸	❸	⑤
	Golden Dragon	"	❸	④	❸
	Harbour City	"	❷	❸	④
	Jade Garden	"	❸	④	❸
	Joy King Lau	"	❷	❸	④
	Keelung	"	❸	❸	❸
	Leong's Legends	*Chinese, Dim sum*	❸	⑤	❸
	ping pong	"	④	④	❸
	Chowki	*Indian*	④	⑤	⑤

	Name	Cuisine	Ratings
	Gopal's of Soho	"	③②④
	Imli	"	③③③
	Masala Zone	"	④③③
	Salaam Namaste	"	③②④
	Centrepoint Sushi	Japanese	②③④
	Itsu	"	③③④
	Kulu Kulu	"	③④⑤
	Misato	"	②⑤⑤
	Sushi Hiroba	"	④④④
	Wagamama	"	④③④
	Hare & Tortoise	Pan-Asian	③④④
	Busaba Eathai	Thai	②③②
	C&R Cafe	"	②③④
£20+	Café in the Crypt	International	④④②
	Gordon's Wine Bar	"	⑤③①
	Bistro 1	Mediterranean	④②③
	Café España	Spanish	③②②
	Ed's Easy Diner	Burgers, etc	③③②
	Gourmet Burger Kitchen	"	③④④
	Hamburger Union	"	④④④
	The Ultimate Burger	"	④④③
	Konditor & Cook	Sandwiches, cakes, etc	②③④
	Leon	"	③③③
	Yalla Yalla	Lebanese	②②③
	Cha Cha Moon	Chinese	④③③
	Wong Kei	"	③⑤②
	India Club	Indian	④④⑤
	Sagar	"	②②④
	Okawari	Japanese	③②③
	Taro	"	③③④
£15+	Square Pie Company	British, Traditional	②②③
	Paolina Café	Italian	③③⑤
	Princi	"	③④①
	Hummus Bros	Mediterranean	③③③
	Food for Thought	Vegetarian	②④④
	Napket	Afternoon tea	④④②
	The Chippy	Fish & chips	③③③
	Bar Italia	Sandwiches, cakes, etc	③③①
	Mrs Marengos	"	②②④
	Just Falafs	Salads	③③④
	Vital Ingredient	"	③③④
	Baozi Inn	Chinese	③④③
	Abokado	Japanese	②④⑤
	Tokyo Diner	"	④③④
	Viet	Vietnamese	②⑤④
£10+	Caffé Vergnano	Italian	③④③
	Nordic Bakery	Scandinavian	③②③
	Fryer's Delight	Fish & chips	③③①
	Kastner & Ovens	Sandwiches, cakes, etc	①②•
	Maison Bertaux	"	②③①
	Monmouth Coffee Co	"	①②②
	Chop'd	Salads	②③④
£5+	Flat White	Sandwiches, cakes, etc	①①②

Mayfair & St James's (Parts of W1 and SW1)

Price	Name	Cuisine			
£120+	Umu	*Japanese*	②	③	③
£110+	Le Gavroche	*French*	②	①	②
£100+	Hélène Darroze	*French*	⑤	④	③
	The Ritz Restaurant	*"*	④	③	①
£90+	Wiltons	*British, Traditional*	③	②	②
	Alain Ducasse	*French*	④	③	④
	G Ramsay at Claridges	*"*	④	③	③
	The Greenhouse	*"*	③	②	②
	Sketch (Lecture Rm)	*"*	⑤	⑤	④
	The Square	*"*	②	②	③
£80+	Dorchester Grill	*British, Modern*	④	③	④
	Hibiscus	*French*	③	③	④
	L'Oranger	*"*	④	④	④
	Kai Mayfair	*Chinese*	③	④	④
	Nobu	*Japanese*	②	④	④
	Nobu Berkeley	*"*	③	④	③
£70+	Bellamy's	*British, Modern*	④	③	③
	The Albemarle	*British, Traditional*	③	②	②
	Galvin at Windows	*French*	③	③	②
	maze Grill	*"*	③	④	④
	La Petite Maison	*"*	②	③	②
	Cipriani	*Italian*	⑤	⑤	④
	Murano	*"*	②	①	③
	Theo Randall	*"*	②	③	⑤
	The Palm	*Steaks & grills*	④	③	④
	China Tang	*Chinese*	④	④	④
	Hakkasan	*"*	②	③	①
	Benares	*Indian*	②	③	③
	Ikeda	*Japanese*	①	②	⑤
	Sake No Hana	*"*	④	④	④
£60+	Nicole's	*British, Modern*	④	③	③
	Patterson's	*"*	③	③	④
	The Pigalle Club	*"*	④	④	②
	Corrigan's Mayfair	*British, Traditional*	③	②	③
	Green's	*"*	③	②	③
	Bentley's	*Fish & seafood*	②	③	③
	Scott's	*"*	②	②	①
	Brasserie Roux	*French*	④	④	④
	maze	*"*	②	②	③
	Dolada	*Italian*	④	④	④
	L'Incontro	*"*	–	–	–
	Luciano	*"*	⑤	⑤	⑤
	Ladurée	*Afternoon tea*	④	④	④
	Mint Leaf	*Indian*	④	④	④
	Kiku	*Japanese*	②	③	⑤
	Matsuri	*"*	③	③	⑤
	Miyama	*"*	③	③	⑤
	Shogun	*"*	③	②	⑤
	Sumosan	*"*	②	③	④

£50+			
Artisan	British, Modern	3 3 4
The Avenue	"	4 4 4
Le Caprice	"	2 0 0
Criterion	"	4 2 2
Hush	"	4 5 4
Just St James	"	5 5 5
Langan's Brasserie	"	5 4 2
Mews of Mayfair	"	3 4 3
Quaglino's	"	5 5 5
Rhodes W1 Brasserie	"	4 4 5
Wild Honey	"	2 2 3
The Wolseley	"	3 2 0
Fortnum's, The Fountain	British, Traditional	4 3 3
Greig's	"	3 3 4
Pescatori	Fish & seafood	3 2 3
Bord'Eaux	French	3 3 5
Boudin Blanc	"	2 3 0
Sketch (Gallery)	"	5 4 4
Alloro	Italian	3 3 4
Cecconi's	"	3 3 2
Franco's	"	4 3 4
Ristorante Semplice	"	2 2 3
Sartoria	"	4 4 3
Serafino	"	4 3 4
Il Vaporetto	"	4 5 3
St Alban	Mediterranean	3 0 2
Gaucho	Steaks & grills	3 3 3
Goodman	"	2 2 4
The Guinea Grill	"	2 3 3
Rowley's	"	4 4 4
Momo	North African	4 5 2
Fakhreldine	Lebanese	4 4 4
Princess Garden	Chinese	2 2 4
Taman Gang	"	3 3 4
Tamarind	Indian	2 2 3
Veeraswamy	"	2 2 2
Quilon	Indian, Southern	2 0 5
Trader Vics	Indonesian	5 3 3
Benihana	Japanese	4 4 4
Mitsukoshi	"	2 3 5
Cocoon	Pan-Asian	3 4 2

£40+			
Automat	American	4 4 3
Hard Rock Café	"	4 4 2
The Duke of Wellington	British, Modern	2 2 2
Inn the Park	"	5 5 3
The Little Square	"	4 4 3
1707	"	3 3 2
Fishworks	Fish & seafood	3 4 4
Brasserie St Jacques	French	4 4 5
Chez Gérard	"	5 5 4
Sotheby's Café	International	2 2 2
Al Duca	Italian	4 4 4
Bar Trattoria Semplice	"	3 3 4
Getti	"	4 4 4
Osteria Dell'Angolo	"	3 0 5
Via Condotti	"	4 4 4
Il Vicolo	"	3 2 4

Dover Street	Mediterranean	⑤	④	④
Rocket	"	④	❸	❷
Truc Vert	"	❸	④	❷
Planet Hollywood	Burgers, etc	–	–	–
Aubaine	Sandwiches, cakes, etc	④	④	④
Sketch (Parlour)	"	④	④	❷
Al Hamra	Lebanese	④	⑤	⑤
Al Sultan	"	❸	❸	⑤
Levant	"	④	④	❶
Noura	"	❸	❷	❸
1001 Nights	"	④	❸	❸
Chor Bizarre	Indian	❷	❸	❷
Patara	Thai	❷	❷	❸

£35+				
The Only Running Footman	British, Modern	❸	❸	❸
The Queens Arms	"	④	❸	❸
Running Horse	"	❸	❸	❸
The Windmill	British, Traditional	❸	❸	④
L'Artiste Musclé	French	④	④	❸
Browns	International	④	④	④
Piccolino	Italian	④	④	④
Delfino	Pizza	❷	❸	④
Richoux	Sandwiches, cakes, etc	⑤	⑤	④
Chisou	Japanese	❷	❷	④
Yoshino	"	❷	❷	④

£30+				
El Pirata	Spanish	❸	❷	❷
Diner	Burgers, etc	④	⑤	❸
Royal Academy	Sandwiches, cakes, etc	⑤	⑤	❸
Sofra	Turkish	④	④	④
Woodlands	Indian	❸	❸	④
Rasa	Indian, Southern	❷	❷	❸
Toku	Japanese	❸	④	④
Thai Square	Thai	④	④	❸

£25+				
tibits	Vegetarian	❸	④	④
Benugo	Sandwiches, cakes, etc	④	④	❷
Itsu	Japanese	❸	❸	④
Sakura	"	❷	⑤	⑤
Wagamama	"	④	❸	④
Jom Makan	Malaysian	⑤	④	④
dim T	Pan-Asian	④	④	❸
Busaba Eathai	Thai	❷	❸	❷
Ekachai	"	❸	④	④

£20+				
Noodle Noodle	Pan-Asian	❸	④	⑤

£15+				
Stock Pot	International	④	❸	④
Napket	Afternoon tea	④	④	❷
Vital Ingredient	Salads	❸	❸	④

£10+				
La Bottega	Italian	❸	❸	④
Crussh	Sandwiches, cakes, etc	❸	❸	④
Fuzzy's Grub	"	❷	❷	④
Chop'd	Salads	❷	❸	④

Fitzrovia & Marylebone (Part of W1)

£90+	Pied à Terre	French	②②③
	Rhodes W1 Restaurant	"	④③④
£80+	Roka	Japanese	②④②
£70+	The Landau	British, Modern	②②②
	Orrery	French	②②③
	Texture	Scandinavian	③③④
	Suka	Malaysian	④④⑤
£60+	The Providores	Fusion	③②④
	5 Cavendish Square	Italian	⑤⑤⑤
	Locanda Locatelli	"	③②③
£50+	Oscar	British, Modern	④④③
	Vanilla	"	②②②
	Odin's	British, Traditional	③①①
	Pescatori	Fish & seafood	③②③
	Elena's L'Etoile	French	⑤④③
	Archipelago	Fusion	③①①
	Michael Moore	International	③②④
	Caffè Caldesi	Italian	③④④
	2 Veneti	"	③②④
	Fino	Spanish	②②②
	Royal China Club	Chinese	②③④
	La Porte des Indes	Indian	③③②
	Crazy Bear	Thai	③③①
£40+	Hardy's Brasserie	British, Modern	④②③
	RIBA Café	"	④④②
	The Union Café	"	③③④
	Back to Basics	Fish & seafood	①③③
	Fishworks	"	③④④
	Seaport	"	④④④
	Trishna	"	①③④
	L'Autre Pied	French	②③④
	Galvin Bistrot de Luxe	"	①①②
	Villandry	"	④⑤⑤
	The Wallace	"	④④①
	Providores (Tapa Room)	Fusion	④④③
	Il Baretto	Italian	③④⑤
	Bertorelli's	"	⑤⑤⑤
	Getti	"	④④④
	Latium	"	①①③
	Sardo	"	②③③
	Garbo's	Scandinavian	④③④
	Ibérica	Spanish	②③③
	Black & Blue	Steaks & grills	③④④
	Reubens	Kosher	④⑤⑤
	Fairuz	Lebanese	③③④
	Tsunami	Japanese	③④③
	Koba	Korean	③②④
	Bam-Bou	Vietnamese	②③①
£35+	Ozer	British, Modern	④③③
	Canteen	British, Traditional	④④④

			Rating		
	Langan's Bistro	French	④	④	④
	Le Relais de Venise	"	❸	④	❸
	Hellenik	Greek	❷	❸	❸
	The Beehive	Italian	④	❸	④
	Salt Yard	Mediterranean	❷	❸	❸
	Maroush	Lebanese	❸	④	④
	Royal China	Chinese	❷	④	④
	Gaylord	Indian	❸	④	·
	Defune	Japanese	⓿	⓿	④
£30+	Eat & Two Veg	International	⑤	④	⑤
	Giraffe	"	④	❸	❸
	Ooze	"	④	④	❸
	Navarro's	Spanish	❸	④	❷
	Eagle Bar Diner	Burgers, etc	❸	④	❸
	Tootsies		④	④	④
	Paradiso Olivelli	Pizza	④	④	④
	Original Tajines	Moroccan	❸	❷	❸
	Efes II	Turkish	❸	❸	④
	Sofra	"	④	④	④
	Indali Lounge	Indian	❸	❷	❸
	Woodlands	"	❸	❸	④
	Rasa Samudra	Indian, Southern	❷	❷	❸
	Dinings	Japanese	⓿	❷	④
	Soho Japan	"	❸	❷	❸
£25+	Real Greek	Greek	⑤	⑤	④
	Benugo	Sandwiches, cakes, etc	④	④	❷
	La Fromagerie Café	"	❷	❸	❷
	Paul	"	❸	④	④
	ping pong	Chinese, Dim sum	④	④	❸
	Ragam	Indian	⓿	⓿	⑤
	Shikara	"	❸	❷	❸
	Wagamama	Japanese	④	❸	④
	dim T	Pan-Asian	④	④	❸
	Monkey & Me	Thai	❷	❷	④
	Siam Central	"	❸	❷	④
	Pho	Vietnamese	④	❸	④
£20+	Vapiano	Italian	④	④	❷
	Hamburger Union	Burgers, etc	④	④	④
	The Ultimate Burger	"	④	④	❸
	Golden Hind	Fish & chips	⓿	⓿	❸
	Leon	Sandwiches, cakes, etc	❸	❸	❸
	Sagar	Indian	❷	❷	④
£15+	Pure	American	❸	❷	④
	Square Pie Company	British, Traditional	❷	❷	❸
	Atari-Ya	Japanese	⓿	❸	④
£10+	Comptoir Libanais	Lebanese	❸	❸	❸

Belgravia, Pimlico, Victoria & Westminster (SW1, except St James's)

£110+	Marcus Wareing	*French*	❶❶❷
£90+	Pétrus	*French*	– – –
£80+	Foliage	*French*	❸❷❸
	Apsleys	*Italian*	④❸❸
	Nahm	*Thai*	④④⑤
£70+	Rib Room	*British, Traditional*	④❷⑤
	One-O-One	*Fish & seafood*	❶❷④
	Roussillon	*French*	❶❶❸
	Mr Chow	*Chinese*	❸④④
£60+	The Fifth Floor Restaurant	*British, Modern*	④④④
	The Goring Hotel	*"*	❸❶❶
	Boxwood Café	*International*	④❸❸
	The Park	*"*	❷❸❸
	Santini	*Italian*	④④④
	Toto's	*"*	❸❷❷
	Zafferano	*"*	❸❸❸
	Boisdale	*Scottish*	④④❷
	Ladurée	*Afternoon tea*	④④④
	The Cinnamon Club	*Indian*	❷❸❷
£50+	The Pantechnicon	*British, Modern*	❸❷❷
	The Thomas Cubitt	*"*	❸❸❷
	Shepherd's	*British, Traditional*	❸❷❸
	La Poule au Pot	*French*	❸❸❶
	Il Convivio	*Italian*	❷❶❸
	Quirinale	*"*	❷❷❸
	Ken Lo's Memories	*Chinese*	❷❷❸
	Amaya	*Indian*	❶❷❷
	Atami	*Japanese*	❸❸④
	Mango Tree	*Thai*	❸❸④
£40+	Chicago Rib Shack	*American*	⑤⑤④
	Atrium	*British, Modern*	④④④
	Bank Westminster	*"*	④④④
	The Botanist	*"*	④⑤④
	Daylesford Organic Café	*"*	④④④
	Ebury Wine Bar	*"*	④④❸
	Footstool	*"*	④④❸
	Tate Britain (Rex Whistler)	*"*	④❸❷
	Grenadier	*British, Traditional*	❸❸❶
	Olivomare	*Fish & seafood*	❷❸❸
	Le Cercle	*French*	❶❷❷
	The Chelsea Brasserie	*"*	⑤⑤④
	Chez Gérard	*"*	⑤⑤④
	The Ebury	*"*	④❸❷
	City Café	*International*	④④④
	Motcombs	*"*	④④④
	Caraffini	*Italian*	❸❶❸
	Como Lario	*"*	❸❸❷
	Gran Paradiso	*"*	④❷❸
	Olivo	*"*	❷❸④

	Name	Cuisine	Rating
	Ottolenghi	"	❶❸④
	Sale e Pepe	"	❸⓿❷
	Signor Sassi	"	❷❷❷
	2 Amici	"	④④④
	Uno	"	④⑤④
	Vivezza	"	④④④
	About Thyme	Mediterranean	❷❷❸
	The Fifth Floor Café	"	④④④
	Oliveto	Pizza	❶❸④
	Beiteddine	Lebanese	❸❷⑤
	Ishbilia	"	❷❷④
	Noura	"	❸❷❸
	Hunan	Chinese	❶❷④
	Salloos	Pakistani	❷❸④
£35+	Grumbles	International	④❷❸
	Oriel	"	⑤④❸
	Pizza on the Park	Italian	❸❸❸
	Baker & Spice	Sandwiches, cakes, etc	❸⑤④
	Texas Embassy Cantina	Mexican/TexMex	⑤⑤⑤
	Kazan	Turkish	❷❸❸
£30+	The Phoenix	British, Modern	❸④④
	Cafe Caramel	International	④④❸
	Goya	Spanish	④❸④
	Seafresh	Fish & chips	❸❷⑤
	Preto	Brazilian	④❸④
	Ranoush	Lebanese	❸④④
	Feng Sushi	Japanese	④④④
	Blue Jade	Thai	❸❶④
£25+	Vincent Rooms	British, Modern	④④④
	Chimes	British, Traditional	④❸❸
	Cyprus Mangal	Turkish	❷❸④
	Jenny Lo's	Chinese	❷❷❸
	Wagamama	Japanese	④❸④
	Thai Café	Thai	❸❸④
	Mekong	Vietnamese	④❸❸
£10+	La Bottega	Italian	❸❸④

WEST

Chelsea, South Kensington, Kensington, Earl's Court & Fulham (SW3, SW5, SW6, SW7, SW10 & W8)

£110+	Gordon Ramsay	*French*	❸❸❸
£100+	Ambassade de l'Ile	*French*	④⑤⑤
	Blakes	*International*	⑤④❷
£90+	Aubergine	*French*	– – –
	Tom Aikens	*"*	❸❸④
£80+	The Capital Restaurant	*French*	❶❷❸
	Rasoi	*Indian*	❷❸④
£70+	Launceston Place	*British, Modern*	❷❷❸
	Brunello	*Italian*	④❷❸
	Bombay Brasserie	*Indian*	❸④④
	Nozomi	*Japanese*	④⑤④
£60+	Babylon	*British, Modern*	④④❷
	Bibendum	*French*	❸❷❶
	Cheyne Walk Bras'	*"*	④④❷
	Lucio	*Italian*	❸❶❸
	Montpeliano	*"*	④④④
	San Lorenzo	*"*	④④❸
	Locanda Ottomezzo	*Mediterranean*	④❷④
	Zuma	*Japanese*	❶❸❶
	The Collection	*Pan-Asian*	⑤④④
£50+	Bibendum Oyster Bar	*British, Modern*	❸❸❷
	Bistro 190	*"*	④④❸
	Bluebird	*"*	⑤⑤⑤
	Bowler Bar & Grill	*"*	❸❸❸
	Clarke's	*"*	❷❷❸
	Marco	*"*	⑤④⑤
	Tom's Kitchen	*"*	❸④④
	Poissonnerie de l'Av.	*Fish & seafood*	❷❷❸
	Le Suquet	*"*	❸❸❸
	Belvedere	*French*	❸❷❶
	L'Etranger	*"*	❸❸❸
	Papillon	*"*	❸❸❸
	Racine	*"*	❷❷❸
	The Ark	*Italian*	④❸❸
	Carpaccio's	*"*	⑤④❸
	Scalini	*"*	❸❸❸
	Gaucho	*Steaks & grills*	❸❸❸
	Good Earth	*Chinese*	❸❸④
	Ken Lo's Memories	*"*	❷❸④
	Min Jiang	*"*	❷❶❶
	Chutney Mary	*Indian*	❷❷❷
	Zaika	*"*	❶❷❸
	Benihana	*Japanese*	④④④
	Awana	*Malaysian*	❸④④
	Mao Tai	*Pan-Asian*	❷❷❷
	Blue Elephant	*Thai*	❸❸❶

£40+				
Big Easy	American	4	3	2
PJ's	"	4	3	3
The Abingdon	British, Modern	3	2	2
Admiral Codrington	"	3	2	2
Brinkley's	"	4	4	3
The Establishment	"	3	3	3
The Farm	"	4	4	3
Gilmour's	"	4	3	2
Kensington Place	"	4	3	4
Kings Road Steakhouse	"	–	–	–
Le Metro	"	4	4	4
The Phoenix	"	4	3	3
Vingt-Quatre	"	4	4	4
Whits	"	2	0	3
Ffiona's	British, Traditional	3	2	0
Maggie Jones's	"	4	3	0
Chez Patrick	Fish & seafood	2	0	3
La Bouchée	French	3	3	2
La Brasserie	"	4	4	4
Le Colombier	"	3	0	2
Langan's Coq d'Or	"	4	4	4
Brompton Quarter Café	International	4	5	4
The Enterprise	"	3	3	2
Foxtrot Oscar	"	5	5	5
606 Club	"	4	4	2
Sushinho	"	4	4	4
The Swag & Tails	"	3	2	2
Daphne's	Italian	3	2	2
Elistano	"	3	2	3
La Famiglia	"	4	3	3
Frantoio	"	3	0	2
Il Giardino	"	3	4	2
Manicomio	"	4	4	4
Osteria dell'Arancio	"	1	3	4
Ottolenghi	"	3	2	3
Pellicano	"	3	0	2
Il Portico	"	2	3	2
Riccardo's	"	3	3	3
Timo	"	3	2	3
Ziani	"	3	2	3
Ognisko Polskie	Polish	4	3	3
Wódka	"	3	2	3
Cambio de Tercio	Spanish	2	2	2
L-Restaurant & Bar	"	3	2	4
Black & Blue	Steaks & grills	3	4	4
El Gaucho	"	3	3	3
Sophie's Steakhouse	"	4	3	2
Friends	Pizza	4	3	3
Aubaine	Sandwiches, cakes, etc	4	4	4
Pasha	Moroccan	5	4	2
Mr Wing	Chinese	3	2	0
The Painted Heron	Indian	1	2	3
Star of India	"	2	4	3
Vama	"	2	2	4
Eight Over Eight	Pan-Asian	2	3	2
Patara	Thai	2	2	3
Sugar Hut	"	3	3	3
Sukho Thai Cuisine	"	0	0	3

£35+			
	Bodean's	*American*	④④④
	Sticky Fingers	"	④④❸
	Brompton Bar & Grill	*British, Modern*	④❷❷
	The Builders Arms	"	④④❷
	Butcher's Hook	"	❸❷❷
	Duke on the Green	"	④④④
	Harwood Arms	"	❷❸❷
	Joe's Brasserie	"	❸❸❷
	Lots Road	"	❸❸❸
	Salisbury	"	❸❸❸
	White Horse	"	❸④❷
	Bumpkin	*British, Traditional*	❸❸❸
	Côte	*French*	④❸④
	The Pig's Ear	"	❸❸❷
	Tartine	"	❸❸❸
	Balans West	*International*	⑤❸④
	The Cabin	"	❷❷❷
	Gallery Mess	"	④④❸
	Glaisters	"	④④❸
	Kensington Wine Rooms	"	④④❷
	The Pembroke	"	❸❷❷
	The Scarsdale	"	④❸❸
	Wine Gallery	"	④❸❷
	Da Mario	*Italian*	④④❸
	De Cecco	"	❸❸❸
	Il Falconiere	"	④❷⑤
	Frankie's Italian Bar & Grill	"	⑤⑤⑤
	Napulé	"	❸④❸
	Nuovi Sapori	"	❸❷④
	Rossopomodoro	"	❸④④
	Santa Lucia	"	⑤④④
	The Atlas	*Mediterranean*	❷❸❷
	Madsen	*Scandinavian*	④④⑤
	Tendido Cero	*Spanish*	❷❷❷
	Tendido Cuatro	"	❸❷❸
	Henry J Beans	*Burgers, etc*	④④❸
	Geale's	*Fish & chips*	❸❸④
	(Ciro's) Pizza Pomodoro	*Pizza*	❸④❷
	Baker & Spice	*Sandwiches, cakes, etc*	❸⑤④
	Bluebird Café	"	⑤⑤⑤
	Richoux	"	⑤⑤④
	Beirut Express	*Lebanese*	❷④⑤
	Maroush	"	❸④④
	Randa	"	❸❷④
	Choys	*Chinese*	④❷④
	Royal China	"	❷④④
	Haandi	*Indian*	❷❸④
	Malabar	"	❸❷④
	Noor Jahan	"	❷❷❸

£30+			
	The Anglesea Arms	*British, Modern*	④❸❷
	Giraffe	*International*	④❸❸
	Aglio e Olio	*Italian*	❷❸❷
	Buona Sera	"	④❸❷
	Made in Italy	"	❷④❷
	Il Pagliaccio	"	④❸❷
	Spago	"	❸④④
	Del'Aziz	*Mediterranean*	④④❷

	Daquise	*Polish*	④	❸	④
	Casa Brindisa	*Spanish*	❸	❸	❸
	La Rueda	*"*	④	④	❸
	La Delizia Limbara	*Pizza*	❸	❸	②
	Troubadour	*Sandwiches, cakes, etc*	⑤	④	❶
	Ranoush	*Lebanese*	❸	④	④
	Yi-Ban	*Chinese*	②	②	②
	kare kare	*Indian*	❸	②	④
	Khan's of Kensington	*"*	❸	②	④
	Memories of India	*"*	❸	❸	④
	Feng Sushi	*Japanese*	④	④	④
	Yumenoki	*"*	④	②	❸
	Tampopo	*Pan-Asian*	❸	②	❸
	Bangkok	*Thai*	❸	②	❸
	Thai Square	*"*	④	④	❸
£25+	Kensington Square Kitchen	*British, Traditional*	❸	②	❸
	Rôtisserie Jules	*French*	④	④	④
	The Windsor Castle	*International*	❸	❸	❶
	Pappa Ciccia	*Italian*	②	②	②
	Rocca Di Papa	*"*	⑤	❸	④
	Lola Rojo	*Spanish*	②	②	❸
	Haché	*Steaks & grills*	②	❸	②
	Byron	*Burgers, etc*	❸	❸	❸
	Basilico	*Pizza*	❸	❸	⑤
	Benugo	*Sandwiches, cakes, etc*	④	④	②
	Paul	*"*	❸	④	④
	Taiwan Village	*Chinese*	❶	❶	❸
	Masala Zone	*Indian*	④	❸	❸
	Monty's	*"*	❸	❸	④
	Shikara	*"*	❸	②	❸
	Tandoori Lane	*"*	②	②	❸
	Itsu	*Japanese*	❸	❸	④
	Kulu Kulu	*"*	❸	④	⑤
	Wagamama	*"*	④	❸	④
	dim T	*Pan-Asian*	④	④	❸
	Addie's Thai Café	*Thai*	②	②	❸
£20+	Costa's Grill	*Greek*	④	❸	④
	Chelsea Bun Diner	*International*	❸	❸	④
	The Chelsea Kitchen	*"*	④	❸	❸
	Mona Lisa	*"*	④	②	❸
	Gourmet Burger Kitchen	*Burgers, etc*	❸	④	④
	Costa's Fish	*Fish & chips*	❸	❸	⑤
	New Culture Rev'n	*Chinese*	④	④	④
	Stick & Bowl	*"*	②	②	④
	Taro	*Japanese*	❸	❸	④
	Café 209	*Thai*	④	②	❶
	Churchill Arms	*"*	②	④	②
£15+	Stock Pot	*International*	④	❸	④
	Napket	*Afternoon tea*	④	④	②
£10+	La Bottega	*Italian*	❸	❸	④
	Crussh	*Sandwiches, cakes, etc*	❸	❸	④

Notting Hill, Holland Park, Bayswater, North Kensington & Maida Vale (W2, W9, W10, W11)

£70+	The Ledbury	French	❶❶❷
£60+	Notting Hill Brasserie	British, Modern	❸❸❷
	Angelus	French	❷❷❸
£50+	Beach Blanket Babylon	British, Modern	⑤⑤❷
	Julie's	"	④④❶
	Le Café Anglais	French	❸④❸
	Assaggi	Italian	❶❶❷
	Essenza	"	❷❷❷
£40+	Commander	British, Modern	④④④
	The Cow	"	❷④❷
	Daylesford Organic	"	④④④
	First Floor	"	④❷❶
	The Frontline Club	"	④❸❷
	The Ladbroke Arms	"	❷④❷
	Paradise, Kensal Green	"	❷❷❶
	The Warrington	"	⑤⑤⑤
	The Waterway	"	④④❸
	The Fat Badger	British, Traditional	❸❷④
	Hereford Road	"	❷❸❸
	Père Michel	French	❸❷④
	Halepi	Greek	④❷❸
	202	International	❸❸❸
	L'Accento Italiano	Italian	❸④④
	Arturo	"	❸❷❸
	Edera	"	❸❸④
	The Green Olive	"	❸❷❸
	Mediterraneo	"	④④④
	The Oak	"	❷❸❶
	Osteria Basilico	"	❸④❷
	Ottolenghi	"	❶❸④
	Trenta	"	❸④④
	Rodizio Rico	Brazilian	④⑤④
	Bombay Palace	Indian	❶❶⑤
	Urban Turban	"	④④④
	E&O	Pan-Asian	❶❸❶
£35+	All Star Lanes	American	④⑤❸
	Bodean's	"	④④④
	Harlem	"	④④❸
	Raoul's Café & Deli	British, Modern	④④❸
	The Westbourne	"	❸④❷
	Bumpkin	British, Traditional	❸❸❸
	The Academy	International	❷❷❷
	Electric Brasserie	"	❸❸❷
	Wine Factory	"	❸❸④
	Luna Rossa	Italian	④⑤❸
	Portobello Ristorante	"	❸④❸
	The Red Pepper	"	❷④④
	Rossopomodoro	"	❸④④
	Mulberry Street	Pizza	④④❸
	Baker & Spice	Sandwiches, cakes, etc	❸⑤④
	Crazy Homies	Mexican/TexMex	❷④❷

	Beirut Express	*Lebanese*	②	④	⑤
	Maroush Gardens	"	③	④	④
	Pearl Liang	*Chinese*	②	②	②
	Royal China	"	②	④	④
	Bombay Bicycle Club	*Indian*	④	④	④
	Noor Jahan	"	②	②	③
	Satay House	*Malaysian*	②	②	④
	The Walmer Castle	*Thai*	③	④	②
£30+	Lucky Seven	*American*	②	③	❶
	Cochonnet	*Mediterranean*	③	②	②
	Galicia	*Spanish*	④	④	②
	El Pirata de Tapas	"	③	③	③
	Tootsies	*Burgers, etc*	④	④	④
	Santo	*Mexican/TexMex*	③	④	④
	Taqueria	"	③	③	③
	Al-Waha	*Lebanese*	②	❶	③
	Ranoush	"	③	④	④
	Mandarin Kitchen	*Chinese*	❶	④	⑤
	Feng Sushi	*Japanese*	④	④	④
	Inaho	"	❶	⑤	④
	Uli	*Pan-Asian*	②	❶	③
	Tawana	*Thai*	③	②	④
£25+	Café Laville	*International*	④	③	②
	Firezza	*Pizza*	②	③	④
	Gail's Bread	*Sandwiches, cakes, etc*	②	③	③
	Tom's Deli	"	④	④	②
	Mandalay	*Burmese*	②	❶	⑤
	The Four Seasons	*Chinese*	②	⑤	⑤
	Magic Wok	"	②	③	④
	ping pong	*Chinese, Dim sum*	④	④	③
	Masala Zone	*Indian*	④	③	③
	Kiasu	*Indonesian*	③	④	⑤
	C&R Cafe	*Thai*	②	③	④
£20+	S & M Café	*British, Traditional*	⑤	④	④
	Gourmet Burger Kitchen	*Burgers, etc*	③	④	④
	Alounak	*Persian*	③	④	④
	New Culture Rev'n	*Chinese*	④	④	④
	Cha Cha Moon	*Chinese, Dim sum*	④	③	③
	Khan's	*Indian*	②	③	③
	Number One Café	*Thai*	❶	④	④
	Yelo Thai Canteen	"	③	③	④
£15+	Fresco	*Lebanese*	②	❶	③
£10+	Comptoir Libanais	*Lebanese*	③	③	③
£5+	Lisboa Pâtisserie	*Sandwiches, cakes, etc*	②	④	③

Hammersmith, Shepherd's Bush, Olympia, Chiswick, Brentford & Ealing (W4, W5, W6, W12, W13, W14, TW8)

£60+	The River Café	*Italian*	②	②	③
£50+	La Trompette	*French*	❶	❶	②

			Rating
	Le Vacherin	"	❸❸❸
£40+	The Anglesea Arms	British, Modern	❷❸❷
	The Carpenter's Arms	"	❸❸❸
	High Road Brasserie	"	④④❸
	Pissarro's	"	④④❶
	Sam's Brasserie	"	④❸❸
	Fish Hook	Fish & seafood	❷❸④
	Charlotte's Place	French	❸❷❸
	Chez Kristof	"	④④④
	Annie's	International	④❸❶
	Bianco Nero	Italian	❷❸❸
	Cibo	"	④❷④
	The Meat & Wine Co	Steaks & grills	⑤④④
	Popeseye	"	❷❸④
£35+	Devonshire House	British, Modern	⑤⑤⑤
	Duke Of Sussex	"	❸❸❸
	Ealing Park Tavern	"	❸❸❸
	The Havelock Tavern	"	❷⑤❸
	Hole in the Wall	"	❸❸❸
	The Roebuck	"	❸❷❸
	Seasons Dining Room	"	❸❷⑤
	Princess Victoria	British, Traditional	❸❸❷
	Balans	International	⑤❸④
	The Thatched House	"	④④④
	Canta Napoli	Italian	❸❸④
	Frankie's Italian Bar & Grill	"	⑤⑤⑤
	Cumberland Arms	Mediterranean	❸❷❸
	The Swan	"	❸❸❷
	Knaypa	Polish	④❷④
	The Gate	Vegetarian	❷❷④
	Chakalaka	South African	❸❸④
	Brilliant	Indian	❷❷④
	Indian Zing	"	❶❶❸
	Madhu's	"	❶❶❸
	Sushi-Hiro	Japanese	❶❸⑤
£30+	Giraffe	International	④❸❸
	Ooze	"	④④❸
	Del'Aziz	Mediterranean	④④❷
	Patio	Polish	④❷❶
	Blah! Blah! Blah!	Vegetarian	❸❸④
	Tootsies	Burgers, etc	④④④
	Fire & Stone	Pizza	❸④❷
	Lola & Simón	Argentinian	❸❸❸
	North China	Chinese	❷❶❸
	Green Chilli	Indian	❸❷④
	Tosa	Japanese	❸④④
	Saigon Saigon	Vietnamese	❸❷❸
£25+	Queen's Head	British, Modern	④④❸
	Port of Manila	Fusion	— — —
	The Real Greek	Greek	⑤⑤④
	Priory House	Mediterranean	❸❸❷
	La Tasca	Spanish	⑤⑤④
	Byron	Burgers, etc	❸❸❸
	Ground	"	❷❸④

	Firezza	Pizza	②	③	④
	Benugo	Sandwiches, cakes, etc	④	④	②
	Wahaca	Mexican/TexMex	❸	②	②
	Adams Café	Moroccan	❸	❶	❸
	Chez Marcelle	Lebanese	❶	④	④
	Mohsen	Persian	❸	❸	⑤
	Anarkali	Indian	②	②	④
	Karma	"	❸	②	④
	Mirch Masala	"	❶	④	⑤
	Monty's	"	❸	❸	④
	Shilpa	Indian, Southern	❶	②	⑤
	Hare & Tortoise	Pan-Asian	❸	④	④
	Esarn Kheaw	Thai	❶	❸	④
	Fat Boy's	"	④	❸	❸
	Latymers	"	②	④	⑤
	Pho	Vietnamese	④	❸	④
£20+	Gourmet Burger Kitchen	Burgers, etc	❸	④	④
	Alounak	Persian	❸	④	④
	Sufi	"	②	❶	❸
	Abu Zaad	Syrian	②	②	❸
	Best Mangal	Turkish	❸	②	❸
	Sagar	Indian	②	②	④
	Okawari	Japanese	❸	②	❸
	Bedlington Café	Thai	❸	②	④
£15+	Square Pie Company	British, Traditional	②	②	❸
	Hammersmith Café	Thai	④	④	⑤
	Old Parr's Head	"	❸	❸	❸
£10+	Crussh	Sandwiches, cakes, etc	❸	❸	④
	Comptoir Libanais	Lebanese	❸	❸	❸

NORTH

Hampstead, West Hampstead, St John's Wood, Regent's Park, Kilburn & Camden Town (NW postcodes)

£70+	Landmark (Winter Gdn)	*British, Modern*	④④❷
£60+	York & Albany	*Italian*	❸④❸
£50+	Odette's	*British, Modern*	❸④④
	L'Aventure	*French*	❷❷❶
	Oslo Court	*"*	❷❶❷
	Gaucho	*Steaks & grills*	❸❸❸
	Good Earth	*Chinese*	❸❸④
	Kaifeng	*"*	❸❸④
	Benihana	*Japanese*	④④④
	Gilgamesh	*Pan-Asian*	④❺❷
£40+	Bradley's	*British, Modern*	④④④
	The Engineer	*"*	❸④❷
	Market	*"*	❷❸❸
	St Pancras Grand	*"*	④④❷
	The Wells	*"*	❸❸❷
	The Wet Fish Cafe	*"*	❸❸❷
	Bull & Last	*British, Traditional*	❶❷❷
	Coast	*Fish & seafood*	– – –
	La Cage Imaginaire	*French*	④❸❷
	twotwentytwo	*International*	④④❺
	Artigiano	*Italian*	❸❷④
	Salt House	*"*	❸❷❷
	The Salusbury	*"*	❸④❸
	Sardo Canale	*"*	④❺❸
	Villa Bianca	*"*	④④④
	Vineria	*"*	– – –
	Camden Brasserie	*Mediterranean*	④❸④
	Black & Blue	*Steaks & grills*	❸④④
	Rôtisserie	*"*	④❸④
	Manna	*Vegetarian*	④④④
	Met Su Yan	*Chinese*	④❸❸
	Atma	*Indian*	❷❷④
	Sushi-Say	*Japanese*	❶❶④
	XO	*Pan-Asian*	❸❸❸
£35+	Belgo Noord	*Belgian*	④④④
	Café Med	*British, Modern*	④④④
	Freemasons Arms	*"*	④④❸
	The Horseshoe	*"*	❸④❸
	The Junction Tavern	*"*	❸❷❷
	The Lansdowne	*"*	❸④❸
	The Lord Palmerston	*"*	❺④④
	The North London Tavern	*"*	❸❸❸
	Walnut	*"*	❸❸④
	Holly Bush	*British, Traditional*	④④❶
	L'Absinthe	*French*	❸❷❷
	Somerstown Coffee House	*"*	❸❸④
	Lemonia	*Greek*	④❷❶
	Retsina	*"*	❸④④

The Arches	*International*	④③②
La Collina	*Italian*	③③④
Fratelli la Bufala	*"*	④④④
Osteria Emilia	*"*	③③④
Sarracino	*"*	②③④
Queen's Head & Artichoke	*Mediterranean*	④③③
Don Pepe	*Spanish*	③②③
Seashell	*Fish & chips*	②③⑤
Baker & Spice	*Sandwiches, cakes, etc*	③⑤④
Richoux	*"*	⑤⑤④
Mestizo	*Mexican/TexMex*	③④④
Cottons	*Afro-Caribbean*	④③③
Mango Room	*"*	③②②
Solly's	*Israeli*	④⑤⑤
Goldfish	*Chinese*	②②③
Phoenix Palace	*"*	②④④
Bombay Bicycle Club	*Indian*	④④④
Eriki	*"*	⓿⓿③
Jin Kichi	*Japanese*	⓿②⑤
Singapore Garden	*Malaysian*	②②③

£30+	The Old Bull & Bush	*British, Modern*	④③②
	Daphne	*Greek*	③⓿②
	Giraffe	*International*	④③③
	L'Artista	*Italian*	④④③
	La Brocca	*"*	③③②
	Caponata	*"*	③②③
	Del'Aziz	*Mediterranean*	④④②
	William IV	*"*	③②②
	El Parador	*Spanish*	②②②
	The Diner	*Burgers, etc*	④⑤③
	Fine Burger Company	*"*	④④④
	Harry Morgan's	*"*	④④④
	Tootsies	*"*	④④④
	Nautilus	*Fish & chips*	⓿②⑤
	Beyoglu	*Turkish*	③③④
	Sofra	*"*	④④④
	Alisan	*Chinese*	②②④
	Gung-Ho	*"*	③⓿②
	Snazz Sichuan	*"*	③③④
	Weng Wah House	*"*	④④④
	Woodlands	*Indian*	③③④
	Abeno	*Japanese*	③②③
	Bento Cafe	*"*	②③③
	Café Japan	*"*	⓿⓿③
	Feng Sushi	*"*	④④④
	Yuzu	*"*	②⑤⑤

£25+	The Swan & Edgar	*British, Traditional*	– – –
	The Czech Restaurant	*Czech*	③④④
	Marine Ices	*Italian*	④②②
	La Porchetta Pizzeria	*"*	③③③
	The Little Bay	*Mediterranean*	④②②
	Stingray Café	*"*	②④③
	Trojka	*Russian*	④⑤③
	Haché	*Steaks & grills*	②③②
	Basilico	*Pizza*	③③⑤
	Benugo	*Sandwiches, cakes, etc*	④④②

			Ratings
	Gail's Bread	"	② ③ ③
	Paul	"	③ ④ ④
	Shish	Turkish	④ ④ ③
	ping pong	Chinese, Dim sum	④ ④ ③
	Chutneys	Indian	③ ③ ④
	Great Nepalese	"	③ ③ ⑤
	Kovalam	"	③ ② ④
	Masala Zone	"	④ ③ ③
	Vijay	"	② ② ④
	Zeen	"	④ ④ ④
	Asakusa	Japanese	② ④ ④
	Wagamama	"	④ ③ ④
	The Banana Tree Canteen	Pan-Asian	③ ③ ③
	dim T	"	④ ④ ③
£20+	Spaniard's Inn	International	④ ③ ②
	Gourmet Burger Kitchen	Burgers, etc	③ ④ ④
	Chamomile	Sandwiches, cakes, etc	③ ② ③
	Kenwood (Brew House)	"	④ ④ ②
	Diwana B-P House	Indian	③ ⑤ ⑤
	Five Hot Chillies	"	② ② ⑤
£15+	Ali Baba	Egyptian	③ ④ ④
	Geeta	Indian	② ② ⑤
	Sakonis	"	③ ④ ⑤
	Atari-Ya	Japanese	❶ ③ ④
£10+	Chop'd	Salads	② ③ ④

Hoxton, Islington, Highgate, Crouch End, Stoke Newington, Finsbury Park, Muswell Hill & Finchley (N postcodes)

			Ratings
£80+	Fifteen Restaurant	Italian	④ ④ ④
£60+	Morgan M	French	❶ ② ③
£50+	Frederick's	British, Modern	④ ③ ②
	Sargasso Sea	Fish & seafood	② ② ②
£40+	The Barnsbury	British, Modern	③ ③ ③
	The Bull	"	④ ④ ④
	The Clissold Arms	"	④ ③ ③
	Cruse 9	"	③ ④ ④
	The Duke of Cambridge	"	④ ④ ③
	The Haven	"	③ ③ ③
	The House	"	④ ④ ③
	Mosaica	"	② ② ②
	Rotunda Bar & Restaurant	"	④ ③ ②
	The Three Crowns	"	④ ④ ④
	Water House	"	④ ④ ②
	The Marquess Tavern	British, Traditional	③ ④ ③
	St Johns	"	③ ② ❶
	The Almeida	French	④ ④ ④
	Bistro Aix	"	③ ③ ②
	Fig	"	② ❶ ②
	Fifteen Trattoria	Italian	④ ④ ③
	Metrogusto	"	④ ③ ③

285

	Ottolenghi	"	❶❸④
	Camino	Spanish	④④❷
	Rôtisserie	Steaks & grills	④❸④
	Rodizio Rico	Brazilian	④⑤④
£35+	The Albion	British, Modern	④❸❷
	Bald Faced Stag	"	❸❸❷
	The Elk in the Woods	"	④❸❸
	The Fellow	"	❸④❸
	Hoxton Apprentice	"	④❸❸
	The Lock Dining Bar	"	❷❷❷
	The Rose & Crown	"	④④④
	Chez Liline	Fish & seafood	❶❷⑤
	Les Associés	French	❸❶❷
	Banners	International	④④❸
	Browns	"	④④④
	Orange Tree	"	④⑤④
	Cantina Italia	Italian	❸❸❸
	San Daniele	"	❸❸❸
	Garufa	Steaks & grills	❸④❸
	Sabor	South American	④❸❸
	Emni	Indian	❸❸④
	Zaffrani	"	❸❷❸
	Isarn	Thai	❷❶❸
£30+	Charles Lamb	British, Modern	❸❸❷
	Villiers Terrace	"	❷❷❸
	The Drapers Arms	British, Traditional	④❸❷
	The Flask	"	❸④❶
	La Petite Auberge	French	④④❷
	Le Sacré-Coeur	"	④❸❸
	Vrisaki	Greek	❸❸❸
	The Fox Reformed	International	⑤④❸
	Giraffe	"	④❸❸
	500	Italian	❷❷④
	Pizzeria Oregano	"	❸❷❸
	Fine Burger Company	Burgers, etc	④④④
	Toff's	Fish & chips	❷❷❸
	Two Brothers	"	❷❷④
	Il Bacio	Pizza	❸❷❷
	Furnace	"	❸❸❸
	Indian Rasoi	Indian	❷❸❸
	Rasa Travancore	Indian, Southern	❷❷❸
	Thai Square	Thai	④④❸
	Yum Yum	"	❸❸❷
£25+	Olympus Fish	Fish & seafood	❸❷⑤
	Le Mercury	French	④❸❶
	The Real Greek	Greek	⑤⑤④
	La Porchetta Pizzeria	Italian	❸❸❸
	Mem & Laz	Mediterranean	④④❸
	Stringray Café	"	❷④❸
	The Islington Tapas Bar	Spanish	⑤⑤④
	Basilico	Pizza	❸❸⑤
	Firezza	"	❷❸④
	Gallipoli	Turkish	❸❸❷
	Izgara	"	❸❸④
	Petek	"	❸❸④

	Masala Zone	Indian	④❸❸
	Rani	"	❷❷④
	Rooburoo	"	❸❸❸
	Rasa	Indian, Southern	❶❶❸
	Wagamama	Japanese	④❸④
	dim T	Pan-Asian	④④❸
	Viet Garden	Vietnamese	❸❸④
£20+	S & M Café	British, Traditional	⑤④④
	La Bota	Spanish	❸❸❷
	Hamburger Union	Burgers, etc	④④④
	Gem	Turkish	❸❷❸
	New Culture Rev'n	Chinese	④④④
	Anglo Asian Tandoori	Indian	❸❶❷
	Dotori	Korean	❸❷④
	Yelo	Thai	❸❸④
	Huong-Viet	Vietnamese	❷⑤④
	Khoai	"	❸❸⑤
£15+	Afghan Kitchen	Afghani	❸④④
£10+	Chilango	Mexican/TexMex	❸❸④

SOUTH

South Bank (SE1)

Price	Name	Cuisine	Ratings
£70+	Oxo Tower (Rest')	British, Modern	⑤⑤④
£60+	Le Pont de la Tour	British, Modern	⑤④❷
	Oxo Tower (Brass')	Mediterranean	⑤⑤❸
£50+	Cantina Vinopolis	British, Modern	④④④
	Skylon	"	④④❷
	Roast	British, Traditional	④④❸
	Gaucho	Steaks & grills	❸❸❸
£40+	Blueprint Café	British, Modern	④④❷
	Garrison	"	❸❸❶
	Mezzanine	"	⑤④④
	RSJ	"	❸❷⑤
	The Swan At The Globe	"	④❸❷
	tamesa@oxo	"	⑤⑤④
	Butlers W'f Chop-house	British, Traditional	⑤④④
	fish!	Fish & seafood	④④④
	Livebait	"	④⑤⑤
	Wright Brothers	"	❶❷❷
	Chez Gérard	French	⑤⑤④
	Magdalen	"	❷❷❸
	Waterloo Brasserie	"	⑤⑤④
	Champor-Champor	Fusion	❷❷❶
	Village East	"	❸④❸
	Tate Modern (Level 7)	International	④④❶
	Vivat Bacchus	"	④❷❸
	Cantina del Ponte	Italian	⑤⑤④
	Tentazioni	"	❷❶❸
	Bermondsey Kitchen	Mediterranean	④④④
	Baltic	Polish	❸④❷
	Black & Blue	Steaks & grills	❸④④
£35+	Arch One	British, Modern	– – –
	Menier Chocolate Factory	"	⑤④❸
	The Anchor & Hope	British, Traditional	❶❸❸
	Canteen	"	④④④
	Applebee's Cafe	International	❷❸④
	Browns	"	④④④
	Tate Modern (Level 2)	"	④④④
	More	"	– – –
	La Lanterna	Italian	❸❷❸
	Tapas Brindisa	Spanish	❷❸❸
	Archduke Wine Bar	Steaks & grills	– – –
	Bengal Clipper	Indian	❷④④
£30+	The Refinery	British, Modern	④❸④
	The Table	"	❷❷❷
	Giraffe	International	④❸❸
	The Wine Theatre	Italian	④❸⑤
	Del'Aziz	Mediterranean	④④❷
	Meson don Felipe	Spanish	④④❷
	Paradiso Olivelli	Pizza	④④④
	Tas	Turkish	④❸❸

			Ratings
	Bangalore Express	Indian	③②②
	Feng Sushi	Japanese	④④④
£25+	Benugo	British, Modern	④④②
	Real Greek	Greek	⑤⑤④
	Gourmet Pizza Co.	Pizza	④④②
	Amano	Sandwiches, cakes, etc	③⑤③
	Ev Restaurant, Bar & Deli	Turkish	④④②
	Tas Pide	"	③④③
	ping pong	Chinese, Dim sum	④④③
	Mango Tree	Indian	②④④
	Inshoku	Japanese	③④⑤
	Wagamama	"	④③④
	dim T	Pan-Asian	④④③
£20+	Masters Super Fish	Fish & chips	②②④
	Leon	Sandwiches, cakes, etc	③③③
£15+	El Vergel	South American	①②②
£10+	Caffé Vergnano	Sandwiches, cakes, etc	③④③
	Fuzzy's Grub	"	②②④
	Monmouth Coffee Co	"	①②②

Greenwich, Lewisham & Blackheath
(All SE postcodes, except SE1)

			Ratings
£50+	Gaucho	steaks & grills	③③③
	Lobster Pot	Fish & seafood	②②②
	The Spread Eagle	French	③④④
	Beauberry House	Fusion	④③④
£40+	Inside	British, Modern	②②④
	The Palmerston	"	②③③
	Rivington	"	③④③
	The Trafalgar Tavern	British, Traditional	⑤⑤③
	Buenos Aires	Steaks & grills	③②②
£35+	Chapters	British, Modern	③②③
	The Dartmouth Arms	"	③②③
	Franklins	"	③④③
	The Rosendale	"	④③④
	Le Chardon	French	④④④
	Joanna's	International	③②②
	Olley's	Fish & chips	②③④
	Babur	Indian	①②②
£30+	The Rye	International	③③②
	The Yellow House	"	②②③
	Le Querce	Italian	②②③
	Barcelona Tapas	Spanish	④④⑤
	Zero Degrees	Pizza	③④③
	Dragon Castle	Chinese	①②②
	Peninsular	"	③④⑤
	Everest Inn	Indian	③③③
	Mela	"	③③③
	Tandoori Nights	"	②②②

£25+	Green & Blue	International	④❸❸
	The Sea Cow	Fish & chips	❸④⑤
	Castello	Pizza	❸④❸
	The Gowlett	"	❷❷❷
	Ganapati	Indian	❷❷❷
	Kennington Tandoori	"	❸❷❸
	Mogul	"	❸❸④
	Thai Corner Café	Thai	❸❷❸
	Thailand	"	④❸④
£20+	S & M Café	British, Traditional	⑤④④

Battersea, Brixton, Clapham, Wandsworth
Barnes, Putney & Wimbledon
(All SW postcodes south of the river)

£50+	Chez Bruce	British, Modern	❶❶❷
	Trinity	"	❷❷❸
	Enoteca Turi	Italian	❷❷❸
	Riva	"	❷❶④
	San Lorenzo Fuoriporta	"	④④④
£40+	The Brown Dog	British, Modern	❸❸❷
	Buchan's	"	❸❷❸
	The Depot	"	④④❷
	The Establishment	"	❸❸❸
	The Fire Stables	"	④④❸
	Four O Nine	"	❷❸❷
	Lamberts	"	❶❶❷
	The Mason's Arms	"	❸❷❸
	Phoenix	"	❸④❸
	Ransome's Dock	"	④❸❸
	Sonny's	"	④❸❸
	Tom Ilic	"	❶❸④
	The Victoria	"	❸❷❷
	Le Bouchon Bordelais	French	④④④
	Le Cassoulet	"	❸❸④
	Upstairs Bar	"	❷❶❶
	Annie's	International	④❸❶
	The Light House	"	❸④④
	Numero Uno	Italian	❷❶❶
	San Remo	"	④❷❸
	The Three Bridges	"	❸❶④
	Butcher & Grill	Steaks & grills	④④④
	Popeseye	"	❷❸④
	La Pampa Grill	Argentinian	❸④④
	Nancy Lam's Enak Enak	Indonesian	❸❸❸
	Tsunami	Japanese	❸④❸
£35+	Bodean's	American	④④④
	Belgo	Belgian	④④④
	Alma	British, Modern	④④❸
	The Bridge	"	④④❸
	The Cadogan Arms	"	❸❷❸
	Earl Spencer	"	❸❸❷
	The East Hill	"	❸❸❷
	Emile's	"	❷❶❸

Harrison's	"	④	④	④
The Prince Of Wales	"	❸	❸	❸
The Roundhouse	"	❸	❸	❸
Sands End	"	❷	❷	❷
Scoffers	"	❸	❷	❷
The Spencer Arms	"	❸	④	❸
Tree House	"	④	④	❸
The Avalon	British, Traditional	④	④	❷
The Bolingbroke	"	❸	❸	❸
Bellevue Rendez-Vous	French	❸	④	❸
Brasserie James	"	❸	❷	❸
Le Chardon	"	④	④	❸
Côte	"	④	❸	④
Gastro	"	④	⑤	❷
Gazette	"	④	❸	❸
Le Provence	"	–	–	–
Brinkley's Kitchen	International	④	④	❸
The Ship	"	❸	❸	❸
The Stonhouse	"	④	④	❸
Donna Margherita	Italian	❷	❷	❸
Frankie's Italian Bar & Grill	"	⑤	⑤	⑤
Isola del Sole	"	❸	❶	❷
Piccolino	"	④	④	④
Pizza Metro	"	❷	❸	④
The Fox & Hounds	Mediterranean	❷	❷	❷
La Mancha	Spanish	④	④	④
Santa Maria del Sur	Argentinian	❷	❷	❷
Chakalaka	South African	❸	❸	④
China Boulevard	Chinese	❸	④	④
Royal China	"	❷	④	④
Bombay Bicycle Club	Indian	④	④	④
Cho-San	Japanese	❷	❶	❸
Suk Saran	Thai	❸	④	④
Thai on the River	"	❸	❸	❸

£30+	The Abbeville	British, Modern	④	④	❷
	The Clarence	"	❸	❷	❸
	The Duke's Head	"	④	❷	❶
	The Fentiman Arms	"	④	❸	❷
	The Lighthouse	"	❷	❷	❷
	Fish Club	Fish & seafood	❷	❷	④
	Giraffe	International	④	❸	❸
	Hudson's	"	⑤	④	❷
	Antipasto & Pasta	Italian	❸	❷	❸
	Buona Sera	"	④	❸	❷
	Rick's Café	"	❷	❷	❷
	Putney Station	Mediterranean	❸	❷	❷
	Rebato's	Spanish	❸	❶	❶
	La Rueda	"	④	④	❸
	Dexter's Grill	Burgers, etc	④	④	❸
	Tootsies	"	④	④	④
	Fish Club	Fish & chips	❸	❷	❸
	Al Forno	Pizza	④	❷	❷
	Bayee Village	Chinese	❸	❷	❸
	Dalchini	"	❸	❷	❸
	Ma Goa	Indian	❷	❶	❷
	Thai Square	Thai	④	④	❸

£25+	Real Greek	Greek	⑤⑤④
	Esca	Italian	❸❸❸
	Pappa Ciccia	"	❷❷❷
	Fish in a Tie	Mediterranean	④❷❷
	The Little Bay	"	④❷❷
	Bar Estrela	Portuguese	④❷❷
	Lola Rojo	Spanish	❷❷❸
	El Rincón Latino	"	❸❶❶
	Brady's	Fish & chips	❸❷❸
	Basilico	Pizza	❸❸⑤
	Eco	"	❸④❸
	Firezza	"	❷❸④
	Dish Dash	Persian	④④❸
	Chutney	Indian	❷❶❸
	Indian Ocean	"	❷❶❸
	Kastoori	"	❶❷④
	Mango & Silk	"	❸❷❸
	Mirch Masala SW16	"	❶④⑤
	Nazmins	"	❷❸④
	Wagamama	Japanese	④④④
	The Banana Leaf Canteen	Pan-Asian	❸❸❸
	Hare & Tortoise	"	❸④④
	Amaranth	Thai	❸❸❸
	Ekachai	"	❸④④
	Fat Boy's	"	④❸❸
	Talad Thai	"	❸❷⑤
	Thai Garden	"	❸❸④
£20+	Gourmet Burger Kitchen	Burgers, etc	❸④④
	Boiled Egg & Soldiers	Sandwiches, cakes, etc	④④④
	Holy Cow	Indian	❷❸❸
	Hot Stuff	"	❶❶❷
	Sree Krishna	"	❷❸❸
	Vijaya Krishna	Indian, Southern	❷❷❸
	Fujiyama	Japanese	❸❸❸
	The Pepper Tree	Thai	❸❷❷
	The Paddyfield	Vietnamese	❸❸⑤
£15+	Trinity Stores	Italian	❷❷❷
	Slurp	Japanese	❸④④
£10+	Franco Manca	Pizza	❶❸❸

Outer western suburbs
Kew, Richmond, Twickenham, Teddington

£50+	The Glasshouse	British, Modern	❶❶❸
	Petersham Hotel	"	❸❸❷
	Petersham Nurseries	"	❷④❶
	A Taste Of McClements	French	❷❷④
	Bingham	International	❸❸❷
	Gaucho	Steaks & grills	❸❸❸
£40+	Rock & Rose	British, Modern	⑤⑤❷
	The Wharf	"	④④❷
	Brula	French	❷❶❶
	A Cena	Italian	❷❷❷

	Kew Grill	*Steaks & grills*	④④❸
	Matsuba	*Japanese*	❸④④
£35+	The Inn at Kew Gardens	*British, Modern*	④❷④
	Loch Fyne	*Fish & seafood*	④④④
	La Buvette	*French*	❸❷❸
	Chez Lindsay	*"*	❸❷❸
	Côte	*"*	④❸④
	Ma Cuisine	*"*	④❸④
	Scarpetta	*Italian*	❸❷❷
	Four Regions	*Chinese*	❸❷④
	Origin Asia	*Indian*	❷❷④
£30+	don Fernando's	*Spanish*	❸❷❸
	Tangawizi	*Indian*	❷❸❸
£25+	O'Zon	*Chinese*	❸❶④
	Fat Boy's	*Thai*	④❸❸
£20+	Brouge	*Belgian*	④❷❸
	Stein's	*German*	④④❸
	Sagar	*Indian*	❷❷④

EAST

Smithfield & Farringdon (EC1)

Price	Restaurant	Cuisine	Ratings
£60+	Club Gascon	French	❷❷❸
£50+	Smiths (Top Floor)	British, Modern	❹❹❸
	St John	British, Traditional	❶❷❸
	Dans le Noir	French	❺❸❷
	The Clerkenwell Dining Rm	Mediterranean	❸❸❸
	Portal	"	❸❸❷
	Gaucho	Steaks & grills	❸❸❸
£40+	The Hat & Feathers	British, Modern	❹❹❹
	The Larder	"	❹❹❹
	Malmaison Brasserie	"	❸❷❸
	Medcalf	"	❸❸❸
	The Modern Pantry	"	❸❸❸
	The Peasant	"	❸❹❷
	Smithfield Bar & Grill	"	❸❹❸
	The Well	"	❸❹❹
	Hix	British, Traditional	❸❹❹
	Fish Shop	Fish & seafood	❸❹❹
	Bleeding Heart	French	❷❷❷
	Café du Marché	"	❷❷❶
	Comptoir Gascon	"	❷❸❷
	Eastside Inn	"	❹❷❹
	Le Rendezvous du Café	"	❸❷❸
	St Germain	"	❹❸❹
	Le Saint Julien	"	❹❹❹
	Alba	Italian	❸❷❹
	Flâneur	Mediterranean	❹❸❹
	The Zetter	"	❸❹❸
	Moro	Spanish	❶❷❷
	Saki Bar & Food Emporium	Japanese	❷❸❺
£35+	Ambassador	British, Modern	❸❷❸
	Coach & Horses	"	❸❸❹
	Vinoteca	"	❸❶❷
	The Fox and Anchor	British, Traditional	❸❷❶
	The Quality Chop House	"	❷❷❸
	Cellar Gascon	French	❸❸❸
	$	International	❹❸❷
	Fabrizio	Italian	❷❷❹
	Potemkin	Russian	❸❹❹
	Smiths (Dining Rm)	Steaks & grills	❹❹❹
	Carnevale	Vegetarian	❸❷❹
	Cottons	Afro-Caribbean	❹❸❸
	54 Farringdon Road	Malaysian	❷❷❹
	Cicada	Pan-Asian	❸❷❸
£30+	Pinchito	Spanish	❹❸❷
	Sofra	Turkish	❹❹❹
	Tas	"	❹❸❸
	Tajima Tei	Japanese	❷❷❹
	Cây Tre	Vietnamese	❸❹❺
£25+	Cock Tavern	British, Traditional	❸❹❹

			Ratings
	Kipferl	East & Cent. European	③②③
	Fish Central	Fish & seafood	③②③
	The Real Greek	Greek	⑤⑤④
	La Porchetta Pizzeria	Italian	③③③
	The Eagle	Mediterranean	③④②
	The Little Bay	"	④②②
	Benugo	Sandwiches, cakes, etc	④④②
	Shish	Turkish	④④③
	Pham Sushi	Japanese	❶②④
	Banana Tree Canteen	Pan-Asian	③③③
	Pho	Vietnamese	④③④
£20+	Smiths (Ground Floor)	British, Modern	④④②
	S & M Café	British, Traditional	⑤④④
	Kolossi Grill	Greek	④③③
£10+	Spianata & Co	Sandwiches, cakes, etc	②②③
£5+	Nusa Kitchen	Sandwiches, cakes, etc	②④⑤

The City (EC2, EC3, EC4)

			Ratings
£70+	1 Lombard Street	British, Modern	③③④
	Prism	"	⑤④⑤
	Rhodes 24	"	④③②
	Bel Canto	French	④④②
£60+	Vertigo 42	British, Modern	④④②
	Green's	British, Traditional	③②③
	Catch	Fish & seafood	④④④
	Bevis Marks	Kosher	③③③
	Mint Leaf	Indian	④④④
£50+	Missouri Angel	American	④④⑤
	High Timber	British, Modern	③②③
	Searcy's Brasserie	"	④③③
	Paternoster Chop House	British, Traditional	④④④
	Chamberlain's	Fish & seafood	③④④
	Coq d'Argent	French	④③③
	1901	"	③②②
	Sauterelle	"	④③③
	L'Anima	Italian	②②②
	Caravaggio	"	④④④
	Refettorio	"	③③④
	Bonds	Mediterranean	③③③
	Boisdale of Bishopsgate	Scottish	③④③
	Eyre Brothers	Spanish	③②③
	Gaucho	Steaks & grills	③③③
	Kenza	Lebanese	④④②
	Cinnamon Kitchen	Indian	❶②③
	Soseki	Japanese	③③②
£40+	The Hoxton Grille	American	– – –
	The Chancery	British, Modern	②②④
	Devonshire Terrace	"	③③③
	The Don	"	②②②
	The Mercer	"	③③③

			Ratings
	Northbank	"	④④❸
	The Princess	"	❸④❸
	Rivington	"	❸④❸
	The White Swan	"	❸❸❸
	Gow's	Fish & seafood	❸❸④
	Sweetings	"	❸❸❷
	Chez Gérard	French	⑤⑤④
	Luc's Brasserie	"	④④④
	Lutyens	"	❸❷❸
	The Royal Exchange	"	④⑤❷
	The Bathhouse	International	– – –
	The East Room	"	❸❷❶
	Vivat Bacchus	"	④❷❸
	Bertorelli	Italian	⑤⑤⑤
	Lena	"	④④④
	Manicomio	"	④④④
	Taberna Etrusca	"	④④④
	Terranostra	"	❸❷⑤
	Rocket	Mediterranean	④❸❷
	Vanilla Black	Vegetarian	❸❷❸
	Imperial City	Chinese	❸❷❷
	City Miyama	Japanese	❷④⑤
	Mugen	"	❸❷④
	Tokyo City	"	❸④④
	D Sum 2	Pan-Asian	④⑤⑤
	Gt Eastern Dining Room	"	❸❸❷
	Pacific Oriental	"	④④④
	Hokkien Chan	Thai	❸❸④
£35+	Bodean's	American	④④④
	The Fox	British, Modern	❸④❸
	George & Vulture	British, Traditional	⑤④❷
	Relais de Venise L'Entrecôte	French	❸④❸
	Browns	International	④④④
	Osteria Appennino	Italian	❷❸④
	Piccolino	"	④④④
	Saf	Vegetarian	④④❸
	Kazan	Turkish	❷❸❸
	Noto Kikuya	Japanese, Teppan-yaki	– – –
£30+	Ye Olde Cheshire Cheese	British, Traditional	④❸❶
	The Restaurant At St Paul's	"	❸❷❸
	Barcelona Tapas	Spanish	④④⑤
	The Diner	Burgers, etc	④⑤❸
	Haz	Turkish	❸❸❸
	Rajasthan II	Indian	❸❷④
	K10	Japanese	❸④④
	Kurumaya	"	❶❷❷
	Thai Square	Thai	④④❸
£25+	Hilliard	British, Modern	❶❷❸
	The Punch Tavern	"	❸④❸
	Simpson's Tavern	British, Traditional	④❷❶
	La Tasca	Spanish	⑤⑤④
	Paul	Sandwiches, cakes, etc	❸④④
	ping pong	Chinese, Dim sum	④④❸
	Wagamama	Japanese	④❸④
	Ekachai	Thai	❸④④

£20+	S & M Café	British, Traditional	⑤④④
	The Wine Library	"	④❷❶
	Gourmet Burger Kitchen	Burgers, etc	❸④④
	Konditor & Cook	Sandwiches, cakes, etc	❷❸④
	Leon		❸❸❸
	Chi Noodle & Wine Bar	Pan-Asian	❷❷❸

£15+	The Place Below	Vegetarian	❸④❸
	Napket	Afternoon tea	④④❷
	Vital Ingredient	Salads	❸❸④

£10+	Crussh	Sandwiches, cakes, etc	❸❸④
	Fuzzy's Grub	"	❷❷④
	Spianata & Co	"	❷❷❸
	Chop'd	Salads	❷❸④
	Chilango	Mexican/TexMex	❸❸④

| £5+ | Nusa Kitchen | Sandwiches, cakes, etc | ❷④⑤ |
| | Pod | " | ❸❸④ |

East End & Docklands (All E postcodes)

| £80+ | Roka | Japanese | ❷④❷ |

| £70+ | Les Trois Garçons | French | ④❸❶ |
| | Quadrato | Italian | ❸❷⑤ |

| £60+ | Plateau | French | ④④❸ |

£50+	Beach Blanket Babylon	British, Modern	⑤⑤❷
	The Boundary	"	❸❸❷
	MPW Steakhouse & Grill	British, Traditional	④④⑤
	Curve	Fish & seafood	④④⑤
	Gaucho	Steaks & grills	❸❸❸
	Hawksmoor	"	❸④④

£40+	The Empress of India	British, Modern	④❸❸
	The Gun	"	❸❸❷
	The Morgan Arms	"	❸④❸
	Wapping Food	"	❸④❶
	Whitechapel Gallery	"	❶❷❸
	The Narrow	British, Traditional	④④❸
	St John Bread & Wine	"	❶❸④
	Forman's	Fish & seafood	– – –
	Bistrotheque	French	❸❸❷
	Le Bouchon Breton	"	④❸④
	Rosemary Lane	"	❸❸④
	Amerigo Vespucci	Italian	④④④
	1 Blossom Street	"	❸④④
	El Faro	Spanish	❶❶❸
	Lower East	Steaks & grills	❸④④
	Buen Ayre	Argentinian	❷❷❸
	Café Spice Namaste	Indian	❷❷❸
	Dockmaster's House	"	❸❷❸

£35+	The Brickhouse	Modern European	④❸❷
	All Star Lanes	American	④⑤❸
	The Prince Arthur	British, Modern	❸❷❸

			Ratings
	Canteen	British, Traditional	④④④
	The Grapes	Fish & seafood	❸❸❷
	Applebee's	International	❷❸④
	Browns	"	④④④
	Il Bordello	Italian	❷❷❷
	La Figa	"	❷❷❸
	Jamie's Italian	"	– – –
	Ark Fish	Fish & chips	❷❷④
	Green & Red Bar & Cantina	Mexican/TexMex	❸④❷
	Lotus	Chinese	❸❸❷
	Royal China	"	❷④④
	Elephant Royale	Thai	❸❷❸
£30+	Giraffe	British, Modern	④❸❸
	LMNT	"	④❸❶
	Albion	British, Traditional	④❸❷
	Faulkner's	Fish & chips	❷❷❸
	Haz	Turkish	❸❸❸
	Yi-Ban	Chinese	❷❷❷
	Rosa's	Thai	❸❸❸
	Namo	Vietnamese	❸❸❸
£25+	Wahaca	Mexican	❸❷❷
	Real Greek	Greek	⑤⑤④
	Stringray Globe Café	Mediterranean	❷④❸
	Story Deli	Organic	❷⑤❷
	La Tasca	Spanish	⑤⑤④
	Gourmet Pizza Co.	Pizza	④④❷
	The Drunken Monkey	Chinese	❷❷❸
	Shanghai	"	❸❸❸
	ping pong	Chinese, Dim sum	④④❸
	The Gaylord	Indian	❸④④
	Memsaheb on Thames	"	❸❸❷
	Mirch Masala	"	❶④⑤
	Itsu	Japanese	❸❸④
	Wagamama	"	④❸④
	New Tayyabs	Pakistani	❶④❷
	Viet Grill	Vietnamese	❸❸❸
	Viet Hoa	"	❸④④
£20+	S & M Café	British, Traditional	⑤④④
	Leon	Sandwiches, cakes, etc	❸❸❸
	Mangal Ocakbasi	Turkish	❶❸④
	Clifton	Indian	❷❸❸
	Lahore Kebab House	Pakistani	❶④④
	Sông Quê	Vietnamese	❷④④
£15+	Square Pie Company	British, Traditional	❷❷❸
	Gourmet San	Chinese	❶④⑤
£10+	E Pellicci	Italian	④❶❶
	Crussh	Sandwiches, cakes, etc	❸❸④
	Spianata & Co	"	❷❷❸
	Chop'd	Salads	❷❸④
	Royal Wok	Chinese	❸❸⑤
£5+	Brick Lane Beigel Bake	Sandwiches, cakes, etc	❶④⑤

MAPS

MAP I – LONDON OVERVIEW

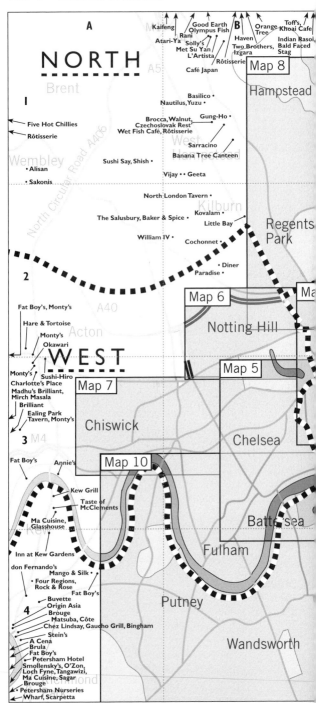

NORTH

Brent

A5

Map 8

Hampstead

Kaifeng
Atari-Ya
Rani
Good Earth
Olympus Fish
Solly's
Met Su Yan
L'Artista
Café Japan
Haven
Two Brothers,
Izgara
Rôtisserie
Orange
Tree
Toff's,
Khoai Cafe
Indian Rasoi,
Bald Faced
Stag

I

← **Five Hot Chillies**
← **Rôtisserie**

Wembley

North Circular Road A406

• **Alisan**
• **Sakonis**

Basilico •
Nautilus, Yuzu •

Brocca, Walnut,
Czechoslovak Rest
Wet Fish Café, Rôtisserie

Gung-Ho •

West
Hampstead

Sarracino •
Banana Tree Canteen •

Sushi Say, Shish •

Vijay • • Geeta

North London Tavern •

Kilburn

The Salusbury, Baker & Spice •

Kovalam •

Little Bay •

Regents
Park

William IV •

Cochonnet •

• Diner

Paradise •

2

A40

Acton

Map 6

Notting Hill

Ma

WEST

Map 5

Fat Boy's, Monty's
Hare & Tortoise
Monty's
Okawari
Monty's
Sushi-Hiro
Charlotte's Place
Madhu's Brilliant,
Mirch Masala
Brilliant
Ealing Park
Tavern, Monty's

Map 7

Chiswick

Chelsea

3

M4

Fat Boy's

Annie's

Map 10

Kew Grill

Taste of
McClements

Ma Cuisine,
Glasshouse

Battersea

Inn at Kew Gardens

don Fernando's
Mango & Silk
Four Regions,
Rock & Rose
Fat Boy's

Buvette
Origin Asia
Brouge
Matsuba, Côte
Chez Lindsay, Gaucho Grill, Bingham
Stein's
A Cena
Brula
Fat Boy's
Petersham Hotel
Smollensky's, O'Zon,
Loch Fyne, Tangawizi,
Ma Cuisine, Sagan
Brouge
Petersham Nurseries
Wharf, Scarpetta

Fulham

Putney

Wandsworth

4

MAP 1 – LONDON OVERVIEW

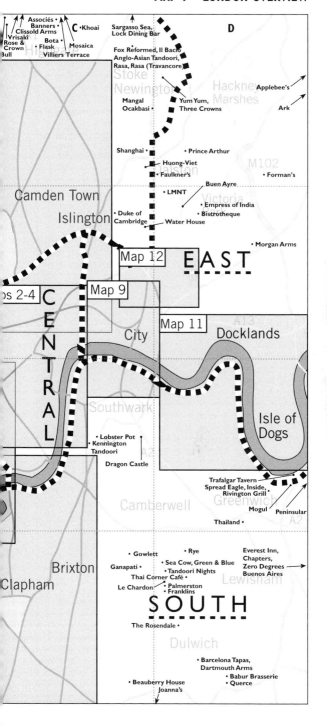

Associés •
Banners •
C •Khoai
Vrisaki
Clissold Arms
Rose &
Bota •
Crown
Flask •
Mosaica
Bull
Villiers Terrace

Sargasso Sea,
Lock Dining Bar

D

Fox Reformed, Il Bacio
Anglo-Asian Tandoori,
Rasa, Rasa (Travancore)

Stoke
Newington

Hackney
Marshes

Applebee's •

Mangal
Ocakbasi •

Yum Yum,
Three Crowns

Ark

Shanghai •

• Prince Arthur

M102

Huong-Viet
Faulkner's

• Forman's

Buen Ayre

• LMNT

Dalston

Victoria

Camden Town

• Duke of
Cambridge

• Empress of India
• Bistrotheque

Islington

Water House

• Morgan Arms

Map 12

EAST

Map 9

City

Map 11

Docklands

os 2-4

**C
E
N
T
R
A
L**

A13

Southwark

Isle of
Dogs

• Lobster Pot •
• Kennington
Tandoori

A2

Dragon Castle

Trafalgar Tavern
Spread Eagle, Inside,
Rivington Grill •

Camberwell

Greenwich

Mogul
Peninsular

A2

Thailand •

Brixton

• Gowlett

• Rye

Ganapati •

• Sea Cow, Green & Blue
• Tandoori Nights

Everest Inn,
Chapters,
Zero Degrees
Buenos Aires

Clapham

Thai Corner Café •
Le Chardon •

• Palmerston
• Franklins

Lewisham

SOUTH

The Rosendale •

Dulwich

• Barcelona Tapas,
Dartmouth Arms

• Babur Brasserie

• Beauberry House
Joanna's

• Querce

MAP 2 – WEST END OVERVIEW

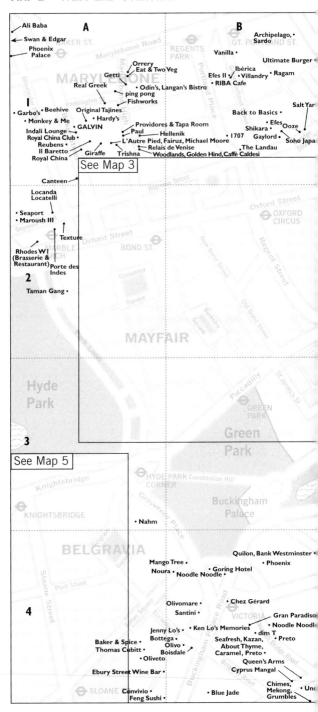

A

Ali Baba

Swan & Edgar

Phoenix Palace

MARYLEBONE

Orrery
Eat & Two Veg
Getti
Real Greek
• Odin's, Langan's Bistro
ping pong
Fishworks

• Garbo's • Beehive
• Monkey & Me   Original Tajines
Indali Lounge   • Hardy's
• GALVIN
Royal China Club   Providores & Tapa Room
Reubens •   Paul   Hellenik
Il Baretto   L'Autre Pied, Fairuz, Michael Moore
Royal China   Giraffe   Relais de Venise
            Trishna   Woodlands, Golden Hind, Caffè Caldesi

See Map 3

Canteen

Locanda
Locatelli

• Seaport
• Maroush III

Texture

Rhodes W1
(Brasserie &
Restaurant)   Porte des
              Indes

2

Taman Gang •

MARBLE ARCH

BOND ST.

MAYFAIR

Hyde
Park

3

See Map 5

Knightsbridge

KNIGHTSBRIDGE

BELGRAVIA

• Nahm

B

Archipelago,
Sardo

Vanilla •

Ultimate Burger •

Ibérica
Efes II   • Villandry   • Ragam
• RIBA Cafe

Salt Yar

Back to Basics •
            • Efes
Shikara •   Ooze
• 1707   Gaylord •   Soho Japa
The Landau

OXFORD
CIRCUS

Oxford Street

HYDE PARK Constitution Hill
CORNER

Buckingham
Palace

Green
Park

Quilon, Bank Westminster •

Mango Tree •   • Phoenix
Noura •   Goring Hotel
        Noodle Noodle •

Olivomare •   • Chez Gérard
Santini •
                    VICTORIA   • Gran Paradiso
                                • Noodle Noodl
Jenny Lo's • • Ken Lo's Memories   • dim T
    Bottega •   Seafresh, Kazan,   • Preto
Baker & Spice •   Olivo •   About Thyme,
Thomas Cubitt •   Boisdale •   Caramel, Preto •
        • Oliveto   Queen's Arms
                            Cyprus Mangal
Ebury Street Wine Bar •
                                Chimes,
SLOANE   Convivio •   Mekong,   • Und
        Feng Sushi •   • Blue Jade   Grumbles

4

MAP 2 – WEST END OVERVIEW

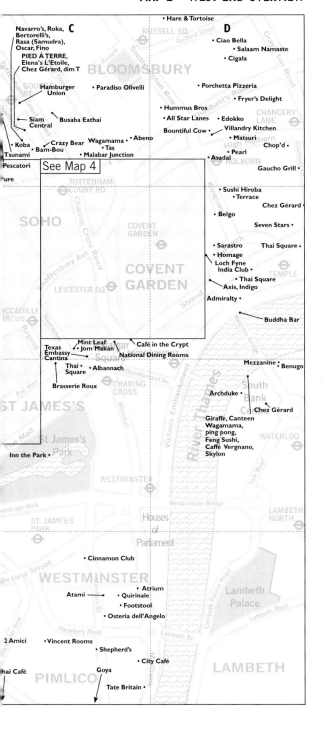

MAP 3 – MAYFAIR, ST JAMES'S & WEST SOHO

Defune •

Fromagerie Café •

A

B

• Union Café

2 Veneti •

• Wallace

Baker St

Levant •

1

Black & Blue •

Wigmore Street

• Comptoir Libanais

• Paradiso Olivelli

Wagamama •

James Street

Tootsies •

ping pong •

• Atari-Ya

• Sofra

Square Pie Company •

• Maroush

Busaba Eathai •

• Ekachai

Oxford Street

Bar Trattoria Semplice

Ristorante Semplice •

• Running Horse

Rasa •

BOND
STREET

New Bond Street

Napket •

Truc Vert •

North Audley Street

Ikeda •

Petite Maison •

MAYFAIR

Hush, Rocket, Mews of Mayfair •

2

• Princess Garden

MAZE, Maze Grill •

Brook Street

• Gordon Ramsay

at Claridge's

Sagar •

GAVROCHE •

*Grosvenor
Square*

Grosvenor Street

Bellamy's •

Greig's •

Cipriani •

Richoux •

Kai •

Shogun •

Guinea •

Hélène Darroze (Connaught) •

• Serafino

← Corrigan's

• SCOTT'S

Delfino •

Berkeley Square

Benares •

← Bord'Eaux

Mount Street

3

• Duke of Wellington

South Audley Street

Only Running Footman •

Park Lane

Crussh •

• Greenhouse

Tamarind •

Murano •

Chop'd •

• Dorchester

(Alain Ducasse,

China Tang, Grill Room)

Benugo, Noura •

Miyama •

• Galvin at Windows,

Trader Vic's

Curzon Street

Boudin Blanc •

Al Hamra •

Al Sultan •

• Sofra

↗ Little Square

• Artiste Muscle

Kiku •

4

*Hyde
Park*

• El Pirata

Piccadilly

Theo Randall (InterContinental) •

• NOBU

• Hard Rock Café

MAP 3 – MAYFAIR, ST JAMES'S & WEST SOHO

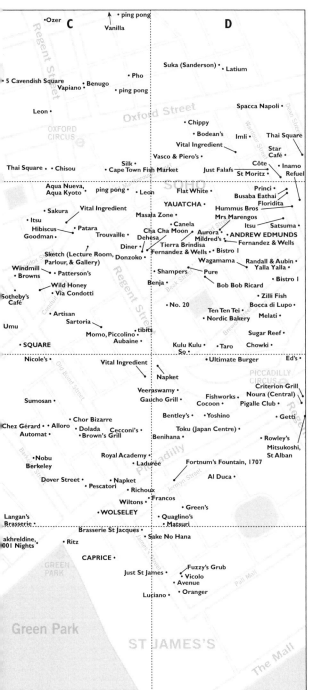

•Ozer · C · ping pong
Vanilla

• Pho
5 Cavendish Square · Benugo
Vapiano · · ping pong

Suka (Sanderson) · · Latium

Leon ·

D

Spacca Napoli ·

OXFORD
CIRCUS

Oxford Street

• Chippy
• Bodean's
Vital Ingredient

Imli ·

Thai Square
Star
Café ·

Vasco & Piero's ·

Thai Square · · Chisou
Silk ·
· Cape Town Fish Market

Just Falafs

Côte
St Moritz ·

· Inamo
Refuel

Aqua Nueva,
Aqua Kyoto · ping pong · · Leon

Flat White ·

Princi ·
Busaba Eathai
Floridita

· Sakura
Vital Ingredient

YAUATCHA ·

Hummus Bros ·

· Itsu
Hibiscus ·
Goodman

· Patara

Masala Zone ·

Mrs Marengos

Trouvaille ·

Cha Cha Moon ·

· Canela
Dehesa

Aurora ·

Itsu Satsuma

· ANDREW EDMUNDS
Mildred's · Fernandez & Wells

Diner ·

Tierra Brindisa
Fernandez & Wells · · Bistro 1

Sketch (Lecture Room,
Parlour, & Gallery)

Donzoko ·

Wagamama ·

Randall & Aubin ·
Yalla Yalla ·

Windmill ·
· Browns
· Patterson's

· Shampers

· Pure

· Bistro 1

Benja ·

Bob Bob Ricard ·

· Wild Honey
· Via Condotti

· Zilli Fish

Sotheby's
Café

Bocca di Lupo ·

· No. 20

Ten Ten Tei ·
· Nordic Bakery

Melati ·

· Artisan
Sartoria

Sugar Reef ·

Umu

· SQUARE

Momo, Piccolino ·
Aubaine ·

tibits ·

Kulu Kulu
So. ·

· Taro

Chowki

Nicole's ·

Vital Ingredient

· Ultimate Burger

Ed's ·

PICCADILLY
CIRCUS

· Napket

Criterion Grill

Veeraswamy ·

Noura (Central) ·

Sumosan ·

Gaucho Grill ·

Fishworks ·
Cocoon ·

Pigalle Club ·

Bentley's ·

· Yoshino

· Getti

· Chor Bizarre

Chez Gérard · · Alloro
Automat ·

· Dolada
· Brown's Grill

Cecconi's ·

Toku (Japan Centre) ·

Benihana ·

· Rowley's
Mitsukoshi,
St Alban

· Nobu
Berkeley

Royal Academy ·
· Ladurée

Fortnum's Fountain, 1707

Dover Street ·

· Napket
· Pescatori

Al Duca ·

Langan's
Brasserie ·

· Richoux
Wiltons · · Francos

· WOLSELEY

· Green's

· Quaglino's
· Matsuri

Brasserie St Jacques ·

akhreldine,
001 Nights

· Ritz

· Sake No Hana

CAPRICE ·

· Fuzzy's Grub

Just St James ·

· Vicolo
· Avenue

Luciano ·

· Oranger

GREEN
PARK

Green Park

ST JAMES'S

The Mall

MAP 4 – EAST SOHO, CHINATOWN & COVENT GARDEN

A   **B**

New Oxford Street

HAKKASAN •

• Eagle Bar Diner

Oxford Street

I

TOTTENHAM CT. RD

• Centrepoint Sushi

• Giaconda Dining Room

Soho Square

• Thai Square

• Gay Hussar

SOHO

Mon Plaisir

• Patara

• Hamburger Union
• Quo Vadis

Monmouth Coffee Company •

• L'Escargot

2 Gopal's
of Soho   • Gourmet Burger Kitchen   Taro •   Souk Medina •

• Bertorelli's   Incognico •   • Mela

Red
Fort   **ARBUTUS**

Barrafina •   • Café Emm   • Bincho Yakitori

Alastair Little •   • Little Italy   • Ed's

Dean Street   • Bar Italia   • Café Bohème   Cambridge

Townhouse   Balans   Circus

Ronnie Scott's   Maison Bertaux •   Rossopomodoro •

Kettners •   • ATELIER DE JOEL ROBUCHON •

Yming •   • Viet

Balans •   Ba Shan •   • Bistro 1   IVY •
• Bar Shu

• French House   • Konditor & Cook

• Café España   • New World

• Jade Garden   Chinese Experience
• Haozhan   • Caffè Vergnano

• Harbour City

3   • Leong's Legends   CHINATOWN   • Tokyo Diner   • Abeno
New Mayflower •

• Imperial China

• Chez Gérard   Mr Kong •

Fung Shing •   Baozi Inn

Wong Kei •   Okawari •

Misato •   • Golden Dragon   Browns •
Beotys •

• C&R Café   • Keelung   LEICESTER

Cork & Bottle •   SQ

Chuen Cheng Ku •   • Joy King Lau   • Gaby's

Tossed •

J SHEEKEY,
J Sheekey Oyster Ba

Leicester
Square

Planet Hollywood

Coventry St

• Wagamama

• Hamburger Union

4

• Wagamama

• Stock Pot
• Woodlands

Portrait •
National Gallery Café •

MAP 4 – EAST SOHO, CHINATOWN & COVENT GARDEN

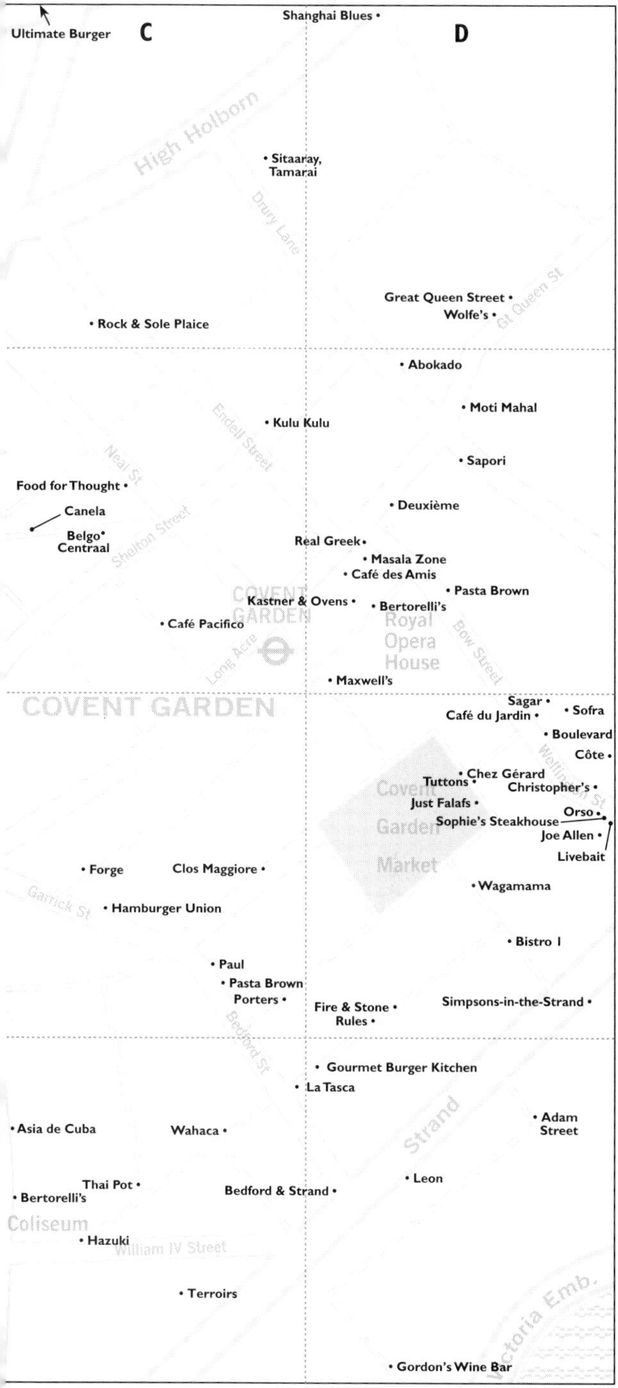
Ultimate Burger
C
Shanghai Blues
D
High Holborn
Sitaaray,
Tamarai
Drury Lane
Great Queen Street
Wolfe's
Gt Queen St
Rock & Sole Plaice
Abokado
Moti Mahal
Kulu Kulu
Endell Street
Neal St
Sapori
Food for Thought
Canela
Deuxième
Belgo
Centraal
Shelton Street
Real Greek
Masala Zone
Café des Amis
Pasta Brown
COVENT
GARDEN
Kastner & Ovens
Bertorelli's
Café Pacifico
Royal
Opera
House
Bow Street
Long Acre
Maxwell's
COVENT GARDEN
Sagar
Sofra
Café du Jardin
Boulevard
Côte
Wellington St
Chez Gérard
Tuttons
Christopher's
Covent
Garden
Market
Just Falafs
Orso
Sophie's Steakhouse
Joe Allen
Livebait
Forge
Clos Maggiore
Wagamama
Garrick St
Hamburger Union
Bistro 1
Paul
Pasta Brown
Porters
Fire & Stone
Rules
Simpsons-in-the-Strand
Bedford St
Gourmet Burger Kitchen
La Tasca
Strand
Adam
Street
Asia de Cuba
Wahaca
Leon
Thai Pot
Bertorelli's
Bedford & Strand
Coliseum
Hazuki
William IV Street
Terroirs
Victoria Emb.
Gordon's Wine Bar

MAP 5 – KNIGHTSBRIDGE, CHELSEA & SOUTH KENSINGTON

A

B

Kensington Gardens

KENSINGTON

Ffiona's •
Feng Sushi •

Maggie Jones's •

Wagamama •

• Min Jiang

Ottolenghi •

Randa •

Zaika

Giraffe

Ranoush • • Côte •

Babylon •

Stick & Bowl •

Crussh

Brunello •
Locanda Ottoemezzo

• Bottega

Launceston Place •

Royal Albert Hall

Wódka •

Etranger • • Pasha

• Bistrot 190

1

• Sticky Fingers

• Byron

• Balans

• L-Restaurant

• Whits

Kensington Square
Kitchen

• Da Mario

Memories of India •

• Abingdon

• Chez Patrick

Spago

Paul

Black &
Blue

Khan's of
Kensington

Madsen

Bangkok

Rôtisserie Jules

Bouchée

• Addie's Thai Café

• Masala Zone

• Gourmet Burger Kitchen

Bombay Brasserie •

Byron

Falconiere
dim T • Beirut Express

Bumpkin •

2

EARLS
COURT

Tendido Cero, Star of India,
kare kare, Noor Jahan

Rocca di Papa Gauche

• Gourmet

Burger Kitche

EARL'S
COURT

Cambio de Tercio •

Pembroke • • Mr Wing

Ambassade de l'Ile

Blakes Hotel •

Anglesea Arms

Langan's Bar & Grill •

Troubadour •

• Balans West

Riccardo's •

Lucio

Taiwan Village

Tampopo

Aglio e Olio

Sophie's
Steakhouse

3

WEST
BROMPTON

• Atlas

Brompton
Cemetery

Glaisters,
Santa Lucia,
Wine Gallery,
Friends,
Brinkley's

Rossopomodoro

Yumenoki •
Feng Sushi •

• Vingt-Quatre

• Haché

• Gilmour's

• Aubergine
Kings Road
Steakhouse & Grill •
Eight over Eight •

Osteria dell' Arancio •

• Chelsea Bun

Sugar Hut

Harwood Arms

• Farm

Chelsea Kitchen •

Famiglia • Vama •

Dine

• Frantoio

Mona Lisa •

Painted Heron

• Del'Aziz

• Marco

• Gourmet Burger Kitchen

• Blue Elephant

Bodean's

Napulé

Masala Zone

• Butcher's Hook

• Chutney Mary

• 606 Club

4

FULHAM

Rueda •

• Lots Road

Chelsea
Harbour

Yi-Ban •

Thai on the
River •

MAP 5 – KNIGHTSBRIDGE, CHELSEA & SOUTH KENSINGTON

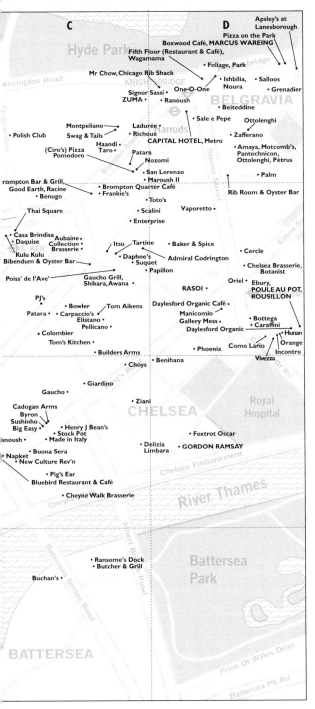

C

D

Apsley's at Lanesborough

Pizza on the Park

Boxwood Café, MARCUS WAREING

Hyde Park

Fifth Floor (Restaurant & Café), Wagamama

• Foliage, Park

Mr Chow, Chicago Rib Shack

KNIGHTSBRIDGE

• Ishbilia, Noura

• Salloos

• Grenadier

Signor Sassi •

One-O-One

ZUMA •

• Ranoush

BELGRAVIA

ensington Road

• Beiteddine

• Sale e Pepe

Ottolenghi

Montpeliano

Ladurée •

• Zafferano

Swag & Tails

• Richoux

Harrods

CAPITAL HOTEL, Metro

• Amaya, Motcomb's, Pantechnicon, Ottolenghi, Pétrus

(Ciro's) Pizza Pomodoro

Haandi •

Taro •

Patara

Nozomi

Polish Club

• Palm

Sloane Street

• San Lorenzo

• Maroush II

Rib Room & Oyster Bar

rompton Bar & Grill, Good Earth, Racine

• Brompton Quarter Café

• Benugo

• Frankie's

• Toto's

Thai Square

• Scalini

Vaporetto •

• Enterprise

• Casa Brindisa

• Daquise

Aubaine •

Collection •

Brasserie •

Itsu

Tartine

• Baker & Spice

• Cercle

S. KEN

Kulu Kulu

• Daphne's

• Chelsea Brasserie, Botanist

Bibendum & Oyster Bar

• Suquet

Admiral Codrington

• Papillon

Oriel •

• Ebury, POULE AU POT, ROUSILLON

Poiss' de l'Ave'

Gaucho Grill, Shikara, Awana •

RASOI •

PJ's

• Bowler

Tom Aikens

Daylesford Organic Café •

Patara •

• Carpaccio's

Elistano •

Pellicano

Manicomio

Gallery Mess •

Daylesford Organic

• Bottega

• Caraffini

• Colombier

Tom's Kitchen •

• Phoenix

Como Lario

•Hunan

Orange

Incontro

Vivezza

• Builders Arms

• Choys

• Benihana

• Giardino

Gaucho •

• Ziani

CHELSEA

Royal Hospital

Cadogan Arms

Byron

Sushinho

Big Easy •

• Henry J Bean's

• Stock Pot

• Made in Italy

• Foxtrot Oscar

anoush •

• Delizia Limbara

• GORDON RAMSAY

• Buona Sera

Napket

• New Culture Rev'n

Chelsea Embankment

• Pig's Ear

Bluebird Restaurant & Café

• Cheyne Walk Brasserie

River Thames

• Ransome's Dock

• Butcher & Grill

Battersea Park

Buchan's •

BATTERSEA

Price Of Wales Drive

Battersea Pk Rd

MAP 6 – NOTTING HILL & BAYSWATER

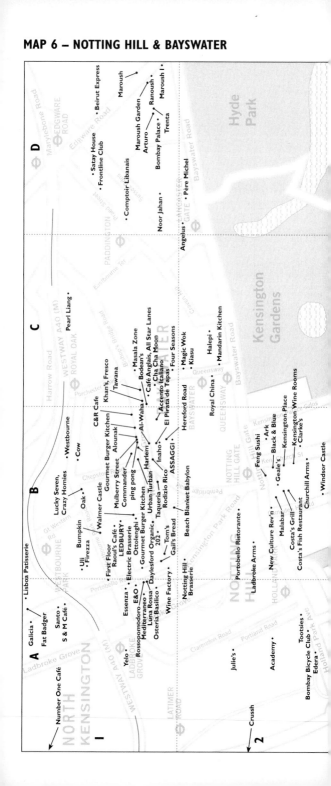

EDGWARE ROAD

Marylebone Road

Hyde Park

Pearl Liang •

Satay House • • Beirut Express

Frontine Club • Maroush

Maroush Garden • Ranoush •

Comptoir Libanais • Arturo • Maroush I •

Bombay Palace • Trenta •

Noor Jahan •

Angelus • • Père Michel

WESTWAY A40 (M)
ROYAL OAK

HARROW ROAD

PADDINGTON

LANCASTER GATE

BAYSWATER ROAD

C&R Cafe

• Westbourne
• Cow

Khan's, Fresco •

Masala Zone •

Bodean's •

Café Anglais, All Star Lanes •

Tawana • Cha Cha Moon •

Al-Waha • Accento Italiano

El Pirata de Tapas

Four Seasons •

Magic Wok •

Halepi • Kiasu •

Mandarin Kitchen •

Lucky Seven, Crazy Homies •

Oak •

Walmer Castle •

Gourmet Burger Kitchen

Mulberry Street • Alounak •

Commander • ping pong

Urban Turban • Harlem •

Taqueria • Inaho •

Rodizio Rico

ASSAGGI •

Hereford Road •

BAYSWATER

Royal China •

Kensington Gardens

Uli • Bumpkin •
Firezza •

First Floor •
Raoul's Café •

Essenza • Electric Brasserie

Rossopomodoro E&O •
Mediterraneo •
Luna Rossa • Daylesford Organic •
Osteria Basilico • 202 •

Tom's •
Wine Factory • Gail's Bread

Beach Blanket Babylon

Notting Hill •
Brasserie

Yelo •

LADBROKE GROVE

WESTWAY A40 (M)

Galicia • • Lisboa Patisserie

Santo •
S & M Café •

Fat Badger •

Number One Café

NORTH KENSINGTON

LATIMER ROAD

Crush

Julie's •

Academy •

Bombay Bicycle Club •
Edera • Tootsies •

Holland Park Ave

Clarendon Road

Portland Road

Kensington Park Road

NOTTING HILL

Ladbroke Arms •

Portobello Ristorante •

New Culture Rev'n •
Malabar •

Costa's Grill •
Costa's Fish Restaurant

Feng Sushi •
• Ark
Geale's • Black & Blue •
Kensington Place •
Kensington Wine Rooms •
Clarke's •

Churchill Arms •

• Windsor Castle

NOTTING HILL GATE

QUEENSWAY

Bayswater Road

MAP 7 – HAMMERSMITH & CHISWICK

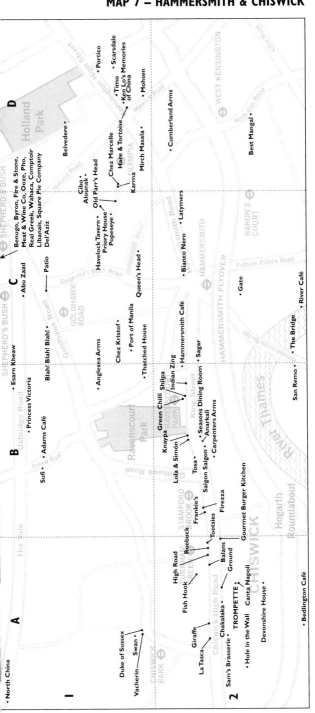

MAP 8 – HAMPSTEAD, CAMDEN TOWN & ISLINGTON

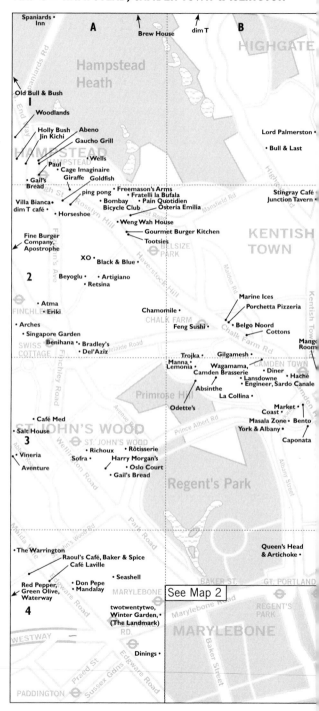

Spaniards • Inn

A

Brew House

dim T

B

HIGHGATE

Hampstead Heath

Old Bull & Bush

Woodlands

Holly Bush • Abeno
Jin Kichi
Gaucho Grill
• Wells
HAMPSTEAD
Paul
• Cage Imaginaire
Giraffe   Goldfish
• Gail's
Bread
ping pong
Villa Bianca
dim T café •
• Horseshoe

Lord Palmerston •

• Bull & Last

• Freemason's Arms
• Fratelli la Bufala
• Bombay   • Pain Quotidien
Bicycle Club • Osteria Emilia
• Weng Wah House

Stingray Café
Junction Tavern •

Fine Burger
Company,
Apostrophe

• Gourmet Burger Kitchen
Tootsies

KENTISH
TOWN

XO
• Black & Blue

BELSIZE
PARK

Beyoglu • • Artigiano
• Retsina

2

• Atma
• Eriki

FINCHLEY

• Arches

• Singapore Garden
Benihana •
Benihana • Bradley's
• Del'Aziz

SWISS
COTTAGE

Chamomile •

CHALK FARM

Feng Sushi •

Marine Ices
Porchetta Pizzeria
• Belgo Noord
Cottons

Mango
Room

Trojka •   Gilgamesh •
Manna •
Lemonia   Wagamama,
Camden Brasserie
Absinthe
La Collina •

CAMDEN TOWN
• Diner
• Haché
• Lansdowne
• Engineer, Sardo Canale

• Café Med

• Salt House

PRIMROSE HILL
Primrose Hill

Odette's

Market •
Coast •
Masala Zone • Bento
York & Albany •
Caponata

ST. JOHN'S WOOD

• Vineria

Aventure

ST. JOHN'S WOOD

• Richoux   • Rôtisserie
Sofra •
Harry Morgan's
• Oslo Court
• Gail's Bread

Regent's Park

3

• The Warrington
Raoul's Café, Baker & Spice
Café Laville

Red Pepper,
Green Olive,
Waterway

• Don Pepe
• Mandalay
• Seashell

MARYLEBONE

4

twotwentytwo,
Winter Garden, •
(The Landmark)

Queen's Head
& Artichoke •

BAKER ST.   GT. PORTLAND

See Map 2

Marylebone Road

REGENT'S
PARK

MARYLEBONE

WESTWAY

Dinings •

PADDINGTON

MAP 8 – HAMPSTEAD, CAMDEN TOWN & ISLINGTON

MAP 9 – THE CITY

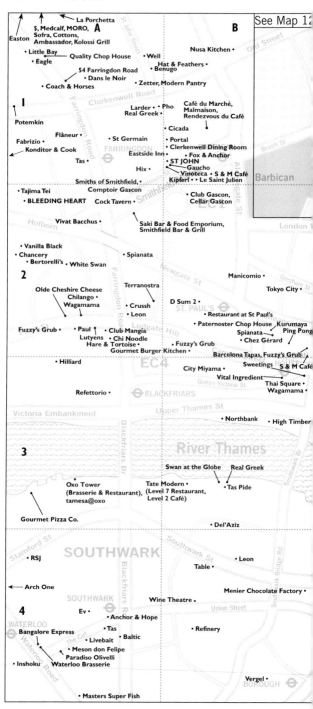

See Map 12

Easton
$, Medcalf, MORO,
Sofra, Cottons,
Ambassador, Kolossi Grill
La Porchetta
A
B
Nusa Kitchen •
Old Street

• Little Bay
Quality Chop House
• Well
• Eagle
Hat & Feathers •
• Benugo

54 Farringdon Road
• Dans le Noir
• Coach & Horses
• Zetter, Modern Pantry

Clerkenwell Road

1

Larder • • Pho
Real Greek
Café du Marché,
Malmaison,
Rendezvous du Café

Potemkin
• Cicada

Fabrizio •
Flâneur •
• St Germain
• Portal
Beech St

Konditor & Cook
FARRINGTON
• Clerkenwell Dining Room
• Fox & Anchor

Eastside Inn •
ST JOHN
Gaucho

Tas •
Vinoteca • S & M Café
Barbican

Hix •
Kipferl • • Le Saint Julien

Smiths of Smithfield, •
Comptoir Gascon
• Tajima Tei
• BLEEDING HEART
Cock Tavern •
• Club Gascon,
Cellar Gascon

EC1

Holborn
Vivat Bacchus •
Saki Bar & Food Emporium,
Smithfield Bar & Grill
London W

• Vanilla Black
• Chancery
• Bertorelli's • White Swan
• Spianata
Manicomio •
Gresham St

2
Newgate St
Tokyo City •

Olde Cheshire Cheese
Chilango •
Wagamama
Terranostra

• Crussh
D Sum 2 •
ST. PAUL'S

• Leon
• Restaurant at St Paul's
• Paternoster Chop House
Kurumaya
Ping Pong

Fuzzy's Grub •
• Paul
Lutyens • Club Mangia
Ludgate Hill
Spianata
Chez Gérard •

Hare & Tortoise •
Chi Noodle
Barcelona Tapas, Fuzzy's Grub •

Gourmet Burger Kitchen •
• Fuzzy's Grub
Sweetings • S & M Café

• Hilliard
City Miyama •
Vital Ingredient •
Thai Square •

Queen Victoria St
Wagamama •

Refettorio •
BLACKFRIARS

EC4

Victoria Embankment
Upper Thames St
• Northbank
• High Timber

River Thames

3
Blackfriars Br
Southwark Br

Swan at the Globe
Real Greek

Oxo Tower
(Brasserie & Restaurant),
tamesa@oxo
Tate Modern •
(Level 7 Restaurant,
Level 2 Café)
• Tas Pide

Gourmet Pizza Co.

• Del'Aziz

Stanford St
SOUTHWARK
Southwark St

• RSJ
• Leon

Table •
Southwark Bridge Rd

← Arch One
Menier Chocolate Factory •

SOUTHWARK
Wine Theatre •
Union Street

4
Ev •
• Anchor & Hope

WATERLOO
• Tas
• Refinery

Bangalore Express
• Baltic

• Livebait
• Meson don Felipe

• Inshoku
Paradiso Olivelli
Waterloo Brasserie

Vergel •
BOROUGH

• Masters Super Fish

MAP 9 – THE CITY

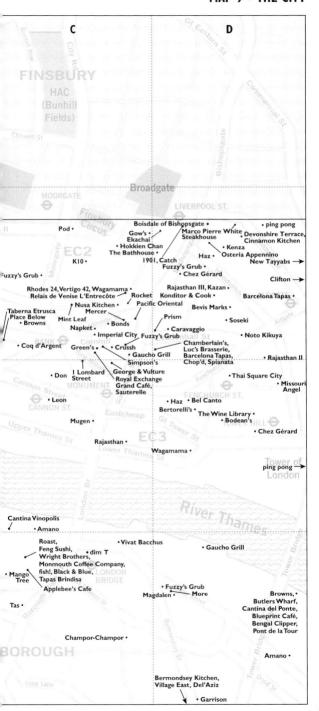

C   D

FINSBURY

HAC
(Bunhill
Fields)

Chiswell St

Broadgate

MOORGATE

LIVERPOOL ST.

Pod •

Finsbury Circus

Boisdale of Bishopsgate •
Gow's,   Marco Pierre White   • ping pong
Ekachai   Steakhouse   Devonshire Terrace,
• Hokkien Chan   • Kenza   Cinnamon Kitchen
The Bathhouse •   1901, Catch   Haz • Osteria Appennino
K10 •   Fuzzy's Grub •   New Tayyabs →
Fuzzy's Grub •   • Chez Gérard   Clifton →

EC2

Rhodes 24, Vertigo 42, Wagamama •   Rajasthan III, Kazan •
Relais de Venise L'Entrecôte •   Konditor & Cook •   Barcelona Tapas •
     Rocket   Pacific Oriental   Bevis Marks •
Taberna Etrusca   Nusa Kitchen •
Place Below   Mint Leaf   Mercer   • Soseki
• Browns   Napket •   • Bonds   Prism •   • Noto Kikuya
     • Imperial City   • Caravaggio
• Coq d'Argent   Green's •   • Crussh   Fuzzy's Grub •
BANK   Cornhill   • Gaucho Grill   Chamberlain's,   • Rajasthan II
      Simpson's   Luc's Brasserie,
• Don   I Lombard   George & Vulture   Barcelona Tapas,
   Street   Royal Exchange   Chop'd, Spianata   • Thai Square City
MONUMENT   Grand Café,   • Missouri
• Leon   Sauterelle   Angel
CANNON ST.   Eastcheap   • Haz   • Bel Canto
     Mugen •   Bertorelli's •   • The Wine Library •
Upper Thames St   • Bodean's
           • Chez Gérard
Rajasthan •   EC3
   Lower Thames St   Wagamama •
            Tower of
          ping pong → London

River Thames

Cantina Vinopolis
• Amano

Roast,   • Vivat Bacchus   • Gaucho Grill
Feng Sushi,   • dim T
Wright Brothers,
Monmouth Coffee Company,
fish!, Black & Blue,   LONDON BRIDGE
• Mango   Tapas Brindisa
Tree   Applebee's Cafe   • Fuzzy's Grub
     Magdalen • — More   Browns, •
Tas •   Butlers Wharf,
          Cantina del Ponte,
          Blueprint Café,
          Bengal Clipper,
          Pont de la Tour

Champor-Champor •

BOROUGH

Long Lane   Amano •

Bermondsey Kitchen,
Village East, Del'Aziz
↓ • Garrison

MAP 10 – SOUTH LONDON (& FULHAM)

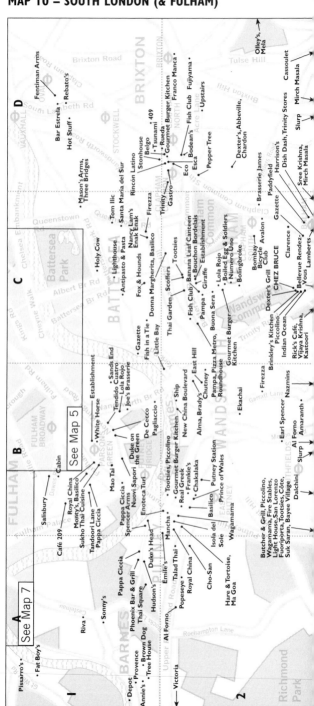

MAP 11 – EAST END & DOCKLANDS

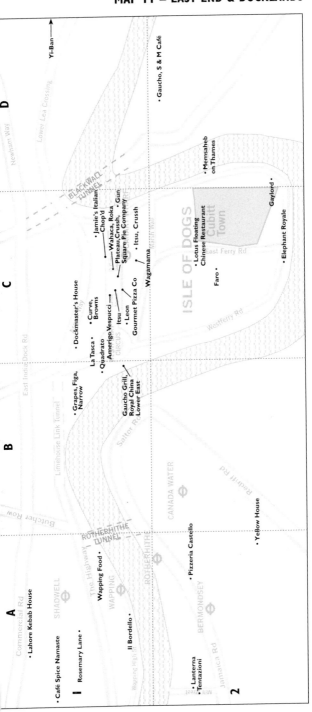

Yi-Ban →

Commercial Rd

• Lahore Kebab House

Newham Way

Lower Lea Crossing

• Gaucho, S & M Café

D

BLACKWALL TUNNEL

• Memsaheb on Thames

• Jamie's Italian •
Chop'd

• Wahaca, Roka

Plateau, Crussh, • Gun
Square Pie Company

• Itsu, Crussh

Wagamama

• Gaylord

Aspen Way

Lotus Floating
Chinese Restaurant

East Ferry Rd

ISLE OF DOGS

Cubitt Town

• Elephant Royale

East India Dock Rd

• Dockmaster's House

• Curve,
Browns

La Tasca •

Quadrato •

Amerigo Vespucci →

CIRCUS

Itsu •

• Leon

Gourmet Pizza Co

C

Faro •

Westferry Rd

Limehouse Link Tunnel

• Grapes, Figa,
Narrow

Salter Rd

Gaucho Grill,
Royal China
Lower East

B

Redriff Rd

CANADA WATER

Butcher Row

The Highway

Wapping Food •

WAPPING

SHADWELL

ROTHERHITHE
TUNNEL

ROTHERHITHE

• Pizzeria Castello

• Yellow House

A

• Café Spice Namaste

• Rosemary Lane •

Wapping High St

Il Bordello •

BERMONDSEY

• Lanterna
Tentazioni

Jamaica Rd

1

2

MAP 12 – SHOREDITCH & BETHNAL GREEN

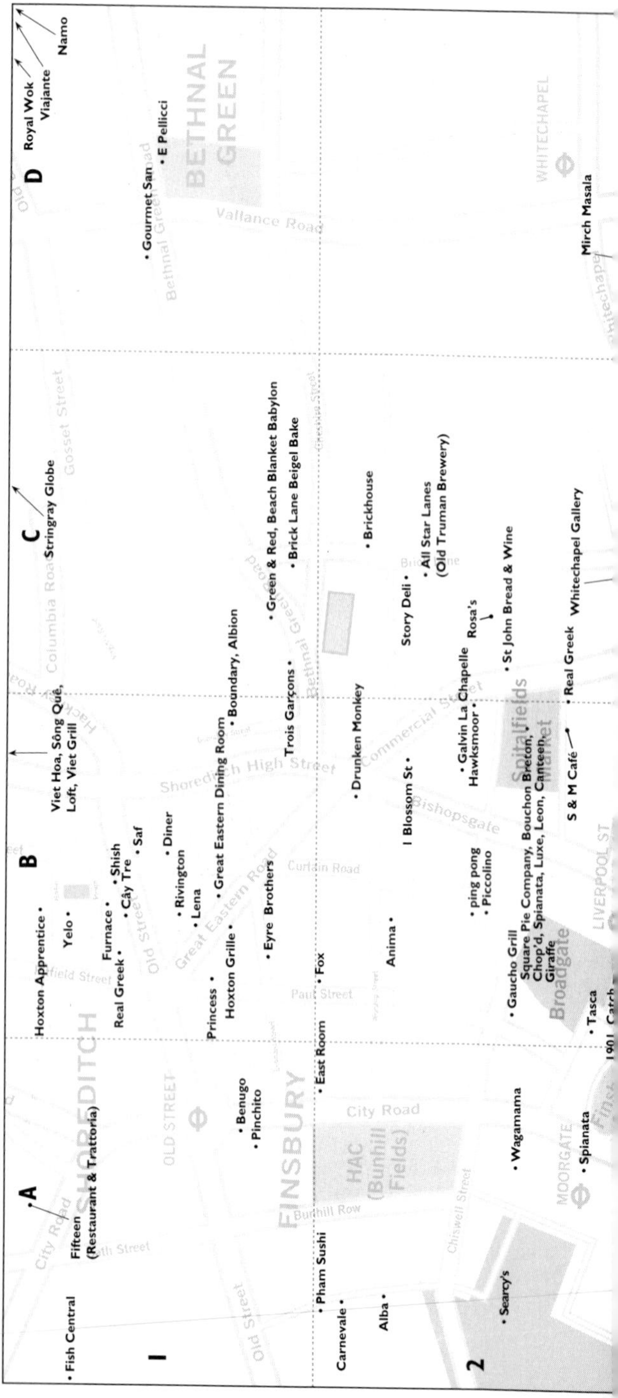

A

Fish Central

Fifteen (Restaurant & Trattoria)

Hoxton Apprentice •
Yelo •

Furnace •   • Shish
Real Greek •   • Cay Tre • Saf

Benugo •
Pinchito •

Princess •   • Diner
Hoxton Grille •   • Lena

Eyre Brothers •

• East Room   • Fox

Pham Sushi •

Carnevale •

Alba •

B

Viet Hoa, Sông Quê, Loft, Viet Grill

• Rivington

Great Eastern Dining Room

• Boundary, Albion

Trois Garçons •

• Drunken Monkey

I Blossom St •

Anima •

• ping pong
• Piccolino

Gaucho Grill •
Square Pie Company, Bouchon Breton,
Chop'd, Spianata, Luxe, Leon, Canteen,
Giraffe

• Tasca
1901 Catch

• Wagamama

• Spianata

Searcy's •

C

Stringray Globe

• Green & Red, Beach Blanket Babylon
• Brick Lane Beigel Bake

• Brickhouse

Story Deli •   • All Star Lanes
(Old Truman Brewery)

• Galvin La Chapelle   Rosa's •
Hawksmoor •

• St John Bread & Wine

S & M Café •   • Real Greek   Whitechapel Gallery •

D

Royal Wok
Viajante
Namo

• Gourmet San   • E Pellicci

BETHNAL GREEN

Vallance Road

Mirch Masala •

SHOREDITCH

FINSBURY

HAC (Bunhill Fields)

MOORGATE

WHITECHAPEL

Spitalfields

Broadgate

LIVERPOOL ST

1

2